PROTEIN CHEMISTRY

PROTEIN CHEMISTRY

By

Sananda Chatterjee

DAE, DCA, CMCNet

Scientific Consultant

Institute for Natural Sciences

Kolkata

(West Bengal)

D P H

DISCOVERY PUBLISHING HOUSE PVT. LTD.

NEW DELHI-110 002

Published by:
Tilak Wasan
DISCOVERY PUBLISHING HOUSE PVT. LTD.
4383/4B, Ansari Road, Darya Ganj
New Delhi-110 002 (India)
Phone : +91-11-23279245, 43596064-65
Fax : +91-11-23253475
E-mail : parul.wasan@gmail.com
discoverypublishinghouse@gmail.com
web : www.discoverypublishinggroup.com

***First Edition:* 2012**

ISBN: 978-93-5056-115-7

Protein Chemistry

Printed at:
Shree Balaji Art Press
Delhi

Preface

Protein chemistry is the large-scale study of proteins, particularly their structures and functions. Proteins are vital parts of living organisms, as they are the main components of the physiological metabolic pathways of cells. The term "proteomics" was first coined in 1997 to make an analogy with genomics, the study of the genes. The word "proteome" is a blend of "protein" and "genome", and was coined by Marc Wilkins in 1994 while working on the concept as a PhD student. The proteome is the entire complement of proteins, including the modifications made to a particular set of proteins, produced by an organism or system. This will vary with time and distinct requirements, or stresses, that a cell or organism undergoes the complexity of the problem.

After geromics, proteomics is considered the next step in the study of biological systems. It is much more complicated than genomics mostly because while an organism's genome is more or less constant, the proteome differs from cell to cell and from time to time. This is because distinct genes are expressed in distinct cell types. This means that even the basic set of proteins which are produced in a cell needs to be determined. In the past this was done by mRNA analysis, but this was found not to correlate with protein content. It is now known that mRNA is not always translated into protein, and the amount of protein produced for a given amount of mRNA depends on the gene it is transcribed from and on the current physiological state of the cell. Proteomics confirms the presence of the protein and provides a direct measure of the quantity present. This book also deals with the Post-translational modifications.

Not only does the translation from mRNA cause differences, many proteins are also subjected to a wide variety of chemical modifications after translation. A lot of these post-translational modifications are critical to the protein's function.

Author

Contents

CHAPTER 1

Introduction to Proteomics

Proteomics is the large-scale study of proteins, particularly their structures and functions. Proteins are vital parts of living organisms, as they are the main components of the physiological metabolic pathways of cells. The term 'proteomics' was first coined in 1997 to make an analogy with genomics, the study of the genes. The word 'proteome' is a blend of *'protein'* and *'genome'*, and was coined by Marc Wilkins in 1994 while working on the concept as a PhD student. The proteome is the entire complement of proteins, including the modifications made to a particular set of proteins, produced by an organism or system. This will vary with time and distinct requirements, or stresses, that a cell or organism undergoes.

Complexity of the Problem

After genomics, proteomics is considered the next step in the study of biological systems. It is much more complicated than genomics mostly because while an organism's genome is more or less constant, the proteome differs from cell to cell and from time to time. This is because distinct genes are expressed in distinct cell types. This means that even the basic set of proteins which are produced in a cell needs to be determined. In the past this was done by mRNA analysis, but this was found not to correlate with protein content. It is now known that mRNA is not always translated into protein, and the amount of protein produced for a given amount of mRNA depends on the gene it is transcribed from and on the current physiological state of the cell. Proteomics confirms the presence of the protein and provides a direct measure of the quantity present.

Post-translational Modifications

Not only does the translation from mRNA cause differences, many proteins are also subjected to a wide variety of chemical modifications after translation. A lot of these post-translational modifications are critical to the protein's function.

Phosphorylation

One such modification is phosphorylation, which happens to many enzymes and structural proteins in the process of cell signaling. The addition of a phosphate to particular amino acids—most commonly serine and threonine mediated by serine/threonine kinases, or more rarely tyrosine mediated by tyrosine kinases—causes a protein to become a target for binding or interacting with a distinct set of other proteins that recognize the phosphorylated domain. Because protein phosphorylation is one of the most-studied protein modifications many 'proteomic' efforts are geared to determining the set of phosphorylated proteins in a particular cell or tissue-type under particular circumstances. This alerts the scientist to the signaling pathways that may be active in that instance.

Ubiquitination

Ubiquitin is a small protein that can be affixed to certain protein substrates by enzymes called E3 ubiquitin ligases. Determining which proteins are poly-ubiquitinated can be helpful in understanding how protein pathways are regulated. This is therefore an additional legitimate 'proteomic' study. Similarly, once it is determined what substrates are ubiquitinated by each ligase, determining the set of ligases expressed in a particular cell type will be helpful.

Additional Modifications

Listing all the protein modifications that might be studied in a 'Proteomics' project would require a discussion of most of biochemistry; therefore, a short list will serve here to illustrate the complexity of the problem. In addition to phosphorylation and ubiquitination, proteins can be subjected to (among others) methylation, acetylation, glycosylation, oxidation and nitrosylation. Some proteins undergo ALL of these modifications, often in time-dependent combinations, aptly illustrating the potential complexity one has to deal with when studying protein structure and function.

Distinct Proteins are Made Under Distinct Settings

Even if one is studying a particular cell type, that cell may make different sets of proteins at different times, or under different conditions. Furthermore, as mentioned, any one protein can undergo a wide range of post-translational modifications. Therefore a 'proteomics' study can become quite complex very quickly, even if the object of the study is very restricted. In more ambitious settings, such as when a biomarker for a tumour is sought—when the proteomics scientist is obliged to study sera samples from multiple cancer patients—the amount of complexity that must be dealt with is as great as in any modern biological project.

Limitations to Genomic Study

Scientists are very interested in proteomics because it gives a much better understanding of an organism than genomics. *First*, the level of transcription of a gene gives only a rough estimate of its level of expression into a protein. An mRNA produced in abundance may be degraded rapidly or translated inefficiently, resulting in a small amount of protein. *Second*, as mentioned above many proteins experience post-translational modifications that profoundly affect their activities; for example some proteins are not active until they become phosphorylated. Methods such as phosphoproteomics and glycoproteomics are used to study post-translational modifications. *Third*, many transcripts give rise to more than one protein, through alternative splicing or alternative post-translational modifications. *Fourth*, many proteins form complexes with other proteins or RNA molecules, and only function in the presence of these other molecules. *Finally*, protein degradation rate plays an important role in protein content.

Methods of Studying Proteins and Determining Proteins Which are Post-translationally Modified

One way in which a particular protein can be studied is to develop an antibody which is specific to that modification. For example, there are antibodies which only recognize certain proteins when they are tyrosine-phosphorylated, known as pan antibodies; also, there are antibodies specific to other modifications. These can be used to determine the set of proteins that have undergone the modification of interest.For sugar modifications, such as glycosylation of proteins, certain lectins have been discovered which bind sugars. These too can be used. A more common way to determine post-translational modification of interest is to subject a complex mixture of proteins to electrophoresis in 'two-dimensions', which simply means that the proteins are electrophoresed first in one direction, and then in another... this allows small differences in a protein to be visualized by separating a modified protein from its unmodified form. This methodology is known as 'two-dimensional gel electrophoresis'. Recently, another approach has been developed called PROTOMAP which combines SDS-PAGE with shotgun proteomics to enable detection of changes in gel-migration such as those caused by proteolysis or post translational modification.

Determining the Existence of Proteins in Complex Mixtures

Classically, antibodies to particular proteins or to their modified forms have been used in biochemistry and cell biology studies. These are among the most common tools used by practicing biologists today. For more quantitative determinations of protein amounts, techniques such as ELISAs can be used. For proteomic study, more recent techniques such as matrix-assisted laser desorption/ionization (MALDI) have been employed for rapid determination of proteins in particular mixtures and increasingly electrospray ionization (ESI).

Establishing Protein-Protein Interactions

Most proteins function in collaboration with other proteins, and one goal of proteomics is to identify which proteins interact. This is especially useful in determining potential partners in cell signaling cascades.Several methods are available to probe protein-protein interactions. The traditional method is yeast two-hybrid analysis. New methods include protein microarrays, immunoaffinity chromatography followed by mass spectrometry, dual polarisation interferometry and experimental methods such as phage display and computational methods.

Practical Applications of Proteomics

One of the most promising developments to come from the study of human genes and proteins has been the identification of potential new drugs for the treatment of disease. This relies on genome and proteome information to identify proteins associated with a disease, which computer software can then use as targets for new drugs. For example, if a certain protein is implicated in a disease, its 3D structure provides the information to design drugs to interfere with the action of the protein. A molecule that fits the active site of an enzyme, but cannot be released by the enzyme, will inactivate the enzyme. This is the basis of new drug-discovery tools, which aim to find new drugs to inactivate proteins involved in disease. As genetic differences among individuals are found, researchers expect to use these techniques to develop personalized drugs that are more effective for the individual. A computer technique which attempts to fit millions of small molecules to the three-dimensional structure of a protein is called 'virtual ligand screening'. The computer rates the quality of the fit to various sites in the protein, with the goal of either enhancing or disabling the function of the protein, depending on its function in the cell. A good example of this is the identification of new drugs to target and inactivate the HIV-1 protease. The HIV-1 protease is an enzyme that cleaves a very large HIV protein into smaller, functional proteins. The virus cannot survive without this enzyme; therefore, it is one of the most effective protein targets for killing HIV.

Biomarkers

The FDA defines a biomarker as, "A characteristic that is objectively measured and evaluated as an indicator of normal biologic processes, pathogenic processes, or pharmacologic responses to a therapeutic intervention". Understanding the proteome, the structure and function of each protein and the complexities of protein-protein interactions will be critical for developing the most effective diagnostic techniques and disease treatments in the future. An interesting use of proteomics is using specific protein biomarkers to diagnose disease. A number of techniques allow to test for proteins produced during a particular disease, which helps to diagnose the disease quickly. Techniques include western blot, immunohistochemical staining, enzyme linked immunosorbent assay (ELISA) or mass spectrometry.

Current Research Methodologies

There are many approaches to attempting to characterize the human proteome, which is estimated to exceed 100,000 unique forms, 25,000 genes plus post-translational modifications.

STRUCTURE OF PROTEINS

For many years, it was thought that proteins were colloids of random structure and that the enzymatic activities of certain crystallized proteins were due to unknown entities associated with an inert protein carrier. In 1934, J.D. Bernal and Dorothy Crowfoot Hodgkin showed that a crystal of the protein *pepsin* yielded a discrete diffraction pattern when placed in an X-ray beam. This result provided the first evidence that pepsin was not a random colloid but an ordered array of atoms organized into a large yet uniquely structured molecule. Even relatively small proteins contain thousands of atoms, almost all of which occupy definite positions in space. The first X-ray structure of a protein, that of sperm whale myoglobin, was reported in 1958 by John Kendrew and co-workers. At the time—only 5 years after James Watson and Francis Crick had elucidated the simple and elegant structure of DNA — protein chemists were chagrined by the complexity and apparent lack of regularity in the structure of myoglobin. In retrospect, such irregularity seems essential for proteins to fulfill their diverse biological roles. However, comparisons of the, 7000 protein structures now known have revealed that proteins actually exhibit a remarkable degree of structural regularity. As we saw that the primary structure of a protein is its linear sequence of amino acids. In discussing protein structure, three further levels of structural complexity are customarily invoked:

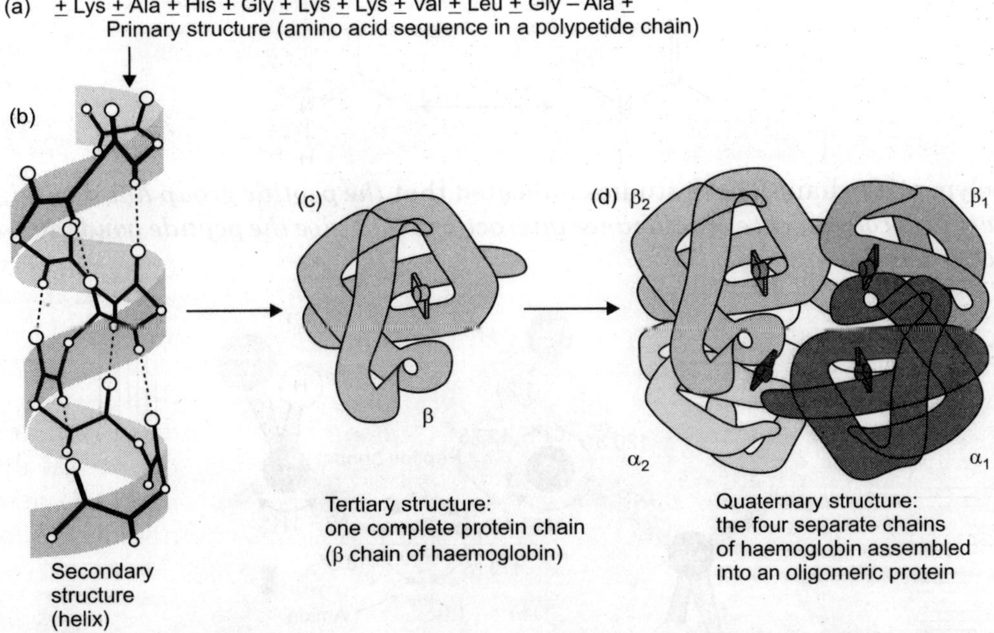

Fig. 1.1 : Levels of protein structure. (*a*) Primary structure, (*b*) secondary structure, (*c*) tertiary structure, and (*d*) quaternary structure

- *Secondary structure* is the local spatial arrangement of a polypeptide's backbone atoms without regard to the conformations of its side chains.

- *Tertiary structure* refers to the three-dimensional structure of an entire polypeptide.
- Many proteins are composed of two or more polypeptide chains, loosely referred to as subunits. A protein's *quaternary structure* refers to the spatial arrangement of its subunits. The four levels of protein structure are summarized in Fig. 1.1.

In this chapter, we explore secondary through quaternary structure, including examples of proteins that illustrate each of these levels. We also introduce methods for determining three-dimensional molecular structure and discuss the forces that stabilize folded proteins.

The Secondary Structure of Protein

Protein secondary structure includes the regular polypeptide folding patterns such as helices, sheets, and turns. However, before we discuss these basic structural elements, we must consider the geometric properties of peptide groups, which underlie all higher order structures.

I. The Peptide Group

In the 1930s and 1940s, Linus Pauling and Robert Corey determined the X-ray structures of several amino acids and dipeptides in an effort to elucidate the conformational constraints on a polypeptide chain. These studies indicated that *the peptide group has a rigid, planar structure as a consequence of resonance interactions that give the peptide bond, 40% double-bond character:*

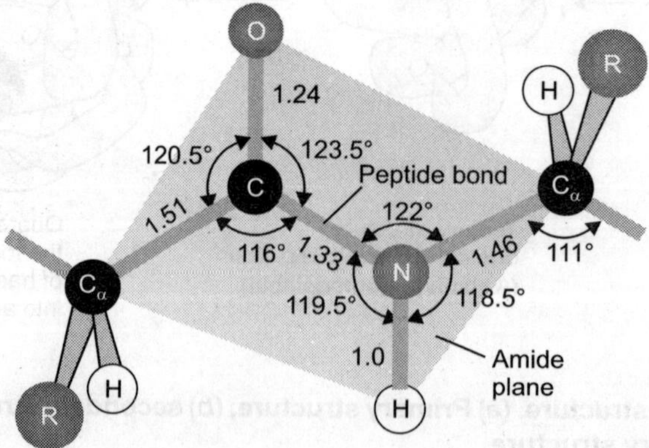

Fig. 1.2 : The trans peptide group. The bond lengths (in angstroms) and angles (in degrees) are derived from X-ray crystal structures

This explanation is supported by the observations that a peptide group's CON bond is 0.13 Å shorter than its NOCa single bond and that its CPO bond is 0.02 Å longer than that of aldehydes and ketones. The planar conformation maximizes p-bonding overlap, which

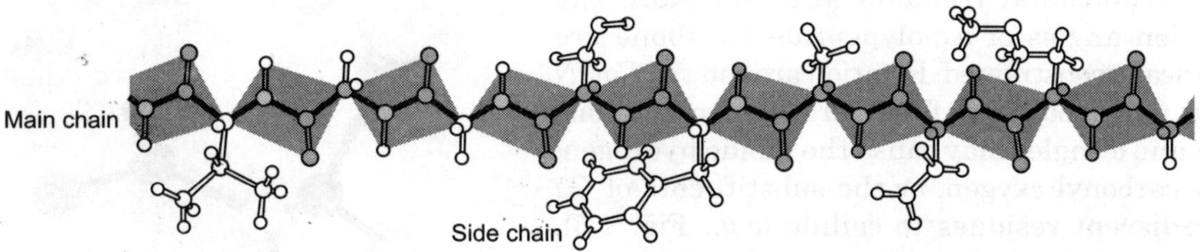

Fig. 1.3 : Extended conformation of a polypeptide. The backbone is shown as a series of planar peptide groups

accounts for the peptide group's rigidity. Peptide groups, with few exceptions, assume the *trans conformation,* in which successive *Ca* atoms are on opposite sides of the peptide bond joining them (Fig. 1.2). The *cis conformation,* in which successive Ca atoms are on the same side of the peptide bond, is 8 kJ mol 21 less stable than the trans conformation because of steric interference between neighbouring side chains. However, this steric interference is reduced in peptide bonds to Pro residues, so,*10% of the Pro residues in proteins follow a cis peptide bond.* Torsion Angles between Peptide Groups Describe Polypeptide Chain Conformations The *backbone* or *main chain* of a protein refers to the atoms that participate in peptide bonds, ignoring the side chains of the amino acid residues. The backbone can be drawn as a linked sequence of rigid planar peptide groups (Fig. 1.3). *The conformation of the backbone can therefore be described by the torsion angles* (also called *dihedral angles* or rotation angles) *around the CaON bond (f) and the CaOC bond (c) of each residue* (Fig. 1.4). These angles, *f* and *c*, are both

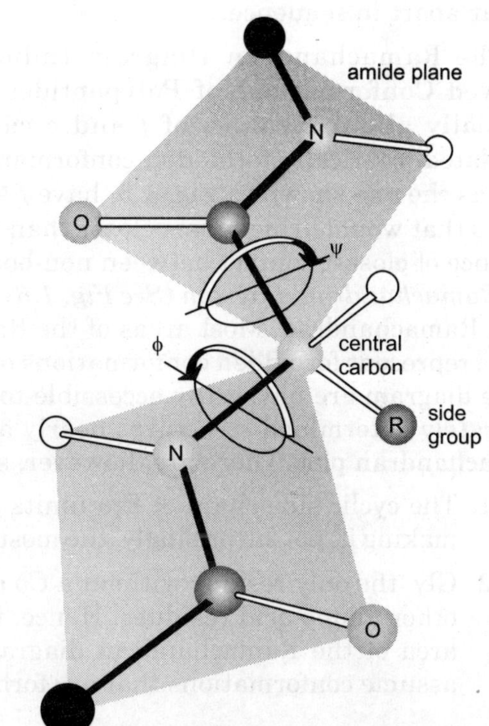

Fig. 1.4 : Torsion angles of the polypeptide backbone. Two planar peptide groups are shown. The only reasonably free movements are rotations around the CaON bond (measured as f) and the CaOC bond (measured as c). By convention, both f and c are 180° in the conformation shown and increase, as indicated, in the clockwise direction when viewed from C.

defined as 180° when the polypeptide chain is in its fully extended conformation and increase clockwise when viewed from *Ca*. The conformational freedom and therefore the torsion angles of a polypeptide backbone are sterically constrained. Rotation around the *CaON* and *CaOC* bonds to form certain combinations of *f* and *c* angles may cause the amide hydrogen, the carbonyl oxygen, or the substituents of *Ca* of adjacent residues to collide (*e.g.,* Fig. 1.5). Certain conformations of longer polypeptides can similarly produce collisions between residues that are far apart in sequence.

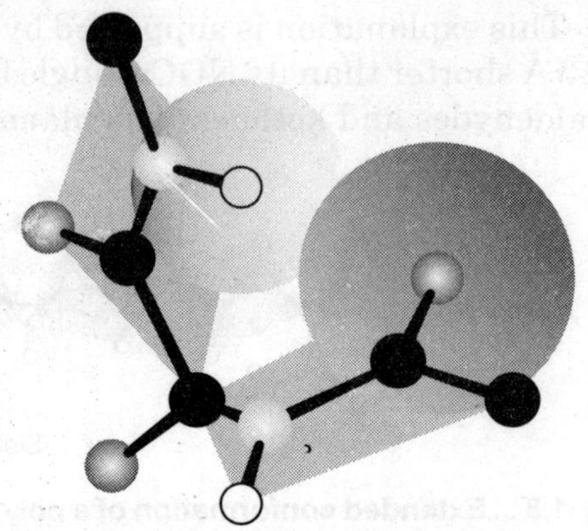

Fig. 1.5 : Steric interference between adjacent peptide groups. Rotation can result in a conformation in which the amide hydrogen of one residue and the carbonyl oxygen of the next are closer than their van der Waals distance

The Ramachandran Diagram Indicates Allowed Conformations of Polypeptides The sterically allowed values of *f* and *c* can be calculated. Sterically forbidden conformations, such as the one shown in Fig. 1.5, have *f* and *c* values that would bring atoms closer than the corresponding van der Waals distance (the distance of closest contact between non-bonded atoms). Such information is summarized in a *Ramachandran diagram* (*See Fig. 1.6 on next page*), which is named after its inventor, G. N. Ramachandran. Most areas of the Ramachandran diagram (most combinations of *f* and *c*) represent forbidden conformations of a polypeptide chain. Only three small regions of the diagram are physically accessible to most residues. The observed *f* and *c* values of accurately determined structures nearly always fall within these allowed regions of the Ramachandran plot. There are, however, some notable exceptions:

1. The cyclic side chain of Pro limits its range of *f* values to angles of around 260°, making it, not surprisingly, the most conformationally restricted amino acid residue.
2. Gly, the only residue without a *Cb* atom, is much less sterically hindered than the other amino acid residues. Hence, its permissible range of *f* and *c* covers a larger area of the Ramachandran diagram. At Gly residues, polypeptide chains often assume conformations that are forbidden to other residues.

Regular Secondary Structure: The α Helix and the β Sheet

A few elements of protein secondary structure are so widespread that they are immediately recognizable in proteins with widely differing amino acid sequences. Both the α *helix* and the β *sheet* are such elements; they are called *regular secondary structures because they are composed of sequences of residues with repeating f and c values.*

The α Helix Only one polypeptide helix has both a favorable hydrogen bonding pattern and *f* and *c* values that fall within the fully allowed regions of the Ramachandran diagram: the α helix. Its discovery by Linus Pauling in 1951, through model building, ranks as one

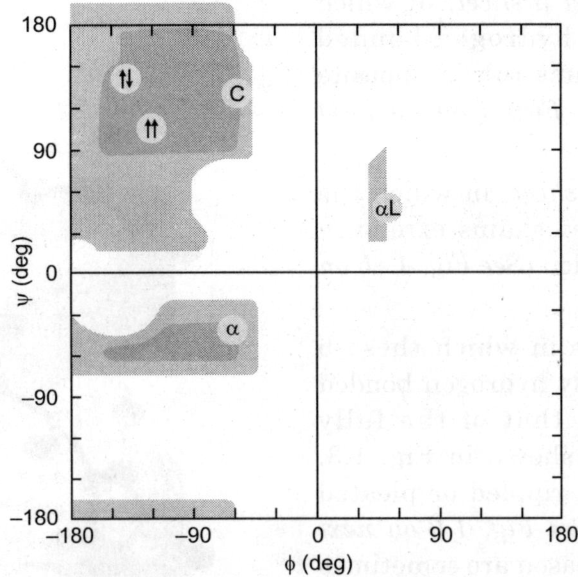

Fig. 1.6 : A Ramachandran diagram. The green-shaded regions indicate the sterically allowed *f* and *c* angles for all residues except Gly and Pro. The coloured circles represent conformational angles of several secondary structures: α, righthanded α helix; *hh*, parallel β sheet; *hg*, antiparallel β sheet; *C*, collagen helix; *aL*, left-handed a helix.

of the landmarks of structural biochemistry. The α helix (See Fig. 1.7 on next page) is right-handed; that is, it turns in the direction that the fingers of a right hand curl when its thumb points in the direction that the helix rises. The a helix has 3.6 residues per turn and a *pitch* (the distance the helix rises along its axis per turn) of 5.4 Å. The a helices of proteins have an average length of, 12 residues, which corresponds to over three helical turns, and a length of, 18 Å. *In the* a *helix, the backbone hydrogen bonds are arranged such that the peptide CPO bond of the nth residue points along the helix axis toward the peptide NOH group of the (n 1 4)th residue.* This results in a strong hydrogen bond that has the nearly optimum NZO distance of 2.8 Å. Amino acid side chains project outward and downward from the helix (Fig. 1.6 to 1.8), thereby avoiding steric interference with the polypeptide backbone and with each other. The core of the helix is tightly packed; that is, its atoms are in van der Waals contact.

β Sheets

In 1951, the same year Pauling proposed the α helix, Pauling and Corey postulated the existence of a different polypeptide secondary structure, the β sheet. Like the α helix, the β sheet uses the full hydrogen-bonding capacity of the polypeptide backbone. *In* β *sheets, however, hydrogen bonding occurs between neighbouring polypeptide chains rather than within one* as in an α helix. Sheets come in two varieties:

1. The *antiparallel* β *sheet,* in which neighbouring hydrogen-bonded polypeptide chains run in opposite directions (*See Fig. 1.8a on next page*).
2. The *parallel* β *sheet,* in which the hydrogen-bonded chains extend in the same direction (*See Fig. 1.8b on next page*).

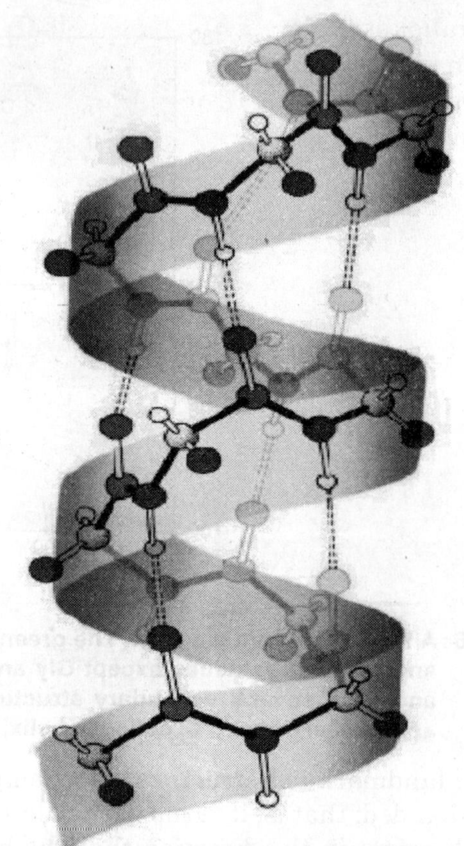

Fig. 1.7 : The α helix. This right-handed helical conformation has 3.6 residues per turn. Dashed lines indicate hydrogen bonds between CPO groups and NOH groups that are four residues farther along the polypeptide chain

The conformations in which these b structures are optimally hydrogen bonded vary somewhat from that of the fully extended polypeptide shown in Fig. 1.3. They therefore have a rippled or pleated edge-on appearance (*See Fig. 1.9 on next page 12*) and for that reason are sometimes called 'pleated sheets.' Successive side chains of a polypeptide chain in a b sheet extend to opposite sides of the sheet with a two-residue repeat distance of 7.0 Å.

β Sheets in proteins contain 2 to >12 polypeptide strands, with an average of 6 strands. Each strand may contain up to 15 residues, the average being 6 residues.

Parallel β sheets containing fewer than five strands are rare. This observation suggests that parallel β sheets are less stable than antiparallel β sheets, possibly because the hydrogen bonds of parallel sheets are distorted compared to those of the antiparallel sheets (See Fig. 1.8 on next page). β Sheets containing mixtures of parallel and antiparallel strands frequently occur. β Sheets almost invariably exhibit a pronounced right-handed twist when viewed along their polypeptide strands (*See Fig. 1.11 on page 13*). Conformational energy calculations indicate that the twist is a consequence of interactions between chiral L-amino acid residues in the extended polypeptide chains. The twist actually distorts and weakens the β sheet's interchain hydrogen bonds. The geometry of a particular β sheet is thus a compromise between optimizing the conformational energies of its polypeptide chains and preserving its hydrogen bonding. The *topology* (connectivity) of the polypeptide strands in a β sheet can be quite complex. The connection between two antiparallel strands may be just a small loop (*See Fig. 1.11a on page 13*), but the link between tandem parallel strands must be a crossover connection that is out of the plane of the b sheet (*See Fig. 1.11b on page 13*). The connecting link in either case can be extensive, often containing helices (*e.g., See Fig. 1.10 on page 13*).

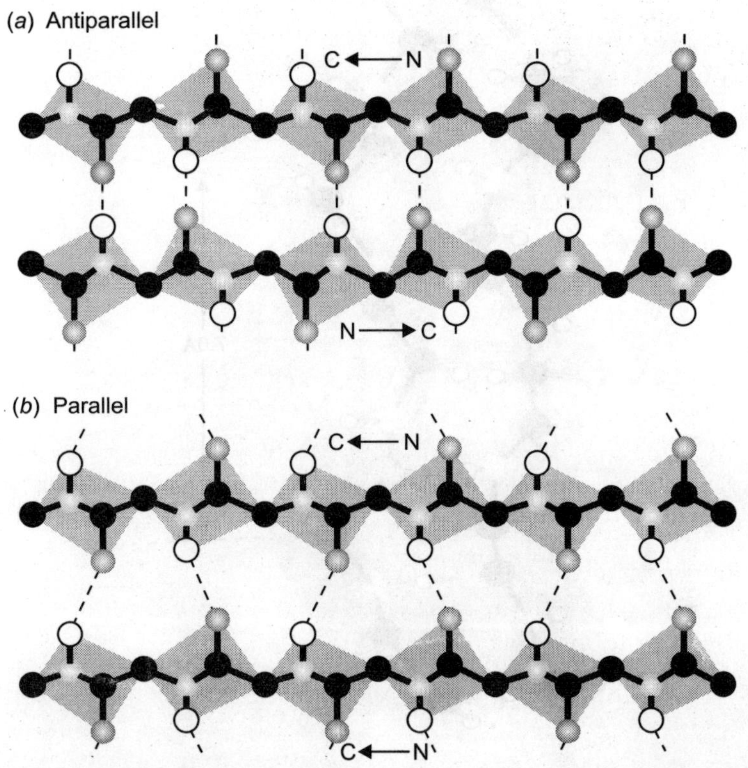

Fig. 1.8: β Sheets. Dashed lines indicate hydrogen bonds between polypeptide strands. Side chains are omitted for clarity. (*a*) An antiparallel β sheet. (*b*) A parallel β sheet

Fibrous Proteins

Proteins have historically been classified as either *fibrous* or *globular,* depending on their overall morphology. This dichotomy predates methods for determining protein structure on an atomic scale and does not do justice to proteins that contain both stiff, elongated, fibrous regions as well as more compact, highly folded, globular regions. Nevertheless, the division helps emphasize the properties of fibrous proteins, which often have a protective, connective, or supportive role in living organisms. The three well-characterized fibrous proteins we discuss here—keratin, silk fibroin, and collagen—are highly elongated molecules whose shapes are dominated by a single type of secondary structure. They are therefore useful examples of these structural elements.

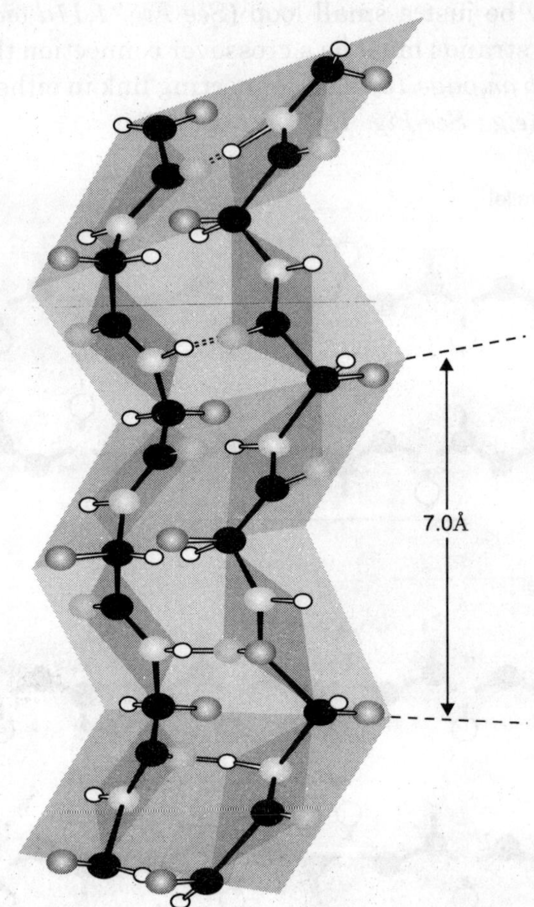

Fig. 1.9: Pleated appearance of a β sheet. Dashed lines indicate hydrogen bonds. The *R* groups (*purple*) on each polypeptide chain alternately extend to opposite sides of the sheet and are in register on adjacent chains

α Keratin—A Coiled Coil *Keratin* is a mechanically durable and chemically unreactive protein that occurs in all higher vertebrates. It is the principal component of their horny outer epidermal layer and its related appendages such as hair, horn, nails, and feathers. Keratins have been classified as either a keratins, which occur in mammals, or b keratins, which occur in birds and reptiles. Mammals each have about 30 keratin variants that are expressed in a tissue-specific manner. The X-ray diffraction pattern of a keratin resembles that expected for an a helix (hence the name a keratin). However, a keratin exhibits a 5.1-Å spacing rather than the 5.4-Å distance corresponding to the pitch of the a helix. This discrepancy is the result of *two a keratin polypeptides, each of which forms an α helix, twisting around each other to form a left-handed coil.* The normal 5.4-Å repeat distance of each α helix in the pair is thereby tilted relative to the axis of this assembly, yielding the observed 5.1- Å spacing. The assembly is said to have a *coiled coil* structure because each a helix itself follows a helical path.

Fig. 1.10: Diagram of a β sheet in bovine carboxypeptidase A. The polypeptide backbone is represented by a ribbon with a helices drawn as coils and strands of the β sheet drawn as arrows pointing toward the C-terminus. Side chains are not shown. The eight-stranded b sheet forms a saddle-shaped curved surface with a right-handed twist

(a) (b)

Fig. 1.11: Connections between adjacent strands in β sheets. (*a*) Antiparallel strands may be connected by a small loop. (*b*) Parallel strands require a more extensive cross-over connection.

because each α helix itself follows a helical path. The conformation of a keratin's coiled coil is a consequence of its primary structure: The central, 310-residue segment of each polypeptide chain has a 7-residue pseudorepeat, *a-b-c-d-e-f-g,* with non-polar residues predominating at positions and *d*. Since an α helix has 3.6 residues per turn, a keratin's *a* and *d* residues line up along one side of each α helix (*See Fig. 1.12a on next page*). The hydrophobic strip along one helix associates with the hydrophobic strip on another helix.

Because the 3.5-residue repeat in a keratin is slightly smaller than the 3.6 residues per turn of a standard α helix, the two keratin helices are inclined about 18° relative to one another, resulting in the coiled coil arrangement. This conformation allows the contacting side chains to interdigitate (Fig. 1.12*b*).

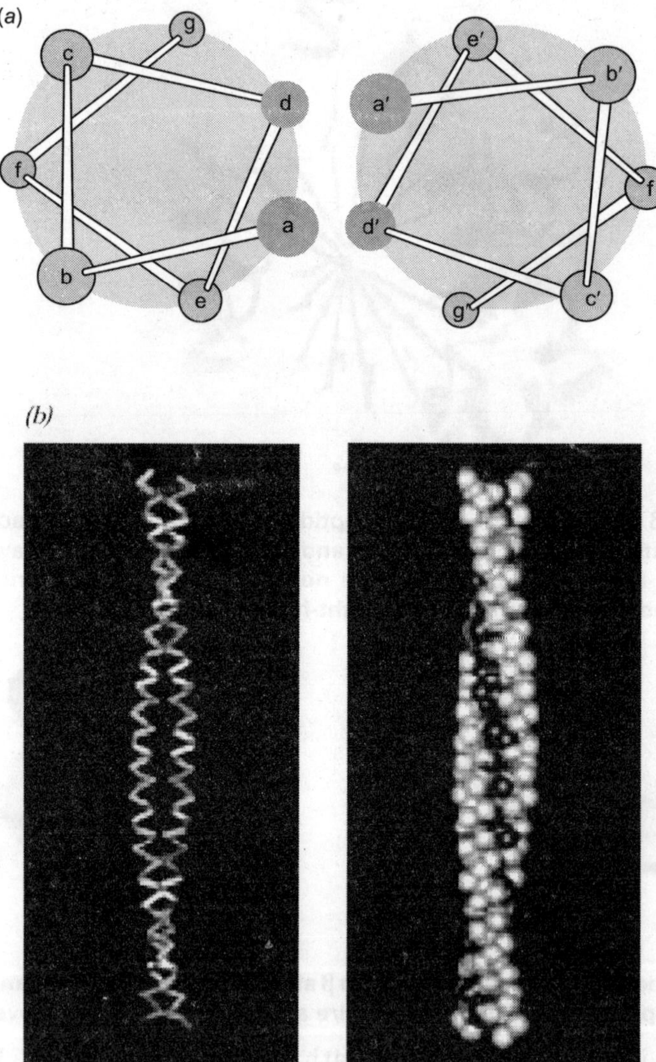

Fig. 1.12 : The coiled coil of a keratin. (*a*) View down the coil axis showing the alignment of non-polar residues along one side of each α helix. The helices have the pseudorepeating sequence *a-b-c-d-e-f-g* in which residues *a* and *d* are predominately non-polar. (*b*) Side view of the polypeptide backbone in skeletal (left) and space-filling (right) forms. Note that the contacting side chains (red spheres in the spacefilling model) interlock

The higher order structure of a keratin is not well understood. The Nand C-terminal domains of each polypeptide facilitate the assembly of coiled coils (dimers) into protofilaments, two of which constitute a protofibril (Fig. 1.13). Four protofibrils constitute a microfibril, which associates with other microfibrils to form a macrofibril. A single mammalian hair consists of layers of dead cells, each of which is packed with parallel macrofibrils.

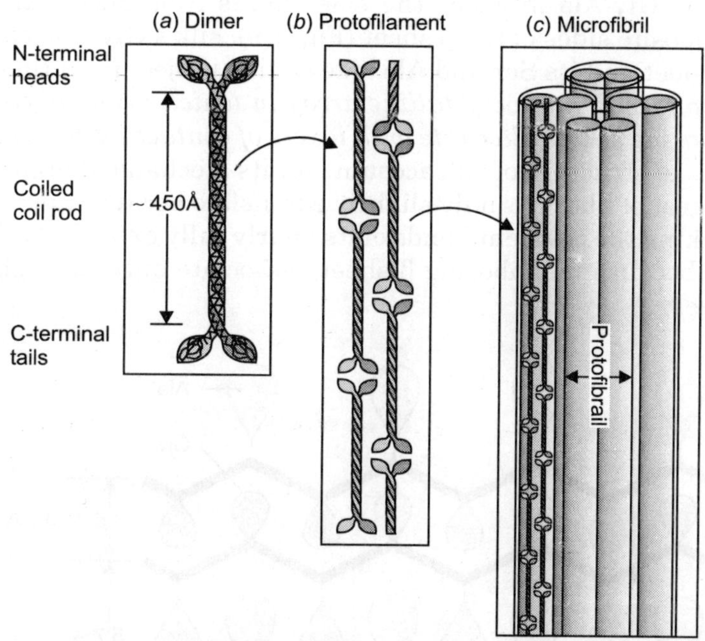

Fig. 1.13: Higher order a keratin structure. (*a*) Two keratin polypeptides form a dimeric coiled coil. (*b*) Protofilaments are formed from two staggered rows of head-to-tail associated coiled coils. (*c*) Protofilaments dimerize to form a protofibril, four of which form a microfibril. The structures of the latter assemblies are poorly characterized

α Keratin is rich in Cys residues, which form disulphide bonds that crosslink adjacent polypeptide chains. The a keratins are classified as 'hard' or 'soft' according to whether they have a high or low sulfur content. Hard keratins, such as those of hair, horn, and nail, are less pliable than soft keratins, such as those of skin and callus, because the disulphide bonds resist deformation. The disulphide bonds can be reductively cleaved with mercaptans. Hair so treated can be curled and set in a 'permanent wave' by applying an oxidizing agent that reestablishes the disulphide bonds in the new 'curled' conformation. Conversely, curly hair can be straightened by the same process. The springiness of hair and wool fibers is a consequence of the coiled coil's tendency to recover its original conformation after being untwisted by stretching. If some of its disulphide bonds have been cleaved, however, an a keratin fiber can be stretched to over twice its original length. At this point, the polypeptide chains assume a β sheet conformation. β Keratin, such as that in feathers, exhibits a b-like pattern in its native state. Silk Fibroin—A β Sheet Insects and arachnids (spiders) produce various silks to fabricate structures such as cocoons, webs, nests, and egg stalks. *Silk fibroin,* the fibrous protein from the cultivated larvae (silkworms) of the moth *Bombyx mori,* consists of antiparallel β sheets whose chains extend parallel to the fiber axis. Sequence studies have shown that long stretches of silk fibroin contain a six-residue repeat:

(-Gly-Ser-Gly-Ala-Gly-Ala-)*n* Since the side chains from successive residues of a β strand extend to opposite sides of the β sheet (Fig. 1.9), silk's Gly side chains project from one surface of a b sheet and its Ser and Ala side chains project from the opposite surface. *The* b*sheets stack to form a microcrystalline array in which layers of contacting Gly side chains from neighboring sheets alternate with layers of contacting Ser and Ala side chains* (Fig. 1.14). The β sheet structure of silk accounts for its mechanical properties. Silk, which is among the strongest of fibers, is only slightly extensible because appreciable stretching would require breaking the covalent bonds of its nearly fully extended polypeptide chains. Yet silk is flexible because neighboring β sheets associate only through relatively weak van der Waals forces.

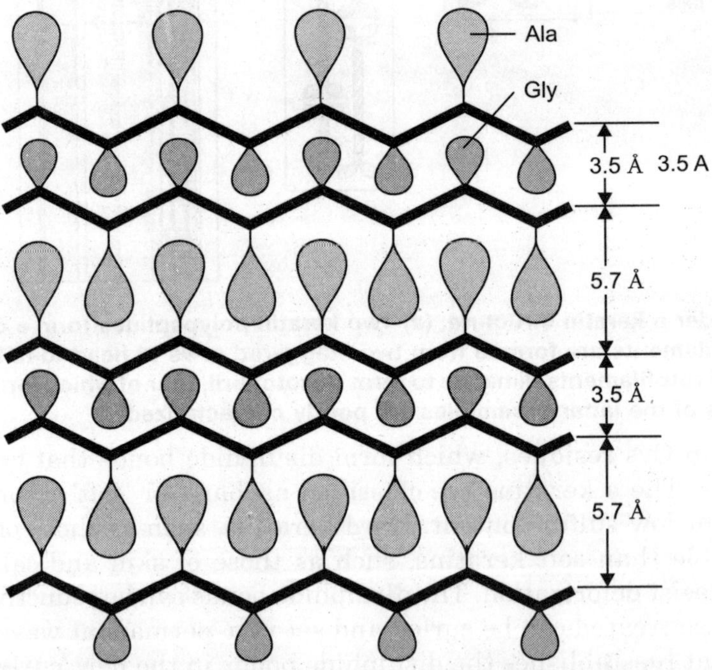

Fig. 1.14 : Schematic side view of silk fibroin β sheets. Alternating Gly and Ala (or Ser) residues extend to opposite sides of each strand so that the Gly side chains (purple) from one sheet nestle efficiently between those of the neighbouring sheet and likewise for the Ser and Ala side chains (brown). The intersheet spacings consequently have the alternating values of 3.5 and 5.7 Å.

Collagen—A Triple Helix

Collagen, which occurs in all multicellular animals, is the most abundant vertebrate protein. Its strong, insoluble fibers are the major stress-bearing components of connective tissues such as bone, teeth, cartilage, tendon, and the fibrous matrices of skin and blood vessels. A single collagen molecule consists of three polypeptide chains. Mammals have about 30 genetically distinct chains that are assembled into at least 19 collagen varieties found in different tissues in the same individual. One of the most common collagens, called Type I, consists of two a1(I) chains and one a2(I) chain. It has a molecular mass of, 285 kD, a width of,14 Å, and a length of, 3000 Å. Collagen has a distinctive amino acid composition: Nearly one-third of its residues are Gly; another 15 to 30% of its residues are Pro and *4-hydroxyprolyl (Hyp). 3-Hydroxyprolyl* and *5-hydroxylysyl (Hyl)* residues also occur in collagen, but in smaller amounts.

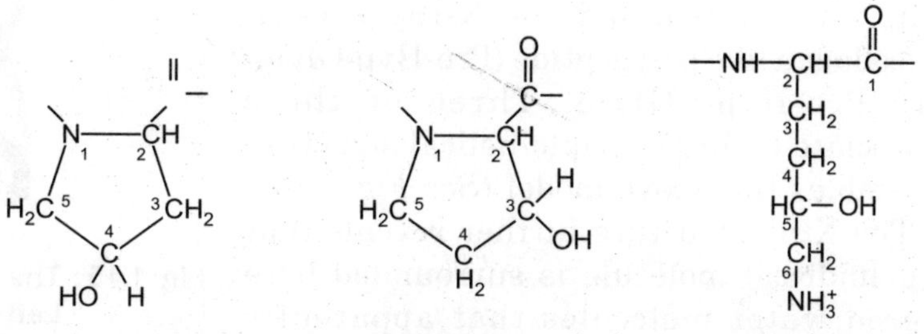

4-Hydroxyprolyl residue (Hyp) | 3-Hydroxyprolyl residue | 5-Hydroxylysyl residue (Hy1)

These non-standard residues are formed after the collagen polypeptides are synthesized. For example, Pro residues are converted to Hyp in a reaction catalyzed by *prolyl hydroxylase.* This enzyme requires *ascorbic acid (vitamin C)* to maintain its activity.

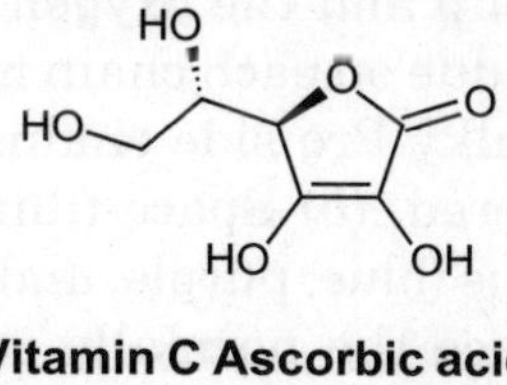

Vitamin C Ascorbic acid

The amino acid sequence of a typical collagen polypeptide consists of monotonously repeating triplets of sequence Gly-*X*-*Y* over a segment of 1000 residues, where *X* is often Pro, and *Y* is often Hyp. Hyl sometimes appears at the *Y* position. Collagen's Pro residues prevent it from forming an a helix (Pro residues cannot assume the a-helical backbone conformation and lack the backbone NOH groups that form the intrahelical hydrogen bonds shown in Fig. 1.7). Instead, the collagen polypeptide assumes a left-handed helical conformation with about three residues per turn. Three parallel chains wind around each other with a gentle, right-handed, ropelike twist to form the triple-helical structure of a collagen molecule (Fig. 1.15). Every third residue of each polypeptide chain passes through the center of the triple helix, which is so crowded that only a Gly side chain can fit there. This crowding explains the absolute requirement for a Gly at every third position of a collagen polypeptide chain. The three polypeptide chains are staggered so that Gly, *X*, and *Y* residues from each of the three chains occur at the same level along the helix axis. The peptide groups are oriented such that the NOH of each Gly makes a strong hydrogen bond with the carbonyl oxygen of an *X* residue on a neighbouring chain (*See Fig. 1.16a on next page*). The bulky and relatively inflexible Pro and Hyp residues confer rigidity on the entire assembly. This model of the collagen structure has been confirmed by Barbara Brodsky and Helen Berman, who determined the X-ray crystal structure of the collagen like polypeptide (Pro-Hyp-Gly)4-(Pro-Hyp-Ala)-(Pro-Hyp- Gly)5. Three of these polypeptides associate to form a triple-helical structure that closely resembles the above model (*See Fig. 1.16b on next page*). The Xray structure further reveals that the 87-Å-long cylindrical molecule is surrounded by a sheath of ordered water molecules that apparently stabilizes the collagen structure. These water molecules form a hydrogen-bonded network that is anchored to the polypeptides in large part through hydrogen bonds to the 4-OH group of Hyp.

Fig. 1.15 : The collagen triple helix. Left handed polypeptide helices are twisted together to form a right-handed superhelical structure.

X, and *Y* occur at every level along the axis. The dashed lines represent hydrogen bonds between each Gly NOH group and the oxygen of the succeeding Pro residue on a neighboring chain. Every third residue on each chain must be Gly because no other residue can fit near the helix axis. The bulky Pro side chains are on the periphery of the helix, where they are sterically unhindered. (*b*) Space-filling model of a collagenlike peptide. The three parallel polypeptide chains (blue, purple, and green) are staggered by one residue. Ala residues (yellow), which replace the normally occurring Gly residue in each chain cause a significant distortion of the normal collagen structure.

Collagen's well-packed, rigid, triple-helical structure is responsible for its characteristic tensile strength. The twist in the helix cannot be pulled out under tension because its component polypeptide chains are twisted in the opposite direction (Fig. 1.6–1.17). Successive levels of fiber bundles in high-quality ropes and cables, as well as in other proteins such as keratin (Fig. 1.6–1.14), are likewise oppositely twisted. Several types of collagen molecules assemble to form loose are likewise oppositely twisted. Several types of collagen molecules assemble to form loose networks or thick fibrils arranged in bundles or sheets, depending on the tissue. The collagen molecules in fibrils are organized in staggered

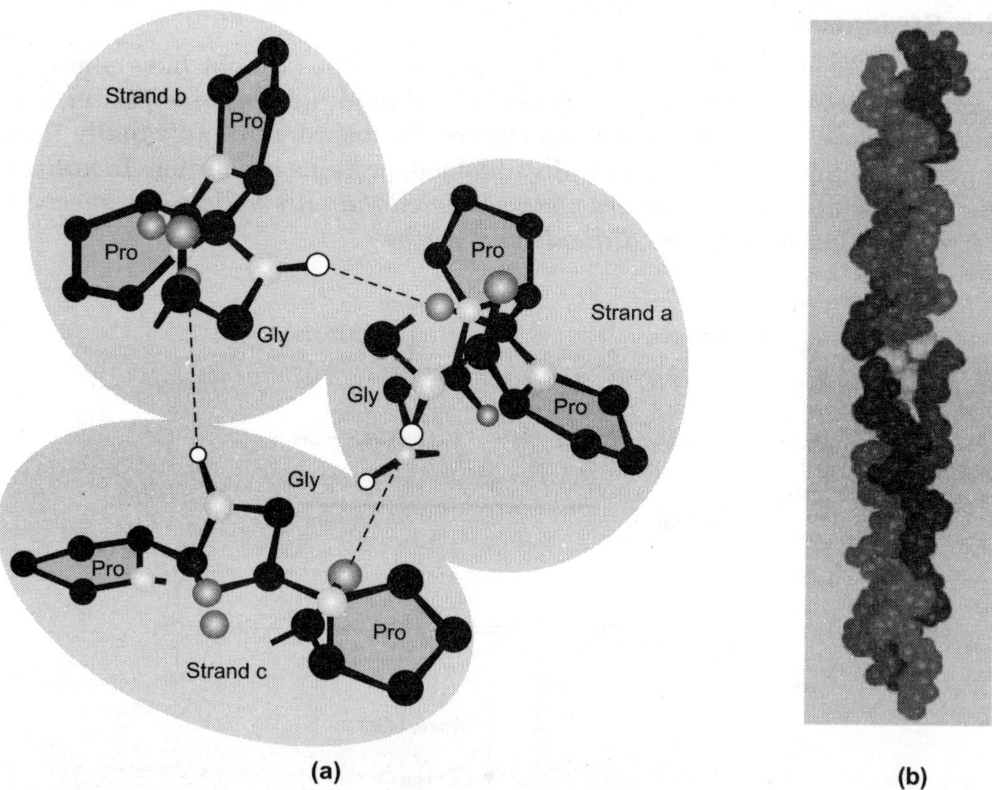

Fig. 1.16 : Molecular interactions in collagen. (*a*) Hydrogen bonding in the collagen triple helix. This view down the helix axis shows one Gly and two Pro residues (*X* and *Y*) in each chain. The residues are staggered so that one Gly

arrays that are stabilized by hydrophobic interactions resulting from the close packing of triple-helical units. Collagen is also covalently cross-linked, which accounts for its poor solubility. The cross-links cannot be disulphide bonds, as in keratin, because collagen is almost devoid of Cys residues. Instead, the cross-links are derived from Lys and His side chains in reactions such as those shown in Fig. 1.6–1.19. *Lysyl oxidase,* the enzyme that converts Lys residues to those of the aldehyde *allysine,* is the only enzyme implicated in this cross-linking process. Up to four side chains can be covalently bonded to each other. The cross-links do not form at random but tend to occur near the N- and C-termini of the collagen molecules. The degree of cross-linking in a particular tissue increases with age. This is why meat from older animals is tougher than meat from younger animals.

Non-repetitive Protein Structure

The majority of proteins are globular proteins that, unlike the fibrous proteins discussed in the preceding section, may contain several types of regular secondary structure, including a helices, β sheets, and other recognizable elements. A significant portion of a protein's structure may also be irregular or unique.

Irregular Structures

Segments of polypeptide chains whose successive residues do not have similar *f* and *c* values are sometimes called coils. However, you should not confuse this term with the appellation *random coil,* which refers to the totally disordered and rapidly fluctuating conformations assumed by *denatured* (fully unfolded) proteins in solution. In *native* (folded) proteins, *non-repetitive structures are no less ordered than are helices or* b *sheets; they are simply irregular and hence more difficult to describe.*

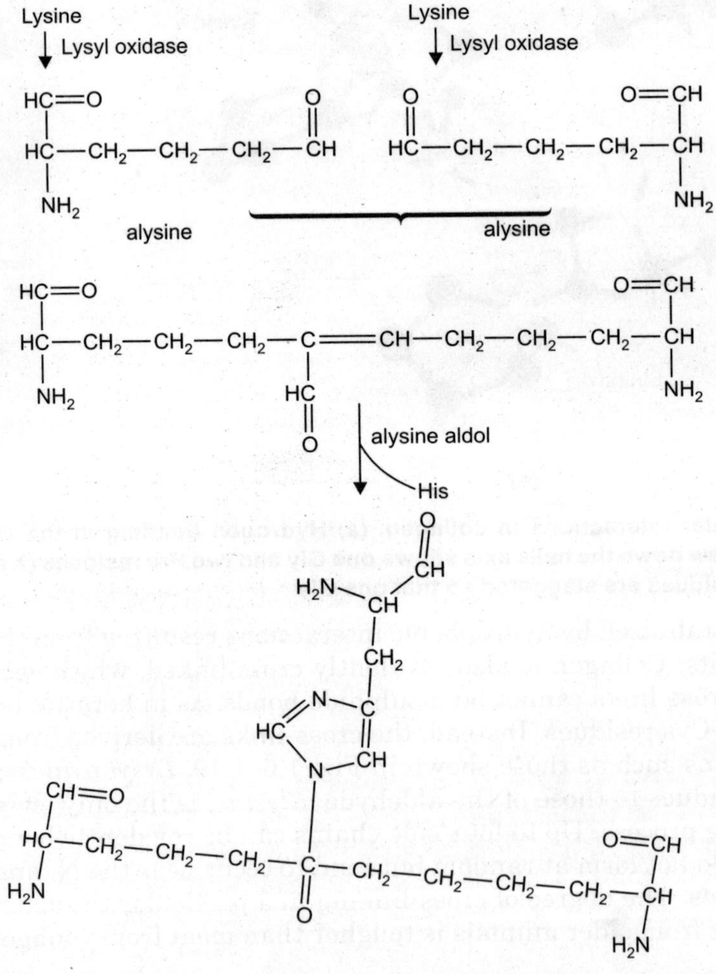

Lysine
Lysyl oxidase
Lysine
Lysyl oxidase
alysine
alysine
alysine aldol
His

The equation in the right shows the reaction between the cross-linking polymers of collagen.

The first step is the lysyl oxidase catalyzed oxidative deamination of Lys to form the aldehyde allysine. Two allysines then undergo an aldol condensation to form allysine aldol. This product can react with His to form aldol histidine, which can in turn react with 5-hydroxylysine to form a Schiff base (an imine bond), thereby cross-linking four side chains.

Protein Structure Prediction and Protein Design

Hundreds of thousands of protein sequences are known either through direct protein sequencing (See the Encyclopaedic architecture of chemistry) or, more commonly, through nucleic acid sequencing (See the Encyclopaedic architecture of chemistry). Yet the structures of only, 7000 of these proteins have as yet been determined by X-ray crystallography or NMR techniques. Determining the function of a newly discovered protein often requires knowledge of its three-dimensional structure. There are currently several major approaches to protein structure prediction. The simplest and most reliablc approach, *homology modelling,* aligns the sequence of interest with the sequence of a homologous protein of known structure —compensating for amino acid substitutions, insertions, and deletions— through modeling and energy minimization calculations. This method yields reliable models for proteins that have as little as 25% sequence identity with a protein of known structure, although, of course, the accuracy of the model increases with the degree of sequence identity. Distantly related proteins may be structurally similar even though they have diverged to such an extent that their sequences show no obvious resemblance. *Threading* is a computational technique that attempts to determine the unknown structure of a protein by ascertaining whether it is consistent with a known protein structure. It does so by placing (threading) the residues of the unknown protein along the backbone of a known protein structure and then determining whether the amino acid side chains of the unknown protein are stable in that arrangement. This method is not yet reliable, although it has yielded encouraging results. Empirical methods based on experimentally determined statistical information such as the a helix and b sheet propensities deduced by Chou and Fasman (Table–1.1) have been moderately successful in predicting the secondary structures of proteins. Their advantage is their simplicity (they don't require a computer).

Since the native structure of a protein depends only on its amino acid sequence, it should be possible, in principle, to predict the structure of a protein based only on its chemical and physical properties (*e.g.,* the hydrophobicity, size, hydrogen-bonding propensity, and charge of each of its amino acid residues). Such *ab initio* (from the beginning) methods are still in their infancy. They are moderately successful in predicting simple structures such as a single α helix but have failed miserably when tested with larger polypeptides whose structures have been experimentally determined. Nevertheless, a recently developed algorithm that simulates the hierarchical protein folding pathway has yielded structural models that are surprisingly similar to those of the corresponding observed protein structures.

Protein design, the experimental inverse of protein structure prediction, has provided insights into protein folding and stability. Protein design begins with a target structure such as a simple sandwich of β sheets or a bundle of four α helices. It attempts to construct an amino acid sequence that will form that structure. The designed polypeptide is then chemically or biologically synthesized, and its structure is determined. Fortunately, protein folding seems to be governed more by extended sequences of amino acids than by individual residues, which allows some room for error in designing polypeptides. Experimental results suggest that the greatest challenge of protein design may lie not in getting the polypeptide to fold to the desired conformation but in preventing it from folding into other, unwanted conformations. In this respect, science lags far behind nature. However, the recent successful design, using computationally based techniques, of a 28-residue polypeptide that stably folds to the desired structure (the smallest known polypeptide that is capable of folding into a unique structure without the aid of disulphide bonds, metal ions, or other subunits) indicates that significant progress in our understanding of protein folding has been made.

Variations in Standard Secondary Structure

Variations in amino acid sequence as well as the overall structure of the folded protein can distort the regular conformations of secondary structural elements. For example, the a helix frequently deviates from its ideal conformation in its initial and final turns of the helix. Similarly, a strand of polypeptide in a b sheet may contain an 'extra' residue that is not hydrogen bonded to a neighboring strand, producing a distortion known as a b *bulge.* Many of the limits on amino acid composition and sequence may be due in part to conformational constraints in the three dimensional structure of proteins. For example, a Pro residue produces a kink in an α helix or β sheet. Similarly, steric clashes between several sequential amino acid residues with large branched side chains (*e.g.,* Ile and Tyr) can destabilize α helices. Analysis of known protein structures by Peter Chou and Gerald Fasman revealed the propensity *P* of a residue to occur in an α helix or a β sheet (*See Tble 1.1 on next page*). Chou and Fasman also discovered that certain residues not only have a high propensity for a particular secondary structure but they tend to disrupt or break other secondary structures. Such data are useful for predicting the secondary structures of proteins with known amino acid sequences. The presence of certain residues outside of α helices or β sheets may also be non-random. For example, α helices are often flanked by residues such as Asn and Gln, whose side chains can fold back to form hydrogen bonds with one of the four terminal residues of the helix, a phenomenon termed *helix capping.* Recall that the four residues at each end of an α helix are not fully hydrogen bonded to neighbouring backbone segments (Fig. 1.7). Turns and Loops Segments with regular secondary structure such as α helices or strands of β sheets are typically joined by stretches of polypeptide that abruptly change direction. Such *reverse turns* or β *bends* (so named because they often connect successive strands of antiparallel β sheets) almost always occur at protein surfaces. Most reverse turns involve four successive amino acid residues more or less arranged in one of two ways, Type I and Type II, that differ by a 180° flip of the peptide unit linking residues 2 and 3 (Fig. 1.6-1.20). Both types of turns are stabilized by a hydrogen bond, although deviations from these ideal conformations often disrupt this hydrogen bond.In Type II turns, the oxygen atom of residue 2 crowds the Cb atom of residue 3, which is therefore usually Gly. Residue 2 of either type of turn is often Pro since it can assume the required conformation. Almost all proteins with more than 60 residues contain one or more loops of 6 to 16 residues, called V *loops.* These loops, which have the necked-in shape of the Greek uppercase letter omega (*See Fig. 1.18 on page 25*), are compactglobular entities because their side chains tend to fill in their internal cavities. Since V loops are almost invariably located on the protein surface, they may have important roles in biological recognition processes.

Table 1.1 : Propensities of Amino Acid Residues for α Helical and β Sheet Conformations

Residue	Pa	Pb
Ala	1.42	0.83
Arg	0.98	0.93
Asn	0.67	0.89
Asp	1.01	0.54
Cys	0.70	1.19
Gln	1.11	1.10
Glu	1.51	0.37
Gly	0.57	0.75
His	1.00	0.87
Ile	1.08	1.60
Leu	1.21	1.30
Lys	1.16	0.74
Met	1.45	1.05
Phe	1.13	1.38
Pro	0.57	0.55
Ser	0.77	0.75
Thr	0.83	1.19
Trp	1.08	1.37
Tyr	0.69	1.47
Val	1.06	1.70

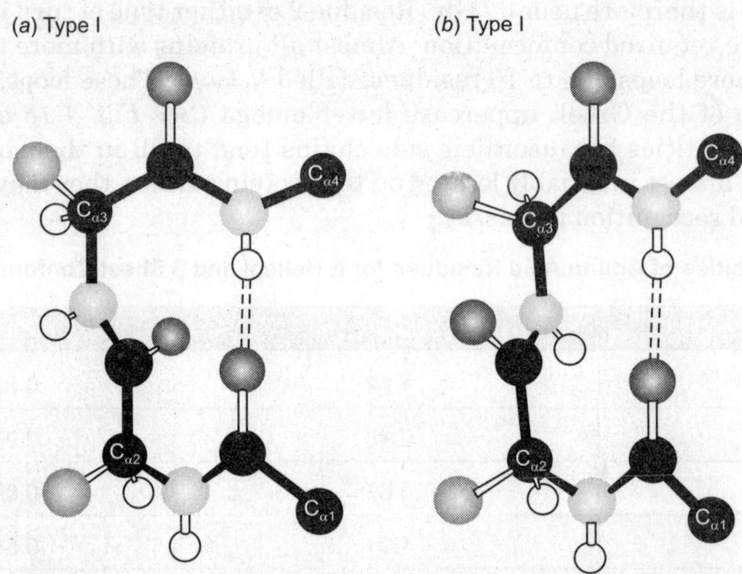

Fig. 1.17 : Reverse turns in polypeptide chains. Dashed lines represent hydrogen bonds. (*a*) Type I. (*b*) Type II

The Tertiary Structure

The tertiary structure of a protein describes the folding of its secondary structural elements and specifies the positions of each atom in the protein, including those of its side chains. The known protein structures have come to light through *X-ray crystallographic* or *nuclear magnetic resonance (NMR)* studies. The atomic coordinates of most of these structures are deposited in a database known as the Protein Data Bank (PDB). These data are readily available via the Internet (http://www.pbd.bnl.gov), which allows the tertiary structures of a variety of proteins to be analyzed and compared. The common features of protein tertiary structure reveal much about the biological functions of the proteins and their evolutionary origins.

Determining Protein Structure

X-Ray crystallography is one of the most powerful methods for studying macromolecular structure. According to optical principles, the uncertainty in locating an object is approximately equal to the wavelength of the radiation used to observe it. X-Rays can directly image a molecule because X-ray wavelengths are comparable to covalent bond distances (,1.5 Å; individual molecules cannot be seen in a light microscope because visible light has a minimum wavelength of 4000 Å). When a crystal of the molecule to be visualized is exposed to a collimated (parallel) beam of X-rays, the atoms in the molecule scatter the X-rays, with the scattered rays canceling or reinforcing each other in a process known as diffraction. The resulting *diffraction pattern* is recorded on photographic film (Fig. 1.18) or by a radiation counter. The intensities of the diffraction maxima (darkness of the spots on the film) are then used to mathematically construct the three-dimensional image of the crystal structure. The photograph in Fig. 1.6-1.22 represents only a small portion of the total diffraction information available from a crystal of myoglobin, a small globular protein. In contrast, fibrous proteins do not crystallize but, instead, can be drawn into fibers whose X-ray diffraction patterns contain only a few spots and thus contain comparatively little structural information. Likewise, the diffraction pattern of a DNA fiber (Fig. 1.3-1.8) is relatively simple.

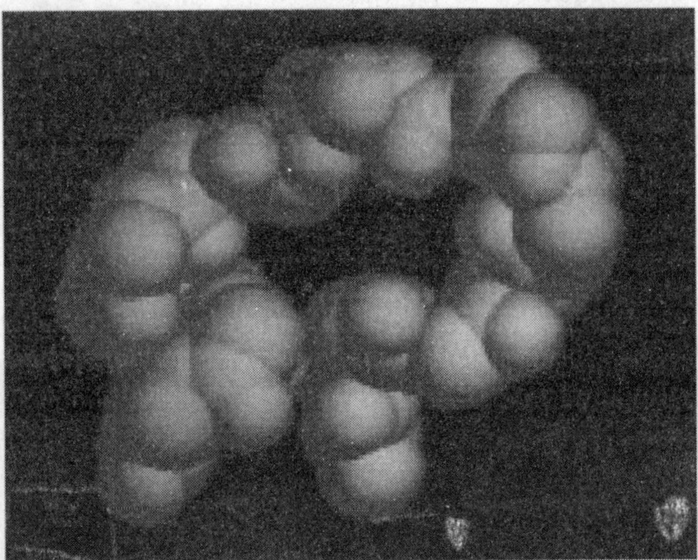

Fig. 1.18: Space-filling model of an V loop. Only backbone atoms are shown; the side chains would fill the loop. This structure is residues 40 to 54 from cytochrome *c*.

X-Rays interact almost exclusively with the electrons in matter, not the atomic nuclei. An X-ray structure is therefore an image of the electron density of the object under study. This information can be shown as a three dimensional *contour map* (Fig. 1.6-1.23). Hydrogen atoms, which have only one electron, are not visible in macromolecular X-ray structures. The X-ray structures of small organic molecules can be determined with a resolution on the order of 1 Å. Few protein crystals have this degree of organization. Furthermore, not all proteins can be coaxed to crystallize, that is, to precipitate in ordered three-dimensional arrays. The protein crystals that do form (Fig. 1.6-1.24) differ from those of most small organic molecules in being highly hydrated; protein crystals are typically 40 to 60% water by volume. The large solvent content gives protein crystals a soft, jellylike consistency so that the molecules are typically disordered by a few angstroms. This limits their resolution to about 2 to 3.5 Å, although a few protein crystals are better ordered (have higher resolution).

A resolution of a few angstroms is too coarse to clearly reveal the positions of individual atoms, but the distinctive shape of the polypeptide backbone can usually be traced. The positions and orientations of its side chains can therefore be deduced. However, since many side chains have similar sizes and shapes, *knowledge of the protein's primary structure is required to fit the sequence of amino acids to its electron density map*. Mathematical techniques can then refine the atomic positions to within, 0.1 Å in high-resolution structures.

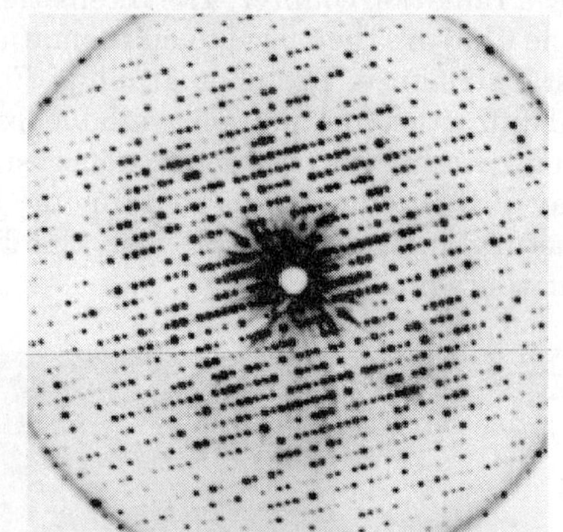

Fig. 1.19: An X-ray diffraction photograph of a crystal of sperm whale myoglobin. The intensity of each diffraction maximum (the darkness of each spot) is a function of the crystal's electron density.

PROTEIN STRUCTURE DETERMINATION BY NUCLEAR MAGNETIC RESONANCE PROCESS

The determination of the three-dimensional structures of small proteins (,250 residues) in aqueous solution has become possible since the mid-1980s, through the development of two-dimensional (2D) NMR spectroscopy (and, more recently, of 3D and 4D techniques), in large part by Kurt Wüthrich. A sample is placed in a magnetic field so that the spins of its protons are aligned. When radiofrequency pulses are applied, the protons are excited and then emit signals whose frequency depends on the molecular environment of the protons. Proteins contain so many atoms that their standard (one-dimensional) NMR spectra consist almost entirely of overlapping signals that are impossible to interpret. In 2D NMR, the characteristics of the applied signal are varied in order to obtain additional information from interactions between protons that are,5 Å apart in space or are covalently connected by only one or two other atoms. The resulting set of distances, together with known

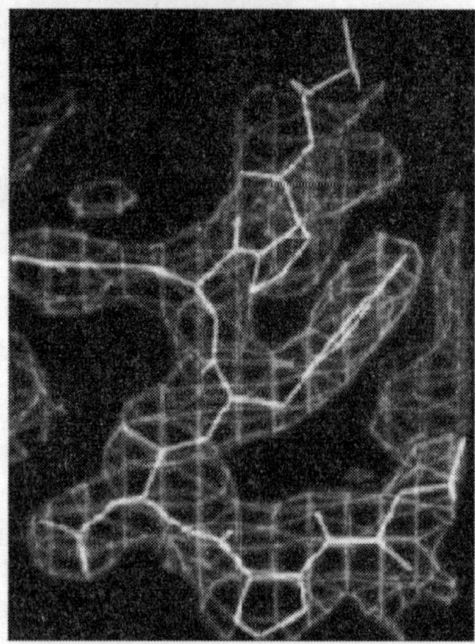

Fig. 1.19A: An electron density map. The three-dimensional outline of the electron density (*orange*) is shown with a superimposed atomic model of the corresponding polypeptide segment (*white*). This structure is a portion of human rhinovirus (the cause of the common cold)

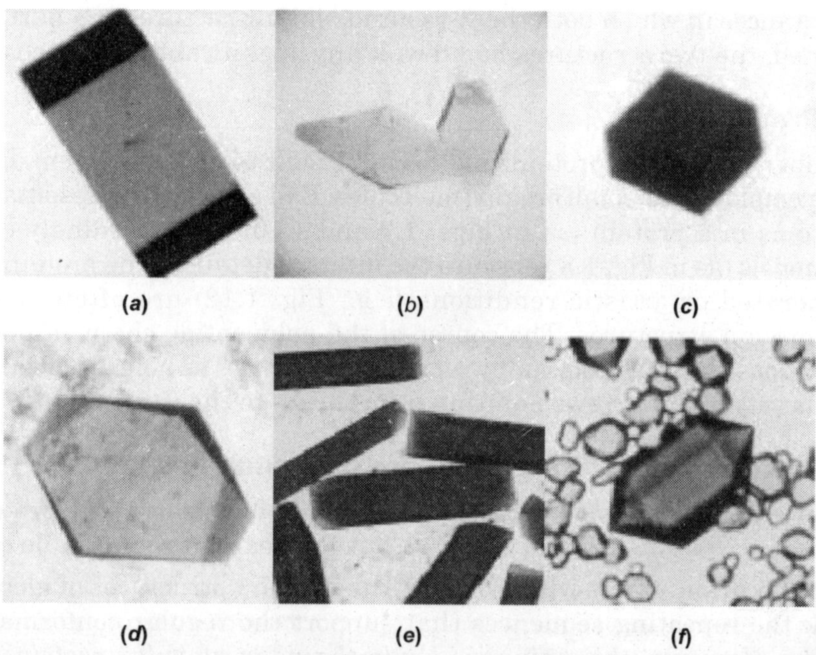

Fig. 1.20 : Protein crystals. (*a*) Azurin from *Pseudomonas aeruginosa,* (*b*) flavodoxin from *Desulfovibrio vulgaris,* (*c*) rubredoxin from *Clostridium pasteurianum,* (*d*) azidomet myohemerythrin from the marine worm *Siphonosoma funafuti,* (*e*) lamprey haemoglobin, and (*f*) bacteriochlorophyll α protein from *Prosthecochloris aestuarii.* These crystals are coloured because the proteins contain light-absorbing groups; proteins are colourless in the absence of such groups

geometric constraints such as covalent bond distances and angles, group planarity, chirality, and van der Waals radii, are used to compute the protein's three-dimensional structure. However, since interproton distance measurements are imprecise, they are insufficient to imply a unique structure. For this reason, the NMR structure of a protein (or any other macromolecule with a well-defined structure) is often presented as an ensemble of closely related structures. The above NMR structure of a 64-residue polypeptide is presented as 20 superimposed Ca traces (*white*), each of which is consistent with the NMR data and geometric constraints. A few side chains (*red, yellow,* and *blue*) are also shown.

Another consequence of the large solvent content of protein crystals is that *crystalline proteins maintain their native conformations and therefore their functions.* Indeed, the degree of hydration of proteins in crystals is similar to that in cells. Thus, the X-ray crystal structures of proteins often provide a basis for understanding their biological activities. Crystal structures have been used as starting points for designing drugs that can interact specifically with target proteins under physiological conditions. Recent advances in NMR spectroscopy have permitted the determination of the structures of proteins and nucleic acids in solution (but limited to a size of, 30 kD). Thus, NMR techniques can be used to elucidate the structures of proteins and other macromolecules that fail to crystallize. In the several instances in which both the X-ray and NMR structures of a particular protein were determined, the two structures had few, if any, significant differences.

Visualizing Proteins

The huge number of atoms in proteins makes it difficult to visualize them using the same sorts of models employed for small organic molecules. Ball and-stick representations showing all or most atoms in a protein (as in Figs. 1.7 and 1.10) are exceedingly cluttered, and space-filling models (as in Fig. 1.8) obscure the internal details of the protein. Accordingly, computer-generated or artistic renditions (*e.g.*, Fig. 1.12) are often more useful for representing protein structures. The course of the polypeptide chain can be followed by tracing the positions of its Ca atoms or by representing helices as helical ribbons or cylinders, and β sheets as sets of flat arrows pointing from the N- to the C-terminal.

B. Motifs (Supersecondary Structures) and Domains

In the years since Kendrew solved the structure of myoglobin, nearly 7000 protein structures have been reported. No two are exactly alike, but they exhibit remarkable consistencies.

Side Chain Location Varies with Polarity The primary structures of globular proteins generally lack the repeating sequences that support the regular conformations seen in fibrous proteins. However, *the amino acid side chains in globular proteins are spatially distributed according to their polarities:*

1. The non-polar residues Val, Leu, Ile, Met, and Phe occur mostly in the interior of a protein, out of contact with the aqueous solvent. The hydrophobic effects that promote this distribution are largely responsible for the three-dimensional structure of native proteins.
2. The charged polar residues Arg, His, Lys, Asp, and Glu are usually located on the surface of a protein in contact with the aqueous solvent. This is because immersing an ion in the virtually anhydrous interior of a protein is energetically unfavourable.
3. The uncharged polar groups Ser, Thr, Asn, Gln, and Tyr are usually on the protein surface but also occur in the interior of the molecule. When buried in the protein, these residues are almost always hydrogen bonded to other groups; in a sense, the formation of a hydrogen bond 'neutralizes' their polarity. This is also the case with the polypeptide backbone. These general principles of side chain distribution are evident in individual elements of secondary structure (Fig. 1.21) as well as in whole proteins

Polar side chains tend to extend toward—and thereby help form—the protein's surface, whereas nonpolar side chains largely extend toward—and thereby occupy—its interior (Fig. 1.22). Most proteins are quite compact, with their interior atoms packed together even more efficiently than the atoms in a crystal of small organic molecules. Nevertheless, the atoms of protein side chains almost invariably have low-energy arrangements.

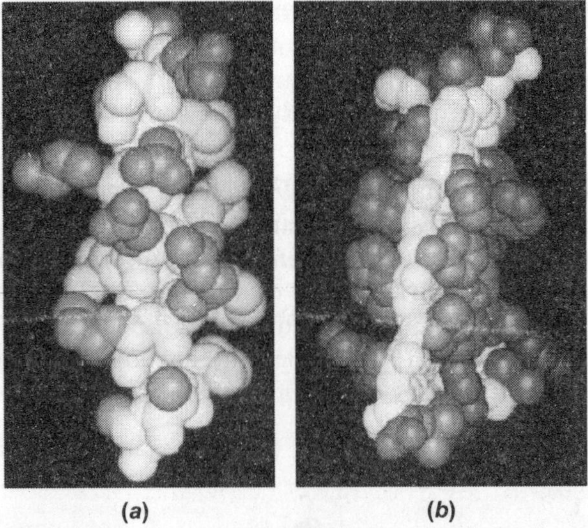

Fig. 1.21 : Side chain locations in an α helix and a β sheet. In these space-filling models, the main chain is white, nonpolar side chains are yellow or brown, and polar side chains are purple. (*a*) An a helix from sperm whale myoglobin. Note that the non-polar residues are primarily on one side of the helix. (*b*) An antiparallel b sheet from concanavalin A (*side view*). The protein interior is to the right and the exterior is to the left

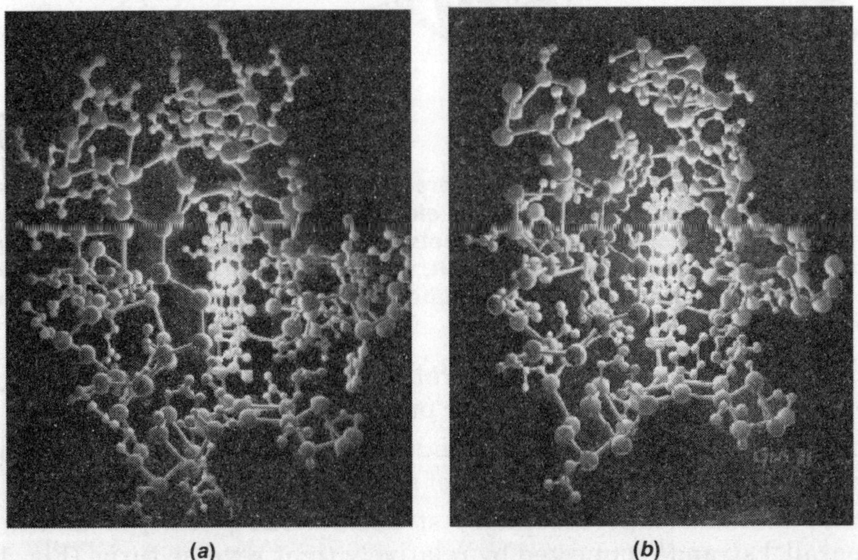

Fig. 1.22 : *Figure 1.6-1.26.* Side chain distribution in horse heart cytochrome *c*. In these paintings, based on the X-ray structure determined by Richard Dickerson, the protein is illuminated by its single iron atom centered in a heme group. Hydrogen atoms are not shown. In (*a*) the hydrophilic side chains are green, and in (*b*) the hydrophobic side chains are orange

Evidently, interior side chains adopt relaxed conformations despite the profusion of intramolecular interactions. Closely packed protein interiors generally exclude water. When water molecules are present, they often occupy specific positions where they can form hydrogen bonds, sometimes acting as a bridge between two hydrogen-bonding protein groups.

Helices and Sheets Can Be Combined in Various Ways The major types of secondary structural elements, α helices and β sheets, occur in globular proteins in varying proportions and combinations. Some proteins, such as hemoglobin subunits, consist only of α helices spanned by short connecting links (Fig. 1.23 *a*). Others, such as *concanavalin A,* have a large proportion of β sheets and are devoid of α helices (Fig. 1.23b). Most proteins, such as *triose phosphate isomerase* (Fig. 1.23c) and carboxypeptidase A (Fig. 1.10), have significant amounts of both types of secondary structure (on average,31% α helix and 28% β sheet).

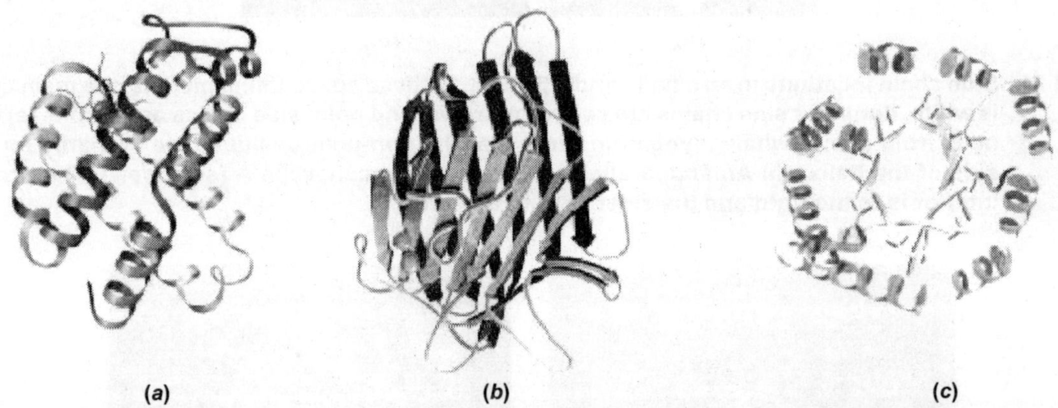

Fig. 1.23: Examples of globular proteins. Different proteins contain different proportions and arrangements of secondary structurai elements. In these models, a helices are drawn as helical ribbons, and strands of β sheets are drawn as flat arrows pointing toward the C-terminus. (*a*) A haemoglobin subunit, with its heme group shown as a skeletal model (*b*) Jack bean concanavalin A. The spheres represent metal ions. (*c*) Triose phosphate isomerase from chicken muscle

Certain groupings of secondary structural elements, called *supersecondary structures* or *motifs,* occur in many unrelated globular proteins:

1. The most common form of supersecondary structure is the bab *motif*, in which an α helix connects two parallel strands of a β sheet (Fig. 1.24*a*).
2. Another common supersecondary structure, the β *hairpin* motif, consists of antiparallel strands connected by relatively tight reverse turns (Fig. 1.24*b*).
3. In an aa *motif*, two successive antiparallel α helices pack against each other with their axes inclined. This permits energetically favourable intermeshing of their contacting side chains (Fig. 1.6–1.28*c*). Such associations stabilize the coiled coil conformation of a keratin.

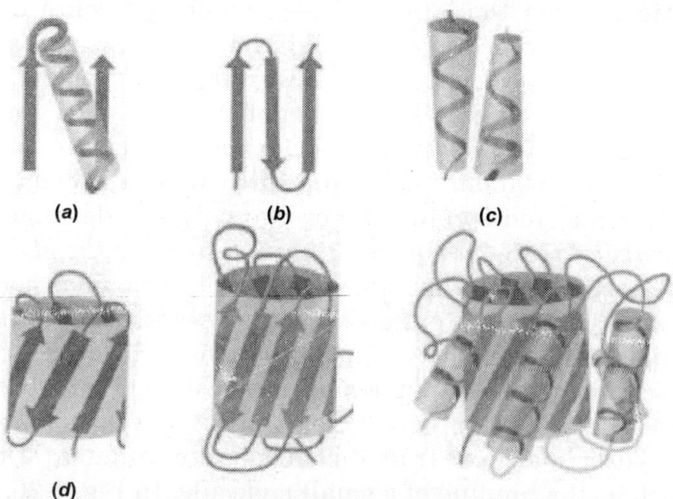

Fig. 1.24 : Protein motifs. (*a*) A bab motif, (*b*) a b hairpin, (*c*) an aa motif, and (*d*) β barrels. The β barrel composed of overlapping bab units (*far right*) is known as an a/b barrel. It is shown in top view in Fig. 1.23*c*.

4. Extended β sheets often roll up to form β *barrels.* Three different types of β barrels are shown in Fig. 1.24*d*. Motifs may have functional as well as structural significance. For example, Michael Rossmann showed that a babab unit, in which the b strands form a parallel sheet with a helical connections, often acts as a nucleotidebinding site. In most proteins that bind dinucleotides (such as nicotinamide adenine dinucleotide, NAD1;), two such babab units combine to form a motif known as a *dinucleotide-binding fold,* or *Rossmann fold* (Fig. 1.25).

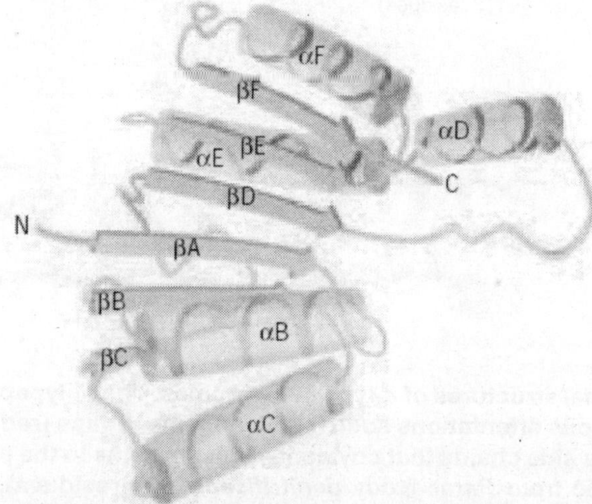

Fig. 1.25 : An idealized dinucleotide-binding (Rossmann) fold. The two structurally similar babab units (*yellow* and *blue*) can each bind a nucleotide portion of the dinucleotide NAD1 (not shown)

Large Polypeptides Form Domains Polypeptide chains containing more than, 200 residues usually fold into two or more globular clusters known as *domains,* which give these proteins a bi- or multilobal appearance. Most domains consist of 100 to 200 amino acid residues and have an average diameter of 25 Å. Each subunit of the enzyme *glyceraldehyde-3-phosphate dehydrogenase,* for example, has two distinct domains (Fig. 1.26). A polypeptide chain wanders back and forth within a domain, but neighboring domains are usually connected by only one or two polypeptide segments. *Consequently, many domains are structurally independent units that have the characteristics of small globular proteins.* Nevertheless, the domain structure of a protein is not necessarily obvious since its domains may make such extensive contacts with each other that the protein appears to be a single globular entity. An inspection of the various protein structures diagrammed in this chapter reveals that domains consist of two or more layers of secondary structural elements. The reason for this is clear: At least two such layers are required to seal off a domain's hydrophobic core from its aqueous environment. Domains often have a specific function such as the binding of a small molecule. In Fig. 1.26, for example, NAD1 binds to the first domain of glyceraldehyde-3-phosphate dehydrogenase (note its dinucleotide-binding fold). In multi-domain proteins, binding sites often occupy the clefts between domains; that is, the small molecules are bound by groups from two domains. In such cases, the relatively pliant covalent connection between the domains allows flexible interactions between the protein and the small molecule.

Protein Families

The thousands of known protein structures, comprising an even greater number of separate domains, can be grouped into families by examining the overall paths followed by their

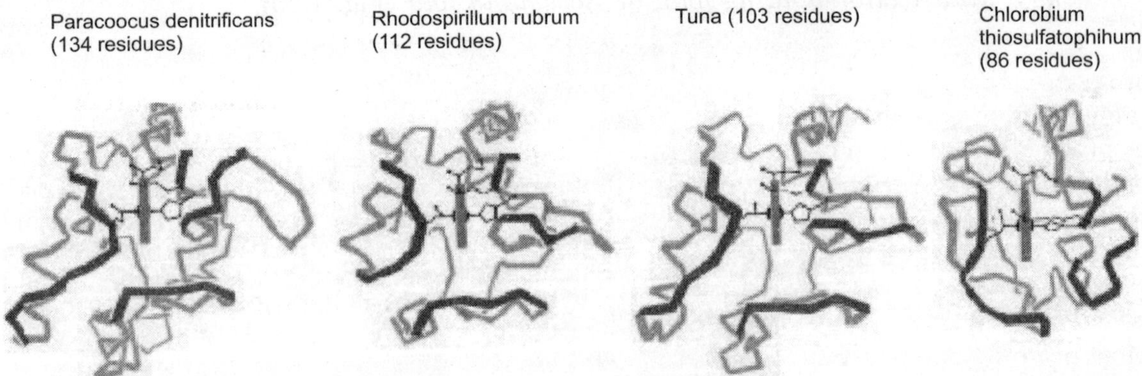

Fig. 1.26 : Three-dimensional structures of *c*-type cytochromes. The polypeptide backbones (*blue*) are shown in analogous orientations such that their heme groups (*red*) are viewed edge-on. The Cys, Met, and His side chains that covalently link the heme to the protein are also shown. (*a*) Cytochrome *c*550 from *Paracoccus denitrificans* (134 residues), (*b*) cytochrome *c*2 from *Rhodospirillum rubrum* (112 residues), (*c*) cytochrome *c* from tuna (103 residues), and (*d*) cytochrome *c*555 from *Chlorobium thiosulfatophilum* (86 residues).

polypeptide chains. When folding patterns are compared without regard to the amino acid sequence or the presence of surface loops, the number of unique structural domains drops to only a few hundred. (Although not all protein structures are known, estimates place an upper limit of about 1000 on the total number of unique protein domains in nature.) Surprisingly, a few dozen folding patterns account for about half of all known protein structures. There are several possible reasons for the limited number of known domain structures. The numbers may reflect database bias; that is, the collection of known protein structures may not be a representative sample of all protein structures. However, the rapidly increasing number of proteins whose structures have been determined makes this possibility less and less plausible.

More likely, the common protein structures may be evolutionary sinks—domains that arose and persisted because of their ability (1) to form stable folding patterns; (2) to tolerate amino acid deletions, substitutions, and insertions, thereby making them more likely to survive evolutionary changes; and (3) to support essential biological functions. Polypeptides with similar sequences tend to adopt similar backbone conformations. This is certainly true for evolutionarily related proteins that carry out similar functions. For example, the cytochromes *c* of different species are highly conserved proteins with closely similar sequences (see Table 1.5-1.6) and three-dimensional structures. Cytochrome *c* occurs only in eukaryotes, but prokaryotes contain proteins known as *c-type cytochromes,* which perform the same general function (that of an electron carrier). The *c*-type cytochromes from different species exhibit only low degrees of sequence similarity to each other and to eukaryotic cytochromes *c*. Yet their X-ray structures are clearly similar,particularly in polypeptide chain folding and side chain packing in the protein interior (*See Fig. 1.27 on next page*). The major structural differences among *c*-type cytochromes lie in the various polypeptide loops on their surfaces. The sequences of the *c*-type cytochromes have diverged so far from one another that, in the absence of their X-ray structures, they can be properly aligned only through the use of recently developed and mathematically sophisticated computer programs. Thus, *it appears that the essential structural and functional elements of proteins, rather than their amino acid residues, are conserved during evolution.*Structural similarities in proteins with only distantly related functions are commonly observed. For example, many NAD1-binding enzymes that participate in widely different metabolic pathways contain similar dinucleotide-binding folds (see Fig. 1.26) coupled to diverse domains that carry out specific enzymatic reactions.

Quaternary Structure and Symmetry

Most proteins, particularly those with molecular masses .100 kD, consist of more than one polypeptide chain. These polypeptide subunits associate with a specific geometry. The spatial arrangement of these subunits is known as a protein's quaternary structure.

There are several reasons why multisubunit proteins are so common. In large assemblies of proteins, such as collagen fibrils, the advantages of subunit construction over the synthesis of one huge polypeptide chain are analogous to those of using prefabricated components in constructing a building:

Defects can be repaired by simply replacing the flawed subunit; the site of subunit manufacture can be different from the site of assembly into the final product; and the only genetic information necessary to specify the entire edifice is the information specifying its few different self-assembling subunits. In the case of enzymes, increasing a protein's size tends to better fix the three-dimensional positions of its reacting groups. *Increasing the size of an enzyme through the association of identical subunits is more efficient than increasing the length of its polypeptide chain since each subunit has an active site. More importantly, the subunit construction of many enzymes provides the structural basis for the regulation of their activities.*

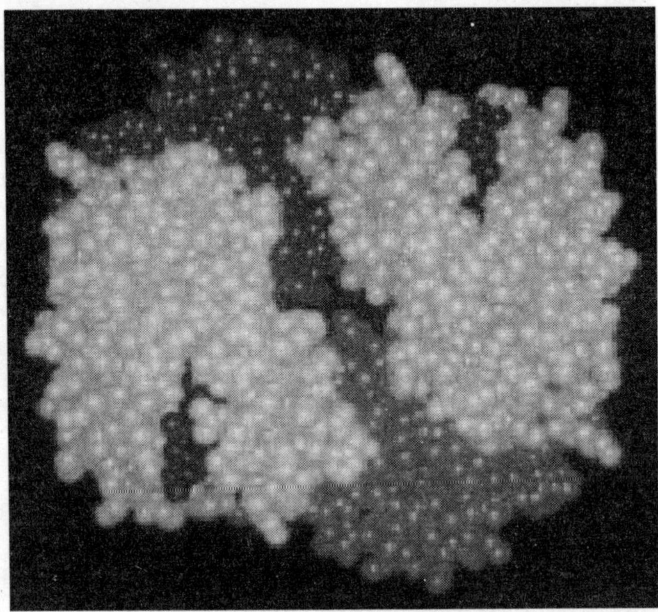

Fig. 1.27 : *Showing* Quaternary structure of haemoglobin. In this space-filling model, the a1, a2, b1, and b2 subunits are coloured yellow, green, cyan, and blue, respectively. Heme groups are red

Subunits Usually Associate Non-covalently A multisubunit protein may consist of identical or non-identical polypeptide chains. Haemoglobin, for example, has the subunit composition a2b2 (Fig. 1.26). Proteins with more than one subunit are called *oligomers,* and their identical units are called *protomers.* A protomer may therefore consist of one polypeptide chain or several unlike polypeptide chains. In this sense, haemoglobin is a dimer of ab protomers. *The contact regions between subunits closely resemble the interior of a single-subunit protein.* They contain closely packed nonpolar side chains, hydrogen bonds involving the polypeptide backbones and their side chains, and, in some cases, interchain disulphide bonds. *Subunits Are Symmetrically Arranged* In the vast majority of oligomeric proteins, *the protomers are symmetrically arranged;* that is, each protomer occupies a geometrically equivalent position in the oligomer. Proteins cannot have inversion or mirror symmetry, however, because bringing the protomers into coincidence would require converting chiral L residues to D residues. Thus, *proteins can have only rotational symmetry.* In the simplest type of rotational symmetry, *cyclic symmetry,* protomers are related by a single axis of rotation (Fig. 1.6-1.28*a*). Objects with two-, three-, or *n*-fold rotational axes are said to have *C*2, *C*3, or *Cn* symmetry, respectively. *C*2 symmetry is the most common; higher cyclic symmetries are relatively rare. *Dihedral symmetry* (D_n), a more complicated type of rotational symmetry, is generated when an *n*-fold rotation axis intersects a two-fold rotation axis at right angles (Fig. 1.6-1.28*b*). An oligomer with *Dn* symmetry consists of 2*n* protomers. *D*2 symmetry is the most common type of dihedral symmetry in proteins. Other possible types of rotational symmetry are those of a tetrahedron, cube, and icosahedron (Fig. 1.6-1.28*c*). Some multienzyme complexes and spherical viruses are built on these geometric plans.

Protein Folding and Stability

Incredible as it may seem, thermodynamic measurements indicate that *native proteins are only marginally stable under physiological conditions.* The free energy required to denature them is, 0.4 kJ/mol21 per amino acid residue, so a fully folded 100-residue protein is only about 40 kJ/mol 21 more stable than its unfolded form (for comparison, the energy required to break a typical hydrogen bond is, 20 kJ/mol21). The various non-covalent influences on proteins—hydrophobic effects, electrostaticinteractions, and hydrogen bonding—each have energies that may total thousands of kilojoules per mole over an entire protein molecule. Consequently, a protein structure is the result of a delicate balance among powerful countervailing forces. In this section, we discuss the forces that stabilize proteins and the processes by which proteins achieve their most stable folded state.

Forces That Stabilize Protein Structure

Protein structures are governed primarily by hydrophobic effects and, to a lesser extent, by interactions between polar residues and other types of bonds.

The Hydrophobic Effect

The hydrophobic effect, which causes non-polar substances to minimize their contacts with water, is the major determinant of native protein structure. The aggregation of non-polar side chains in the interior of a protein is favoured by the increase in entropy of the water molecules that would otherwise form ordered 'cages' around the hydrophobic groups. The combined hydrophobic and hydrophilic tendencies of individual amino acid residues in proteins can be expressed as *hydropathies* (*See Table 1.2 on page 37*). The greater a side chain's hydropathy, the more likely it is to occupy the interior of a protein and vice versa. Hydropathies are good predictors of which portions of a polypeptide chain are inside a protein, out of contact with the aqueous solvent, and which portions are outside (Fig. 1.6-1.34). Site-directed mutagenesis experiments in which individual interior residues have been replaced by a number of others suggest that the factors that affect stability are, in order, the hydrophobicity of the substituted residue, its steric compatibility, and, last, the volume of its side chain.

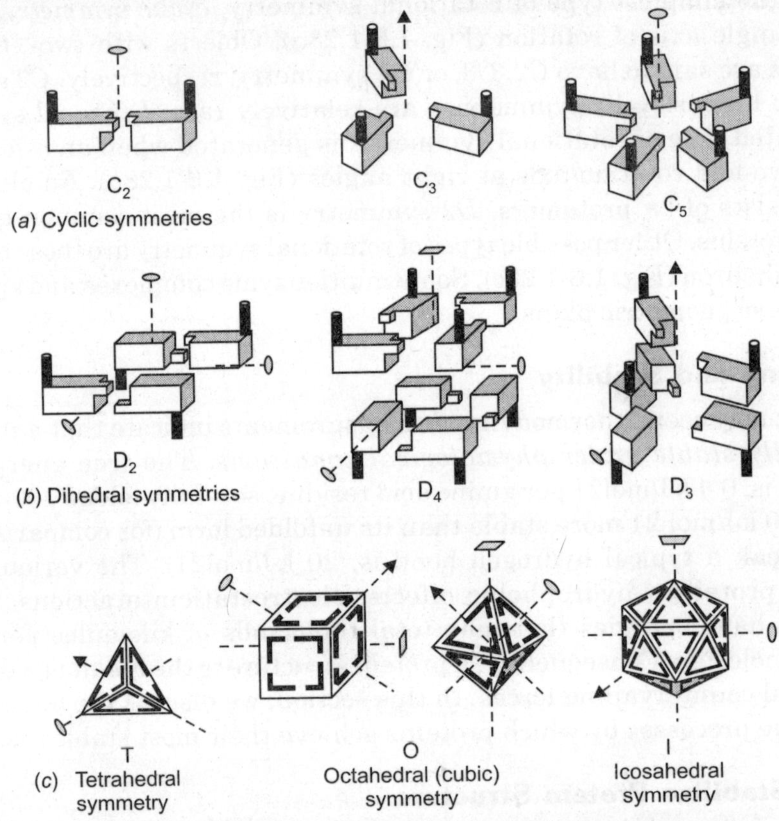

Fig. 1.28 : Some symmetries for oligomeric proteins. The oval, the triangle, the square, and the pentagon at the ends of the dashed green lines indicate, respectively, the unique two-fold, three-fold, four-fold, and five-fold rotational axes of the objects shown. (*a*) Assemblies with cyclic (*C*) symmetry. (*b*) Assemblies with dihedral (*D*) symmetry. In these objects, a 2-fold axis is perpendicular to another rotational axis. (*c*) Assemblies with the rotational symmetries of a tetrahedron (*T*), a cube or octahedron (*O*), and an icosahedron (*I*)

Electrostatic Interactions

In the closely packed interiors of native proteins, van der Waals forces, which are relatively weak are nevertheless an important stabilizing influence. This is because these forces act over only short distances and hence are lost when the protein is unfolded. Perhaps surprisingly, *hydrogen bonds, which are central features of protein structures, make only minor contributions to protein stability*. This is because hydrogen-bonding groups in an unfolded protein form energetically equivalent hydrogen bonds with water molecules. Nevertheless, hydrogen bonds are important determinants of native protein structures, because if a protein folded in a way that prevented a hydrogen bond from forming, the

Table 1.2 : Hydropathy Scale for Amino Acid

Side Chain	Hydropathy
Ile	4.5
Val	4.2
Leu	3.8
Phe	2.8
Cys	2.5
Mct	1.9
Ala	1.8
Gly	20.4
Thr	20.7
Ser	20.8
Trp	20.9
Tyr	21.3
Pro	21.6
His	23.2
Glu	23.5
Gln	23.5
Asp	23.5
Asn	23.5
Lys	23.9
Arg	24.5

stabilizing energy of that hydrogen bond would be lost. Hydrogen bonding therefore fine-tunes tertiary structure by "selecting" the unique native structure of a protein from among a relatively small number of hydrophobically stabilized conformations. The association of two ionic protein groups of opposite charge (*e.g.*, Lys and Asp) is known as an *ion pair* or *salt bridge.* About 75% of the charged residues in proteins are members of ion pairs that are located mostly on the protein surface. Despite the strong electrostatic attraction between the Fig. 1.29. A hydropathic index plot for bovine chymotrypsinogen. The sum of the hydropathies of nine consecutive residues is plotted versus residue sequence number. A large positive hydropathic index indicates a hydrophobic region of the polypeptide, whereas a large negative value indicates a hydrophilic region. The upper bars denote the protein's interior regions, as determined by X-ray crystallography, and the lower bars denote the protein's exterior regions.

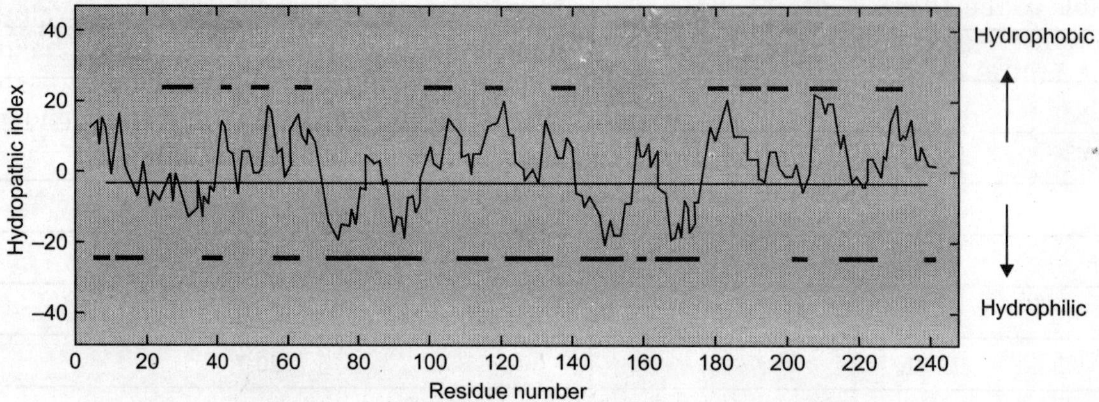

Fig. 1.29 : A hydropathic index plot for bovine chymotrypsinogen. The sum of the hydropathies of nine consecutive residues is plotted versus residue sequence numner. A large positive hydropathic index indicates a hydrophobic region of the polypeptide, whereas a large negative value indicates a hydrophilic region. The upper bars denote the protein's interior regions, as determined by X-ray crystallography, and the lower bars denote the protein's exterior regions.

Oppositely charged members of an ion pair, these interactions contribute little to the stability of a native protein. This is because the free energy of an ion pair's charge–charge interactions usually fails to compensate for the loss of entropy of the side chains and the loss of solvation free energy when the charged groups form an ion pair. This accounts for the observation that ion pairs are poorly conserved among homologous proteins.

Chemical Cross-links

Disulphide bonds within and between polypeptide chains form as a protein folds to its native conformation. Some polypeptides whose Cys residues have been derivatized to prevent disulphide bond formation can still assume their fully active conformations, suggesting that disulphide bonds are not essential stabilizing forces. They may, however, be important for 'locking in' a particular backbone folding pattern as the protein proceeds from its fully extended state to its mature form. Disulphide bonds are rare in intracellular proteins because the cytoplasmis a reducing environment. Most disulphide bonds occur in proteins that are secreted from the cell into the more oxidizing extracellular environment.

The relatively hostile extracellular world (*e.g.,* uncontrolled temperature and pH) apparently requires the additional structural constraints conferred by disulphide bonds. *Metal ions may also function to internally cross-link proteins.* For example, at least ten motifs collectively known as *zinc fingers* have been described in nucleic acid–binding proteins. These structures contain about 25–60 residues arranged around one or two Zn21 ions that are tetrahedrally coordinated by the side chains of Cys, His, and occasionally Asp or Glu (Fig. 1.30). The Zn21 allows relatively short stretches of polypeptide chain to fold into stable units that can interact with nucleic acids. Zinc fingers are too small to be stable in the absence of Zn21. Zinc is ideally suited to its structural role in intracellular proteins: Its filled *d* electron shell permits it to interact strongly with a variety of ligands (e.g., sulfur, nitrogen, or oxygen) from different amino acid residues. In addition, zinc has only one stable oxidation state (unlike, for example, copper and iron), so it does not undergo oxidation–reduction reactions in the cell.

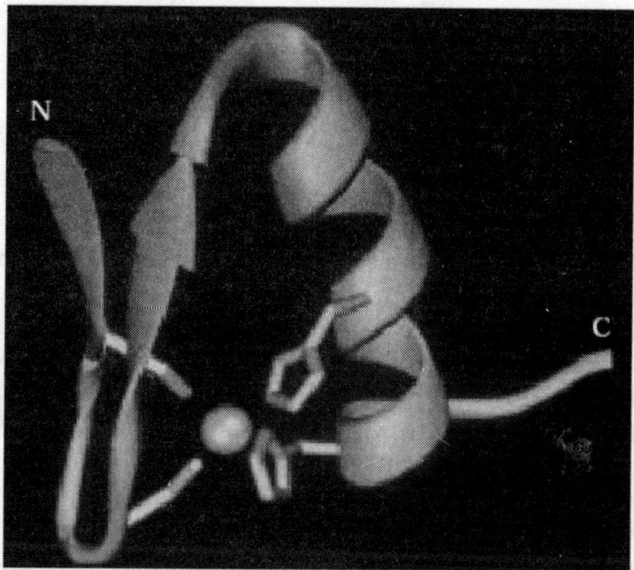

Fig. 1.30 : A zinc finger motif. This structure, from the DNA-binding protein Zif268, is known as a Cys2–His2 zinc finger because the zinc atom (*silver*) is coordinated by two Cys residues (*yellow*) and two His residues (*cyan*)

Denaturation and Renaturation of Protein

The low conformational stabilities of native proteins make them easily susceptible to denaturation by altering the balance of the weak nonbonding forces that maintain the native conformation. Proteins can be denatured by a variety of conditions and substances:

1. Heating causes a protein's conformationally sensitive properties, such as optical rotation, viscosity, and UV absorption, to change abruptly over a narrow temperature range. Such a sharp transition indicates that the entire polypeptide unfolds or 'melts' cooperatively, that is, nearly simultaneously. Most proteins havemelting points well below 100°C. Among the exceptions are the proteins of thermophilic bacteria, organisms that inhabit hot springs or submarine volcanic

vents with temperatures near 100°C. Amazingly, the X-ray structures of these heat-stable proteins are only subtly different from those of their low-temperature homologs.

2. pH variations alter the ionization states of amino acid side chains, thereby changing protein charge distributions and hydrogen bonding requirements.
3. Detergents associate with the nonpolar residues of a protein, thereby interfering with the hydrophobic interactions responsible for the protein's native structure.
4. The chaotropic agents guanidinium ion and urea,

$$H_2N-\overset{\overset{NH}{||}}{C}-NH_2 \qquad H_2N-\overset{\overset{O}{||}}{C}-NH_2$$

guanidine urea

in concentrations in the range 5 to 10 M, are the most commonly used protein denaturants. Chaotropic agents are ions or small organic molecules that increase the solubility of non-polar substances in water.

Their effectiveness as denaturants stems from their ability to disrupt hydrophobic interactions, although their mechanism of action is not well understood. *Denatured Proteins can be Renatured* In 1957, the elegant experiments of Christian Anfinsen on *ribonucleaseA (RNase A)* showed that proteins can be denatured reversibly. RNase A, a 124-residue single-chain protein, is completely unfolded and its four disulphide bonds reductively cleaved in an 8 M urea solution containing 2-mercaptoethanol (*See Fig. 1.31 on next page*). Dialyzing away the urea and reductant and exposing the resulting solution to O2 at pH 8 (which oxidizes the SH groups to form disulphides) yields a protein that is virtually 100% enzymatically active and physically indistinguishable from native RNase A. The protein must therefore *renature* spontaneously. The renaturation of RNase A demands that its four disulphide bonds reform. The probability of one of the eight Cys residues randomly forming a disulphide bond with its proper mate among the other seven Cys residues is 1/7; that one of the remaining six Cys residues then randomly forming its proper disulphide bond is 1/5; etc. The overall probability of RNase A reforming its four native disulphide links at random is

$$\frac{1}{7}\times\frac{1}{5}\times\frac{1}{3}\times 1=\frac{1}{105}$$

Clearly, the disulphide bonds do not randomly re-form under renaturing conditions, since, if they did, only 1% of the refolded protein would be catalytically active. Indeed, if the RNase A is reoxidized in 8 M urea so that its disulphide bonds re-form while the polypeptide chain is a random coil, then after removal of the urea, the RNase A is, as expected, only, 1% active. This 'scrambled' protein can be made fully active by exposing it to a trace of 2-mercaptoethanol, which breaks the improper disulphide bonds and allows the proper bonds to form. *Anfinsen's work demonstrated that proteins can fold spontaneously into their native conformations under physiological conditions. This implies that a protein's primary structure dictates itsthree-dimensional structure.*

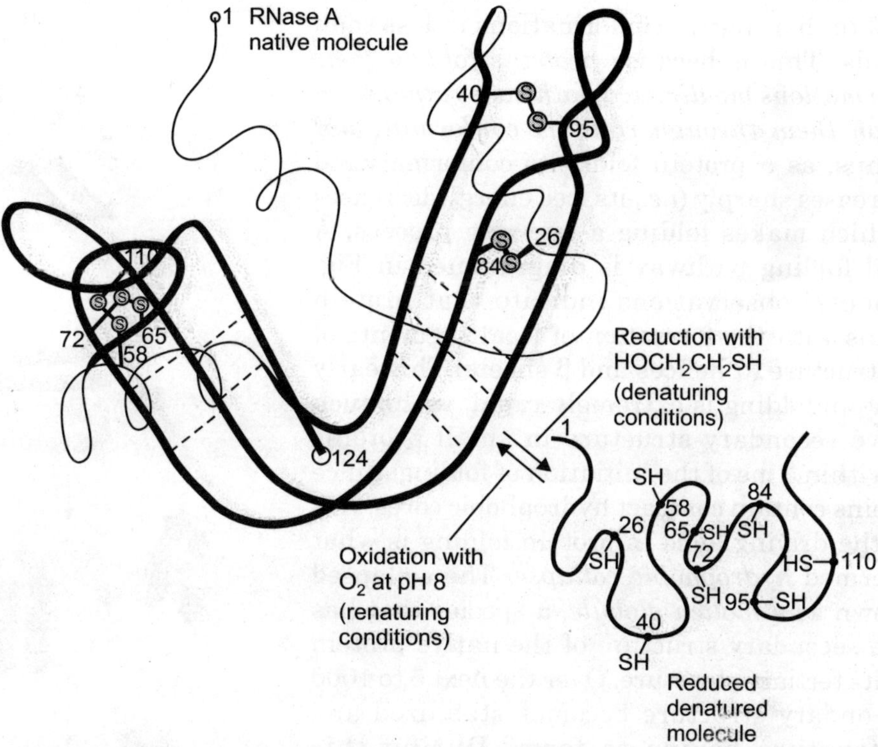

Fig. 1.31 : The reductive denaturation and oxidative renaturation of RNase A

Protein Folding Pathways

Studies of protein stability and renaturation suggest that protein folding is directed largely by the residues that occupy the interior of the folded protein. But *how* does a protein fold to its native conformation? One might guess that this process occurs through the protein's random exploration of all the conformations available to it until it eventually stumbles onto the correct one. A simple calculation first made by Cyrus Levinthal, however, convincingly demonstrates that this cannot possibly be the case: Assume that an n-residue protein's $2n$ torsion angles, f and c, each have three stable conformations. This yields $32n < 10n$ possible conformations for the protein(a gross underestimate because we have completely neglected its side chains). Then, if the protein could explore a new conformation every 10213s (the rate at which single bonds reorient), the time t, in seconds, required for the protein to explore all the conformations available to it is

$$t = \frac{10^n}{10^{13}}$$

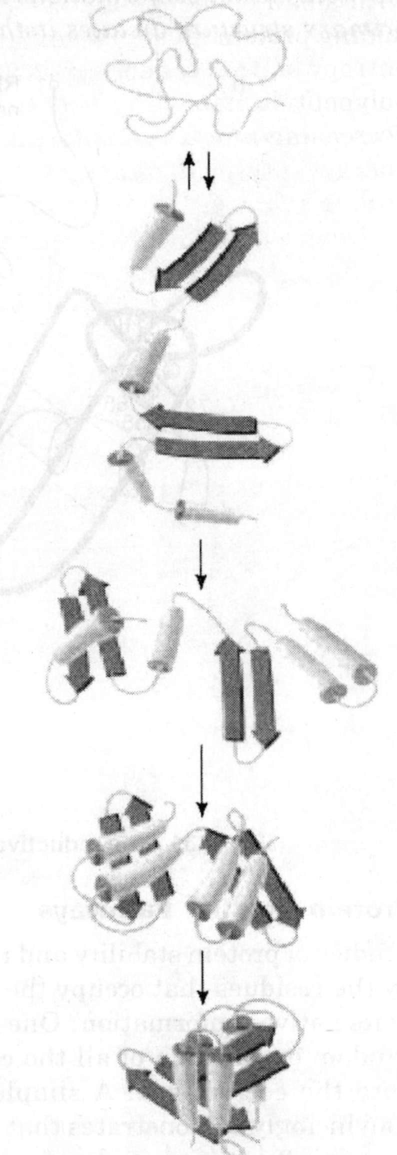

Fig. 1.32 : **Showing Hypothetical protein folding pathway. This example shows a linear pathway for folding a two-domain protein**

For a small protein of 100 residues, *t* 5 1087 s, which is immensely greater than the apparent age of the universe (20 billion years, or 6 3 1017 s).In fact, many proteins fold to their native conformations in less than a few seconds. This is because *proteins fold to their native conformations via directed pathways rather than stumbling on them through random conformational searches.* Thus, as a protein folds, its conformational stability increases sharply (*i.e.,* its free energy decreases sharply), which makes folding a one-way process. A hypothetical folding pathway is diagrammed in Fig. 32.Experimental observations indicate that protein folding begins with the formation of local segments of secondary structure (α helices and β sheets).This early stage of protein folding is extremely rapid, with much of the native secondary structure in small proteins appearing within 5 ms of the initiation of folding. Since native proteins contain compact hydrophobic cores, it is likely that the driving force in protein folding is what has been termed *hydrophobic collapse.* The collapsed state is known as a *molten globule,* a species that has much of the secondary structure of the native protein but little of its tertiary structure. Over the next 5 to 1000 ms, the secondary structure becomes stabilized and tertiary structure begins to form. During this intermediate stage, the native like elements are thought to take the form of subdomains that are not yet properly docked to form domains. In the final stage of folding, which for small single-domain proteins occurs over the next few seconds, the protein undergoes a series of complex motions in which it attains its relatively rigid internal side chain packing and hydrogen bonding while it expels the remaining water molecules from its hydrophobic core. In multidomain and multisubunit proteins, the respective units then assemble in a similar manner, with a few slight conformational adjustments required to produce the protein's native tertiary or quaternary structure. Thus, *proteins appear to fold in a hierarchical manner, with small local elements of structure forming and then coalescing to yield larger elements, which coalesce with other such elements to form yet larger elements, etc.* Folding, like denaturation, appears to be a cooperative process, with small elements of structure accelerating the formation of additional structures. A folding protein must proceed from a high-energy, high-entropy state to a low-energy, low-entropy state. This energy–entropy relationship is diagrammed in Fig. 1.33. An unfolded polypeptide has many possible conformations (high entropy). As it folds into an ever-decreasing number of possible conformations, its entropy and free energy decrease. The energy–entropy diagram is not a smooth valley but a jagged landscape. Minor clefts and gullies represent conformations that are temporarily trapped until, through random thermal activation, they overcome a slight 'uphill' free energy barrier and can then proceed to a lower energy conformation. Evidently, *proteins have evolved to have efficient folding pathways as well as stable native conformations.* Nevertheless, misfolded proteins do occur in nature, and their accumulation is believed to be the cause of a variety of neurological diseases

Protein Disulphide Isomerase Even under optimal experimental conditions, proteins often fold moreslowly *in vitro* than they fold *in vivo.* One reason is that folding proteins often form disulphide bonds not present in the native proteins, which then slowly form native disulphide bonds through the process of disulphide interchange.

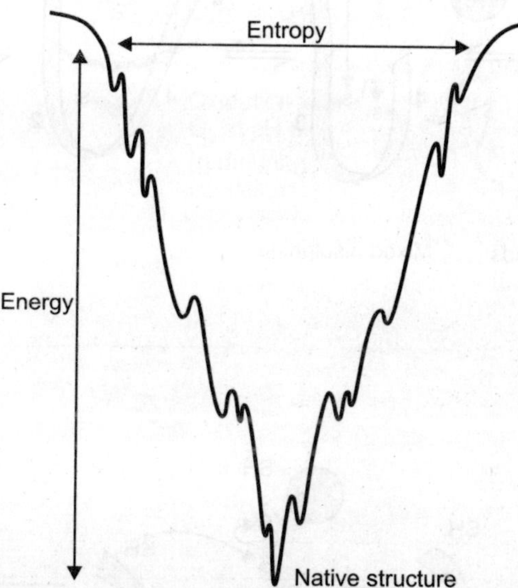

Fig. 1.33 : Energy–entropy diagram for protein folding. The width of the diagram representsentropy, and the depth, the energy. The unfolded polypeptide proceeds from a high-entropy, disordered state (*wide*) to a single low-entropy (*narrow*), low-energy native conformation

Protein disulphide isomerase (PDI) catalyzes this process. Indeed, the observation that RNase A folds so much faster *in vivo* than *in vitro* led Anfinsen to discover this enzyme. PDI binds to a wide variety of unfolded polypeptides via a hydrophobic patch on its surface. A Cys OSH group on PDI reacts with a disulphide groupon the polypeptide to form a mixed disulphide and a Cys OSH group on thepolypeptide (Fig. 1.34*a*). Another disulphide group on the polypeptide, brought into proximity by the spontaneous folding of the polypeptide, is attacked by this Cys OSH group. The newly liberated Cys OSH group then repeats this process with another disulphide bond, and so on, ultimately yielding the polypeptide containing only native disulphide bonds, along with regenerated PDI. Oxidized (disulphide-containing) PDI also catalyzes the initial formation of a polypeptide's disulphide bonds by a similar mechanism (Fig. 1.34*b*). In this case, the reduced PDI reaction product must be reoxidized by cellular oxidizing agents in order to repeat the process. Molecular Chaperones Proteins begin to fold as they are being synthesized, so the renaturation of a denatured protein *in vitro* may not mimic the folding of a protein *in vivo*. In addition, proteins fold *in vivo* in the presence of extremely high concentrations of other proteins with which they can potentially interact.

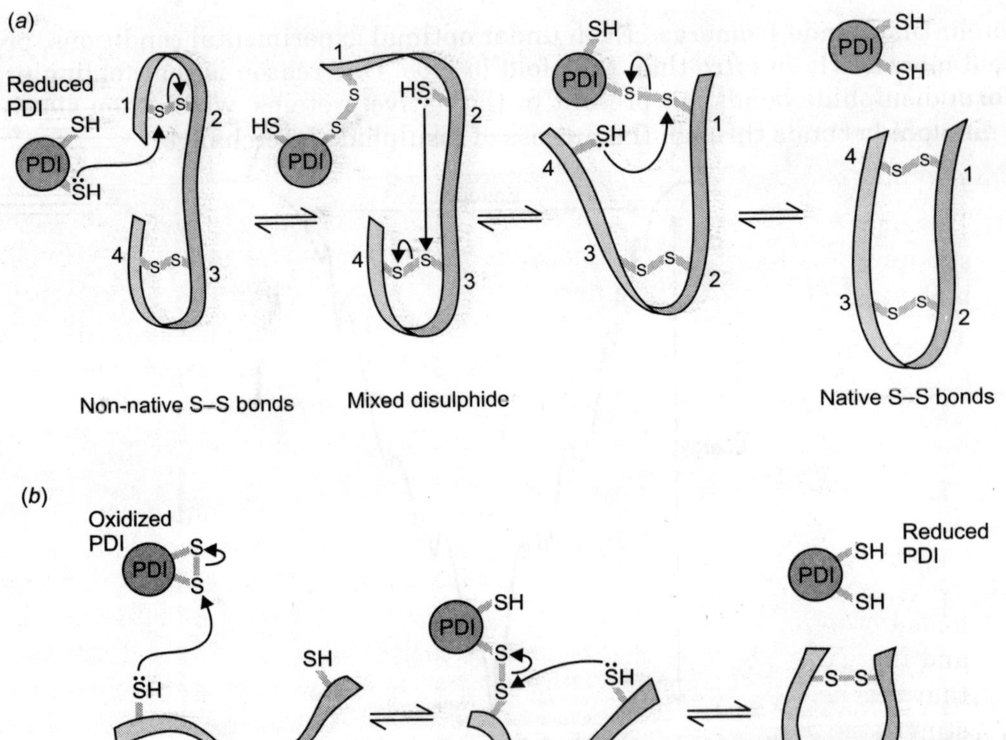

Fig. 1.34: Mechanism of protein disulphide isomerase. (*a*) Reduced (SH-containing) PDI catalyzes the rearrangement ofa polypeptide's non-native disulphide bonds via disulphide interchange reactions to yield native disulphide bonds. (*b*) Oxidized (disulphide-containing) PDI catalyzes the initial formation of a polypeptide's disulphide bonds through the formation of a mixed disulphide. Reduced PDI can then react with a cellular oxidizing agent to regenerate oxidized PDI.

Molecular chaperones are essential proteins that bind to unfolded and partially folded polypeptide chains to prevent the improper association of exposed hydrophobic segments that might lead to non-native folding as well as polypeptide aggregation and precipitation. This is especially important for multidomain and multisubunit proteins, whose components must fold fully before they can properly associate with each other. Molecular chaperones also allow misfolded proteins to refold into their native conformations. Many molecular chaperones were first described as *heat shock proteins (Hsp)* because their rate of synthesis is increased at elevated temperatures. Presumably, the additional chaperones are required to recoverheat-denatured proteins or to prevent misfolding under conditions of environmental stress. There are two major classes of molecular chaperones in both prokaryotes and eukaryotes: the *Hsp70* family of 70-kD protcins and the *chaperonins,* which are large multisubunit proteins.

An Hsp70 protein binds to a newly synthesized polypeptide, possibly as soon as the first 30 amino acids have been polymerized at the ribosome. The Hsp70 chaperone probably helps prevent premature folding.

Chaperonins consist of two types of proteins:

1. The *Hsp60 proteins (GroEL in E. coli),* which are composed of 14 identical, 60-kD subunits arranged in two stacked rings of 7 subunits each, thereby forming a hollow cylinder with *D*7 symmetry
2. The *Hsp10 proteins (GroES in E. coli),* which consist of 7 identical, 10-kD subunits arranged with 7-fold rotational (*C*7) symmetry to form a dome-shaped complex. The X-ray structure of the GroEL–GroES complex determined by Paul Sigler shows, in agreement with previous electron microscopy studies, that one open end of the GroEL cylinder is capped by a GroES complex (Fig. 1.35). The interior of the cylinder provides a protected environment in which a protein can fold without aggregating with other partially foldod proteins. The interior of the GroEL cylinder contains hydrophobic patches that bind the exposed groups of its enclosed and improperly folded protein. The GroEL subunits bind ATP and catalyze its hydrolysis to ADP and inorganic phosphate (P*i*), a process that motivates a conformational change that masks the hydrophobic patches. The bound protein is thereby released and stimulated to continue folding. The binding and release, in effect, frees the partially folded protein from its entrapment in a local free energy minimum,such as those in Fig. 1.6 to 1.38, which permits the folding protein to continue its descent down its funnel toward the native state. In the protected environment inside the hollow GroEL–GroES (Hsp60–Hsp10) barrel, a .70-kD protein can fold out of contact with other proteins with which it otherwise might aggregate. *This cycle of ATP-driven binding, release, and refolding is repeated until the protein achieves its native conformation.* The Hsp70 proteins are thought to follow a similar pathway of binding and ATPdriven release of a folding protein.

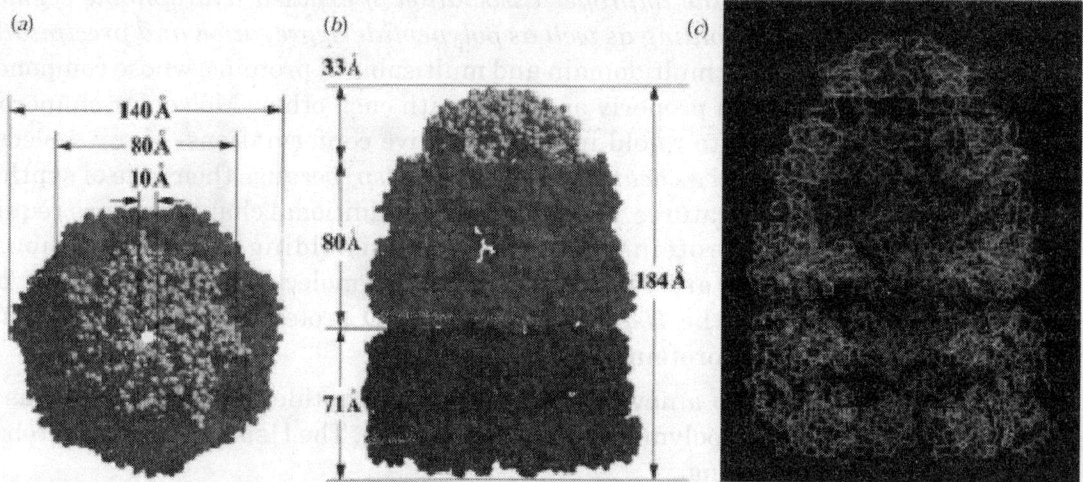

Fig. 1.35: The X-ray structure of the GroEL–GroES– (ADP)7 chaperonin complex. Two seven-membered rings of GroEL subunits stack to form a hollow cylinder that is capped at one end by a seven-membered ring of GroES subunits. (*a*) A space-filling representation of the complex as viewed down its 7-fold axis of rotation. The GroES ring is gold, its adjacent GroEL ring is green, and the adjoining GroEL ring is red. (*b*) As in *a* but viewed perpendicularly to the 7-fold axis. Note the different conformations of the two GroEL rings. (*c*) The Ca backbones of the complex as viewed perpendicularly to the 7-fold axis and cut away in the plane containing this axis. The ADPs, which are bound to the lower portion of each subunit in the upper GroEL ring, are shown in space-filling form. Note the large cavity formed by the GroES cap and the upper GroEL ring in which a polypeptide can fold in isolation

Protein Dynamics

The precision with which protein structures are determined may leave the false impression that proteins have fixed and rigid structures. In fact, *proteins are flexible and rapidly fluctuating molecules whose structural mobilities are functionally significant.* Groups ranging in size from individual side chains to entire domains or subunits may be displaced by up to several angstroms through random intramolecular movements or in response to a trigger such as the binding of a small molecule. Extended side chains, such as Lys, and the N- and C-termini of polypeptide chains are especially prone to wave around in solution because there are few forces holding them in place. Theoretical calculations by Martin Karplus indicate that a protein's native structure probably consists of a large collection of rapidly interconverting conformations that have essentially equal stabilities (Fig.36). Conformational flexibility, or *breathing,* with structural displacement of up to, 2 Å, allows small molecules to diffuse in and out of the interior of certain proteins.

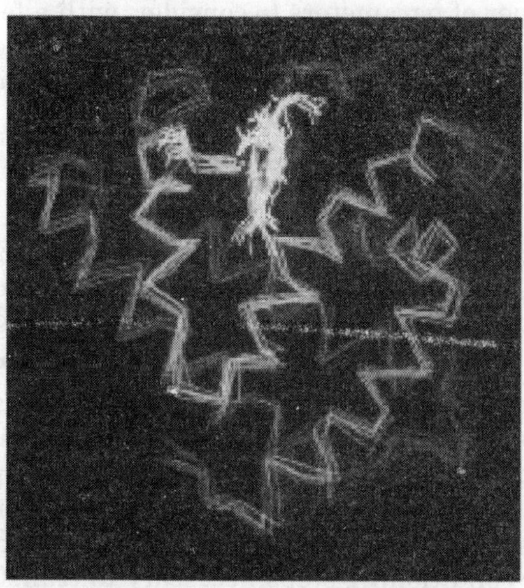

Fig. 1.36 : Molecular dynamics of myoglobin. Several 'snapshots' of the protein calculated at intervals of 5 3 10212 s are superimposed. The backbone is blue, the heme group is yellow, and the His side chain linking the heme to the protein is orange

PROTEIN FRACTIONATION AND PURIFICATION

Introduction

The development of techniques and methods for protein purification has been an essential pre-requisite for many of the advancements made in biotechnology. This book provides advice and examples for a smooth path to protein purification. Protein purification varies from simple one-step precipitation procedures to large scale validated production processes. Often more than one purification step is necessary to reach the desired purity. The key to successful and efficient protein purification is to select the most appropriate techniques, optimize their performance to suit the requirements and combine them in a logical way to maximize yield and minimize the number of steps required. Most purification schemes involve some form of chromatography. As a result chromatography has become an essential tool in every laboratory where protein purification is needed. Different chromatography techniques with different selectivities can form powerful combinations for the purification of any biomolecule. The development of recombinant DNA techniques has revolutionized the production of proteins in large quantities. Recombinant proteins are often produced in forms which facilitate their subsequent chromatographic purification. However, this has not removed all challenges. Host contaminants are still present and problems related to solubility, structural integrity and biological activity can still exist. Although there may appear to be a great number of parameters to consider, with a few simple guidelines and application of the Three Phase Purification Strategy the process can be planned and performed simply and easily, with only a basic knowledge of the details of chromatography techniques.

Purification Strategies the Simple Approach

A systematic approach to development of a purification strategy

The first step is to describe the basic scenario for the purification. General considerations answer questions such as: What is the intended use of the product? What kind of starting material is available and how should it be handled? What are the purity issues in relation to the source material and intended use of the final product? What has to be removed? What must be removed completely? What will be the final scale of purification? If there is a need for scale-up, what consequences will this have on the chosen purification techniques? What are the economical constraints and what resources and equipment are available? Most purification protocols require more than one step to achieve the desired level of product purity. This includes any conditioning steps necessary to transfer the product from one technique into conditions suitable to perform the next technique. Each step in the process will cause some loss of product. For example, if a yield of 80% in each step is assumed, this will be reduced to only 20% overall yield after 8 processing steps as shown in Figure 1. Consequently, to reach the targets for yield and purity with the *minimum* number of steps and the *simplest* possible design, it is not efficient to add one step to another until purity requirements have been fulfilled. Occasionally when a sample is readily available purity can be achieved by simply adding or repeating steps. However, experience shows that, even for the most challenging applications, high purity and yield can be achieved efficiently in fewer than four well-chosen and optimized purification steps. Techniques should be organized in a logical sequence to avoid the need for conditioning steps and the chromatographic techniques selected appropriately to use as few purification steps as possible.

Preparation

Limit the number of steps in a purification procedure

The need to obtain a protein, efficiently, economically and in sufficient purity and quantity, applies to every purification. It is important to set *objectives* for purity, quantity and maintenance of biological activity and to define the economical and time framework for the work. All information concerning *properties of the target protein and contaminants* will help during purification development. Some simple experiments to characterize the sample and target molecule are an excellent investment. Development of fast and reliable *analytical assays* is essential to follow the progress of the purification and assess its effectiveness. *Sample preparation* and *extraction procedures* should be developed prior to the first chromatographic purification step. With background information, assays and sample preparation procedures in place the Three Phase Purification Strategy can be considered.

Three Phase Purification Strategy

Imagine the purification has three phases Capture, Intermediate Purification and Polishing.

In the Three Phase Strategy specific objectives are assigned to each step within the process: In the *capture* phase the objectives are to *isolate, concentrate and stabilize* the target product. During the *intermediate purification* phase the objective is to *remove most of the bulk impurities* such as other proteins and nucleic acids, endotoxins and viruses. In the *polishing* phase the objective is to *achieve high purity* by removing any remaining trace impurities or closely related substances. The selection and optimum combination of purification techniques for Capture, Intermediate Purification and Polishing is crucial to ensure fast method development, a shorter time to pure product and good economy. The final purification process should ideally consist of sample preparation, including extraction and clarification when required, followed by three major purification steps, as shown in Figure 1.36a. The number of steps used will always depend upon the purity requirements and intended use for the protein.

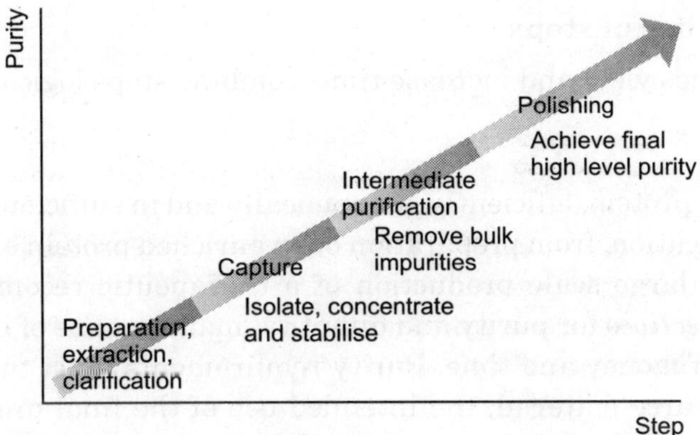

Fig. 1.36a : Showing the Process of Protein Purification in steps

Guidelines for Protein Purification

The guidelines for protein purification shown here can be applied to any purification process and are a suggestion as to how a systematic approach can be applied to the development of an effective purification strategy. As a reminder these guidelines will be highlighted where appropriate throughout the following subheads.

Define objectives

For purity, activity and quantity required of final product to avoid over or under developing a method

Define properties of target protein and critical impurities

To simplify technique selection and optimization

Develop analytical assays

For fast detection of protein activity/recovery and critical contaminants

Minimize sample handling at every stage

to avoid lengthy procedures which risk losing activity/reducing recovery

Minimize use of additives

Additives may need to be removed in an extra purification step or may interfere with activity assays

Remove damaging contaminants early

for example, proteases

Use a different technique at each step

to take advantage of sample characteristics which can be used for separation (size, charge, hydrophobicity, ligand specificity)

Minimize number of steps

Extra steps reduce yield and increase time, combine steps logically

Procedure

The need to obtain a protein, efficiently, economically and in sufficient purity and quantity, applies to any purification, from preparation of an enriched protein extract for biochemical characterization to large scale production of a therapeutic recombinant protein. It is important to set *objectives* for purity and quantity, maintenance of biological activity and economy in terms of money and time. Purity requirements must take into consideration the nature of the source material, the intended use of the final product and any special safety issues. For example, it is important to differentiate between contaminants which must be removed and those which can be tolerated. Other factors can also influence the prioritization of objectives. High yields are usually a key objective, but may be less crucial in cases where a sample is readily available or product is required only in small quantities. Extensive method development may be impossible without resources such as an ÄKTA™design chromatography system. Similarly, time pressure combined with a slow assay turnaround will steer towards less extensive scouting and optimization. All information concerning *properties* of the target protein and contaminants will help during purification development, allowing faster and easier technique selection and optimization, and avoiding conditions which may inactivate the target protein. Development of fast and reliable analytical assays is essential to follow the progress of the purification and assess effectiveness (yield, biological activity, recovery).

The statement that a protein is >95% pure (*i.e.* target protein constitutes 95% of total protein) is far from a guarantee that the purity is sufficient for an intended application. The same is true for the common statement "the protein was homogenous by Coomassie™ stained SDS-PAGE". Purity of 95% may be acceptable if the remaining 5% consists of harmless impurities. However, even minor impurities which may be biologically active could cause significant problems in both research and therapeutic applications. It is therefore important to differentiate between contaminants which must be removed completely and those which can be reduced to acceptable levels. Since different types of starting material will contain different contaminant profiles they will present different contamination problems.

It is better to over-purify than to under-purify.

Although the number of purification steps should be minimized, the quality of the end product should not be compromised. Subsequent results might be questioned if sample purity is low and contaminants are unknown. The need to maintain biological activity must be considered at every stage during purification development. It is especially beneficial if proteases are removed and target protein transferred into a friendly environment during the first step. A downstream production process must achieve the required purity and recovery with complete safety and reliability, and within a given economic framework. Economy is a very complex issue. In commercial production the time to market can override issues such as optimization for recovery, capacity or speed. Robustness and reliability are also of great concern since a batch failure can have major consequences. Special safety issues may be involved in purification of biopharmaceuticals, such as detection or removal of infectious agents, pyrogens, immunogenic contaminants and tumourigenic hazards. It may be necessary to use analytical techniques targeted towards specific contaminants in order to demonstrate that they have been removed to acceptable levels.

Contaminants which degrade or inactivate the protein or interfere with analyses should be removed as early as possible.

Define Properties of Target Protein and Critical Impurities

All information concerning the target protein and contaminant properties will help to guide the choice of separation techniques and experimental conditions for purification. Database information for the target, or related proteins, may give size, isoelectric point (pI) and hydrophobicity or solubility data. Native one and two dimensional PAGE can indicate sample complexity and the properties of the target protein and major contaminants. Particularly important is a knowledge of the *stability window* of the protein so that irreversible inactivation is avoided. It is advisable to check the target protein stability window for at least pH and ionic strength. Table 1.3 shows how different target protein properties can affect a purification strategy.

Table 1.3 : Protein properties and their effect on development of purification strategies

Sample and target protein properties	Influence on purification strategy
Temperature stability	Need to work rapidly at lowered temperature
pH stability	Selection of buffers for extraction and purification
	Selection of conditions for ion exchange, affinity or reversed phase chromatography
Organic solvents stability	Selection of conditions for reversed phase chromatography
Detergent requirement	Consider effects on chromatographic steps and the need or detergent removal. Consider choice of detergent.
Salt (ionic strength)	Selection of conditions for precipitation techniques, ion exchange and hydrophobic interaction chromatography
Co-factors for stability or activity	Selection of additives, pH, salts, buffers
Protease sensitivity	Need for fast removal of proteases or addition of inhibitors
Sensitivity to metal ions	Need to add EDTA or EGTA to buffers
Redox sensitivity	Need to add reducing agents
Molecular weight	Selection of gel filtration media
Charge properties	Selection of ion exchange conditions
Biospecific affinity	Selection of ligand for affinity medium
Post translational modifications	Selection of group-specific affinity medium
Hydrophobicity	Selection of medium for hydrophobic interaction Chromatography

Develop Analytical Assays

To progress efficiently during method development the effectiveness of each step should be assessed. The laboratory should have access to the following assays:

- A rapid, reliable assay for the target protein
- Purity determination
- Total protein determination
- Assays for impurities which must be removed

The importance of a reliable assay for the target protein cannot be over- emphasized. When testing chromatographic fractions ensure that the buffers used for separation do not interfere with the assay. Purity of the target protein is most often estimated by SDS-PAGE, capillary electrophoresis, reversed phase chromatography or mass spectrometry. Lowry or Bradford assays are used most frequently to determine the total protein. The Bradford assay is particularly suited to samples where there is a high lipid content which may interfere with the Lowry assay. For large scale protein purification the need to assay for target proteins and critical impurities is often essential. In practice, when a protein is purified for research purposes, it is too time consuming to identify and set up specific assays for harmful contaminants. A practical approach is to purify the protein to a certain level, and then perform SDS-PAGE after a storage period to check for protease cleavage. Suitable control experiments, included within assays for bio-activity, will help to indicate if impurities are interfering with results.

Sample Extraction and Clarification

Minimise sample handling
Minimise use of additives
Remove damaging contaminants early

The need for *sample preparation* prior to the first chromatographic step isdependent upon sample type. In some situations samples may be taken directly tothe first capture step. For example cell culture supernatant can be applied directlyto a suitable chromatographic matrix such as Sepharose™ Fast Flow and mayrequire only a minor adjustment of the pH or ionic strength. However, it is mostoften essential to perform some form of *sample extraction and clarification* procedure. If sample extraction is required the chosen technique must be robust and suitable for all scales of purification likely to be used. It should be noted that a technique such as ammonium sulphate precipitation, commonly used in small scale, may be unsuitable for very large scale preparation. Choice of buffers and additives must be carefully considered if a purification is to be scaled up. In these cases inexpensive buffers, such as acetate or citrate, are preferable to the more complex compositions used in the laboratory. It should also be noted that dialysis and other common methods used for adjustment of sample conditions are unsuitable for very large or very small samples.

1. For repeated purification, use an extraction and clarification technique that is robust and able to handle sample variability. This ensures a reproducible product for the next purification step despite variability in starting material.
2. Use additives only if essential for stabilisation of product or improved extraction. Select those which are easily removed. Additives may need to be removed in an extra purification step.
3. Use pre-packed columns of Sephadex™ G-25 gel filtration media, for rapid sample clean-up at laboratory scale, as shown in Table 1.4.

Table 1.4 : Pre-packed columns for sample collection

Pre-packed column	Sample volume loading per run	Sample volume recovery per run	Code No.
HiPrep™ Desalting 26/10	2.5 - 15 ml	7.5 - 20 ml	17-5087-01
HiTrap™ Desalting	0.25 - 1.5 ml	1.0 - 2.0 ml	17-1408-01
Fast Desalting PC 3.2/10	0.05 - 0.2 ml	0.2 - 0.3 ml	17-0774-01
PD-10 Desalting	1.5 - 2.5 ml	2.5 - 3.5 ml	17-0851-01

Sephadex G-25 gel filtration media are used at laboratory and production scale for sample preparation and clarification of proteins >5000. Sample volumes of up to 30%, or in some cases, 40% of the total column volume are loaded. In a single step, the sample is desalted, exchanged into a new buffer, and low molecular weight materials are removed. The high volume capacity, relative insensitivity to sample concentration, and speed of this step enable very large sample volumes to be processed rapidly and efficiently. Using a high sample volume load results in a separation with minimal sample dilution (approximately 1:1.4). contains further details on sample storage, extraction and clarification procedures. Sephadex G-25 is also used for sample conditioning, *e.g.* rapid adjustment of pH, buffer exchange and desalting between purification steps.

Sephadex G 25 gel filtration

For fast group separations between high and low molecular weight substances Typical flow velocity 60 cm/h (Sephadex G-25 Superfine, Sephadex G-25 Fine),150 cm/h (Sephadex G-25 Medium).

Combine Sample Clean-up and Capture in a Single Step

If large sample volumes will be handled or the method scaled-up in the future, consider using STREAMLINE™ expanded bed adsorption. This technique is particularly suited for large scale recombinant protein and monoclonal antibody purification. The crude sample containing particles can be applied to the expanded bed without filtration or centrifugation. STREAMLINE adsorbents are specially designed for use in STREAMLINE columns. Together they enable the high flow rates needed for high productivity in industrial applications of fluidized beds. The technique requires no sample clean up and so combines sample preparation and capture in a single step. Crude sample is applied to an expanded bed of STREAMLINE media. Target proteins are captured whilst cell debris, cells, particulate matter, whole cells, and contaminants pass through. Flow is reversed and the target proteins are desorbed in the elution buffer.

Media for consideration:

STREAMLINE (IEX, AC, HIC)

For sample clean-up and capture direct from crude sample. STREAMLINE adsorbents are designed to handle feed directly from both fermentation homogenate and crude feedstock from cell culture/fermentation at flow velocities of 200 - 500 cm/h, according to type and application.

Note: *cm/h: flow velocity (linear flow rate) = volumetric flow rate/ cross sectional area of column.*

Three Phase Purification Strategy

Principles

With background information, assays, and sample preparation and extraction procedures in place the Three Phase Purification Strategy can be applied. This strategy is used as an aid to the development of purification processes for therapeutic proteins in the pharmaceutical industry and is equally efficient as an aid when developing purification schemes in the research laboratory.

In the Three Phase Strategy a specific objective is assigned to each step. The purification problem associated with a particular step will depend greatly upon the properties of the starting material. Thus, the objective of a purification step will vary according to its position in the process, *i.e.* at the beginning for *isolation* of product from crude sample, in the middle for *further purification* of partially purified sample, or at the end for *final cleanup* of an almost pure product. The Three Phase Strategy ensures faster method development, a shorter time to pure product and good economy. In the *capture phase* the objectives are to *isolate, concentrate and stabilize* the target product. The product should be concentrated and transferred to an environment which will conserve potency/activity. At best, significant removal of other critical contaminants can also be achieved.

During the *intermediate purification phase* the objectives are to *remove most of the bulk impurities,* such as other proteins and nucleic acids, endotoxins and viruses. In the *polishing phase* most impurities have already been removed except for trace amounts or closely related substances. The objective is to *achieve final purity.* It should be noted that this Three Phase Strategy does not mean that all strategies must have three purification steps. For example, capture and intermediate purification may be achievable in a single step, as may intermediate purification and polishing. Similarly, purity demands may be so low that a rapid capture step is sufficient to achieve the desired result, or the purity of the starting material may be so high that only a polishing step is needed. For purification of therapeutic proteins a fourth or fifth purification step may be required to fulfill the highest purity and safety demands. The optimum selection and combination of purification techniques for *Capture, Intermediate Purification and Polishing* is crucial for an efficient purification process.

Protein propety	Technique
Charge	Ion exchange (IEX)
Size	Gel filtration (GF)
Hydrophobicity	Hydrophobic interaction (HIC), Reversed phase (RPC)
Biorecognition (ligand specificity)	Affinity (AC)
Charge, ligand specificity or hydrophobicity	Expanded bed adsorption (EBA) follows the principles of AC, IEX or HIC

Selection and Combination of Purification Techniques

For any chromatographic separation each different technique will offer different performance with respect to recovery, resolution, speed and capacity. A technique can be optimized to focus on one of these parameters, for example resolution, or to achieve the best balance between two parameters, such as speed and capacity. A separation optimized for one of these parameters will produce results quite different in appearance from those produced using the same technique, but focused on an alternative parameter. See, for example, the results shown on page 49 where ion exchange is used for a capture and for a polishing step.

Capacity, in the simple model shown, refers to the amount of target protein loaded during purification. In some cases the amount of sample which can be loaded may be limited by volume (as in gel filtration) or by large amounts of contaminants rather than the amount of the target protein.

Speed is of the highest importance at the beginning of purification where contaminants such as proteases must be removed as quickly as possible.

Recovery becomes increasingly important as the purification proceeds because of the increased value of the purified product. Recovery is influenced by destructive processes in the sample and unfavourable conditions on the column.

Resolution is achieved by the selectivity of the technique and the efficiency of the chromatographic matrix to produce narrow peaks. In general, resolution is most difficult to achieve in the final stages of purification when impurities and target protein are likely to have very similar properties. Every technique offers a balance between resolution, speed, capacity and recovery and should be selected to meet the objectives for each purification step. In general, optimization of any one of these four parameters can only be achieved at the expense of the others and a purification step will be a compromise. The importance of each parameter will vary depending on whether a purification step is used for capture, intermediate purification or polishing. This will steer the optimization of the critical parameters, as well as the selection of the most suitable media for the step. Proteins are purified using chromatographic purification techniques which separate according to differences in specific properties, as shown in Table 1.5.

The product should be eluted from the first column in conditions suitable for the start conditions of the next column.The start conditions and end conditions for the techniques are shown in Table 1.5. For example, if the sample has a low ionic strength it can be applied to an IEX column. After elution from IEX the sample will usually be in a high ionic strength buffer and can be applied to a HIC column (if necessary the pH can be adjusted and further salt can be added). In contrast, if sample is eluted from a HIC column, it is likely to be in high salt and will require dilution or a buffer exchange step in order to further decrease the ionic strength to a level suitable for IEX. Thus it is more straightforward to go from IEX to HIC than vice-versa. Ammonium sulphate precipitation is a common sample clarification and concentration step at laboratory scale and in this situation HIC (which requires high salt to enhance binding to the media) is ideal as the capture step. The salt concentration and the total sample volume will be significantly reduced after elution from the HIC column. Dilution of the fractionated sample or rapid buffer exchange using a Sephadex G-25 desalting column will prepare it for the next IEX or AC step.

Table 1.5 : Suitability of purification techniques for the Three Phase Purification Strategy

Tech-nique	Main features	Capture	Interme-diate	Polish	Sample Start condition	Sample End condition
IEX	high resolution high capacity high speed	HHH	HHH	HHH	low ionic strength sample volume not limiting	high ionic strength or pH change *concentrated*
HIC	good resolution good capacity high speed	HHH	HHH	H	high ionic strength sample volume not limiting	low ionic strength *concentrated*
AC	high resolution high capacity high speed	HHH	HHH	HH	specific binding conditions sample volume not limiting	specific elution conditions *concentrated*
GF	high resolution using Superdex™		H	HHH	limited sample volume (<5% total column volume) and flow rate range	buffer exchanged (if required) *diluted*
RPC	high resolution		H	HHH	requires orgnic solvents	in organic solvent, risk loss of biological activity *concentrated*

GF is well suited for use after any of the concentrating techniques (IEX, HIC, AC) since the target protein will be eluted in a reduced volume and the components from the elution buffer will not affect the gel filtration separation (gel filtration is a non-binding technique with limited volume capacity and unaffected by buffer conditions). Selection of the final strategy will always depend upon specific sample properties and the required level of purification. Logical combinations of techniques are shown in Figure 1.37.

For any capture step, select the technique showing the strongest binding to the target protein while binding as few of the contaminants as possible, i.e. the technique with the highest selectivity and/or capacity for the protein of interest. A sample is purified using a combination of techniques and alternative selectivities. For example, in an IEX-HIC-GF Three Phase Strategy the capture step selects according to differences in charge (IEX), the intermediate purification step according to differences in hydrophobicity (HIC) and the final polishing step according to differences in size (GF). Figure 1.38 shows a standard Three Phasestrategy purification *(See on page 59).*

If nothing is known about the target protein use IEX-HIC-GF. This combination of techniques can be regarded as a standard protocol. Consider the use of both anion and cation exchange chromatography to give different selectivities within the same purification strategy. IEX is a technique which offers different selectivities using either anion or cation

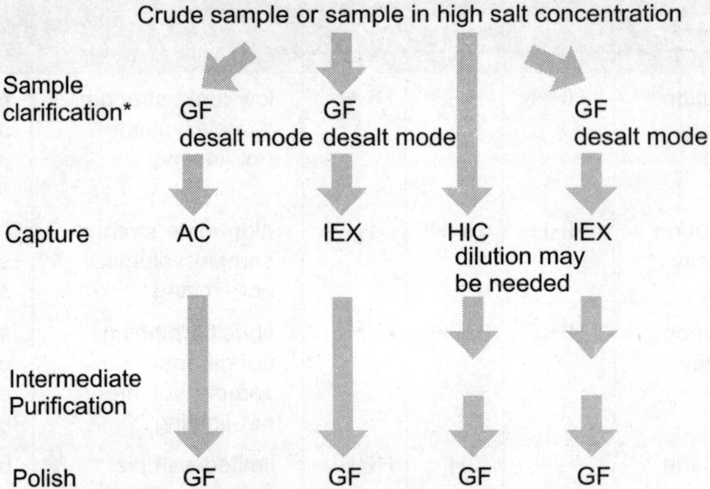

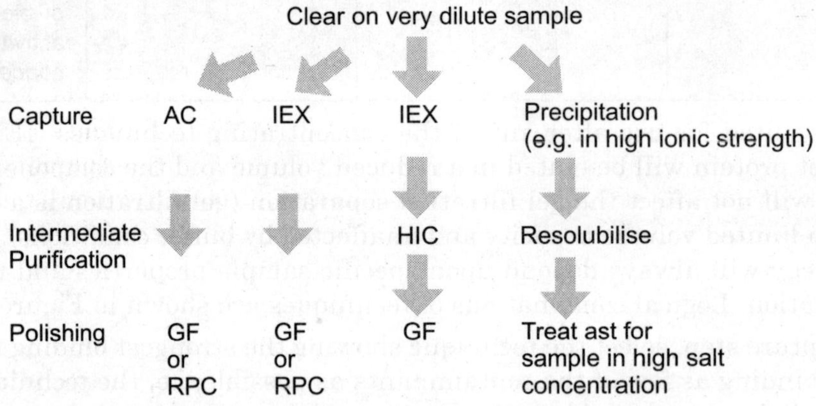

Fig. 1.37 : Logical combinations of chromatographic steps

exchangers. The pH of the separation can be modified to alter the charge characteristics of the sample components. It is therefore possible to use IEX more than once in a purification strategy, for capture, intermediate purification or polishing. IEX can be used effectively both for rapid separation in low resolution mode during capture, and in high resolution mode during polishing in the same purification scheme. Figure 6 shows an example for the purification of cellulase in which advantage is taken of the different selectivities of anion and cation exchange to create a simple two step process.

Capture by IEX
Basic proteins
STREAMLINE SP or SP Sepharose XL
Suggested binding butter: 20 mM sodium phosphate, pH 7
Suggested elution butter: Binding butter + 0.5 M NaCl
Acidic proteins
STREAMLINE DEAE or Q Sepharose XL
Suggested binding butter: 50 mM Tris.HCl, pH 8
Suggested elution butter: Binding butter + 0.5 M NaCl

Intermediate purification by HIC
Phenyl Sepharose 6 Fast Flow (high sub)
Suggested binding butter: 50 mM sodium phosphate, pH 7 + 1.5 M ammonium sulphate
Suggested elution butter: 50 mM sodium phosphate, pH 7

Polishing by GF
Superdex 75 prep grade or Superdex 200 prep grade
Suggested butter: as required by subsequent use

Fig. 1.38 : A standard purification protocol

Sample: 500 ml of Trichoderma reesei crude cellulases in buffer A, 2.5 mg
Column: Mono QTM HR 5/5
Flow: 1.0 ml/min
Buffer A: 20 mM Tris-HCl, pH 7.6
Buffer B: A + 0.5 M NaCl
Gradient: 0% B for 4 min, 0-40% in 21 min, 40-100% B in 15 min

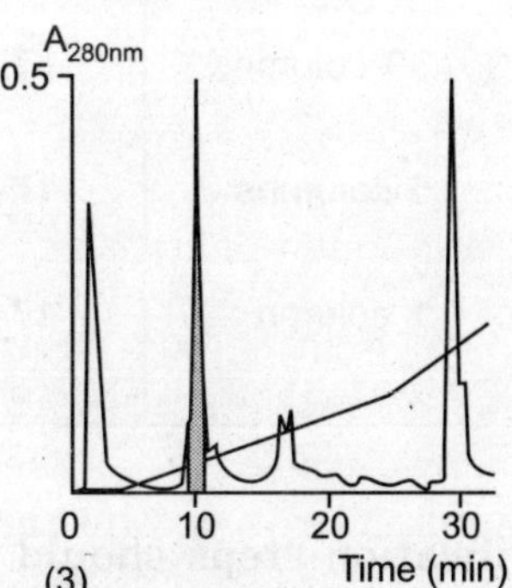

Sample: Peak 3 from step 1
Column: Mono S[TM] HR 5/5
Flow rate: 1.0 ml/min
Buffer A: 20 mM acetate pH 3.6
Buffer B: A + 0.2 M NaCl
Gradient: 0-100% B in 26 min

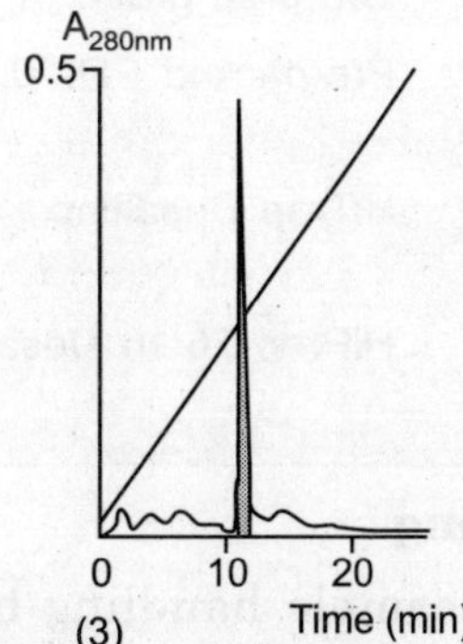

Fig. 1.39 : Two step purification of a cellulase

Consider RPC for a polishing step provided that the target protein can withstand the run conditions.

Reversed phase chromatography (RPC) separates proteins and peptides on the basis of hydrophobicity. RPC is a high selectivity (high resolution) technique, requiring the use of organic solvents. The technique is widely used for purity check analyses when recovery of activity and tertiary structure are not essential.

Since many proteins are denatured by organic solvents, the technique is not generally recommended for protein purification where recovery of activity and return to a correct tertiary structure may be compromised. However, in the polishing phase, when the majority of protein impurities have been removed, RPC can be excellent, particularly for small target proteins which are often not denatured by organic solvents. If a purification is not intended for scale up (*i.e.* only milligram quantities ofproduct are needed), use high performance, pre-packed media such as Sepharose High Performance (IEX, HIC), SOURCE™ (IEX, HIC), MonoBeads™ (IEX), or Superdex (GF) for all steps.

Recommended media for a standard protocol

Purification step	Media	Quantity	Code No.
Capture	STREAMLINE SP	300 ml	17-0993-01
Capture	STREAMLINE DEAE	300 ml	17-0994-01
Capture	HiPrep™ 16/10 SP XL	1 column	17-5093-01
Capture	HiPrep 16/10 Q XL	1 column	17-5092-01
Intermediate purification	HiPrep 16/10 Phenyl FF (high sub)	1 column	17-5095-01
Polishing	HiLoad™ 16/60 Superdex 75 prep grade	1 column	17-1068-01
Polishing	HiLoad 16/60 Superdex 200 prep grade	1 column	17-1069-01
Sample clarification/ conditioning	Pre-packed PD-10 Column	30 columns	17-0851-01
Sample clarification/ conditioning	HiTrap Desalting	5 columns	17-1408-01
Sample clarification/ conditioning	HiPrep 26/10 Desalting	1 column	17-5087-01

Sample Conditioning

Although additional sample handling between purification steps should be avoided, it may be necessary to adjust the buffer conditions of an eluted product (pH, ionic strength and/or buffering ions) to ensure compatibility with the following purification technique. Sephadex G-25 is an ideal media for *rapid desalting and pH adjustment* by buffer exchange between purification steps. Sample volumes of up to 30%, or in some cases 40%, of the total column volume are loaded. In a single step, the sample is desalted, exchanged into a new buffer, and low molecular weight materials are removed. Figure 7 shows a typical desalt/buffer exchange separation. The high volume capacity and speed of this step enable very large sample volumes to be processed rapidly and efficiently. The high sample volume load results in a separation with minimal sample dilution. Sephadex G-25 is also used for rapid sample clean-up at laboratory scale.

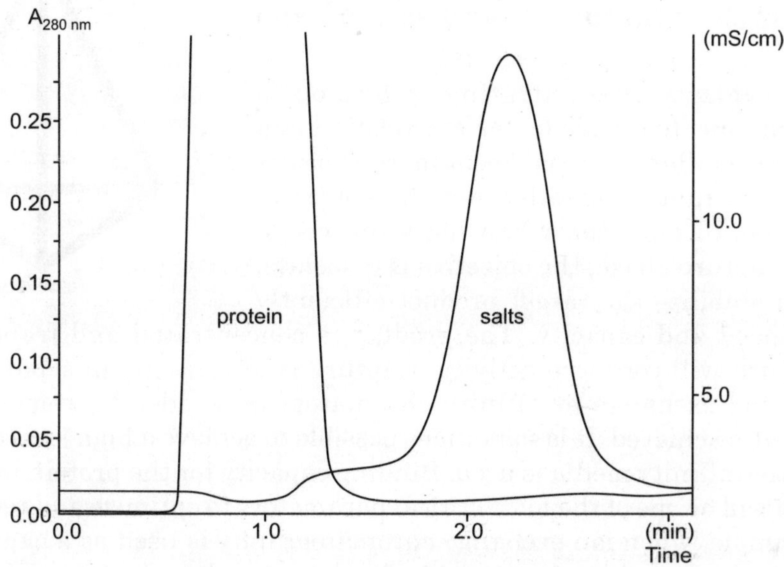

Table 1.6: Used pre packed columns of Sephadex G-25 for rapid sample conditioning at laboratory scale

Pre-packed column	Sample volume loading per run	Sample volume recovery per run	Code No.
HiPrep Desalting 26/10	2.5 -15 ml	7.5 - 20 ml	17-5087-01
HiTrap Desalting	0.25 - 1.5 ml	1.0 - 2.0 ml	17-1408-01
Fast Desalting PC 3.2/10	0.05 - 0.2 ml	0.2 - 0.3 ml	17-0774-01
PD-10 Desalting	1.5 - 2.5 ml	2.5 - 3.5 ml	17-0851-01

Dilution can be used as an alternative to desalting before application to an ion exchange column.

Sephadex G-25 Gel Filtration

For fast group separations between high and low molecular weight substances. Typical flow velocities 60

> **Note:** *cm/h: flow velocity (linear flow rate) = volumetric flow rate/ cross sectional area of column.*

cm/h (Sephadex G-25 Superfine, Sephadex G-25 Fine), 150 cm/h (Sephadex G-25 Medium). In the following chapters Capture, Intermediate Purification and Polishing are discussed in more detail.

Remove Damaging Contaminants Early

Definition: Initial purification of the target molecule from crude or clarified source material.

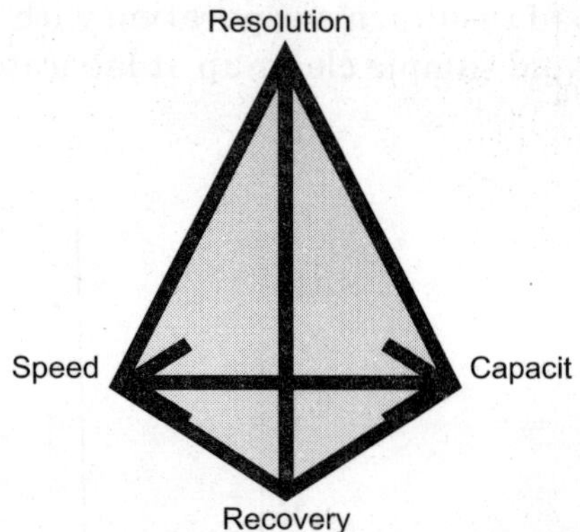

Goals: Rapid isolation, stabilisation and concentration.

Use a high capacity, concentrating technique to reduce sample volume, to enable faster purification and to allow the use of smaller columns. Focus on robustness and simplicity in the first purification step. Do not try to solve all problems in one step when handling crude material. In the capture phase, the objective is to isolate, concentrate and stabilise the target product efficiently by optimising speed and capacity. The product is concentrated and transferred to an environment which will conserve activity. Capture is often a group separation using a step elution on ion exchange or affinity chromatography. Ideally, removal of critical contaminants is also achieved. It is sometimes possible to achieve a high level of purification if a highly selective affinity media is used. Binding capacity for the protein in the presence of the impurities will be one of the most critical parameters to optimise and reduce the scale of work. For example, when ion exchange chromatography is used as a capture step, the goal is to adsorb the target protein quickly from the crude sample and isolate it from critical contaminants such as proteases and glycosidases. Conditions are selected to avoid binding of contaminants so that the capacity for the target protein is maximised. High speed may be required to reduce sample application time, particularly if proteolysis or other destructive effects threaten the integrity of the target protein. Transfer to a step elution during method development to increase speed and capacity of the capture step.

The most common technique for a capture step is ion exchange chromatography (IEX) which has high binding capacity. IEX media are resistant to harsh cleaning conditions which may be needed after purification of crude samples. Typically proteins are eluted from an IEX column using a salt gradient. However, during method development, a transfer to a step elution will give a simple, robust separation with a shorter run time and decreased buffer consumption. It is often possible to use high sample loadings since the focus is not on resolution (high sample loadings will decrease resolution). High speed and capacity and low buffer consumption are particularly advantageous for large scale purification, as shown in Figure 1.40.

For large scale capture, throughput will often be the focus during method development. It is important to consider all aspects: sample extraction and clarification, sample loading

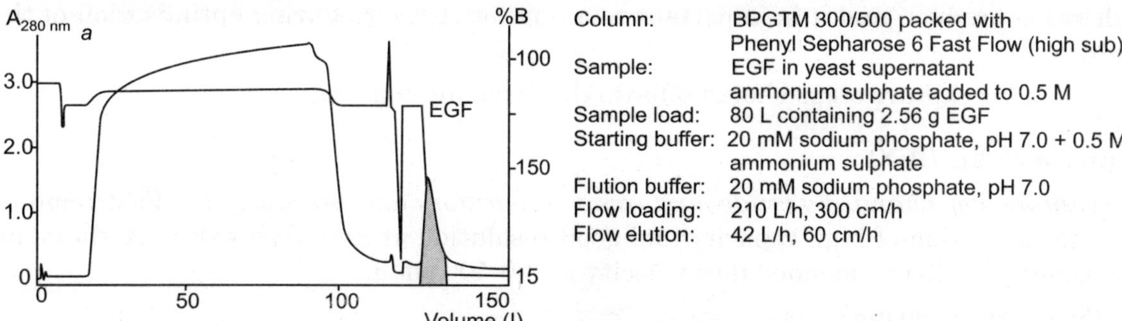

a) Purification of recombinant epidemal growth factor (EGF) - capture step.

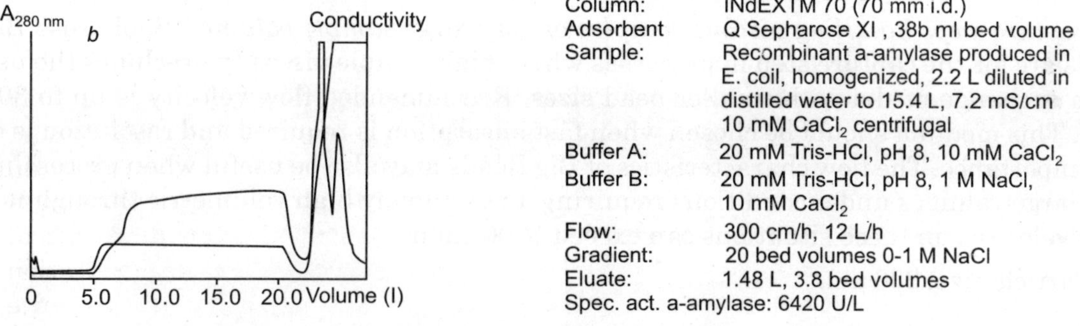

b) Pilot scale purification of recombinánt α-amylase from E. coil - capture step.

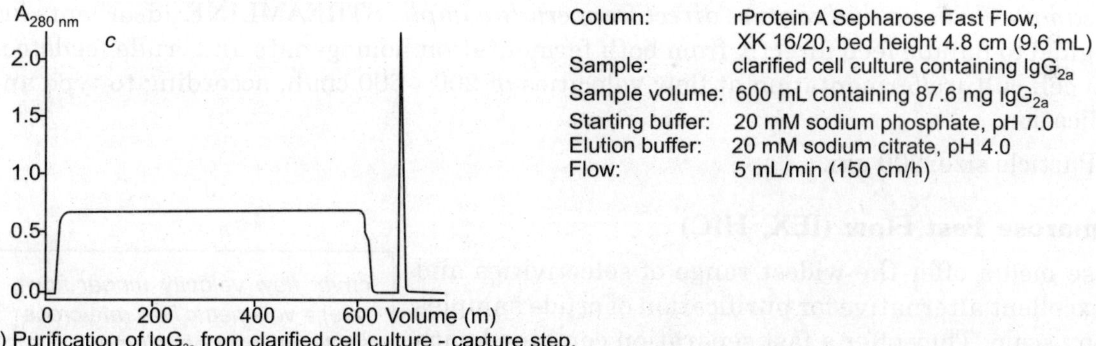

c) Purification of IgG_{2a} from clarified cell culture - capture step.

Fig. 1.40 : Examples of capture steps

capacity, flow rate during equilibration, binding, washing, elution and cleaning, and the need for cleaning-in-place procedures.

In principle, a capture step is designed to maximise capacity and/or speed at the expense of some resolution. However, there is usually significant resolution and purification from molecules which have significant physicochemical differences compared to the target protein.

Recovery will be of concern in any preparative situation, especially for production of a high value product, and it is important to assay for recovery during optimisation of the capture step.

Media for capture steps should offer high speed and high capacity.

Sepharose XL (IEX)

For capture steps handling crude mixtures at laboratory and process scale. Fast removal and a combination of high capacity and good resolution at high flow rates are the main characteristics. Recommended flow velocity is 100-500 cm/h.

Particle size: 90 μm.

Sepharose Big Beads (IEX)

For capture steps handling viscous samples or very large sample volumes. Sepharose Big Beads are for the capture step in processes where high sample viscosity precludes the use of ion exchange media with smaller bead sizes. Recommended flow velocity is up to 300 cm/h. This medium should be chosen when fast adsorption is required and resolution is of less importance. The flow characteristics of Big Beads may also be useful when processing very large volumes under conditions requiring an extremely high volumetric throughput. Flow velocities in these situations can exceed 1000 cm/h.

Particle size: 200 μm.

Streamline (IEX, AC, HIC)

For sample clean-up and capture direct from crude sample. STREAMLINE adsorbents are designed to handle feed directly from both fermentation homogenate and crude feedstock from cell culture/fermentation at flow velocities of 200 - 500 cm/h, according to type and application.

Particle size: 200 μm.

Sepharose Fast Flow (IEX, HIC)

These media offer the widest range of selectivities and an excellent alternative for purification of crude samples at any scale. They offer a fast separation combined with good resolution. Recommended flow velocity is 100-300 cm/h.

cm/h: flow velocity (linear flow rate) = volumetric flow rate/cross sectional area of column.

Particle size: 90 μm.

- If purification is not intended for scale up (i.e. milligram quantities of product are needed), use high performance media such as Sepharose High Performance (IEX, HIC) or MonoBeads (IEX), or SOURCE (IEX, HIC). All these media are available in pre-packed columns. For micro scale purification use MonoBeads or MiniBeads™

(IEX), Phenyl Superose™ (HIC) or NHS-activated Superose (AC) columns. For 'one time' purification or with a readily available sample, sacrifice yield for purity by taking a narrow cut from a chromatographic peak during the first purification step. Use HiTrap Ion Exchange and HiTrap HIC Test Kits for media screening and simple method optimization.

- If the starting material is reasonably clean, a single step purification on highest resolution MonoBeads (IEX) may be sufficient to achieve required purity at laboratory scale.
- If a bio specific ligand is available, consider using affinity chromatography as the capture step. If the media is to be used routinely, ensure that any contaminants from the crude sample can be removed by column regeneration procedures which do not damage the affinity ligand. AC will give a highly selective capture step to improve resolution from contaminants, but speed may need to be reduced to maintain a high binding capacity.
- If the starting material is reasonably clean a single step purification on a prepacked HiTrap affinity column may be sufficient to achieve required purity at the milligram scale, as shown in Figure 1.41.
- If the starting material is concentrated, has a low volume and there is no intention to scale up, Superdex gel filtration media can offer a mild first step, requiring little or no optimization. Conversely, gel filtration is not suitable in a typical capture step where the sample volume is large or will be scaled up.

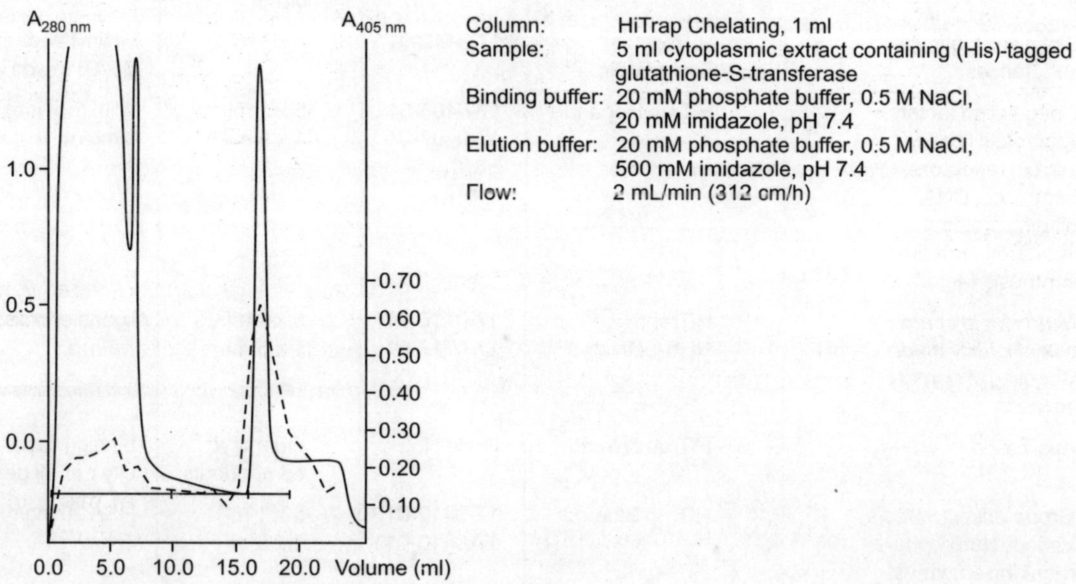

Fig. 1.41: HiTrap Chelating column used to purify histidine-tagged glutathione-S-transferase from cytoplasmic extract

Table 1.7 : Recommended HiTrap affinity columns for laboratory scale separation

Application	HiTrap column	Code No.	Quantity/ components	Approximate binding capa- city per ml gel
1	2	3	4	5
Group Specific Media	HiTrap Blue	17-0412-01	5 x 1 ml	HSA 20 mg/ml
Various Nucleotide-requiring enzymes, coagulation factors, DNA binding proteins, $2^{\text{-macroglobulin}}$		17-0413-01	1 x 5 ml	
Proteins and peptides	HiTrap Chelating	17-0408-01	5 x 1 ml	$^{\text{(His)}}6^{\text{-tagged}}$
with exposed amino acids: His (Cys, Trp) e.g. ?$2^{\text{-macroglobulin}}$ and interferon		17-0409-01	1 x 5 ml	protein (27.6 kD) 12 mg /ml
Histidine-tagged fusion proteins	HisTrap™	17-1880-01	HiTrap Chelating column (1 ml), accessories, pre-made buffers	as above
Biotin and biotinylated substances	HiTrap Streptavidin	17-5112-01	5 x 1 ml	biotinylated BSA 6 mg/ml
Coagulation factors, lipoprotein lipases, steroid receptors, hormones, DNA binding proteins, interferon, protein synthesis factors	HiTrap Heparin	17-0406-01 17-0407-01	5 x 1 ml 1 x 5 ml	ATIII (bovine) 3 mg/ml
Matrix for preparation of affinity media Coupling of primary amines	HiTrap NHS-activated	17-0716-01 17-0717-01	5 x 1 ml 1 x 5 ml	ligand specific
Application	HiTrap column	Code No.	Quantity/ components	binding capa- city per ml gel
Group Specific Media Various Nucleotide-requiring enzymes, coagulation factors, DNA binding proteins, ?$2^{\text{-macroglobulin}}$	HiTrap Blue	17-0412-01 17-0413-01	5 x 1 ml 1 x 5 ml	HSA 20 mg/ml

(Contd...)

1	2	3	4	5
Proteins and peptides with exposed amino acids: His (Cys, Trp) e.g. ?2-macroglobulin and interferon	HiTrap Chelating	17-0408-01 17-0409-01	5 x 1 ml 1 x 5 ml	(His)6-tagged protein (27.6 kD) 12 mg /ml
Histidine-tagged fusion proteins	HisTrap™	17-1880-01	HiTrap Chelating column (1 ml), accessories, pre-made buffers	as above
Biotin and biotinylated substances	HiTrap Streptavidin	17-5112-01	5 x 1 ml	biotinylated BSA 6 mg/ml
Coagulation factors, lipoprotein lipases, steroid receptors, hormones, DNA binding proteins, interferon, protein synthesis factors	HiTrap Heparin	17-0406-01 17-0407-01	5 x 1 ml 1 x 5 ml	ATIII (bovine) 3 mg/ml
Matrix for preparation of affinity media Coupling of primary amines	HiTrap NHS-activated	17-0716-01 17-0717-01	5 x 1 ml 1 x 5 ml	ligand specific

Recommended separation conditions All HiTrap columns are supplied with a detailed protocol to ensure optimum results Maximum flow rates: HiTrap 1 ml column: up to 4 ml/min HiTrap 5 ml column: up to 20 ml/min

STREAMLINE expanded bed adsorption is particularly suited for large scale recombinant protein and monoclonal antibody purification. STREAMLINE adsorbents are specially designed for use in STREAMLINE columns. The technique requires no sample clean up and so combines sample preparation and capture in a single step. As shown in Figure 1.42 (*See on next page*), crude sample is applied to an expanded bed of STREAMLINE media, target proteins are captured whilst cell debris, particulate matter, whole cells, and contaminants pass through. Flow is reversed and the target protein is desorbed in the elution buffer.

Intermediate Purification

In the intermediate purification phase the focus is to separate the target protein from most of the bulk impurities such as other proteins, nucleic acids, endotoxins and viruses. The ability to resolve similar components is of increased importance. The requirements for resolution will depend upon the status of the sample produced from the capture step and the purity requirements for the final product. Capacity will still be important to maintain productivity. Speed is less critical in intermediate purification since the impurities causing

System: BioProcessTM Modular
Column: STREAMLINE 200 (i.d. 200 mm)
Medium: STREAMLINE DEAE, 4.7 L
Sample: 4.7 kg of cells were subjected to osmotic shock and suspended in a final volume of 180 L 50 mM Tris
Buffer A: 50 mM Tris buffer, pH 7.4
Buffer B: 50 mM Tris, 0.5 M sodium chloride, pH 7.4
Flow: 400 cm/h during sample application and wash
100 cm/h during elution

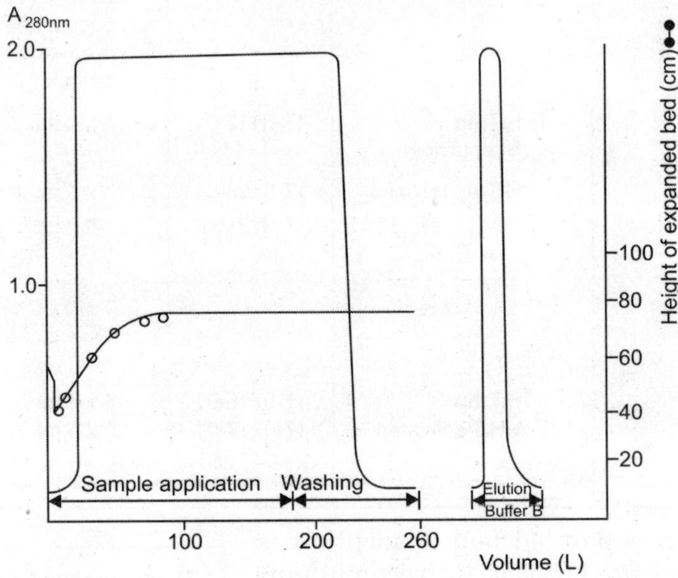

Fig. 1.42 : Purification of a recombinant protein *Pseudomonas aeruginosa* exotoxin A - capture step

proteolysis or other destructive effects should have been removed, and sample volume should have been reduced, in the capture step.The optimal balance between capacity and resolution must be defined for each specific application. This then decides how the separation conditions should be optimised during method development.The technique must give a high resolution separation. Elution by a continuous gradient will usually be required. As in a capture step, selectivity during sample adsorption will be important, not only to achieve high binding capacity, but also to contribute to the purification by achieving a further separation during sample application. However, in contrast to a capture step, selectivity during sample desorption from the column is also important and is usually achieved by applying a more selective desorption principle, such as a continuous gradient or a multi-step elution procedure, as shown in Figure 142A. Examples of Intermediate Purification steps are shown later. Use a technique with a complementary selectivity to that which was used for the capture step.

a) Purification of recombinant protein Pseudomonas aeruginosa exotoxin A -intermediate purification step.

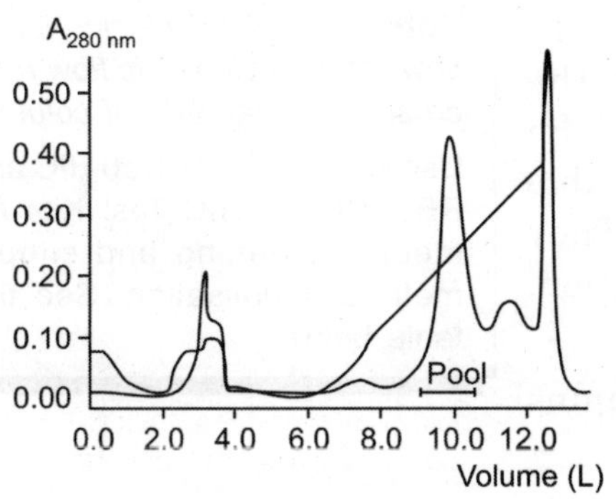

Column:	FineLINE™ 100 (i.d. 100 mm)
Medium:	SOURCE 30Q, 375 mL (50 mm bed height)
Sample:	from the previous pool, diluted 1 to 3 with distilled water 1.5 L/cycle were applied
Buffer A:	20 mM phosphate, pH 7.4
Buffer B:	Buffer A + 1.0 M sodium chloride
Gradient:	0 to 50% B, 20 column volumes
Flow:	600 cm/h

b) Purification of recombinant Annexin V - intermediate purification step.

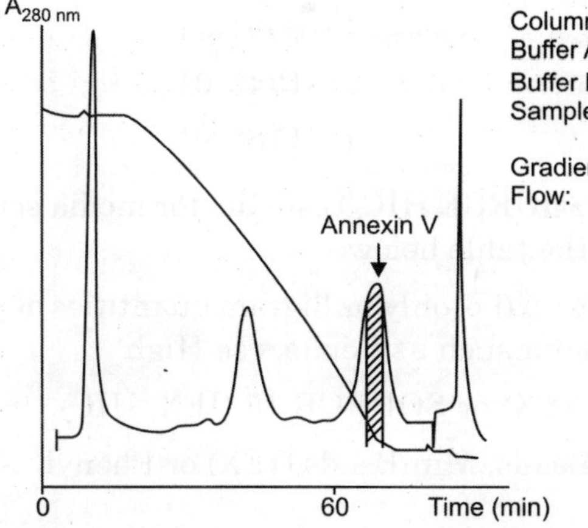

Column:	XK 16/20 Butyl Sepharose 4 Fast Flow
Buffer A:	20 mM Sodium phosphate, pH 7.0, 1 M $(NH_4)_2SO_4$
Buffer B:	20 mM Sodium phosphate, pH 7.0,
Sample:	Partially purified Annexin V expressed in E. coli, 5 ml
Gradient:	0 to 50% B, 20 column volumes
Flow:	100 cm/h

Fig. 1.42A

Source (IEX)

For fast, high resolution and high capacity intermediate purification. SOURCE media are for high throughput, high capacity and high resolution purification. Frequently, if filtered samples are used, the intermediate purification step can be combined with the capture step. A flow velocity up to 2000 cm/h is possible. SOURCE 30 is also a good choice at large scale for intermediate purification.

Particle size: 15 µm. Available in pre-packed columns and as bulk media.

Particle size: 30 µm. Available as bulk media.

Sepharose High Performance (IEX, HIC, AC)

For high resolution and high capacity intermediate purification. These media are ideal for intermediate purification at large scale and should be used when resolution and capacity are a priority. Recommended flow velocity is up to 150 cm/h.

Particle size: 34 µm. Available in pre-packed columns and as bulk media.

Sepharose Fast Flow (IEX, HIC, AC)

Proven in large scale production of pharmaceuticals during intermediate purification steps. These media are the accepted standard for general applications in the laboratory and at large scale. They are available in the widest range of techniques and selectivities and are able to withstand harsh cleaning-in-place conditions. They offer a fast separation combined with good resolution. Recommended flow velocity is 100-300 cm/h.

> **Note:** *cm/h: flow velocity (linear flow rate) = volumetric flow rate/ cross sectional area of column.*
>
> Use HiTrap IEX, HiTrap HIC and RESOURCE HIC Test Kits for media screening and simple method optimisation. See the table below.

Particle size: 90 μm. Available in pre-packed columns and as bulk media.

Kit	Code No.
HiTrap IEX Test Kit	17-6001-01
HiTrap HIC Test Kit	17-1349-01
RESOURCE HIC Test Kit	17-1187-01

- Use HiTrap IEX, HiTrap HIC and RESOURCE HIC Test Kits for media screening and simple method optimisation. See the table below.
- If a purification is not intended for scale up (i.e. only milligram quantities of product are needed), use high performance media such as Sepharose High
- Performance (IEX, HIC) MonoBeads (IEX) or SOURCE 15 (IEX, HIC).
- For microscale purification use MonoBeads, MiniBeads (IEX) or Phenyl
- Superose PC (HIC) columns.

Polishing

In the polishing phase the focus is almost entirely on high resolution to achieve final purity. Most contaminants and impurities have already been removed except for trace impurities such as leachable, endotoxins, nucleic acids or viruses, closely related substances such as micro heterogeneous structural variants of the product, and reagents or aggregates. To achieve resolution it may be necessary to sacrifice sample load or even recovery (by peak cutting). Recovery of the final product is also a high priority and a technique must be selected which ensures the highest possible recovery. Product losses at this stage are more costly than in earlier stages. Ideally the product should be recovered in buffer conditions ready for the next procedure. The technique chosen must discriminate between the target protein and any remaining contaminants The high resolution required to achieve this discrimination is not always reached by using a high selectivity technique alone, but usually requires selection of a high efficiency medium with small, uniform bead sizes.

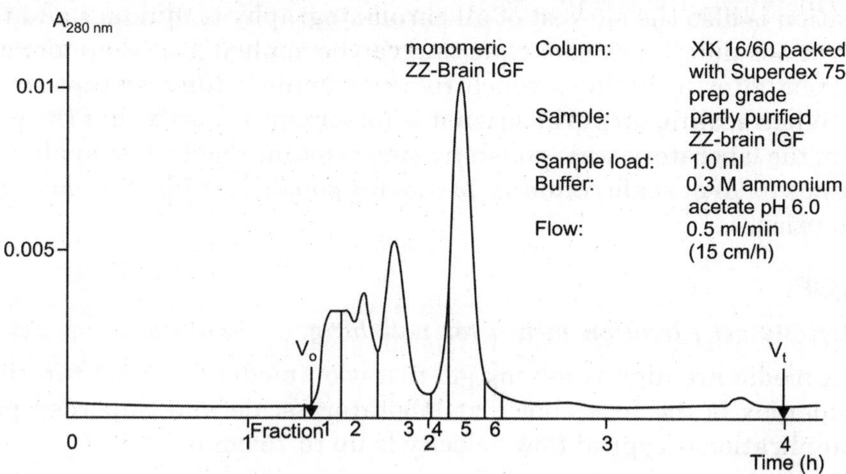

Fig. 1.43 : Separation of dimers and multimers-polishing step

Typically, separations by charge, hydrophobicity or affinity will have already been used so that high resolution gel filtration is ideal for polishing. The product is purified and transferred into the required buffer in one step and dimers or aggregates can often be removed, as shown in Figure 1.43. To remove contaminants of similar size, an alternative high resolution technique using elution with shallow gradients is usually required, as shown in Figure 1.44.

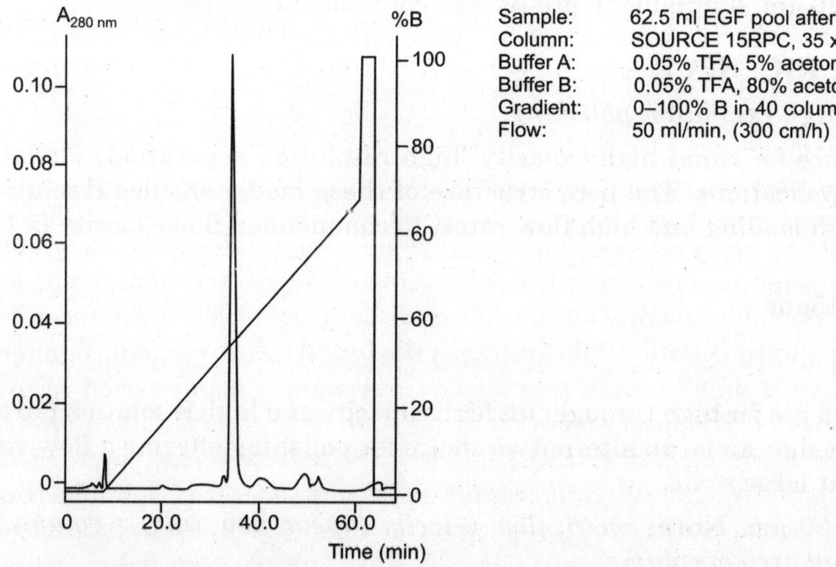

Fig. 1.44 : Final polishing step of recombinant epidermal growth factor, using reversed phase chromatography. Method developed on pre-packed RESOURCE™ RPC and scaled up on SOURCE 15RPC

Gel filtration is also the slowest of all chromatography techniques and the size of the column determines the volume of sample that can be applied. It is therefore most logical to use gel filtration after techniques which reduce sample volume so that smaller columns can be used. When scaling up purification it is important to verify that the high resolution achieved from the laboratory scale polishing step is maintained when applying preparative sample volumes to large scale columns. Media for polishing steps should offer the highest possible resolution.

Superdex (GF)

High productivity gel filtration media for polishing.

Superdex media are high resolving gel filtration media for short run times and good recovery. Superdex is the first choice at laboratory scale and Superdex prep grade for large scale applications. Typical flow velocity is up to 75 cm/h.

Particle size Superdex: 13 μm.

Particle size Superdex prep grade: 34 μm.

MonoBeads (IEX)

Media for polishing at laboratory scale when highest resolution is essential.

These media offer high capacity and high resolution separations at laboratory scale. Typical flow velocity is 150-600 cm/h.

Particle size: 10 μm. Available in pre-packed columns.

Source 15 (IEX, HIC, RPC)

Media for rapid high resolution polishing.

SOURCE 15 are for rapid high capacity, high resolution separations for laboratory and large scale applications. The pore structure of these media enables resolution to be maintained at high loading and high flow rates. Recommended flow velocity is 150-1800 cm/h.

Particle size: 15μm.

Source 30 (IEX)

SOURCE 30 media are for high throughput, high capacity and high resolution purification. However, these media can be an alternative choice for polishing offering a flow velocity of up to 2000 cm/h at large scale.

Particle size: 30 μm. **Note:** *cm/h: flow velocity (linear flow rate) = volumetric flow rate/cross sectional area of column.*

For microscale purification use Superdex PC (GF), MiniBeads (IEX) or Phenyl Superose PC (HIC) columns.

Examples of Protein Purification Strategies

The Three Phase Purification Strategy has been successfully applied to many purification schemes from simple laboratory scale purification to large, industrial scale production. Examples highlighted in this chapter demonstrate applications in which a standard protocol was applied, *i.e.* sample extraction and clarification, capture, intermediate purification and polishing. There are also examples where strategies were developed requiring even fewer steps, by following the general guidelines for protein purification given in this handbook and selecting the most appropriate technique and media to fulfil the purification objectives. In most of these examples methods were developed using ÄKTAdesign chromatography systems.

Three step purification of a recombinant enzyme. This example demonstrates one of the most common purification strategies:

IEX for capture, HIC for intermediate purification and GF for the polishing step.

The objective of this purification was to obtain highly purified protein for crystallisation and structural determination.

A more detailed description of this work can be found in Application Note 18-1128-91.

Target Molecule

Deacetoxycephalosporin C synthase (DAOCS), an oxygen-sensitive enzyme.

Source Material

Recombinant protein over-expressed in soluble form in the cytoplasm of *E. coli* bacteria.

Sample Extraction and Clarification

Cells were suspended in lysis buffer (50 mM Tris-HCl, 1 mM EDTA, 2 mM DTT, 0.2 M benzamidine-HCl, 0.2 mM PMSF, pH 7.5) and lysed using ultrasonication. Streptomycin sulphate (1%) and polyethyleneimine (0.1%) were added to precipitate DNA. The extract was clarified by centrifugation.

EDTA, DTT, Benzamidine-HCl and PMSF were used in the lysis buffer to inhibit proteases and to minimise damage to the oxygen-sensitive enzyme. Keeping the sample on ice also reduced protease activity.

Capture

The capture step focused on the rapid removal of the most harmful contaminants from the relatively unstable target protein. This, together with the calculated isoelectric point of DAOCS (pI = 4.8), led to the selection of an anion exchange purification. A selection of anion exchange columns, including those from HiTrap IEX Test Kit, were screened to select the optimum medium (results not shown) before using a larger column for the optimisation of the capture step. Q Sepharose XL, a high capacity medium, well suited for capture, was chosen. As shown in Figure 1.45, optimisation of the capture step allowed the use of a step elution at high flow rate to speed up the purification. This was particularly.

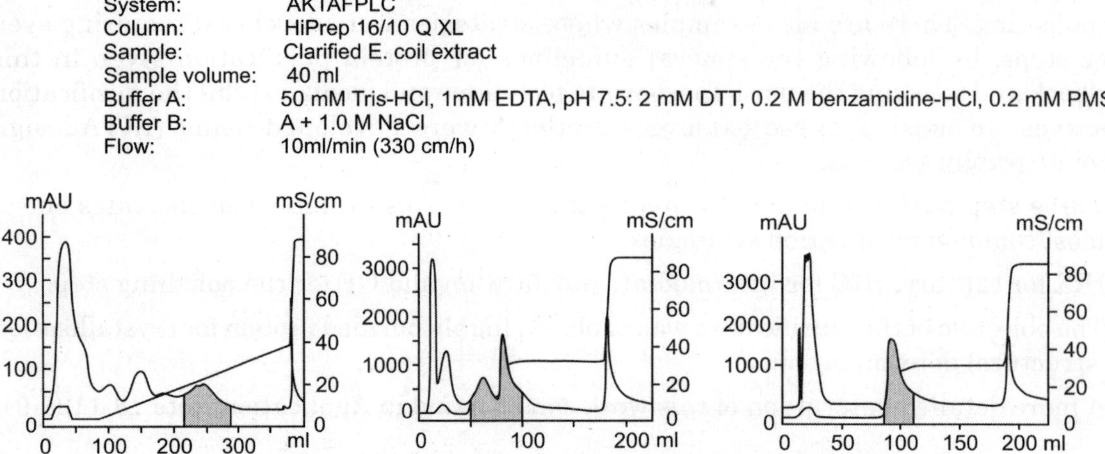

Fig. 1.45: Capture using IEX and optimisation of purification conditions. The elution position of DAOCS is shaded

Intermediate Purification

Hydrophobic interaction chromatography (HIC) was selected because the separation principle is complementary to ion exchange and because a minimum amount of sample conditioning was required. Hydrophobic properties are difficult to predict and it is always recommended to screen different media. The intermediate purification step was developed by screening pre-packed hydrophobic interaction media (RESOURCE HIC Test Kit) to select the optimum medium for the separation (results not shown). SOURCE 15ISO was selected on the basis of the resolution achieved. In this intermediate step, shown in Figure 1.46, the maximum possible speed for separation was sacrificed in order to achieve higher resolution and to allow significant reduction of remaining impurities *(See Fig. on next page)*.

Polishing

The main goal of the polishing step was to remove aggregates and minor contaminants and to transfer the purified sample into a buffer suitable for use in further structural studies. Superdex 75 prep grade, a gel filtration medium giving high resolution at relatively short separation times, was selected since the molecular weight of DAOCS (34 500) is within the optimal separation range for this medium. Figure 1.47 shows the final purification step.

System:	AKTAFPLC
Column:	SOURCE 15ISO, packed in HR 16/10 column
Sample:	DAOCS pool from HiPrep 16/10 Q XL
Sample volume:	40 ml
Buffer A:	1.6 M ammonium sulphate, 10% glycerol, 50 mM Tris-HCl, 1 mM EDTA, 2 mM DTT, 0.2 mM benzamidine-HCl 2mM PMSF, pH 7.5
Buffer B:	50 mM Tris-HCl, 10% glycerol, 1 mM EDTA, 2 mM DTT, 0.2 mM benzamidine-HCl, 0.2 mM PMSF, pH 7.5
Gradient:	0–16% B in 4 CV, 16–24% B in 8 CV, 24–35% B in 4 CV, 100% B in 4 CV
Flow:	5 ml/min (150 cm/h)

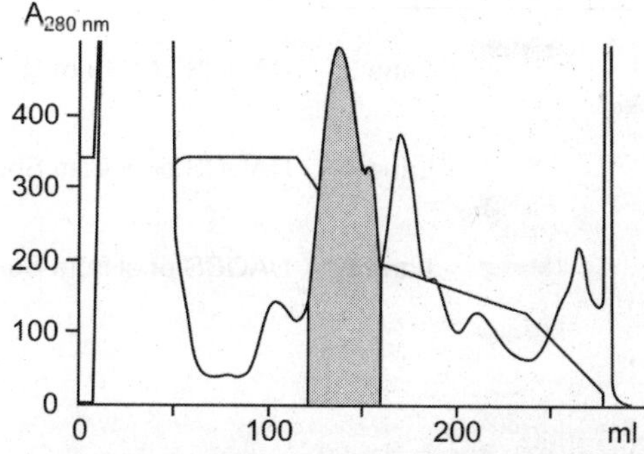

Fig. 1.46 : Intermediate purification using HIC

System:	AKTAFPLC
Column:	HiLoad 16/60 Superdex 75 prep grade
Sample:	Concentrated DAOCS pool from SOURCE 15ISO
Sample volume:	3 ml
Buffer:	100 mM Tris-HCl, 1 mM EDTA, 2 mM DTT, 0.2 mM benzamidine-HCl, 0.2 mM PMSF, pH 7.5
Flow:	1 ml/min (30 cm/h)

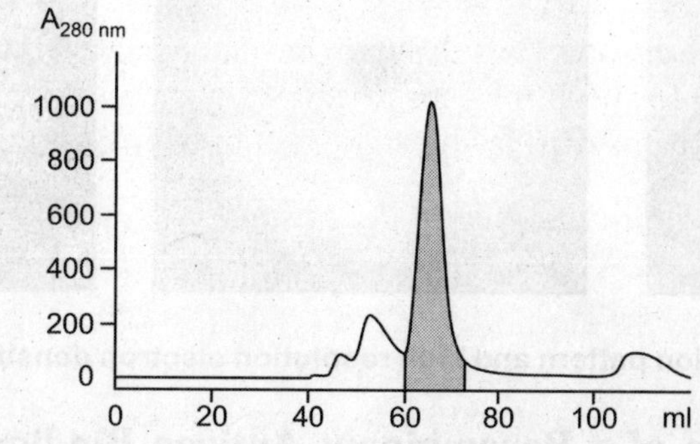

Fig. 1.47 : Polishing using gel filtration

Analytical Assays

Figure 1.48 shows the analysis of collected fractions by SDS-PAGE and silver staining using Multiphor™ II, following the separation and staining protocols supplied with the instruments.

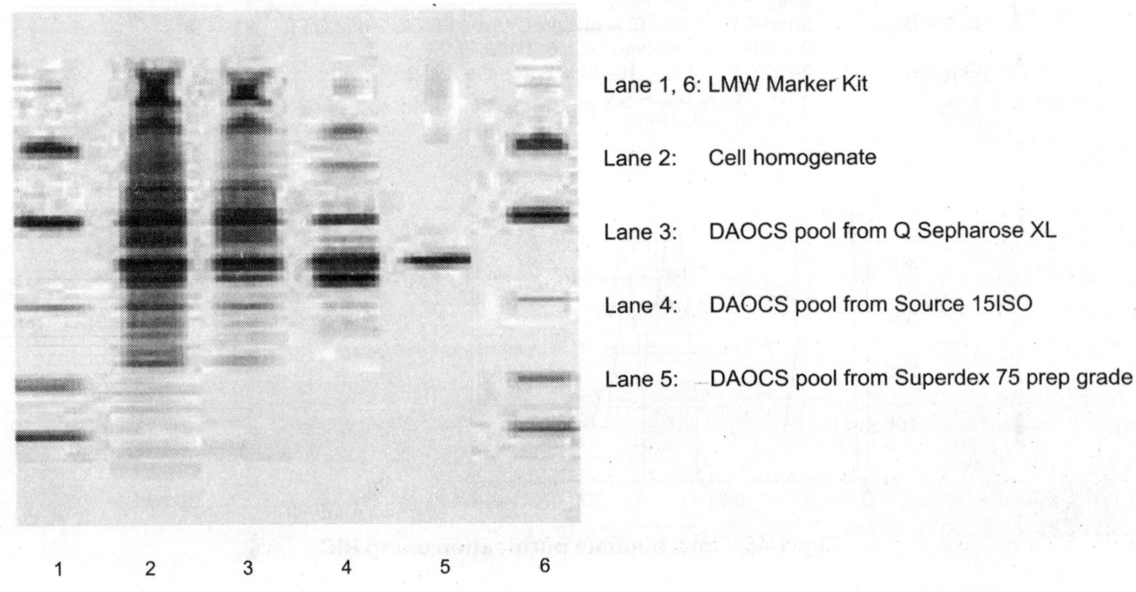

Fig. 1.48 : Analysis of purification steps using ExcelGel™ SDS Gradient 8-18

The final product was used successfully in X-ray diffraction studies, Figure 1.49.

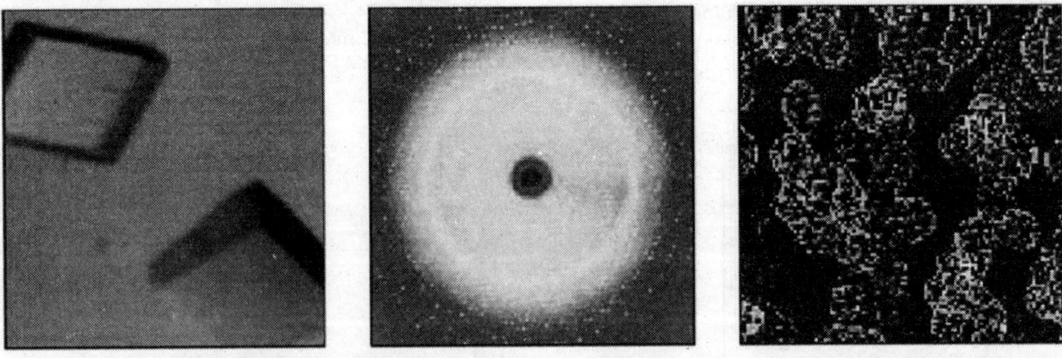

Fig. 1.49 : Crystals, diffraction pattern and high resolution electron density map of purified DAOCS

Three Step Purification of a Recombinant Antigen Binding Fragment

This example demonstrates a three stage purification strategy in which the same purification principle is used in two different modes in the capture and polishing step : IEX for capture, HIC for intermediate purification and IEX for the polishing step. The objective of this purification was to scale up the purification for use as a routine procedure. A more detailed description of this work can be found in Application Note 18-1111-23.

Target Molecule

Recombinant antigen binding fragment (Fab) directed against HIV gp-120.

Source Material

The anti-gp 120 Fab was expressed in the periplasm of the E. coli strain BM170

MCT61. E. coli pellets were stored frozen after being harvested and washed once.

Sample Extraction, Clarification and Capture

Thawed cells were lysed and the lysate was treated with DNase in the presence of 2 mM MgCl2 at pH 7.5, before the capture step.

The Fab fragment was captured from non-clarified homogenate by using expanded bed adsorption with STREAMLINE SP (cation exchanger).Expanded bed adsorption was chosen because the target protein could be captured directly from the crude homogenate in a single step, without centrifugation or other preparatory clean-up steps. The technique is well suited for large scale purification. The result of the capture step is shown in Figure 1.50. The Fab fragment is concentrated and transferred rapidly into a stable environment, using step elution.

Column:	STREAMLINE 200 (i.d. 200 mm)
Adsorbent:	STREAMLINE SP, 4.6 L
Sample:	60 L high pressure homogenized E. coli suspension
Buffer A:	50 mM sodium acetate, pH 5.0
Buffer B;	50 mM sodium acetate, pH 5.0, 1 M NaCl
Flow:	300 cm/h during sample application and wash, 100 cm/h during elution

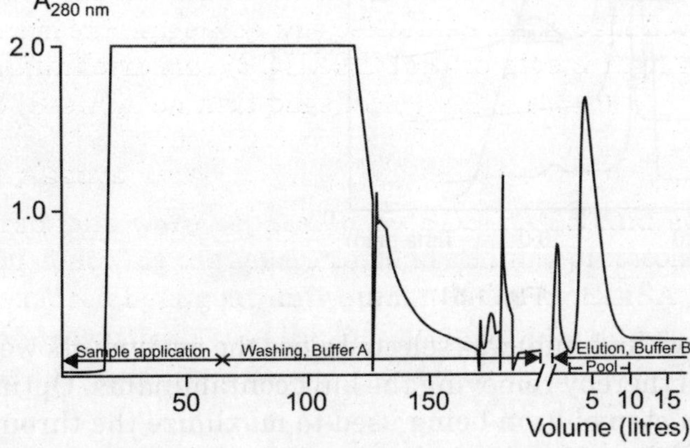

Fig. 1.50

Hydrophobic interaction chromatography (HIC) was selected because the separation principle is complementary to ion exchange and because a minimum amount of sample conditioning was required since the sample was already in a high salt buffer after elution from STREAMLINE SP. Hydrophobic properties are difficult to predict and it is always recommended to screen different media. A HiTrap HIC Test Kit (containing five 1 ml columns pre-packed with different media suitable for production scale) was used to screen for the most appropriate medium. Buffer pH was kept at pH 5.0 to further minimize the need for sample conditioning after capture. Results of the media screening are shown in Figure 1.51.

System:	AKTAexplorer
Sample:	Fab fraction form STREAMLINE SP,2 ml
Columns:	HiTrap HIC Test Kit (1 ml columns), Phenyl Sepharose High Performance, Phenyl Sepharose 6 Fast Flow (low sub), Phenyl Sepharose 6 Fast Flow (high sub), Butyl Sepharosa 4 Fast Flow, Octyl Sepharose 4 Fast Flow
Buffer A:	1 ml (NH4)2SO4, 50 mM NaAc, pH 5.0
Buffer B:	50 mM NaAc, pH 5.0
Gradient:	20 column volumes
Flow:	2 ml/min (300 cm/hr)

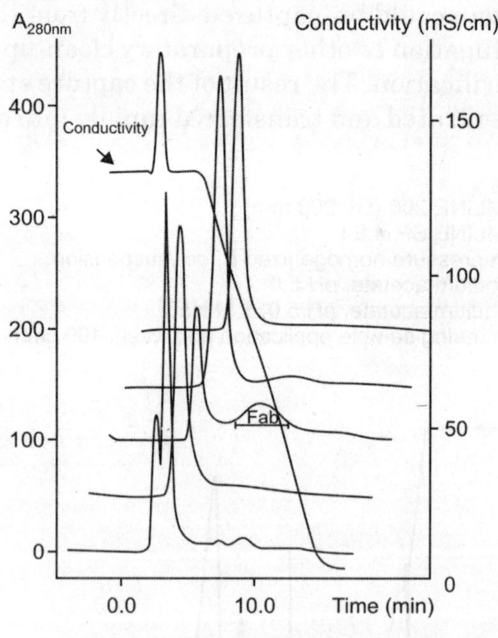

Fig. 1.51

Phenyl Sepharose 6 Fast Flow (high sub) was selected since the medium showed excellent selectivity for the target protein thereby removing the bulk contaminants. Optimization of elution conditions resulted in a step elution being used to maximize the throughput and the concentrating effect of the HIC purification technique. Figure 1.52 shows the optimized elution and the subsequent scale up of the intermediate purification step.

System:	AKTAexplorer
Sample:	Fab fraction from STREAMLINE SP, 80 ml
Columns:	Phenyl Sepharose 6 Fast Flow (high sub) in XK 16/20 (10 cm bed height)
Buffer A:	1 M $(NH_4)_2SO_4$, 50 mM NaAc, pH 5.0
Buffer B:	50 mM NaAc, pH 5.0
Gradient:	Step gradient to 50% B
Flow:	5 ml/min

System:	AKTAexplorer
Sample:	Fab fraction from STREAMLINE SP, 80 ml
Columns:	Phenyl Sepharose 6 Fast Flow (high sub) in XK 50/20
Buffer A:	1 M $(NH_4)_2SO_4$, 50 mM NaAc, pH 5.0
Buffer B:	50 mM NaAc, pH 5.0
Gradient:	Step gradient to 50% B
Flow:	Equilibration: 100 ml/min Loading and elution: 50 ml/min

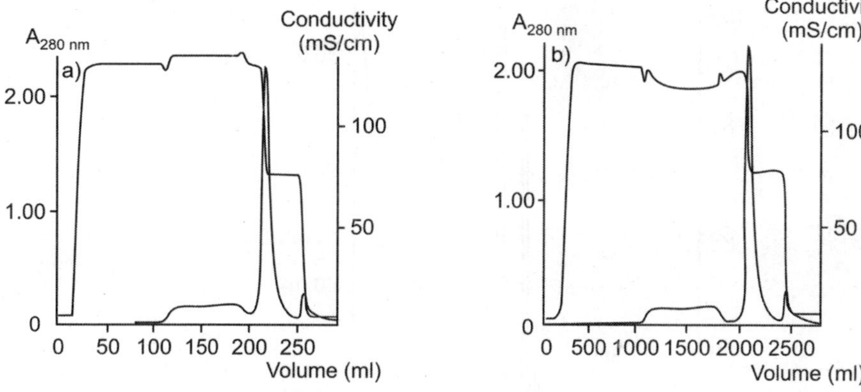

Fig. 1.52 : Intermediate purification using HIC: optimisation and scale-up

Polishing

Gel filtration was investigated as the natural first choice for a final polishing step to remove trace contaminants and transfer the sample to a suitable storage conditions. However, in this example, gel filtration could not resolve a contaminant (Mr 52 000) from the Fab fragment (Mr 50 000) (results not shown). As an alternative another cation exchanger SOURCE 15S was used. In contrast to the cation exchange step at the capture step, the polishing cation exchange step was performed using a shallow gradient elution on a medium with a small,uniform size (SOURCE 15S) to give a high resolution result, as shown in Figure 1.53 (*See Fig. on next page).*

Analytical Assays

Collected fractions were separated by SDS-PAGE and stained by Coomassie™ using PhastSystem, following the separation and staining protocols supplied with the instrument. Fab was measured by a goat-anti-human IgG Fab ELISA, an anti-gp120 ELISA and an in vitro assay which measured the inhibition of HIV-1 infection of T-cells. Nucleic acid was routinely monitored by measuring A260/A280. The correlation ofa high A260/A280 ratio (>1) with the presence of DNA was verified for selected samples by agarose gel electrophoresis and ethidium bromide staining. Endotoxin determination employed a kinetic chromogenic Limulus assay (Coamatic™, Chromogenix AB, Mölndal, Sweden).

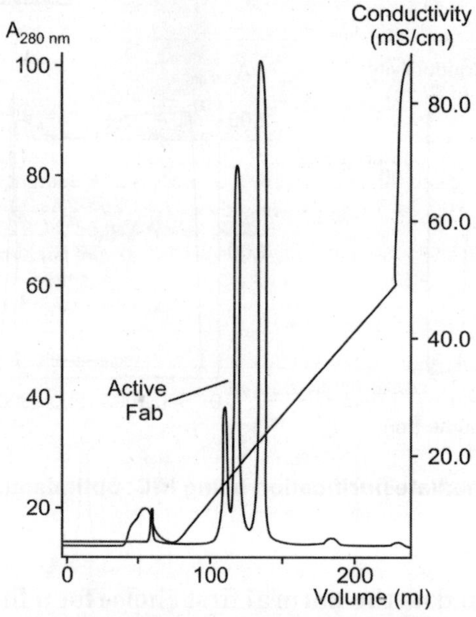

Fig. 1.53 : Optimised Fab polishing step

Two step purification of a monoclonal antibody

This example demonstrates the effectiveness of using a high selectivity affinity chromatography technique as a capture step, since only a gel filtration polishing step was needed to achieve the required level of purity. The objective of this work was to produce an efficient, routine procedure for monoclonal antibody purification. A more detailed description of this work can be found in Application Note 18-1128-93.

Target Molecule

Mouse monoclonal IgG1 antibodies.

Source Material

Cell culture supernatant.

Sample Extraction and Clarification

Salt concentration and pH were adjusted to those of the binding buffer in the capture step. Samples were filtered through a 0.45 μm filter before chromatography.

Capture

Affinity or ion exchange chromatography are particularly suitable for samples such as cell culture supernatants as they are binding techniques which concentrate the target protein and significantly reduce sample volume. For monoclonal antibody purification capture of the target protein can be achieved by using a highly selective affinity chromatography medium. In this example a HiTrap rProtein A column was used. Although general standard protocols were supplied with this pre-packed columns, it was decided to further optimise the binding and elution conditions for the specific target molecule. Most mouse monoclonal antibodies of the IgG1 sub-class require high salt concentrations to bind to immobilised Protein A, therefore a salt concentration was selected which gave the largest elution peak area and absence of antibodies in the flow-through. Results from the scouting for optimal binding conditions are shown in Figure 1.54. Scouting for the optimum elution pH also helped to improve antibody recovery. Optimisation of binding and elution conditions gave a well resolved peak containing IgG1, as shown in Figure 1.55 *(See on next page).*

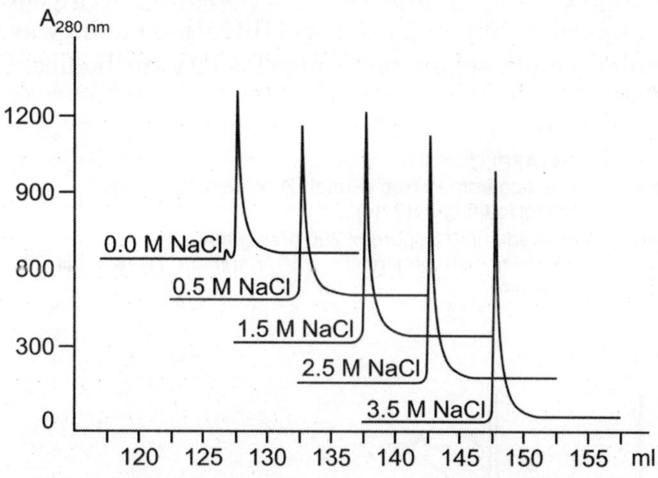

Fig. 1.54 : Automatic scouting for optimal binding conditions

Intermediate Purification

No intermediate purification was required as the high selectivity of the capture step also removed contaminating proteins and low-molecular substances giving a highly efficient purification.

System: AKTAFPLC
Sample: Cell culture supernatant containing monoclonal IgG_1, 100 ml
Column: HiTrap rProtein A, 1 ml
Binding buffer: 100 mM sodium phosphate, 2.5 M sodium chloride pH, 7.4
Elution buffer: 100 mM sodium citrate, pH 4.5
Flow: 1 ml/min

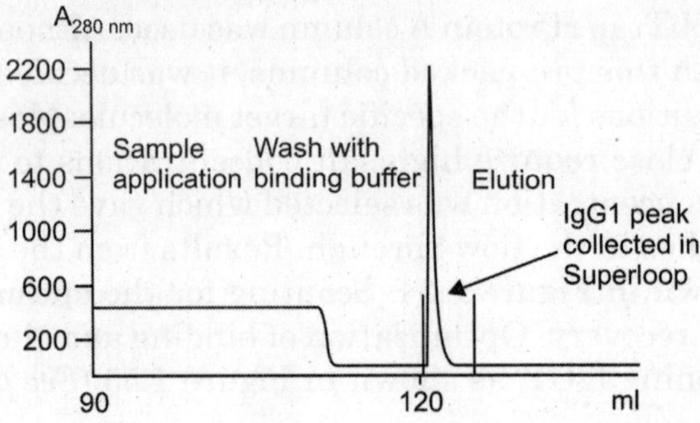

Fig. 1.55 : Optimised capture step on HiTrap rProtein A

Polishing

In most antibody preparations there is a possibility that IgG aggregates and/or dimers are present. It was therefore essential to include a gel filtration polishing step, despite the high degree of purity achieved during capture. The polishing step removes low or trace levels of contaminants. Superdex 200 prep grade gel filtration media was selected as it has the most suitable molecular weight separation range for IgG antibodies. Figure 1.56 shows the final purification step.

System: AKTAFPLC
Sample: Fraction from HiTrap rProtein A column containing monoclonal IgG_1 (3 ml)
Column: HiLoad 16/60 Superdex 200 prep grade
Buffer: 50 mM sodium phosphate, 0.15 M sodium chloride, pH 7.4
Flow: 1 ml/min

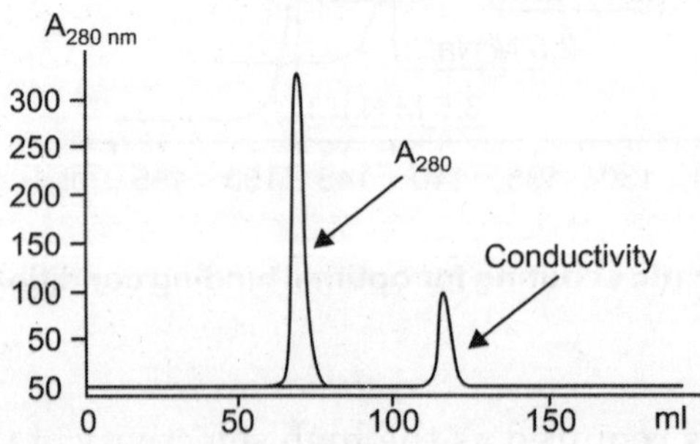

Fig. 1.56 : Gel filtration on HiLoad 16/60 Superdex 200 prep grade

Analytical assay

Collected fractions were separated by SDS-PAGE and silver stained using PhastSystem, following the separation and staining protocols supplied with the instrument.

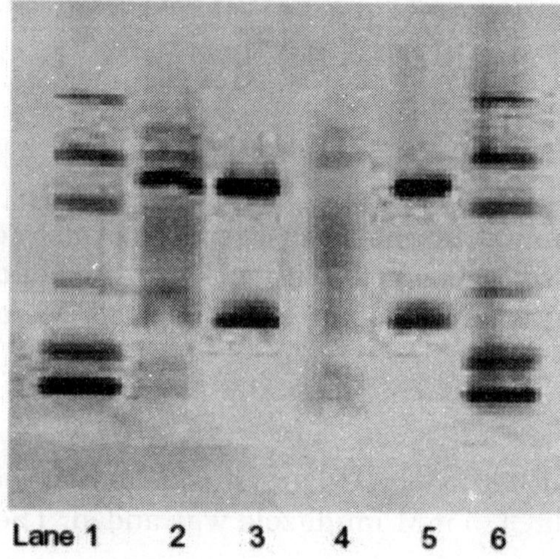

Lane 1. LMW-standard
Lane 2. Starting material (diluted 2 x)
Lane 3. Eluted IgG_1 peak from HiTrap rProtein A column (diluted 10 x)
Lane 4. Flow through, HiTrap rProtein A
Lane 5. Eluted IgG_1 peak from HiLoad Superdex 200 prep grade (diluted 6 x)
Lane 6. LMW-standard
Gel: 10–15 % SDS-PAGE PhastGel
System: PhastSystem

Fig. 1.57

One Step Purification of an Integral Membrane Protein

This example demonstrates that, with the use of a suitably tagged recombinant protein, selected detergents and an appropriate chromatographic medium, a successful purification can be achieved in a single chromatographic step. The objective was to purify a recombinant histidine-tagged integral membrane protein to allow characterisation under non-denaturing conditions. A more detailed description of this work, including results for size and charge homogeneity, can be found in Application Note 18-1128-92.

Target Molecule

Histidine-tagged cytochrome bo 3 ubiquinol oxidase from E. coli.

Source Material

The histidine-tagged cytochrome bo 3 ubiquinol oxidase accumulated in the membrane of E. coli.

Sample Extraction and Clarification

Membrane Preparation

Integral membrane proteins require the use of detergents for extraction. The concentration and type of detergent that is suitable for a particular extraction must be tested for each situation. Cells were harvested by centrifugation and frozen at -80°C.

Frozen cells were mixed with 200 mM Tris-HCl, pH 8.8, 20 mM Na2-EDTA, 500 mM sucrose and brought to room temperature, stirring gently.

10 mg/ml lysozyme in buffer was added and the solution was stirred for 30 min.

Cells were sedimented by centrifugation and supernatant was removed.

Pellets were resuspended in 5 mM Na_2-EDTA, pH 8.0, with PMSF, and stirred for 10 min.

$MgCl_2$ (final concentration 10 mM) and a few crystals of DNase I were added and stirred for 5 min.

The solution was sonicated for 3 × 1 min. Unbroken cells were removed by centrifugation Membrane particles were isolated by high speed centrifugation, resuspended in 50 mM Tris-HCl (pH 8.0), 250 mM NaCl and sedimented again at high speed. Membrane pellets were stored frozen.

Membrane Solubilisation

Membrane pellets were thawed, ice cold 1% dodecyl-?-D-maltoside (a non-ionic detergent) in 20 mM Tris-HCl, pH 7.5, 300 mM NaCl, 5 mM imidazole was added. The solution was stirred on ice for 30 min.

Insoluble material was removed by centrifugation. The presence of non-ionic detergent avoided denaturing conditions and interference with purification steps whilst maintaining membrane protein solubility.

Capture

Due to the instability of membrane proteins and their tendency to associate it is often essential to use fast purification protocols at low temperatures. Attachment of a histidine tag allowed the use of a HiTrap Chelating column giving a highly selective affinity chromatography capture step, shown in Figure 1.58. This technique also removed contaminating proteins, DNA, lipids and low-molecular substances and allowed equilibration of detergent-protein complexes with the detergent solution. The technique was unaffected by the presence of the

System:	AKTAFPLC
Column:	Hi Trap Chelating, 1 ml
Sample:	Detergent extracts of E, coli membranes
Binding buffer:	20 mM Tris-HCl, pH 7.5, 5 mM imidazole, 0.03% dodecyl-b-D-maltoside, 300 mM NaCl
Elution buffer:	20 mM Tris-HCl, pH 7.5, 500 mM imidazole, 0.03% dodecyl-b-D-maltoside, 300 mM NaCl
Gradient:	0–60% 20 column volumes
Temperature:	+5 °C
Flow:	1 ml/min

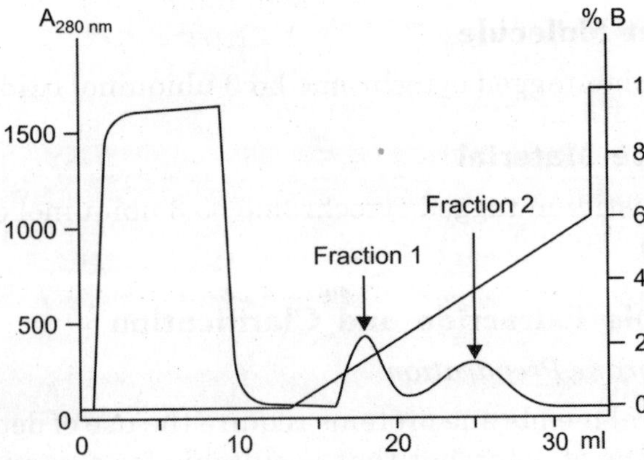

Fig. 1.58

non-ionic detergent. Buffers and separation procedure followed the recommendations provided with the HiTrap Chelating column.

Intermediate Purification and Polishing

No intermediate or polishing steps were needed as the high selectivity of the capture step produced a membrane protein of sufficient purity to allow further characterisation, *i.e.* a single step purification was achieved (as shown by electrophoresis).

Analytical assay

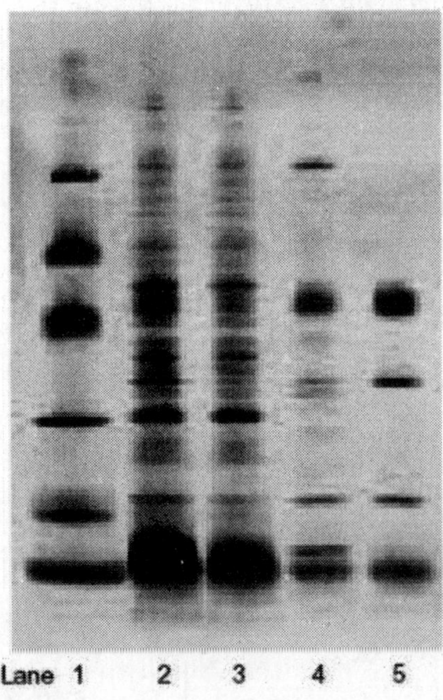

Lane 1: Low Molecular Weight Calibration kit (LMW) 14 400, 20 100, 30 000, 43 000, 67 000, 94 000
Lane 2: Detergent extract of *Escherichia coli* membranes
Lane 3: Flow-through material
Lane 4: Fraction 1 from HiTrap Chelating 1 ml
Lane 5: Fraction 2 from HiTrap Chelating 1 ml

Fig. 1.59 : SDS electrophoresis on PhastSystem using PhastGel 8-25%, silver staining

To confirm final purity, collected fractions were separated by SDS-PAGE and silver stained by PhastSystem™, following the separation and staining protocols supplied with the instrument. Figure 1.59 shows that four subunits of cytochrome bo 3 were present in both fractions. Fraction 2 was essentially pure, whereas contaminants were seen in Fraction 1.

Sample Storage Conditions and some Recommendations for Biological Samples

Keep refrigerated in a closed vessel to minimise bacterial growth and protease activity. Avoid conditions close to stability limits (for example, extreme pH, pH values close to the isoelectric point of the target protein or salt concentrations, reducing or chelating agents).

For storage times longer than 24 hours a bacteriostatic agent may be added, but this should be selected with care to ensure compatability with subsequent procedures. For long term storage keep proteins frozen or freeze dried in small aliquots (to avoid repeated freeze/thawing or freeze drying/re-dissolving which may reduce biological activity). Samples which will be freeze dried should be dissolved in volatile buffers, examples shown in Table 1.8. It should also be noted that concentration gradients can develop during freezing and thawing which may create extreme conditions causing protein denaturation. If essential add stabilising agents. These are more often required for storage of purified proteins.

Table 1.8 : Volatile buffer systems

pH range	Volatile buffer systems used in ion exchange chromatography		
	Buffer system	Counter-ion	pK-values for buffering ions
2.0	Formic acid	H^+	3.75
2.3-3.5	Pyridine/formic acid	$HCOO^-$	3.75; 5.25
3.0-5.0	Trimethylamine/formic acid	$HCOO^-$	3.75; 9.25
3.0-6.0	Pyridine/acetic acid	CH_3COO^-	4.76; 5.25
4.0-6.0	Trimethylamine/acetic acid	CH_3COO^-	4.76; 9.25
6.8-8.8	Trimethylamine/HCl	Cl^-	9.25
7.0-8.5	Ammonia/formic acid	$HCOO^-$	3.75; 9.25
8.5-10.0	Ammonia/acetic acid	CH_3COO^-	4.76; 9.25
7.0-12.0	Trimethylamine/carbonate	CO_3^{2-}	6.50; 9.25
7.9	Ammonium bicarbonate	HCO_3^-	6.50; 9.25
8.0-9.5	Ammonium carbonate/ammonia	CO_3^{2-}	6.50; 9.25
8.5-10.5	Ethanolamine/HCl	Cl^-	10.0
8.5	Ammonium carbonate	CO_3^{2-}	6.50; 9.25

Store in high concentration of ammonium sulphate (*e.g.* 4 M). Freeze in 50% glycerol, especially suitable for enzymes. Add stabilising agents, *e.g.* glycerol (5-20%), serum albumin (10 mg/ml), ligand (concentration is selected based on the concentration of the active protein). Sterile filter to avoid bacterial growth.

Sample Extraction and Clarification Procedures

Extraction procedures should be selected according to the source of the protein, such as bacterial, plant or mammalian, intracellular or extracellular. Use procedures which are as gentle as possible since disruption of cells or tissues leads to the release of proteolytic enzymes and general acidification. Selection of an extraction technique is dependent as much upon the equipment available and scale of operation as on the type of sample. Examples of common extraction processes are shown in Table 1.9. Extraction should be performed quickly, at sub-ambient temperatures, in the presence of a suitable buffer to maintain pH and ionic strength and to stabilise the sample. Samples should be clear and free from particles before beginning a chromatographic separation.

Table 1.9 : Common sample extraction processes

Extraction process	Typical conditions	Protein source	Comment
Gentle Cell lysis (osmotic shock)	2 volumes water to 1 volume packed pre-washed cells	erythrocytes, E.coli periplasm: intracellular proteins	lower product yield but reduced protease release
Enzymatic digestion	lysozyme 0.2 mg/ml, 37 °C, 15 mins.	bacteria: intracellular proteins	lab scale only, often combined with mechanical disruption
Hand homogenisation	follow equipment instructions	liver tissue	
Mincing (grinding)	"	muscle	
Moderate Blade homogeniser	follow equipment instructions	muscle tissue, most animal tissues, plant tissues	
Grinding with abrasive e.g. sand	"	bacteria, plant tissues	
Vigorous Ultrasonication or bead milling	follow equipment instructions	cell suspensions: intracellular proteins in cytoplasm, periplasm, inclusion bodies	small scale, release of nucleic acids may cause viscosity problems inclusion bodies must be resolubilised
Manton-Gaulin homogeniser	follow equipment instructions	cell suspensions	large scale only
French press	follow equipment instructions	bacteria, plant cells	
Fractional precipitation	see section on fractional precipitation	extracellular: secreted recombinant proteins, monoclonal antibodies, cell lysates	precipitates must be resolubilised

Buffers and Additives

With knowledge of the target protein stability window and other properties, additives can be kept to a minimum. This can help to avoid problems of interference with assays or other procedures and will avoid the need for an extrapurification step to remove additives at a later stage in purification. Examples of buffers and additives, together with their use, are shown in Table 1.10 below:

Table 1.10: Examples of Buffers and Additives, together with their use

	Typical conditions for use	Purpose
Buffer components Tris	20 mM, pH 7.4	maintain pH, minimise acidification caused by lysosomal disruption
NaCl	100 mM	maintain ionic strength of medium
EDTA	10 mM	reduce oxidation damage, chelate metal ions
Sucrose or glucose	25 mM	stabilise lysosomal membranes, reduce protease release
Detergents	See Table 1.11	extraction and purification of integral
Ionic or non-ionic detergents		membrane proteins solubilisation of poorly soluble proteins
DNase and RNase	1 μg/ml	degradation of nucleic acids, reduce viscosity of sample solution
*Protease inhibitors**		*Inhibits*
PMSF	0.5 - 1 mM	serine proteases
APMSF	0.4 - 4 mM	serine proteases
Benzamidine-HCl	0.2 mM	serine proteases
Pepstatin	1 μM	aspartic proteases
Leupeptin	10 - 100 μM	cysteine and serine proteases
Chymostatin	10 - 100 μM	chymotrypsin, papain, cysteine proteases
Antipain-HCl	1 - 100 μM	papain, cysteine and serine proteases
EDTA	2 - 10 mM	metal dependent proteases, zinc and iron
EGTA	2 - 10 mM	metal dependent proteases e.g. calcium

(Contd...)

	Typical conditions for use	Purpose
Reducing agents	1 - 10 mM	keep cysteine residues
1,4 dithiothreitol, DTT		reduced
1,4 dithioerythritol, DTE	1 - 10 mM	"
Mercaptoethanol	0.05%	"
Others		
Glycerol	5 - 10%	for stabilisation, up to 50% can be used if required

PMSF Phenylmethylsulfonyl fluoride
APMSF—4-Aminophenyl-methylsulfonyl fluoride
PMSF is a hazardous chemical. Half-life time in aqueous solution is 35 min. PMSF is usually stored as 10 mM or 100 mM stock solution (1.74 or 17.4 mg/ml in isopropanol) at - 20° C.
* Protease inhibitors are available in pre-made mixes from several suppliers.
Details taken from Protein Purification, Principles and Practice, R.K. Scopes. 1994, Springer., Protein Purification, Principles, High Resolution Methods and Applications, J-C. Janson and L. Rydén, 1998, 2nd ed. Wiley VCH and other sources.

Detergents

Non-ionic detergents are used most commonly for extraction and purification of integral membrane proteins. Selection of the most suitable detergent is often a case of trial and error. The detergent should be used at concentrations near or above its critical micelle concentration, *i.e.* the concentration at which detergent monomers begin to associate with each other. This concentration is dependent upon the type of detergent and the experimental conditions. Examples of ionic and non-ionic detergents are shown in Table 1.11. Adjustment of the detergent concentration necessary for optimum results is often a balance between the activity and yield of the protein. During purification procedures it may be possible to reduce the concentration of detergent compared to that used for extraction. However, some level of detergent is usually essential throughout purification procedures to maintain solubility. Detergents can be exchanged by adsorption techniques (Ref: Phenyl Sepharose mediated detergent exchange chromatography: its application to exchange of detergents bound to membrane protein

Table 1.11: Examples of Ionic and Non-ionic Detergents

Sodium dodecyl sulphate	0.1 - 0.5%	denatures proteins, used for SDS-PAGE use non-ionic detergents to avoid denaturation
Triton™ X-100	0.1 %	non-ionic detergent for membrane solubilisation. *Note:* may absorb strongly at 280 nm!
NP-40	0.05 - 2%	"
Dodecyl βD-maltoside	1%	"
Octyl βD-glucoside	1 - 1.5%	"

Sample Clarification

Centrifugation

Use before first chromatographic step

Removes lipids and particulate matter

For small sample volumes and those which adsorb non-specifically to filters:

Centrifuge at 10000g for 15 minutes

For cell homogenates:

Centrifuge at 40 000-50 000g for 30 minutes

Ultrafiltration

Use before first chromatographic step

Removes salts, concentrates sample

Ultrafiltration membranes are available with different cut off limits for separation of molecules from Mr1000 up to 300000. The process is slower than gel filtration and membranes may clog.

Check the recovery of the target protein in a test run.

Some proteins may adsorb non-specifically to filter surfaces.

Filtration

Use before first chromatographic step

Removes particulate matter

Suitable for small sample volumes.

For sample preparation before chromatography select filter size according to the bead size of the chromatographic medium.

Filter size Bead size of chromatographic medium

1 μm 90 μm and upwards

0.45 μm 3, 10, 15, 34 μm

0.22 μm sterile filtration or extra clean samples

Check the recovery of the target protein in a test run. Some proteins may adsorb non-specifically to filter surfaces.

Gel filtration (for sample clarification or conditioning)

Use before or between chromatographic purification steps.

For rapid processing of small or large sample volumes.

Removes salts from samples Mr >5000.

Sephadex G-25 is used at laboratory and production scale for sample preparation and clarification. Typically sample volumes of up to 30% of the total column volume are loaded. In a single step, the sample is desalted, exchanged into a new buffer, and low molecular weight materials are removed. The high volume capacity and speed of this step enable very large sample volumes to be processed rapidly and efficiently. The high sample volume load results in a separation with minimal sample dilution. A typical elution is shown in Figure 1.60.

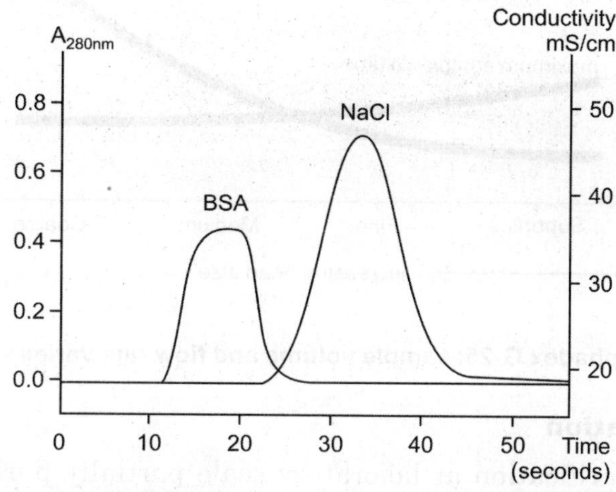

Fig. 1.60 : Typical elution profile for sample desalting and buffer exchange

Methodology

Select a pre-packed desalting column from the table below or pack a column.

Pre-packed column	Sample volume loading per run	Sample volume recovery per run	Code No.
HiPrep Desalting 26/10	2.5 -15 ml	7.5 - 20 ml	17-5087-01
HiTrap Desalting	0.25 - 1.5 ml	1.0 - 2.0 ml	17-1408-01
Fast Desalting PC 3.2/10	0.05 - 0.2 ml	0.2 - 0.3 ml	17-0771 01
PD-10 Desalting	1.5 - 2.5 ml	2.5 - 3.5 ml	17-0851-01

Column Packing

The following guidelines apply at all scales of operation:

Column dimensions = typically 10 - 20 cm bed height.

Quantity of gel = five times volume of sample.

For column packing Sephadex G-25 is available in a range of bead sizes (Superfine, Fine, Medium and Coarse). Changes in bead size alter flow rates and sample volumes which can be applied (see Figure 1.61). For laboratory scale separations use Sephadex G-25 Fine with an average bed height of 15 cm.

Individual product packing instructions contain more detailed information on packing Sephadex G-25.

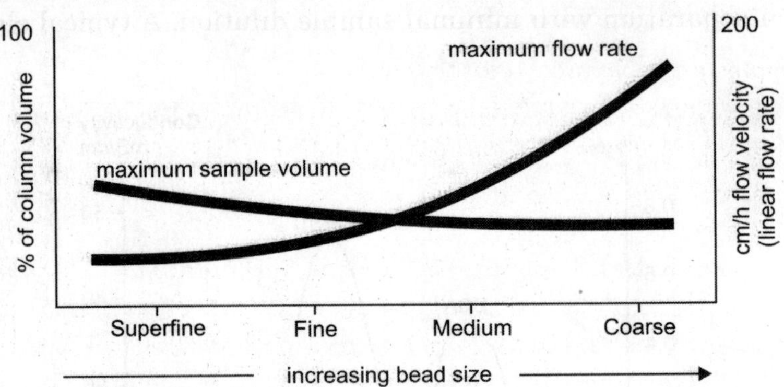

Fig. 1.61 : Sephadex G-25: sample volume and flow rate varies with bead size.

Fractional Precipitation

For extraction and clarification at laboratory scale partially purifies sample, may also concentrate Use before the first chromatographic step most precipitation techniques are not suitable for large scale preparations. Precipitation techniques are affected by temperature, pH and sample concentration. These parameters must be controlled to ensure reproducible results. Precipitation can be used in three different ways, as shown in Figure 1.62.

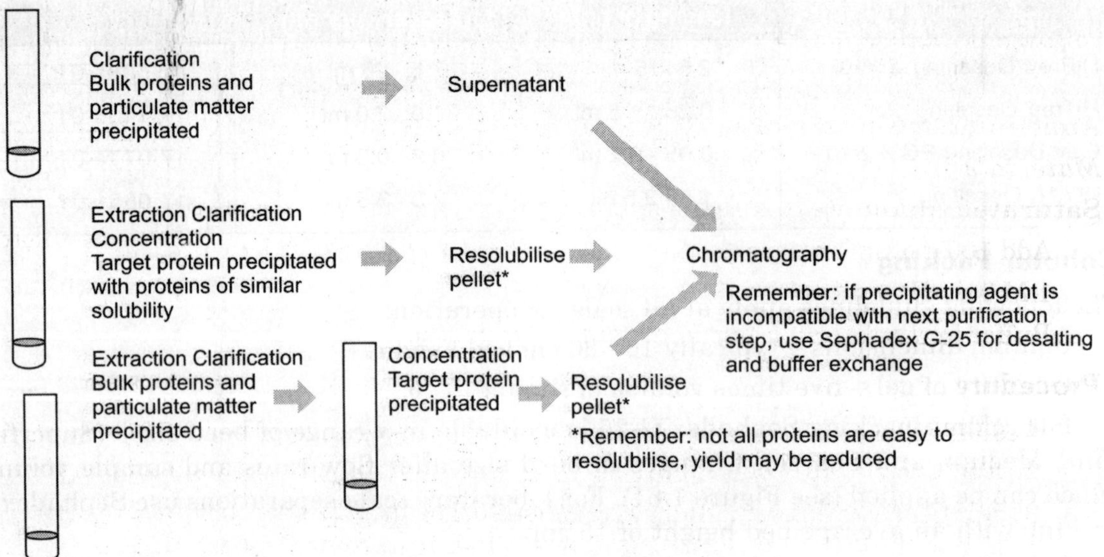

Fig. 1.62 : Three ways to use precipitation

Precipitation techniques are reviewed in Table 1.12 and the two common methods are described in more detail.

Table 1.12: Examples of precipitation techniques

Precipitation agent	Typical conditions for use	Sample type	Comment
Ammonium sulphate	as described	>1mg/ml proteins especially immuno-globulins	stabilizes proteins, no denaturation, super-natant can go directly to HIC
Dextran sulphate	as described	samples with high levels of lipoprotein, *e.g.* ascites	precipitates lipoprotein
Polyvinylpyrrolidine	Add 3% (w/v), stir 4 hours, centrifuge, discard pellet	"	alternative to dextran Sulphate
Polyethylene glycol (PEG, M.W. >4000)	up to 20% wt/vol	plasma proteins	no denaturation, super-natant goes direct to IEX or AC. Complete removal may be difficult
Acetone	up to 80% vol/vol at 0°C	useful for peptide precipitation or con-centration of sample for electrophoresis	may denature protein Irreversibly
Polyethyleneimine	0.1% w/v		precipitates aggregated Nucleoproteins
Protamine sulphate	1%		"
Streptomycin sulphate	1%		precipitation of nucleic Acids

Ammonium sulphate precipitation

Materials

Saturated ammonium sulphate solution

Add 100 g ammonium sulphate to 100 ml distilled water, stir to dissolve

1 M Tris-HCl pH 8.0

Buffer for first chromatographic purification step

Procedure

1. Filter (0.45μm) or centrifuge (refrigerated, 10000 g) sample.
2. Add 1 part 1 M Tris-HCl pH 8.0 to 10 parts sample volume to maintain pH.
3. Stir gently. Add ammonium sulphate solution, drop by drop (solution becomes milky at about 20% saturation). Add up to 50% saturation*. Stir for 1 hour.
4. Centrifuge 20 minutes at 10000g.

5. Discard supernatant. Wash pellet twice by resuspension in an equal volume of ammonium sulphate solution of the same concentration (*i.e.* a solution that will not redissolve the precipitated protein or cause further precipitation).

   Centrifuge again.
6. Dissolve pellet in a small volume of the chromatographic buffer.
7. Ammonium sulphate is removed during clarification/buffer exchange steps with Sephadex G-25 or during hydrophobic interaction separations.

*The % saturation can be adjusted either to precipitate a target molecule or to precipitate contaminants.

The quantity of ammonium sulphate required to reach given degrees of saturation varies according to temperature. Table 1.13 shows the quantities required at 20 °C.

Table 1.13: Quantities of ammonium sulphate required to reach given degrees of saturation at 20°C

	Final percent saturation to be obtained																
	20	25	30	35	40	45	50	55	60	65	70	75	80	85	90	95	100
Starting per cent saturation	Amount of ammonium sulphate to add (grams) per liter of solution at 20 °C																
0	113	144	176	208	242	277	314	351	390	430	472	516	561	608	657	708	761
5	85	115	146	179	212	246	282	319	358	397	439	481	526	572	621	671	723
10	57	86	117	149	182	216	251	287	325	364	405	447	491	537	584	634	685
15	28	58	88	119	151	185	219	255	293	331	371	413	456	501	548	596	647
20	0	29	59	89	121	154	188	223	260	298	337	378	421	465	511	559	609
25		0	29	60	91	123	157	191	228	265	304	344	386	429	475	522	571
30			0	30	61	92	125	160	195	232	270	309	351	393	438	485	533
35				0	30	62	94	128	163	199	236	275	316	358	402	447	495
40					0	31	63	96	130	166	202	241	281	322	365	410	457
45						0	31	64	98	132	169	206	245	286	329	373	419
50							0	32	65	99	135	172	210	250	292	335	381
55								0	33	66	101	138	175	215	256	298	343
60									0	33	67	103	140	179	219	261	305
65										0	34	69	105	143	183	224	267
70											0	34	70	107	146	186	228
75												0	35	72	110	149	190
80													0	36	73	112	152
85														0	37	75	114
90															0	37	76
95																0	38

Dextran Sulphate Precipitation

Materials

10% dextran sulphate

1 M calcium chloride

Buffer for first chromatographic purification step.

Procedure

1. Add 0.04 ml dextran sulphate solution and 1 ml calcium chloride solution to every 1 ml of sample. Mix 15 minutes.
2. Centrifuge (10000 g, 10 minutes), discard precipitate.

Dextran sulphate is removed during a clarification/buffer exchange Sephadex G-25 step.

Resolubilisation of Protein Precipitates

Many proteins are easily resolubilised in a small amount of the buffer to be used in the next chromatographic step. However, an agent, selected from Table 1.14, may be required for less soluble proteins. Specific conditions will depend upon the specific protein. These agents must always be removed to allow complete re-folding of the protein and to maximize recovery of mass and activity. A chromatographic step often removes a denaturant during purification.

Table 1.14

Denaturing agent	Typical conditions for use	Removal/comment
Urea	2 - 8 M	remove using Sephadex G-25
Guanidine hydrochloride	3 - 8 M	remove using Sephadex G-25 or during IEX
Triton X-100	2%	"
Sarcosyl	1.5%	"
N-octyl glucoside	2%	"
Sodium dodecyl sulphate	0.1 - 0.5%	exchange for non-ionic detergent during first chromatographic step, avoid anion exchange chromatography
alkaline pH	> pH 9, NaOH	may need to adjust pH during chromatography to maintain solubility

Expanded Bed Adsorption (STREAMLINE)

For large scale recombinant protein and monoclonal antibody purification. The technique requires no sample clean up and enables clarification, concentration and capture in a single step. EBA can be regarded as a technique in which sample preparation and capture are combined in a single step. Crude sample is applied to an expanded bed of STREAMLINE media, target proteins are captured whilst cell debris, cells, particulate matter, whole cells, and contaminants pass through. Flow is reversed and the target proteins are desorbed in the elution buffer.

Ion Exchange (Iex) Chromatography

IEX separates proteins with differences in charge to give a very high resolution separation with high sample loading capacity. The separation is based on the reversible interaction between a charged protein and an oppositely charged chromatographic medium. Proteins bind as they are loaded onto a column.

Conditions are then altered so that bound substances are eluted differentially. This elution is usually performed by increases in salt concentration or changes in pH. Changes are made stepwise or with a continuous gradient. Most commonly, samples are eluted with salt (NaCl), using a gradient elution (Figure 1.63). Target proteins are concentrated during binding and collected in a purified, concentrated form.

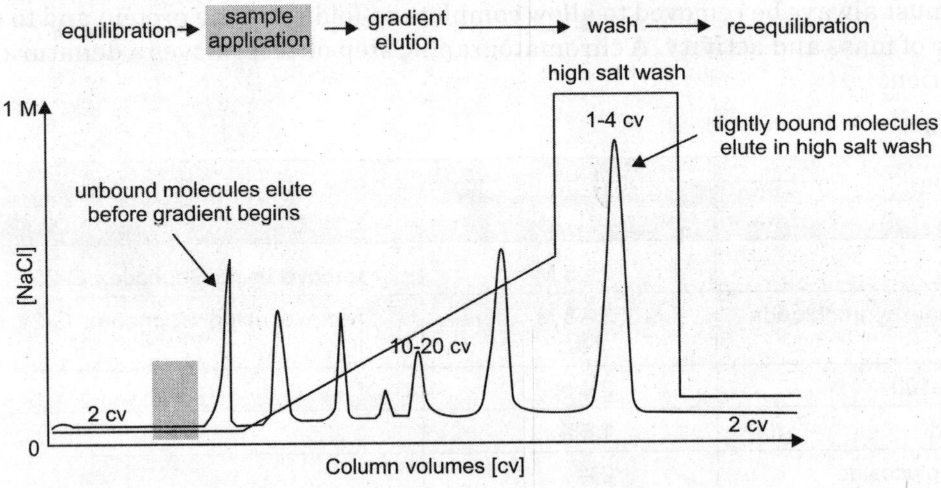

Fig. 1.63 : Typical IEX gradient elution

The net surface charge of proteins varies according to the surrounding pH. When above its isoelectric point (pI) a protein will bind to an anion exchanger, when below its pI a protein will behind to a cation exchanger. Typically IEX is used to bind the target molecule, but it can also be used to bind impurities if required. IEX can be repeated at different pH values to separate several proteins which have distinctly different charge properties, as shown in Figure 1.64. This can be used to advantage during a multi-step purification.

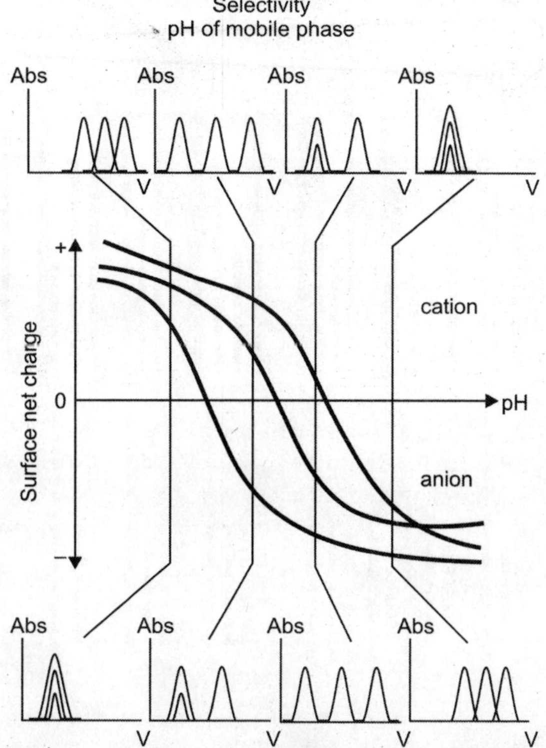

Fig. 1.64 : Effect of pH on protein elution

Choice of Ion Exchanger

For most purification steps it is recommended to begin with a strong exchanger, allowing work over a broad pH range during method development. Use a strong anion exchanger (Q) to bind the target if the isoelectric point is below pH 7.0 or unknown.

Strong Ion Exchangers

Q (anion exchange), S and SP (cation exchange) are fully charged over a broad pH range (pH 2 - 12).

Weak ion Exchangers

DEAE (anion exchange) and CM (cation exchange) are fully charged over a narrower pH range (pH 2 - 9 and pH 6 - 10, respectively), but give alternative selectivities for separations. Sample volume and capacity Ion exchange chromatography is a binding technique, independent of sample volume provided that the ionic strength of the sample is low and the target molecule is highly charged. The total amount of protein which is loaded and binds to the column should not exceed the total binding capacity of the column. For optimal separations when performing gradient elution, use approximately one-fifth of the total binding capacity of the column.

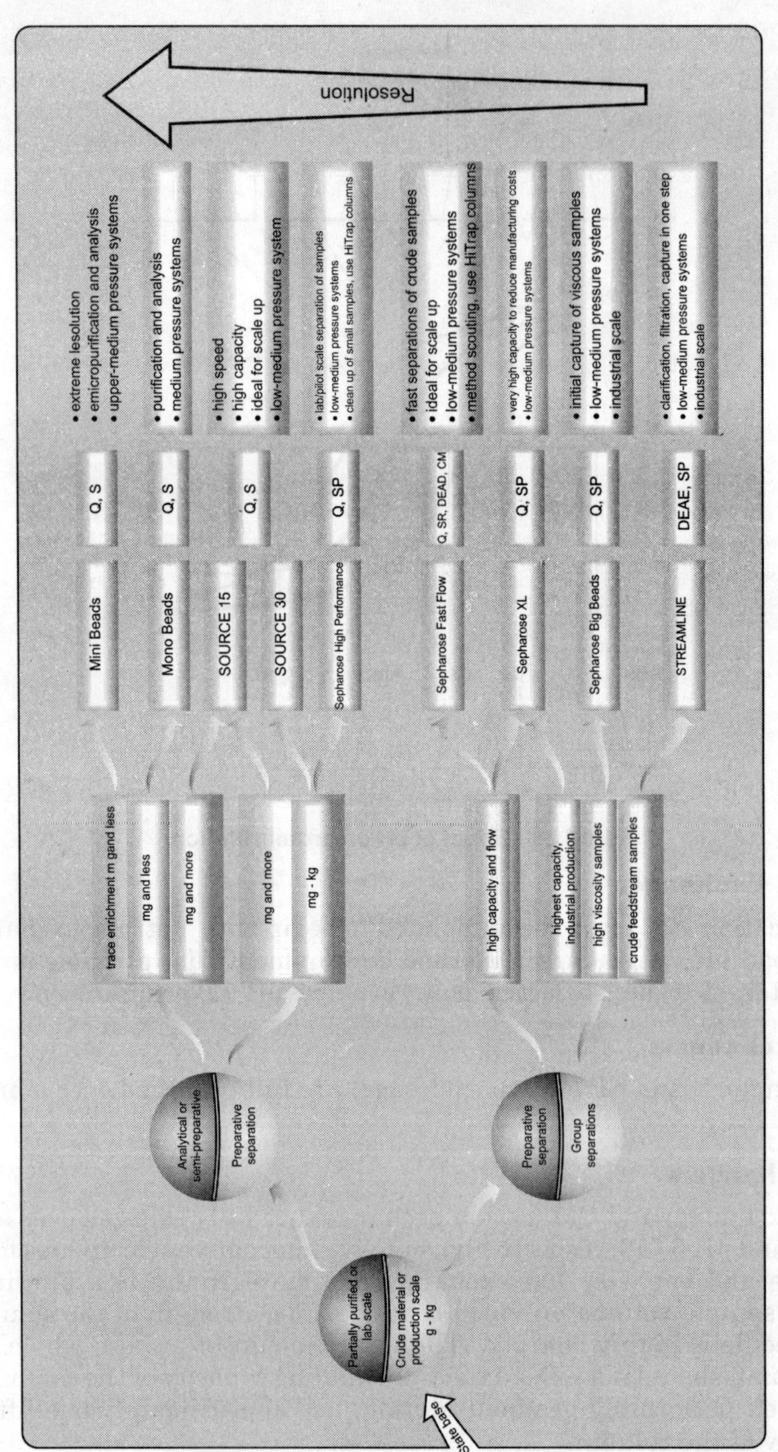
Resolution
Mini Beads
Q, S
• extreme lesolution
• emicropurification and analysis
• upper-medium pressure systems
Mono Beads
Q, S
• purification and analysis
• medium pressure systems
SOURCE 15
Q, S
• high speed
• high capacity
• ideal for scale up
• low-medium pressure system
SOURCE 30
Q, SP
Sepharose High Performance
• lab/pilot scale separation of samples
• low-medium pressure systems
• clean up of small samples, use HiTrap columns
Sepharose Fast Flow
Q, SR, DEAD, CM
• fast separations of crude samples
• ideal for scale up
• low-medium pressure systems
• method scouting, use HiTrap columns
Sepharose XL
Q, SP
• very high capacity to reduce manufacturing costs
• low-medium pressure systems
Sepharose Big Beads
Q, SP
• initial capture of viscous samples
• low-medium pressure systems
• industrial scale
STREAMLINE
DEAE, SP
• clarification, filtration, capture in one step
• low-medium pressure systems
• industrial scale
trace enrichment m gand less
mg and less
mg and more
mg and more
mg - kg
high capacity and flow
highest capacity, industrial production
high viscosity samples
crude feedstream samples
Analytical or semi-preparative
Preparative separation
Preparative separation
Group separations
Partially purified or lab scale
Crude material or production scale g - kg

Media Selection

Parameters such as scale of purification, resolution required, speed of separation, sample stability and media binding capacity, should be considered when selecting a chromatographic medium. Figure 1.65 on page 75 shows a guide to selecting ion exchange media.

Sample Preparation

Correct sample preparation ensures good resolution and extends the life of the column. To ensure efficient binding during sample application samples should be at the same pH and ionic strength as the starting buffer. Samples must be free from particulate matter, particularly when working with bead sizes of 34 μm or less (see page 65 for details of sample clarification procedures).

Column Preparation

Pre-packed columns

To increase speed and efficiency in method development, use small pre-packed columns for media scouting and method optimisation. HiTrap IEX Test Kit is ideal for this type of work, as shown in Figure 1.65.

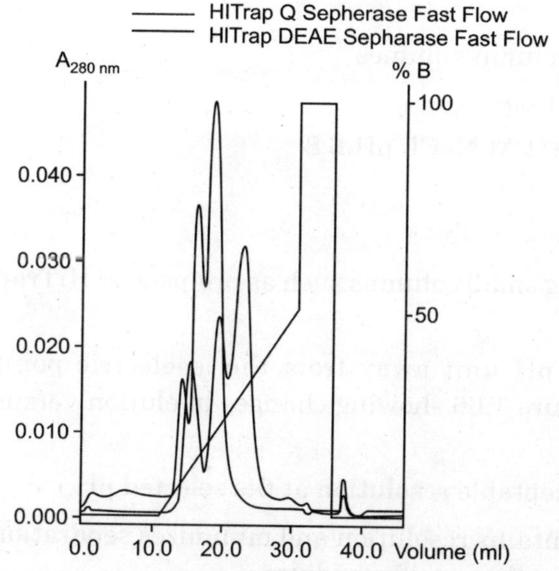

Sample:	Ribonuclease A, human apo-transfemin, a-lactalbumin
Columns:	HiTrap IEX Test Kit
Buffer A:	20 mM piperazine, pH 9.7
Buffer B:	20 mM piperazine, 1 M NaCl pH 9.7
Flow:	2 ml/mi9n (310 cm/h)

Fig. 1.65 : Media selection using 2 columns from HiTrap IEX Test Kit

Using pre-packed columns at any scale will ensure reproducible results and high performance.

Column Packing

The following guidelines apply at all scales of operation: Column dimensions = typically 5 - 15 cm bed height. Quantity of gel = estimate amount of gel required to bind the sample, use five times this amount to pack a column. See individual product packing instructions for more detailed information on a specific medium.

Buffer Preparation

Buffering ions should have the same charge as the selected medium, with a pKa within 0.6 pH units of the working pH. Buffer concentration should be sufficient to maintain buffering capacity and constant pH during sample application and while an increase in salt concentration is applied. When working with a sample of unknown charge characteristics, try these conditions first:

Anion Exchange

Gradient: 0-100% elution buffer B in 10 - 20 column volumes

Start buffer A: 20 mM Tris-HCl, pH 8.0

Elution buffer B: 20 mM Tris-HCl + 1 M NaCl, pH 8.0

Cation Exchange

Gradient: 0-100% elution buffer B in 10 - 20 column volumes

Start buffer A: 20 mM $Na_2HPO_4.2H_2O$, pH 6.8

Elution buffer B: 20 mM $Na_2HPO_4.2H_2O$ + 1 M NaCl, pH 6.8

Method Development (in Priority Order)

1. Select the optimum ion exchanger using small columns such as pre-packed HiTrap columns to save time and sample.
2. Scout for optimum pH. Begin 0.5-1 pH unit away from the isoelectric point of the target protein if known (see Figure 1.66 showing changes in elution versus pH).
3. Select the steepest gradient to give acceptable resolution at the selected pH.
4. Select the highest flow rate which maintains resolution and minimizes separation time. Check recommended flow rates for the specific medium.
5. For large scale purification and to reduce separation times and buffer consumption, transfer to step elution after method optimisation as shown in Figure 1.67. It is often possible to increase sample loading when using step elution.

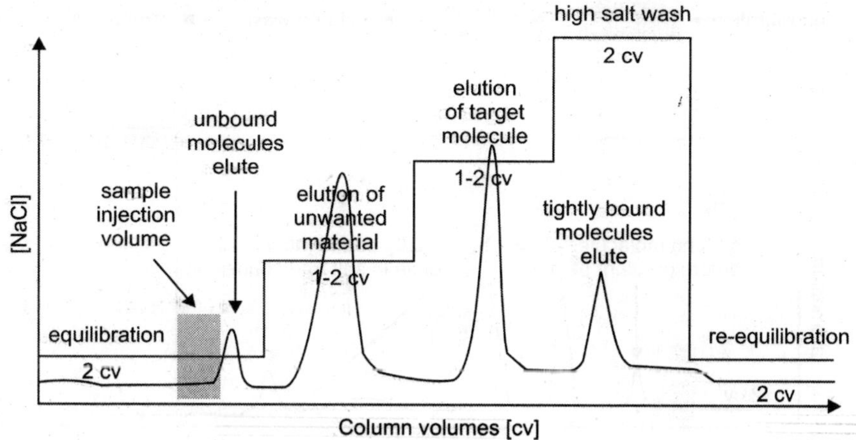

Fig. 1.66 : Effect of pH on protein elution 1

Cleaning, Sanitisation and Sterilisation

Procedures vary according to type of sample and medium. Guidelines are supplied with the medium or pre-packed column.

Storage of Media and Columns

Recommended conditions for storage are supplied with the medium or pre-packed column.

Further Information

Ion Exchange Chromatography: Principles and Methods Code no. 18-1114-21.

Hydrophobic Interaction Chromatography(HIC)

HIC separates proteins with differences in hydrophobicity. The technique is ideal for the capture or intermediate steps in a purification. The separation is based on the reversible interaction between a protein and the hydrophobic surface of achromatographic medium. This interaction is enhanced by high ionic strength buffer which makes HIC an ideal 'next step' after precipitation with ammonium sulphate or elution in high salt during IEX. Samples in high ionic strengthsolution (*e.g.* 1.5 M ammonium sulphate) bind as they are loaded onto a column.Conditions are then altered so that the bound substances are eluted differentially. Elution is usually performed by decreases in salt concentration (Figure 1.67). Changes are made stepwise or with a continuous decreasing salt gradient. Most commonly, samples are eluted with a decreasing gradient of ammonium sulphate.Target proteins are concentrated during binding and collected in a purified,concentrated form. Other elution procedures include reducing eluent polarity(ethylene glycol gradient up to 50%), adding chaotropic species (urea, guanidinehydrochloride) or detergents, changing pH or temperature.

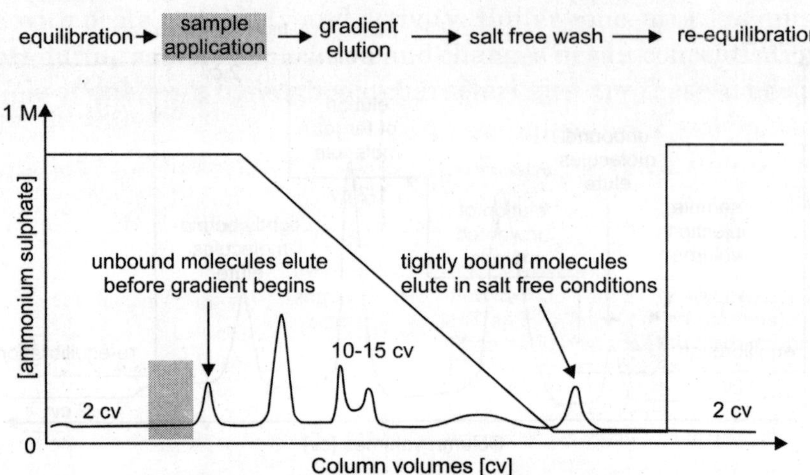

Fig. 1.67: Typical HIC gradient elution

Choice of Hydrophobic Ligand

Very hydrophobic proteins bind tightly to very hydrophobic ligands and may require extreme elution conditions, *e.g.* chaotropic agents or detergents, for the target protein or contaminants. To avoid this problem it is recommended to screen several hydrophobic media, using HiTrap HIC Test Kit or RESOURCE

HIC Test Kit. Begin with a medium of low hydrophobicity if the sample has very hydrophobic components. Select the medium which gives the best resolution and loading capacity at a reasonably low salt concentration. Typically the strength of binding of a ligand to a protein increases in the order: ether, isopropyl, butyl, octyl, and phenyl. However, the nature of the binding, both the selectivity and the binding strength, can vary and must be tested in individual cases.

Sample Volume and Capacity

HIC is a binding technique and therefore rather independent of sample volume, provided that conditions are chosen to bind the target protein strongly. The total amount of protein which is loaded and binds to the column should not exceed the total binding capacity of the column. For optimal separations when performing gradient elution, use approximately one fifth of the total binding capacity of the column.

Media Selection

In HIC the characteristics of the chromatographic matrix as well as the hydrophobic ligand affect the selectivity of the medium. This should be considered, together with parameters such as sample solubility, required resolution, scale of purification and availability of the medium at the scale intended. Figure 1.68 on page 81 shows a guide to selecting HIC media.

Sample Preparation

Correct sample preparation ensures good resolution and extends the life of the column. To ensure efficient binding during sample application samples should be at the same pH as the starting buffer and in high ionic strength solution (*e.g.* 1.5 M ammonium sulphate or 4 M NaCl). Samples must be free from particulate matter, particularly when working with bead sizes of 34 μm or less.

Column Preparation Pre-packed columns

To increase speed and efficiency in method development use small pre-packed columns for media scouting and method optimisation. HiTrap HIC Test Kit and RESOURCE HIC Test Kit are ideal for this work. Using pre-packed columns at any scale will ensure reproducible results and high performance. Figure 1.69 shows an example of media screening with HiTrap HIC Test Kit *(See Fig. on next page).*

Column Packing

The following guidelines apply at all scales of operation:

> See individual product packing instructions for more detailed information on a specific medium.

Column dimensions = typically 5 - 15 cm bed height.

Quantity of gel = estimate amount of gel required to bind the sample, use five times this amount to pack a column.

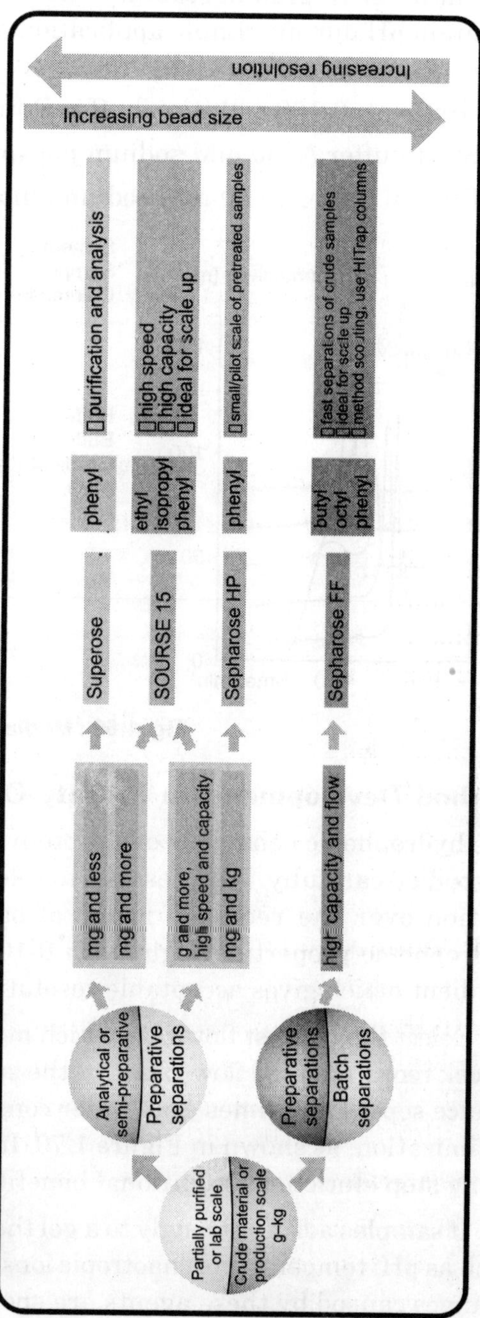

Fig. 1.68 : Hydrophobic interaction media selection guide

Buffer Preparation

Buffering ion selection is not critical for hydrophobic interaction. Select a pH compatible with protein stability and activity. Buffer concentration must be sufficient to maintain pH during sample application and changes in salt concentration. When working with a sample of unknown hydrophobic characteristics, try these conditions first:

Gradient: 0-100% elution buffer B in 10 - 20 column volumes

Start buffer A: 50 mM sodium phosphate pH 7.0 + 1 - 1.5 M ammonium sulphate

Elution buffer B: 50 mM sodium phosphate pH 7.0

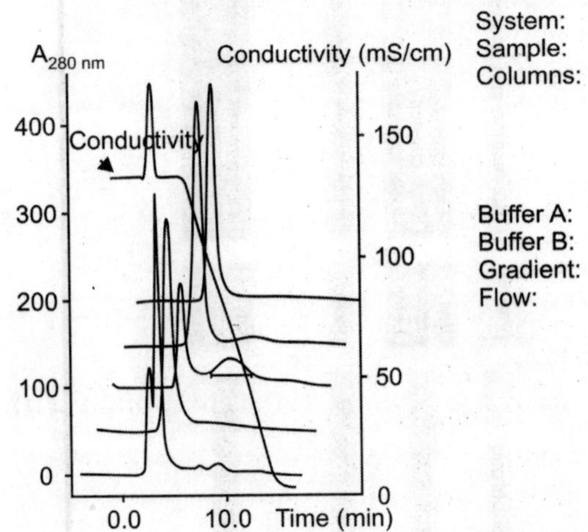

System:	AKTAexplorer
Sample:	Fab fraction from STREAMLINE SP, 2 ml
Columns:	HiTrap HIC Test Kit (1 ml columns), Phnenyl Sepharose High Performance, Phenyl Sepharose 6 Fast Flow (low sub), Phenyl Sepharose 6 (high sub), Butyl Sepharose 4 Fast Flow, Octyl Sepharose 4 Fast Flow
Buffer A:	1 ml (NH4)2SO4. 50 mM NaAc, pH 5.0
Buffer B:	50 mM NaAc, pH 5.0
Gradient:	20 column volumes
Flow:	2 ml/min (300 cm/hr)

Fig. 1.69 : Media screening with HiTrap HIC

Method Development (in Priority Order)

The hydrophobic behaviour of a protein is difficult to predict and binding conditions must be studied carefully. HIC Test Kit to select the medium which gives optimum binding and elution over the required range of salt concentration. For proteins with unknown hydrophobic properties begin with 0-100%B(0%B=1 M ammonium sulphate).Select the gradient which gives acceptable resolution.

Select the highest flow rate which maintains resolution and minimize separation time. Check recommended flow rates for the specific medium. For large scale purification and to reduce separation times and buffer consumption, transfer to a step elution after method optimization, as shown in Figure 1.70. It is often possible to increase sample loading when using step elution, an additional benefit for large scale purification.

If samples adsorb strongly to a gel then conditions which cause conformational changes, such as pH, temperature, chaotropic ions or organic solvents can be altered. Conformational changes caused by these agents are specific to each protein. Use screening procedures to investigate the effects of these agents.

Alternatively, change to a less hydrophobic medium.

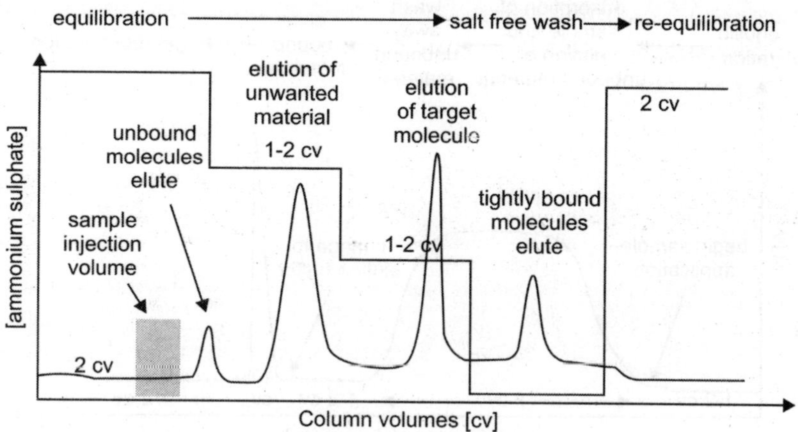

Fig. 1.70 : The Step Elution

Cleaning, Sanitisation and Sterilisation

Procedures vary according to type of sample and medium. Guidelines are supplied with the medium or pre-packed column.

Affinity Chromatography (AC)

AC separates proteins on the basis of a reversible interaction between a protein (or group of proteins) and a specific ligand attached to a chromatographic matrix. The technique is ideal for a capture or intermediate step and can be used whenever a suitable ligand is available for the protein(s) of interest. AC offers high selectivity, hence high resolution, and usually high capacity for the protein(s) of interest.

The target protein(s) is specifically and reversibly bound by a complementary binding substance (ligand). The sample is applied under conditions that favour specific binding to the ligand. Unbound material is washed away, and the bound target protein is recovered by changing conditions to those favouring desorption. Desorption is performed specifically, using a competitive ligand, or non specifically, by changing the pH, ionic strength or polarity. Samples are concentrated during binding and protein is collected in purified, concentrated form. The key stages in a separation are shown in Figure 1.71. Affinity chromatography is also used to remove specific contaminants, for example Benzamidine Sepharose 6B removes serine proteases.

Sample Volume and Capacity

AC is a binding technique, independent of sample volume provided that conditions are chosen to bind the target protein strongly.

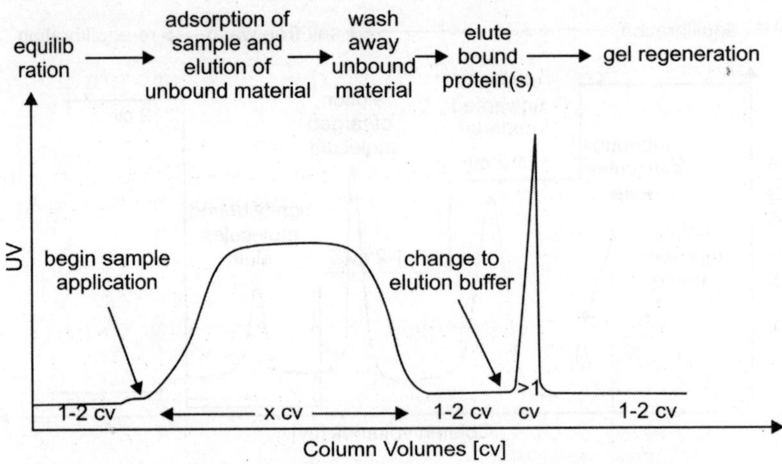

Fig. 1.71 : Showing the Typical Affinity Separation

Media Selection

Parameters such as scale of purification and commercial availability of affinity matrices should be considered when selecting affinity media. To save time and ensure reproducibility, use prepacked columns for method development or small scale purification. HiTrap affinity columns are ideal for this work. Specific affinity media are prepared by coupling a ligand to a selected gel matrix, following recommended coupling procedures.

Sample Preparation

Correct sample preparation ensures efficient binding and extends the life of a column. Removal of contaminants which may bind non-specifically to the column, such as lipids, is crucial. Stringent washing procedures may damage the ligand of an affinity medium, destroying the binding capacity of the column.

Samples must be free from particulate matter

Column Preparation

Pre-packed columns

Pre-packed columns ensure reproducible results and highest performance.

Column packing

The following guidelines apply at all scales of operation:

Column dimensions = short and wide

Quantity of gel = calculate according to known binding capacity of medium, use 2-5 times excess capacity.

Buffer Preparation

Binding, elution and regeneration buffers are specific to each affinity medium.

Follow instructions supplied with the medium or column.

1. Select the correct specificity for the target protein. Follow the manufacturer's instructions for binding or elution conditions and check recommended flow rates for the specific medium;
2. Select optimum flow rate to achieve efficient binding;
3. Select optimum flow rate for elution to maximise recovery;
4. Select maximum flow rate for column regeneration to minimise run times.

Cleaning, sanitisation and sterilisation

Procedures vary according to type of sample and medium. Guidelines are supplied with the medium or pre-packed column

Gel Filtration (GF)

GF separates proteins with differences in molecular size. The technique is ideal for the final polishing steps in a purification when sample volumes have been reduced (sample volume significantly influences speed and resolution in gel filtration). Samples are eluted isocratically (single buffer, no gradient Figure 1.72). Buffer conditions are varied to suit the sample type or the requirements for further purification, analysis or storage step, since buffer composition does not directly affect resolution. Proteins are collected in purified form in the chosen buffer.

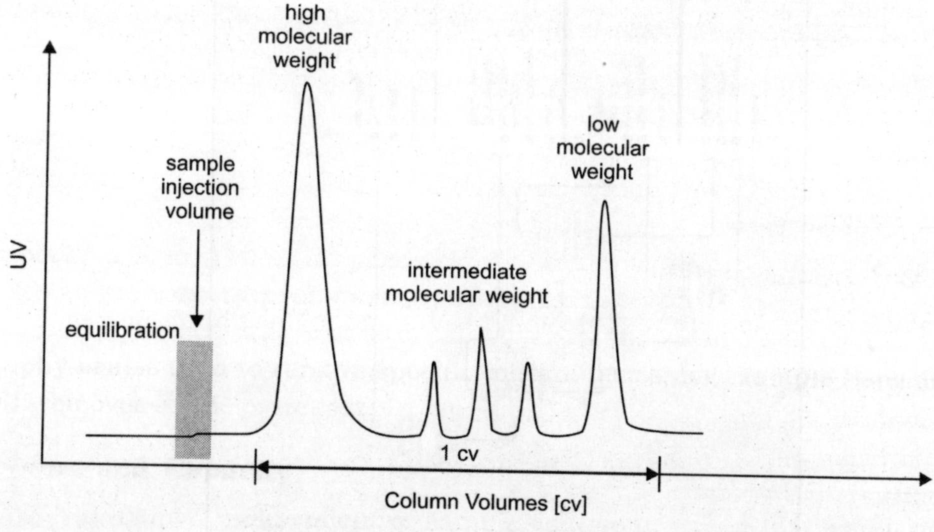

Fig. 1.72 : Typical GF elution

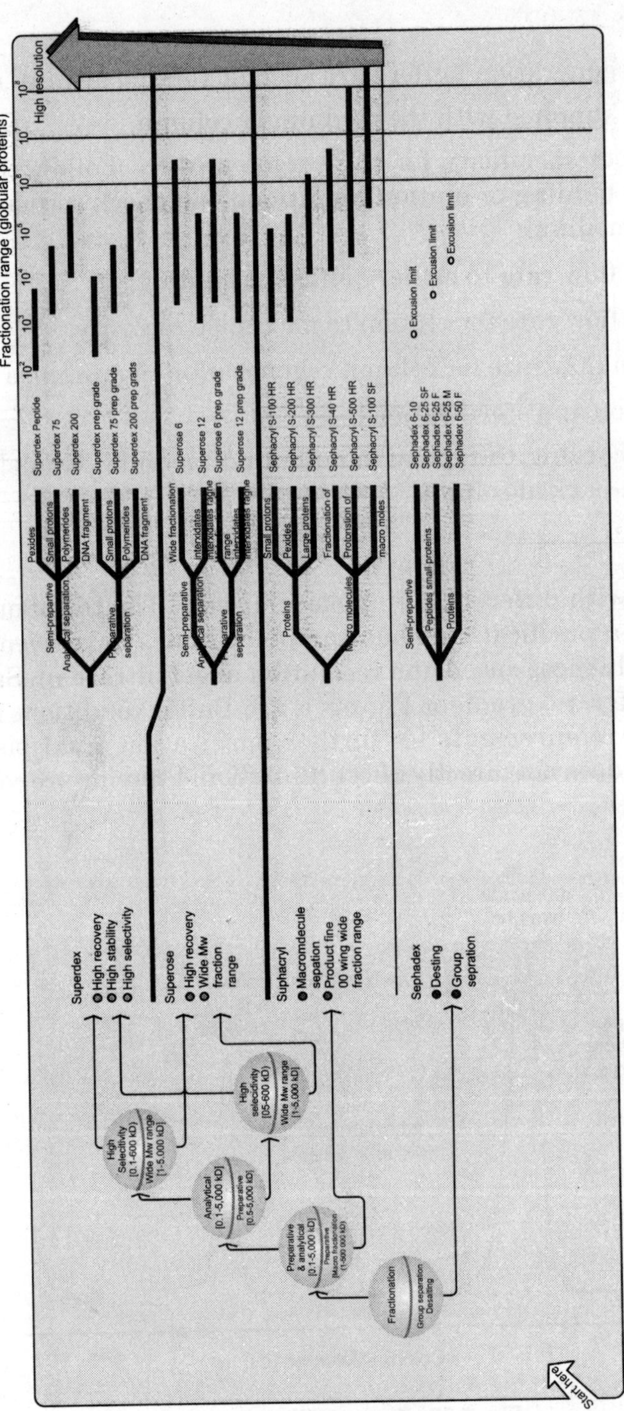

Fractionation range (globular proteins)
High resolution
Superdex Peptide
Superdex 75
Superdex 200
Superdex prep grade
Superdex 75 prep grade
Superdex 200 prep grade
Superose 6
Superose 12
Superose 6 prep grade
Superose 12 prep grade
Sephacryl S-100 HR
Sephacryl S-200 HR
Sephacryl S-300 HR
Sephacryl S-40 HR
Sephacryl S-500 HR
Sephacryl S-100 SF
Sephadex 6-10
Sephadex 6-25 SF
Sephadex 6-25 F
Sephadex 6-25 M
Sephadex 6-50 F
Excusion limit
Excusion limit
Excusion limit
Semi-preparative
Analytical separation
Preparative separation
Pexides
Small protons
Polymendes
DNA fragment
Wide fractionation
Small protons
Large proteins
Proteins
Macro molecules
macro moles
Peptides small proteins
Superdex
High recovery
High stability
High selectivity
Superose
High recovery
Wide Mw fraction range
Suphacryl
Macromdecule sepation
Product fine 00 wing wide fraction range
Sephadex
Desting
Group sepration
High Selectivity [0.1-600 kD]
Wide Mw range [1-5,000 kD]
Analytical [0.1-5,000 kD]
Preparative [0.5-5,000 kD]
High selectivity [05-600 kD]
Preparative & analytical [0.1-5,000 kD]
Fractionation
Group separation Desalting
Start here

Fig. 1.72A

Sample Volume and Capacity

To achieve the highest resolution the sample volume must not exceed 5% of the total column volume. Gel filtration is independent of sample concentration, although above 50 mg/ml protein viscosity effects may cause 'fingering'. Extremely viscous samples should be diluted.

Media Selection

Parameters such as molecular weight of target proteins and contaminants, resolution required, scale of purification should be considered when selecting gel filtration media. Figure 1.72A on page 108 shows a guide to selecting of GF media.

Sample Preparation

Correct sample preparation ensures good resolution and extends the life of the column. Sample buffer composition does not directly affect resolution. During separation the sample buffer is exchanged with buffer in the column. Viscous samples, which could cause an increase in back pressure and affect column packing, should be diluted. Samples must be free from particulate matter, particularly when working with bead sizes of 34 μm or less (see page 65 for details of sample clarification procedures)

Column Preparation

Pre-packed columns

Pre-packed columns ensure reproducible results and highest performance.

Column packing

In gel filtration good column packing is essential. The resolution between two separated zones increases as the square root of column length. The following guidelines apply:

Column dimensions: = minimum 50 cm bed height (Sephacryl)mminimum 30 cm bed height (Superdex, Superose)

Bed volume = depending on sample volume per run (up to 5% of bed volume)

See individual product packing instructions for more detailed information on a specific medium.

Buffer Preparation

Selection of buffering ion does not directly affect resolution. Select a buffer in which the purified product should be collected and which is compatible with protein stability and activity.

Buffer concentration must be sufficient to maintain buffering capacity and constant pH.

Ionic strength can be up to 150 mM NaCl in the buffer, to avoid non-specific ionic interactions with the matrix (shown by delays in peak elution).

When working with a new sample try these conditions first

Buffer: 50 mM sodium phosphate, pH 7.0 + 0.15 M NaCl

or select the buffer in which the sample should be eluted for the next step

Method Development (in priority order)

1. Select the medium which gives the best separation of target proteins from contaminants.
2. Select the highest flow rate which maintains resolution and minimizes separation time. Check recommended flow rates for the specific medium.
   Lower flow rates improve resolution of high molecular weight components, faster flow rates may improve resolution of low molecular weight components.
3. Determine the maximum sample volume which can be loaded without reducing resolution (sample volume should be 0.5-5% of total column volume).
4. To further improve resolution increase column length by connecting two columns in series Cleaning, sanitisation and sterilisation.

Procedures vary according to type of sample and medium. Guidelines are supplied with the medium or pre-packed column.

Storage of media and columns

Recommended conditions for storage are supplied with the medium or pre-packed column.

Reversed Phase Chromatography (RPC)

RPC separates proteins and peptides with differing hydrophobicity based on their reversible interaction with the hydrophobic surface of a chromatographic medium. Samples bind as they are loaded onto a column. Conditions are then altered so that the bound substances are eluted differentially. Due to the nature of the reversed phase matrices, the binding is usually very strong and requires the use of organic solvents and other additives (ion pairing agents) for elution. Elution is usually performed by increases in organic solvent concentration, most commonly acetonitrile. Samples, which are concentrated during the binding and separation process, are collected in a purified, concentrated form. The key stages in a separation are shown in Figure 1.73.

RPC is often used in the final polishing of oligonucleotides and peptides and is ideal for analytical separations, such as peptide mapping.RPC is not recommended for protein purification if recovery of activity and return to a correct tertiary structure are required, since many proteins are denatured in the presence of organic solvents.

Choice of hydrophobic ligand Select hydrocarbon ligands according to the degree of hydrophobicity required. Highly hydrophobic molecules bind tightly to highly hydrophobic

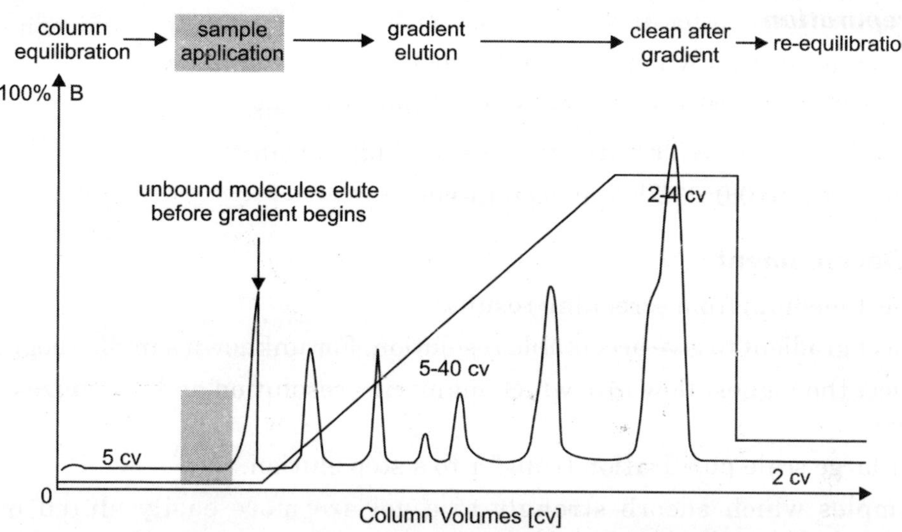

Fig. 1.73 : Showing the Typical RPC gradient elution

ligands, *e.g.* C18. Screen several RPC media. Begin with a medium of low hydrophobicity, if the sample has very hydrophobic components (more likely with larger biomolecules, such as proteins). Select the medium which gives the best resolution and loading capacity. A polymer based medium such as SOURCE RPC can offer significant advantages over silica based media as it can be used across the pH range 1-14 providing not only an alternative selectivity to silica but also a wider working pH range for method optimization.

Sample Volume and Capacity

RPC is a binding technique, often independent of sample volume. Total capacity is strongly dependent upon experimental conditions and the properties of the and sample. For optimal conditions during gradient elution, screen for a sample loading this does not reduce resolution.

Media Selection

In RPC the chromatographic medium as well as the hydrophobic ligand affects selectivity. Screening of different RPC media is recommended.

Sample Preparation

Samples should be free from particulate matter and, when possible, dissolved in the start buffer.

Column Preparation

Reversed phase columns should be 'conditioned' for first time use, after long term storage or when changing buffer systems.

Buffer Preparation

Try these conditions first when sample characteristics are unknown:

Gradient: 2-80% elution buffer B in 20 column volumes

Start buffer A: 0.065% TFA (trifluoroacetic acid) in water

Elution buffer B: 0.05% TFA in acetonitrile

Method Development

1. Select medium from screening results.
2. Select gradient to give acceptable resolution. For unknown samples begin 0-100%B.
3. Select the highest flow rate which maintains resolution and minimizes separation time.
4. For large scale purification transfer to a step elution.
5. Samples which adsorb strongly to a gel are more easily eluted from a less hydrophobic medium.

Cleaning, sanitisation and sterilisation

Procedures vary according to type of sample and medium. Guidelines are supplied with the medium or pre-packed column. Storage of media and columns

Recommended conditions for storage are supplied with the medium or pre-packed column.

Expanded Bed Adsorption (EBA)

EBA is a single pass operation in which target proteins are purified from crude sample, without the need for separate clarification, concentration and initial purification to remove particulate matter. Crude sample is applied to an expanded bed of STREAMLINE adsorbent particles within a specifically designed STREAMLINE column. Target proteins are captured on the adsorbent. Cell debris, particulate matter, whole cells, and contaminants pass through and target proteins are then eluted. Figure 1.74 shows the steps involved in an EBA purification and Figure 1.75 shows a typical EBA elution pattern *(See Both Figs. on next page)*.

Selection of STREAMLINE Adsorbent

Selection of adsorbent is based on the same principles that are used for chromatography. Select the medium with the strongest binding to the target protein and which binds as few of the contaminants as possible, *i.e.* the mediumwith the highest selectivity and/or capacity for the protein of interest. Sample volume and capacityAll STREAMLINE media are binding techniques, independent of sample volume.

The total amount of protein which is loaded should not exceed the total binding capacity of the column.

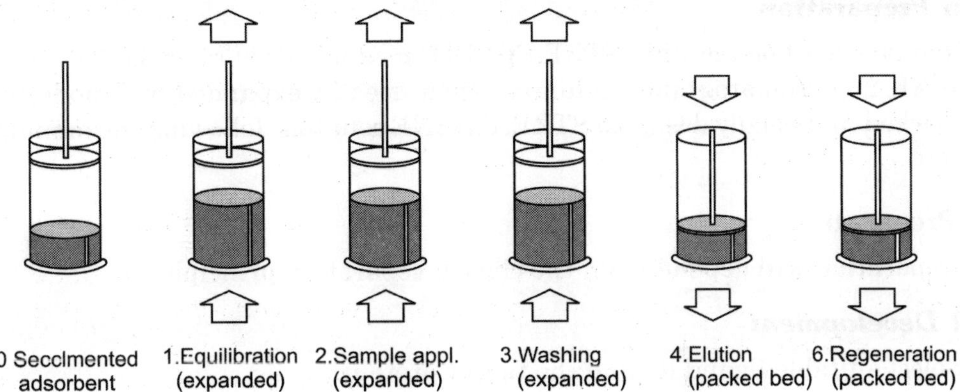

Fig. 1.74 : Steps in an EBA purification process

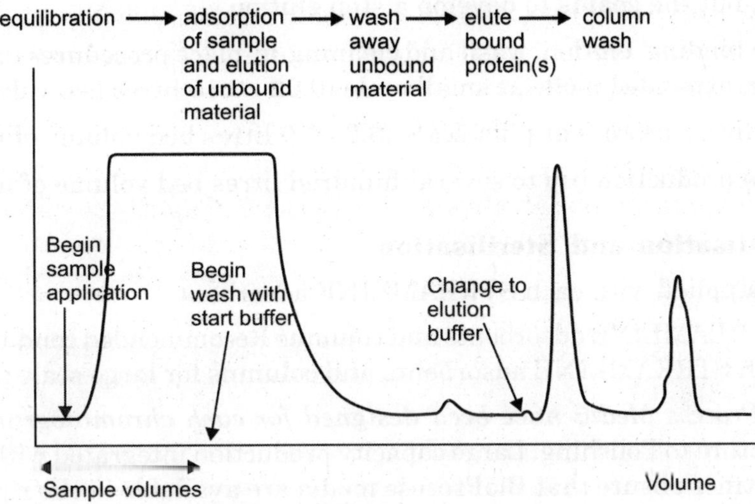

Fig. 1.75 : Typical EBA elution

Sample Volume and Capacity

All STREAMLINE media are binding techniques, independent of sample volume.

The total amount of protein which is loaded should not exceed the total binding capacity of the column.

Sample Preparation

STREAMLINE is able to handle crude, particulate feedstock, reducing the need for significant sample preparation steps. Adjustment of pH or ionic strength be required according to the separation principle being used (IEX, AC, HIC)

Column Preparation

For preliminary method scouting STREAMLINE media is used in packed bed mode in an XK 16 or XK 26 chromatography column. When used in expanded bed mode the media must be packed in specially designed STREAMLINE columns, following the manufacturer's instructions.

Buffer Preparation

Buffer preparation will depend upon the chosen separation principle.

Method Development

1. Select suitable ligand to bind the target protein.
2. Scout for optimal binding and elution conditions using clarified material in packed column (0.02 - 0.15 litres bed volume of media). Gradient elutions be used during scouting, but the goal is to develop a step elution.
3. Optimise binding, elution, wash and cleaning-in-place procedures using unclarified sample in expanded mode at small scale (0.02 - 0.15 litres bed volume of media)
4. Begin scale up process at pilot scale (0.2 - 0.9 litres bed volume of media)
5. Full scale production (up to several hundred litres bed volume of media)

Cleaning, Sanitisation and Sterilisation

Guidelines are supplied with each STREAMLINE adsorbent.

Storage of STREAMLINE adsorbents and columns Recommended conditions for storage are supplied with STREAMLINE adsorbents and columns for large scale production

Specific BioProcess Media have been designed for each chromatographic stage in a process from Capture to Polishing. Large capacity production integrated with clear ordering and delivery routines ensure that BioProcess media are available in the right quantity, at the right place, at the right time. Amersham Biosciences can assure future supplies of BioProcess Media, making them a safe investment for long term production. The media are produced following validated methods and tested under strict control to fulfil high performance specifications. A certificate of analysis is available with each order.

Regulatory support files contain details of performance, stability, extractable compounds and analytical methods. The essential information in these files gives an invaluable starting point for process validation, as well as providing support for submissions to regulatory authorities. Using BioProcess Media for every stage results in an easily validated process. High flow rates, high capacity and high recovery contribute to the overall economy of an industrial process. All BioProcess Media have chemical stability to allow efficient cleaning and sanitisation procedures. Packing methods are established for a wide range of scales and compatible large scale columns and equipment are available.

PROTEIN MODIFICATIONS

Secreted and Membrane—Associated Proteins

Proteins that are membrane bound or are destined for excretion are synthesized by ribosomes associated with the membranes of the endoplasmic reticulum (ER). The ER associated with ribosomes is termed rough ER (RER). This class of proteins all contain an N-terminus termed a *signal sequence* or *signal peptide*. The signal peptide is usually 13-36 predominantly hydrophobic residues. The signal peptide is recognized by a multi-protein complex termed the signal recognition particle (SRP). This signal peptide is removed following passage through the endoplasmic reticulum membrane. The removal of the signal peptide is catalyzed by signal peptidase. Proteins that contain a signal peptide are called preproteins to distinguish them from proproteins. However, some proteins that are destined for secretion are also further proteolyzed following secretion and, therefore contain pro sequences. This class of proteins is termed preproproteins.

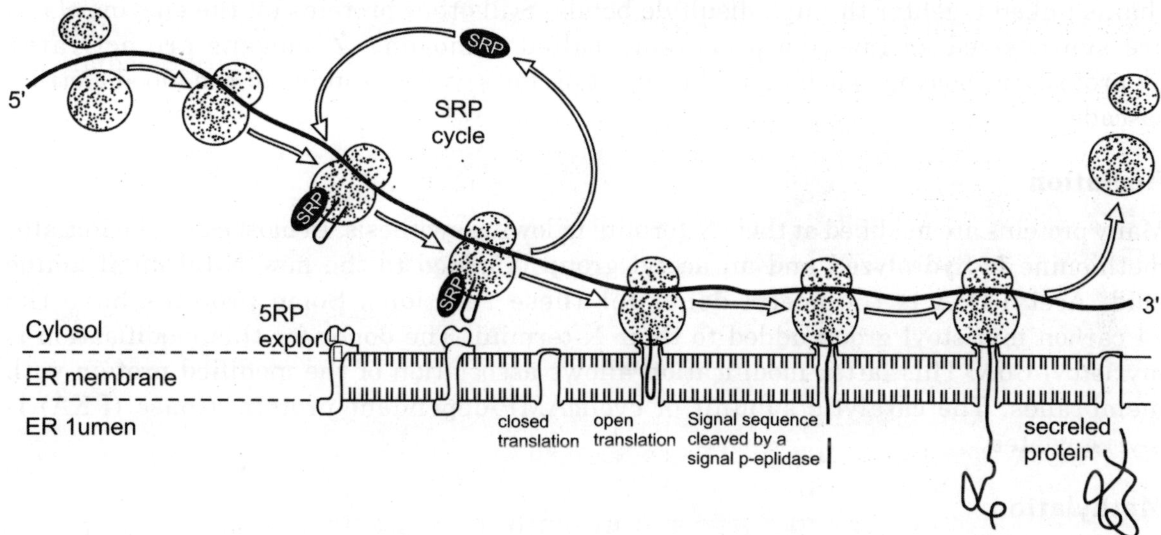

Fig. 1.76 : Showing the Protein Modification

Proteolytic Cleavage

Most proteins undergo proteolytic cleavage following translation. The simplest form of this is the removal of the initiation methionine. Many proteins are synthesized as inactive precursors that are activated under proper physiological conditions by limited proteolysis. Pancreatic enzymes and enzymes involved in clotting are examples of the latter. Inactive precursor proteins that are activated by removal of polypeptides are termed proproteins. A complex example of post-translational processing of a preproprotein is the cleavage of prepro-opiomelanocortin (POMC) synthesized in the pituitary (see the Peptide Hormones in the Encyclopedic architecture of chemistry). This preproprotein undergoes complex cleavages, the pathway of which differs depending upon the cellular location of POMC synthesis.

Mechanism of synthesis of membrane bound or secreted proteins. Ribosomes engage the ER membrane through interaction of the signal recognition particle, SRP in the ribosome with the SRP receptor in the ER membrane. As the protein is synthesized the signal sequence is passed through the ER membrane into the lumen of the ER. After sufficient synthesis the signal peptide is removed by the action of signal peptidase. Synthesis will continue and if the protein is secreted it will end up completely in the lumen of the ER. If the protein is membrane associated a stop transfer motif in the protein will stop the transfer of the protein through the ER membrane. This will become the membrane spanning domain of the protein.

Another is example of a preproprotein is insulin. Since insulin is secreted from the pancreas it has a prepeptide. Following cleavage of the 24 amino acid signal peptide the protein folds into proinsulin. Proinsulin is further cleaved yielding active insulin which is composed of two peptide chains linked togehter through disulfide bonds. Still other proteins (of the enzyme class) are synthesized as inactive precursors called zymogens. Zymogens are activated by proteolytic cleavage such as is the situation for several proteins of the blood clotting cascade.

Acylation

Many proteins are modified at their N-termini following synthesis. In most cases the initiator methionine is hydrolyzed and an acetyl group is added to the new N-terminal amino acid. Acetyl-CoA is the acetyl donor for these reactions. Some proteins have the 14 carbon myristoyl group added to their N-termini. The donor for this modification is myristoyl-CoA. This latter modification allows association of the modified protein with membranes. The catalytic subunit of cyclicAMP-dependent protein kinase (PKA) is myristoylated.

Methylation

Post-translational methylation of proteins occurs on nitrogens and oxygens. The activated methyl donor is S-adenosylmethionine (SAM). The most common methylations are on the ?-amine of lysine residues. Methylation of lysine residues in histones in DNA is an important regulator of chromatin structure and consequently of transcriptional activity. Lysine methylation was originally thought to be a permanent covalent mark, providing long-term signaling, including the histone-dependent mechanism for transcriptional memory. However, recent evidence has shown that lysine methylation, similar to other covalent modifications, can be transient and dynamically regulated by an opposing de-methylation activity. Recent findings indicate that methylation of lysine residues affects gene expression not only at the level of chromatin, but also by modifying transcription factors.

Additional nitrogen methylations are found on the imidazole ring of histidine, the guanidino moiety of arginine and the R-group amides of glutamate and aspartate. Methylation of the oxygen of the R-group carboxylates of gutamate and aspartate also takes place and forms methyl esters. Proteins can also be methylated on the thiol R-group of cysteine.

As indicated below, many proteins are modified at their C-terminus by prenylation near a cysteine residue in the consensus CAAX. Following the prenylation reaction the protein is cleaved at the peptide bond of the cysteine and the carboxylate residue is methylated by a prenylated protein methyltransferase. One such protein that undergoes this type of modification is the proto-oncogene RAS.

Phosphorylation

Post-translational phosphorylation is one of the most common protein modifications that occurs in animal cells. The vast majority of phosphorylations occur as a mechanism to regulate the biological activity of a protein and as such are transient. In other words a phosphate (or more than one in many cases) is added and later removed. Physiologically relevant examples are the phosphorylations that occur in glycogen synthase and glycogen phosphorylase in hepatocytes in response to glucagon release from the pancreas. Phosphorylation of synthase inhibits its activity, whereas, the activity of phosphorylase is increased. These two events lead to increased hepatic glucose delivery to the blood.

The enzymes that phosphorylate proteins are termed kinases and those that remove phosphates are termed phosphatases. Protein kinases catalyze reactions of the following type:

$$\text{ATP + protein} \leftrightarrow \text{phosphoprotein + ADP}$$

In animal cells serine, threonine and tyrosine are the amino acids subject to phosphorylation. The largest group of kinases are those that phsophorylate either serines or threonines and as such are termed serine/threonine kinases. The ratio of phosphorylation of the three different amino acids is approximately 1000/100/1 for serine/threonine/tyrosine.

Although the level of tyrosine phosphorylation is minor, the importance of phosphorylation of this amino acid is profound. As an example, the activity of numerous growth factor receptors is controlled by tyrosine phosphorylation.

Sulphation

Sulphate modification of proteins occurs at tyrosine residues such as in fibrinogen and in some secreted proteins (eg gastrin). The universal sulphate donor is 3'-phosphoadenosyl-5'-phosphosulphate (PAPS).

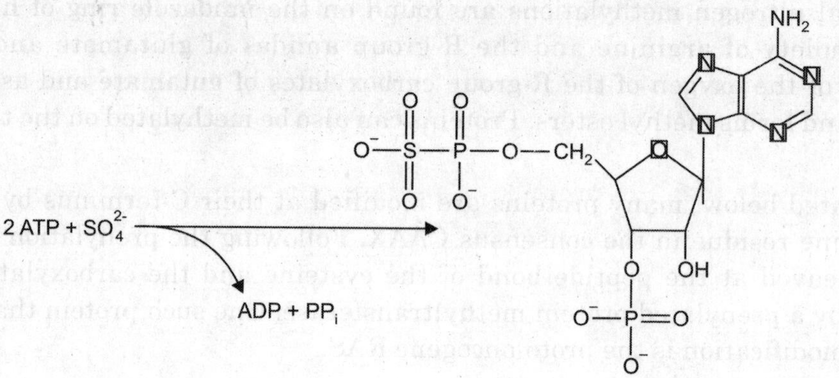

$2\ ATP + SO_4^{2-} \rightarrow$ (ADP + PP_i)

3'-phosphoadensine 5'-phosphosulfate (PAPS)

Since sulphate is added permanently it is necessary for the biological activity and not used as a regulatory modification like that of tyrosine phosphorylation.

Prenylation

Prenylation refers to the addition of the 15 carbon farnesyl group or the 20 carbon geranylgeranyl group to acceptor proteins, both of which are isoprenoid compounds derived from the cholesterol biosynthetic pathway. The isoprenoid groups are attached to cysteine residues at the carboxy terminus of proteins in a thioether linkage (C-S-C). A common consensus sequence at the C-terminus of prenylated proteins has been identified and is

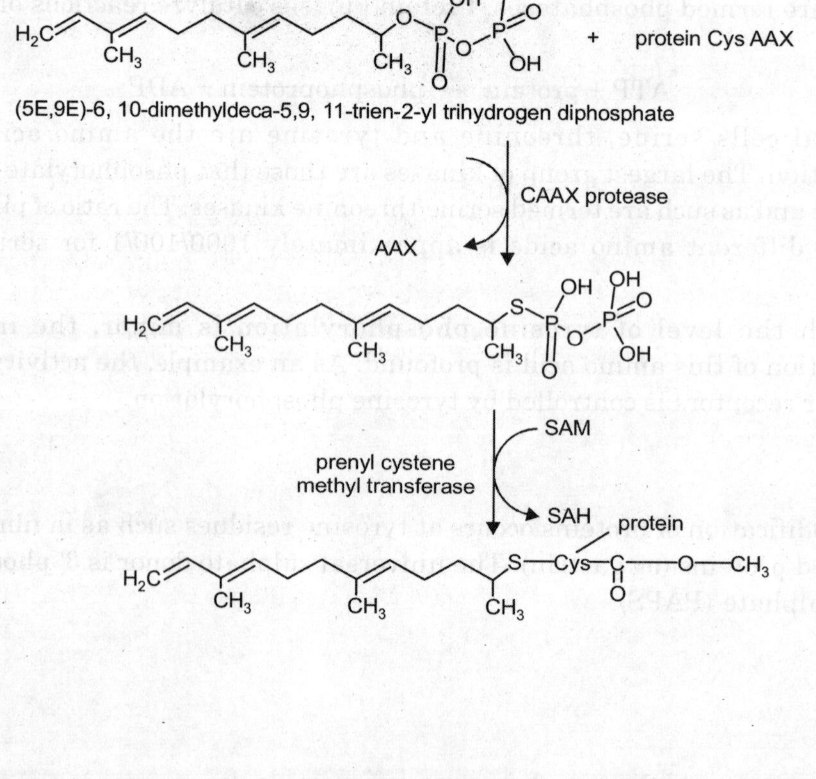

\+ protein Cys AAX

(5E,9E)-6, 10-dimethyldeca-5,9, 11-trien-2-yl trihydrogen diphosphate

CAAX protease

AAX

SAM

prenyl cystene methyl transferase

SAH

protein

composed of CAAX, where C is cysteine, A is any aliphatic amino acid (except alanine) and X is the C-terminal amino acid. In order for the prenylation reaction to occur the three C-terminal amino acids (AAX) are first removed. Following attachment of the prenyl group the carboxylate of the cysteine is methylated in a reaction utilizing S-adenosylmethionine as the methyl donor.

In addition to numerous prenylated proteins that contain the CAAX consensus, prenylation is known to occur on proteins of the RAB family of RAS-related G-proteins. There are at least 60 proteins in this family that are prenylated at either a CC or CXC element in their C-termini. The RAB family of proteins are involved in signaling pathways that control intracellular membrane trafficking.Some of the most important proteins whose functions depend upon prenylation are those that modulate immune responses. These include proteins involved in leukocyte motility, activation, and proliferation and endothelial cell immune functions. It is these immune modulatory roles of many prenylated proteins that are the basis for a portion of the anti-inflammatory actions of the statin class of cholesterol synthesis-inhibiting drugs due to a reduction in the synthesis of farnesylpyrophosphate and geranylpyrophosphate and thus reduced extent of inflammatory events. Other important examples of prenylated proteins include the oncogenic GTP-binding and hydrolyzing protein RAS and the ?-subunit of the visual protein transducin, both of which are farnesylated. In addition, numerous GTP-binding and hydrolyzing proteins (termed G-proteins) of signal transduction cascades have γ-subunits modified by geranylgeranylation.

Vitamin C-Dependent Modifications

Modifications of proteins that depend upon vitamin C as a cofactor include proline and lysine hydroxylations and carboxy terminal amidation. The hydroxylating enzymes are identified as prolyl hydroxylase and lysyl hydroxylase. The donor of the amide for C-terminal amidation is glycine. The most important hydroxylated proteins are the collagens. Several peptide hormones such as oxytocin and vasopressin have C-terminal amidation.

Vitamin K-Dependent Modifications

Vitamin K is a cofactor in the carboxylation of glutamic acid residues. The result of this type of reaction is the formation of a γ-carboxyglutamate (gamma-carboxyglutamate), referred to as a gla residue.

CH
CH_2
CH
$^{\ominus}OOC$ $COO^{\ominus}$

Structure of gla-Residue

The formation of gla residues within several proteins of the blood clotting cascade is critical for their normal function. The presence of gla residues allows the protein to chelate calcium ions and thereby render an altered conformation and biological activity to the protein. The coumarin-based anticoagulants, warfarin and dicumarol function by inhibiting the carboxylation reaction.

Selenoproteins

Selenium is a trace element and is found as a component of several prokaryotic and eukaryotic enzymes that are involved in redox reactions. The selenium in these selenoproteins is incorporated as a unique amino acid, selenocysteine, during translation. A particularly important eukaryotic selenoenzyme is glutathione peroxidase. This enzyme is required during the oxidation of glutathione by hydrogen peroxide (H_2O_2) and organic hydroperoxides.

NH
|
CH—CH_2—Se—H
|
C=O

Structure of Silinocysteine Residue

Incorporation of selenocysteine by the translational machinery occurs via an interesting and unique mechanism. The tRNA for selenocysteine is charged with serine and then enzymatically selenylated to produce the selenocysteinyl-tRNA. The anticodon of selenocysteinyl-tRNA interacts with a stop codon in the mRNA (UGA) instead of a serine codon. The selenocysteinyl-tRNA has a unique structure that is not recognized by the termination machinery and is brought into the ribosome by a dedicated specific elongation factor. An element in the 3' non-translated region (UTR) of selenoprotein mRNAs determines whether UGA is read as a stop codon or as a selenocysteine codon.

Ubiquitin and Targeted Protein Degradation

Proteins are in a continual state of flux, being synthesized and degraded. In addition, when proteins become damaged they must be degraded to prevent aberrant activities of the defective proteins and/or other proteins associated with those that have been damaged. One of the major mechanisms for the destruction of cellular proteins involves a complex structure referred to as the proteosome. In eukayotic cells the proteosome is found in the cytosol and the nucleus and has a large mass such that it has a sedimentation coefficient of 26*S*. The 26*S* proteosome comprises a 20*S* barrel-shaped catalytic core as well as 19*S* regulatory complexes at both ends. Degradation of proteins in the proteosome occurs via an ATP-dependent mechanism.Proteins that are to be degraded by the proteosome are first tagged by attachment of multimers of the 76 amino acid polypeptide ubiquitin. Many proteins involved in cell cycle regulation, control of proliferation and differentiation, programmed cell death (apoptosis), DNA repair, immune and inflammatory processes and

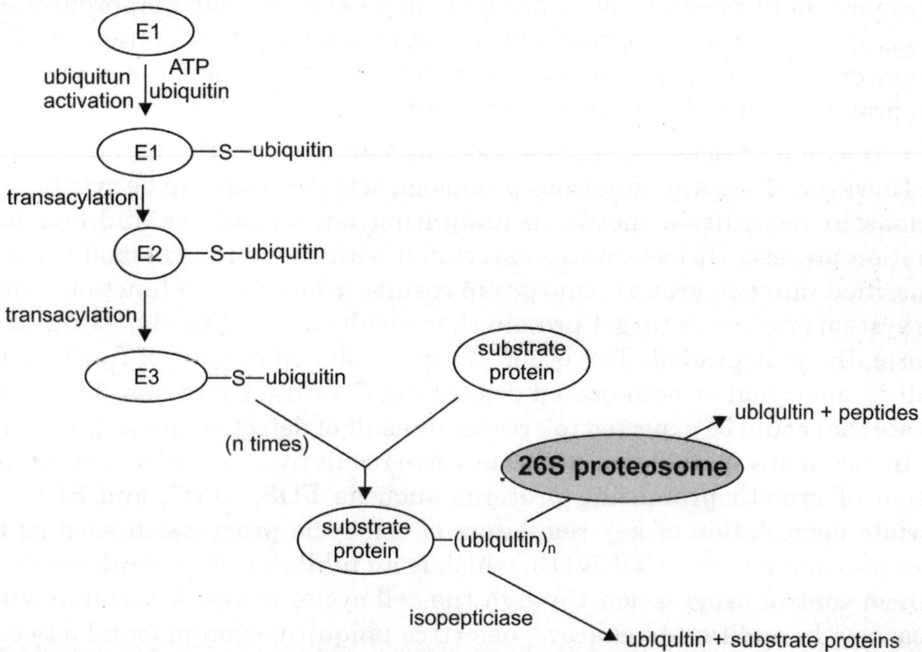

Fig. 1.77 : Showing the Process of ubiquitination and proteosome-mediated protein degradation

organelle biogenesis have been discovered to undergo regulated degradation via the 26S proteosome. Of clinical significance are the recent findings that deregulation of the functions of the proteosome can contribute to the pathogenesis of various human diseases such as cancer, myeloproliferative diseases, and neurodegenerative diseases.The degradation of proteins via the 26*S* proteosome involves a two-step process starting with ubiquitination of the protein followed by entry into and degradation by the proteosome complex with release of ubiquitin monomers that can be re used to tag additional proteins. The process of ubiquitin addition to the substrate protein involves multiple ubiquitin additions such that the targeted protein is polyubiquitinated.Attachment of ubiquitin involves a series of three enzyme activities. The first, identified as E1 (also called ubiquitin-activating enzymes), activates ubiquitin in an ATP-dependent manner such that the ubiquitin is bound to the E1 enzyme via a high-energy thiol ester. The next class of enzyme, referred to as E2 (also called ubiquitin-conjugating enzymes or ubiquitin-carrier proteins), transfers the ubiquitin via an E2 thiol ester intermediate to the substrate protein. The substrate proteins are recognizable by E2 because they are bound by the third class of enzyme called E3 or ubiquitin-protein ligases. The E3 enzymes carry out the final step in the process which is the covalent attachment of ubiquitin to the substrate protein. The ubiquitin is generally transferred to the ε-amino group of an internal lysine residue in the substrate protein. There are however, examples where the ubiquitin is attached to the N-terminal amino group in a substrate protein. Whereas, ubiquitination targets proteins for degradation in the proteosome there needs to be a mechanism to ensure that inappropriately tagged proteins, *i.e.* those that are not destined for degradation, can be untagged. There are a family of enzymes called isopeptidases that carry out this vital function of removing ubiquitin from from proteins to which it is mistakenly attached.

Inactivation of a critical activity such as that catalyzed by the E1 enzymes results in lethality. However, there are numerous pathological states that can be attributed, in part, to mutations in recognition motifs in ubiquitination substrates and enzymes in the ubiquitination process. Disease states associated with the ubiquitin modification system can be classified into two groups. One group results from a loss of function mutation in a ubiquitin system enzyme or target protein that results in stabilization of the protein that should normally be degraded. The other group results from gain of function mutations that result in abnormal or accelerated degradation of target proteins. The most obvious disease state that could be expected to arise as a result of defective ubiquitination processes is cancer. In fact, many malignancies are known to result from defective ubiquitin-mediated degradation of growth promoting proteins such as FOS, MYC, and SRC. Likewise, inappropriate degradation of key regulators of cell cycle progression such as the tumor suppressor p53 and p27^{KIPI} (CDKN1B), which is an inhibitor of cyclin-dependent kinases (CDKs which control progression through the cell cycle) is also associated with various types of cancer. In addition to cancers, defective ubiquitination is found associated with neurodegenerative diseases such as Parkinson disease, Alzheimer disease, and amyotrophic lateral sclerosis.

Protein Modification by SUMO

As discussed in the above section, many proteins are post-translationally modified via the addition of ubiquitin. Over the past several years numerous ubiquitin-like (Ubl) proteins have been identified. Like ubiquitin, Ubls are added to other proteins via post-translational reactions. However, unlike ubiquitination which targets proteins for degradation in the proteosome, Ubl modifications do not. Although there are several types of Ubls, those with the broadest range of functions and the largest number of known substrates are members of the SUMO (small ubiquitin-related modifier) proteins. There have been over 50 proteins, that function in a variety of different capacities within cells, shown to be modified by SUMOylation. Modification of proteins by SUMO addition has been shown to occur in all tissues and at all developmental stages. There are four SUMO proteins in mammalian cells designated SUMO-1 to SUMO-4. SUMO-1 is also identified as UBL1, PIC1 [promyelocytic leukemia (PML) interacting clone 1], sentrin, GMP1 [GTPase activating protein (GAP) modifying protein 1], and Smt3c (suppressor of mif two 3 homolog 1c). SUMO-2 is also identified as sentrin 2, Smt3b, and GMP-related protein. SUMO-3 is also identified as sentrin 3 and Smt3a. SUMO-2 and SUMO-3 differ only at three N-terminal amino acid residues and are, therefore, often referred to collectively as SUMO-2/3. SUMO-2/3 share only 50% amino acid similarity to SUMO-1. SUMO-4 is based upon DNA sequence analysis and exhibits 87% amino acid similarity to SUMO-2. It is believed that the SUMO-

4 gene is actually a pseudogene since it does not contain any introns. Although SUMO-4 mRNA has been detected in tissues such as spleen and lymph nodes, no protein product has been detected. Following de novo synthesis, SUMO proteins must undergo a C-terminal cleavage processing event in order to render the proteins biologically active. The C-terminal cleavage reactions are catalyzed by a family of proteins called SENP (sentrin/SUMO-specific protease). There are at least six SENP proteins in mammals. The removal of the C-terminal amino acids reveals a di-glycine (-G-G) motif that allows the SUMO protein to subsequently conjugate to lysine (K) residues in target proteins. SUMO conjugation to target proteins requires a series of enzymatic steps that is similar in mechanism to the conjugation of ubiquitin to target proteins. SUMO proteins are initially activated via an ATP-dependent reaction catalyzed by the E1 activating complex. This complex is a heterodimer composed of SUMO-activating enzyme E1 (SAE1) and SAE2. This activating reaction forms a covalent bond between an active site cysteine in SAE2 and the C-terminal glycine of the SUMO protein. The next step involved the transfer of the SUMO protein to an active site cysteine of the protein identified as Ubc9 (ubiquitin-conjugating 9). As yet Ubc9 is the only known SUMO-conjugating enzyme in mammalian tissues. Ubc9 brings the SUMO protein to the target protein by recognizing, and binding to, the consensus SUMOylation motif in target proteins. The consensus motif for SUMOylation is the following: ψKxD/E where ψ is a large hydrophobic amino acid and x is any amino acid. Approximately 75% of all SUMOylated proteins contain this target motif, however, not all proteins that contain this miotif are SUMOylated and some proteins are SUMOylated on lysine residues that do not lie in this motif.

As described above for ubiquitination, there are three classes of enzyme involved in the process: E1, E2, and E3. Since Ubc9 can directly conjugate SUMO proteins to their targets it was thought that no E3-like activity was required. However, SUMO E3 ligases have been identified and although they do not function directly in the enzymatic process of SUMO attachment to target they do act as a scaffold. SUMO E3 ligases bring Ubc9-SUMO complexes into contact with target proteins. The mammalian SUMO E3 proteins are members of the PIAS [protein inhibitor of activated STAT (signal transducer and activator of transcription)] family of proteins. There are currently five members of the mammalian PIAS protein family. Whereas, ubiquitination of a protein results in is destruction in the proteosome, SUMOylation is a dynamic process and once attached the SUMO residue can be removed. Removal of SUMO from a target protein is accomplished by the same SENP enzymes that are required for the activation step of SUMO processing. SENP1 and SENP2 have broad specificity for SUMO-1 and SUMO-2/3 and are involved in their processing and deconjugation. SENP3 and SENP5 exhibit a preference for SUMO-2/3. Although SENP6 and SENP7 exhibit the same preference for SUMO-2/3 they are only minimally involved in deconjugation reactions. The primary functions of SENP6 and SENP7 are in editing the length of poly-SUMO-2/3 chains on target proteins. Therefore, it seems clear that SENP1 and SENP2 are responsible for maturation of SUMO proteins and deconjugation of SUMO-1 and SUMO-2/3 conjugated targets. SENP3 and SENP5 function in the removal of monomeric SUMO-2/3 from target proteins. SENP6 and SENP7 function as editors of SUMO-2/3 chains in target proteins. The exact functional consequences of SUMOylation of a particular target protein is difficult to predict. However, modification of target proteins by SUMO addition is likely to lead to at least three non-mutually exclusive effects. The attachment of SUMO can result in the masking of a site in the target protein that is required for binding or interaction with a substrate protein. The addition of SUMO may alternatively result in the formation of an attachment site allowing for the recruitment of proteins that can now interact with the SUMOylated protein. The third consequence could be that the conformation of the SUMOylated protein is altered such that activity is regulated in some way.

Mammalian Substrates for SUMO

The following Table is not intended to represent a complete list of all known SUMO target proteins it is just a representative list.

Protein Symbol & Name	Protein Function	Role of SUMOylation
1	2	3
Androgen receptor	transcriptional activation	Ireduces the transcriptional activation activity of the receptor
GLUT1 glucose transporter 1	glucose transport	exact consequence not fully defined but GLUT1 protein levels are down-regulated by Ubc9
GLUT4 glucose transporter 4	glucose transport	exact consequence not fully defined but GLUT4 protein levels are up-regulated by Ubc9
HIPK2 homeodomain-interacting protein kinase 2	transcriptional co-repression	mediates the localization of HIPK2 nuclear bodies, also called promyelocytic leukemia (PML) bodies
IκBα inhibitory κBα	inhibitor of NF-κB (nuclear factor κB) signal transduction	inhibits ubiquitination of IκBα thereby blocking NF-κB activity
Mdm2 originally isolated from mouse tumorigenic cell line 3T3DM	E3 ubiquitin ligase for tumor suppressor p53	inhibits ubiquitylation of Mdm2 resulting in activation of the E3 function of Mdm2
p53	tumour suppressor, is a transcription factor activated in response to DNA damage	activates p53 transactivation leading to increased apoptosis

(Contd...)

1	2	3
PML promyelocytic leukemia	tumor suppressor	allows for the formation of nuclear bodies and the recruitment p53
Topo I topoisomerase I	topoisomerase involved in DNA replication and repair	exact consequence not fully defined but SUMOylation is induced after DNA damage with camptothecin
Topo II topoisomerase II	topoisomerase involved in DNA replication and repair	exact consequence not fully defined but SUMOylation is induced after DNA damage with teniposide

Post Translational Modifications

Most of the proteins that are translated from mRNA undergo chemical modifications before becoming functional in different body cells. The modifications collectively, are known as post-translational modifications. The protein post translational modifications play a crucial role in generating the heterogeneity in proteins and also help in utilizing identical proteins for different cellular functions in different cell types. How a particular protein sequence will act in most of the eukaryotic organisms is regulated by these post translational modifications. Post Translational modifications occurring at the peptide terminus of the amino acid chain play an important role in translocating them across biological membranes. These include secretory proteins in prokaryotes and eukaryotes and also proteins that are intended to be incorporated in various cellular and organelle membranes such as lysosomes, chloroplast, mitochondria and plasma membranes.Expression of proteins is important in diseased conditions. Post translational modifications play an important part in modifying the end product of expression and contribute towards biological processes and diseased conditions. The amino terminal sequences are removed by proteolytic cleavage when the proteins cross the membranes. These amino terminal sequences target the proteins for transporting them to their actual point of action in the cell.

Protein Post translational modifications may happen in several ways. Some of them are listed below:

1. *Glycosylation*: Many proteins, particularly in eukaryotic cells, are modified by the addition of carbohydrates, a process called glycosylation. Glycosylation in proteins results in addition of a glycosyl group to either asparagine, hydroxylysine, serine, or threonine. Software for studying glycosylation by glycan structure prediction.
2. *Acetylation*: the addition of an acetyl group, usually at the N-terminus of the protein.
3. *Alkylation*: The addition of an alkyl group (*e.g.* methyl, ethyl).
4. *Methylation*: The addition of a methyl group, usually at lysine or arginine residues. (This is a type of alkylation.)
5. *Biotinylation*: Acylation of conserved lysine residues with a biotin appendage.

6. *Glutamylation*: Covalent linkage of glutamic acid residues to tubulin and some other proteins.
7. *Glycylation*: Covalent linkage of one to more than 40 glycine residues to the tubulin C-terminal tail of the amino acid sequence.
8. *Isoprenylation*: The addition of an isoprenoid group (e.g. farnesol and geranylgeraniol).
9. *Lipoylation*: The attachment of a lipoate functionality.
10. *Phosphopantetheinylation*, The addition of a 4'-phosphopantetheinyl moiety from coenzyme A, as in fatty acid, polyketide, non-ribosomal peptide and leucine biosynthesis.
11. *Phosphorylation*, the addition of a phosphate group, usually to serine, tyrosine, threonine or histidine.
12. *Sulfation*: The addition of a sulfate group to a tyrosine.
13. Selenation
14. C-terminal amidation

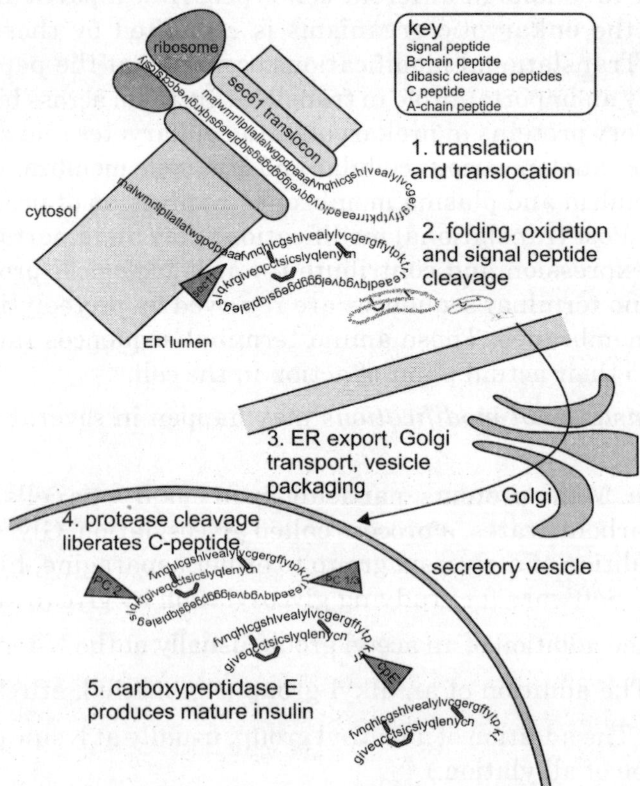

Fig. 1.78 : Showing the Post translational Modifications

PTMs involving addition by an enzyme *in vivo*

- acylation, *e.g.* *O*-acylation (esters), *N*-acylation (amides), *S*-acylation (thioesters)
  - – acetylation, the addition of an acetyl group, either at the *N*-terminus of the protein or at lysine residues. See also histone acetylation. The reverse is called deacetylation.
  - – formylation
  - – lipoylation, attachment of a lipoate (C_8) functional group
  - – myristoylation, attachment of myristate, a C_{14} saturated acid
  - – palmitoylation, attachment of palmitate, a C_{16} saturated acid
- alkylation, the addition of an alkyl group, *e.g.* methyl, ethyl
  - – methylation the addition of a methyl group, usually at lysine or arginine residues. The reverse is called demethylation.
  - – isoprenylation or prenylation, the addition of an isoprenoid group (e.g. farnesol and geranylgeraniol)
    - farnesylation
    - geranylgeranylation
    - amidation at C-terminus
    - amino acid addition
  - – arginylation, a tRNA-mediation addition
  - – polyglutamylation, covalent linkage of glutamic acid residues to tubulin and some other proteins. (See tubulin polyglutamylase)
  - – polyglycylation, covalent linkage of one to more than 40 glycine residues to the tubulin C-terminal tail
- diphthamide formation
- gamma-carboxylation dependent on Vitamin K
- glycosylation, the addition of a glycosyl group to either asparagine, hydroxylysine, serine, or threonine, resulting in a glycoprotein. Distinct from glycation, which is regarded as a nonenzymatic attachment of sugars.
  - – polysialylation, addition of polysialic acid, PSA to NCAM
- glypiation, glycosylphosphatidylinositol (GPI) anchor formation
- heme moiety may be covalently attached
- hydroxylation
- iodination (*e.g.* of thyroid hormones)

- nucleotides or derivatives thereof may be covalently attached
  - adenylation
  - ADP-ribosylation
  - flavin attachment
- nitrosylation
- oxidation
- phosphopantetheinylation, the addition of a 4'-phosphopantetheinyl moiety from coenzyme A, as in fatty acid, polyketide, non-ribosomal peptide and leucine biosynthesis
- phosphorylation, the addition of a phosphate group, usually to serine, tyrosine, threonine or histidine
- pyroglutamate formation
- sulfation, the addition of a sulfate group to a tyrosine.
- selenoylation (co-translational incorporation of selenium in selenoproteins)

PTMs involving non-enzymatic additions *in vivo*

- glycation, the addition of a sugar molecule to a protein without the controlling action of an enzyme.

PTMs involving non-enzymatic additions *in vitro*

- biotinylation, acylation of conserved lysine residues with a biotin appendage
- pegylation

PTMs involving addition of other proteins or peptides

- ISGylation, the covalent linkage to the ISG15 protein (Interferon-Stimulated Gene 15)
- SUMOylation, the covalent linkage to the SUMO protein (Small Ubiquitin-related MOdifier)
- ubiquitination, the covalent linkage to the protein ubiquitin.
- Neddylation, the covalent linkage to Nedd

PTMs involving changing the chemical nature of amino acids

- citrullination, or deimination the conversion of arginine to citrulline
- deamidation, the conversion of glutamine to glutamic acid or asparagine to aspartic acid

- eliminylation, the conversion to an alkene by beta-elimination of phosphothreonine and phosphoserine or dehydration of threonine and serine as well as by decarboxylation of cysteine.

PTMs involving Structural Changes

- disulfide bridges, the covalent linkage of two cysteine amino acids
- proteolytic cleavage, cleavage of a protein at a peptide bond
- racemization of proline by prolyl isomerase

Case Examples

- Cleavage and formation of disulfide bridges during the production of insulin
- PTM of histones as regulation of transcription: RNA polymerase control by chromatin structure
- PTM of RNA polymerase II as regulation of transcription
- Cleavage of polypeptide chains as crucial for lectin specificity.

TANDEM MASS SPECTROMETRY

Mass spectrometers can be divided into three fundamental parts, namely the *ionization source*, the *analyzer*, and the *detector*.

The sample has to be introduced into the ionization source of the instrument. Once inside the ionization source, the sample molecules are ionized, because ions are easier to manipulate than neutral molecules. These ions are extracted into the analyzer region of the mass spectrometer where they are separated according to their *mass (m) -to-charge (z) ratios (m/z)*. The separated ions are detected and this signal sent to a data system where the m/z ratios are stored together with their relative abundance for presentation in the format of an *m/z spectrum*.

The analyzer and detector of the mass spectrometer, and often the ionization source too, are maintained under high vacuum to give the ions a reasonable chance of travelling from one end of the instrument to the other without any hindrance from air molecules. The entire operation of the mass spectrometer, and often the sample introduction process also, is under complete *data system* control on modern mass spectrometer

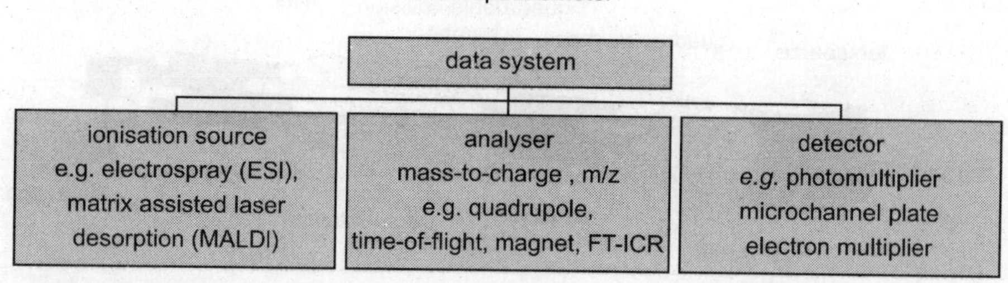

Fig. 1.79 : Showing the Functional Block Diagram of the Mass Spectrometry Process

Sample Introduction

The method of sample introduction to the ionisation source often depends on the ionisation method being used, as well as the type and complexity of the sample.

The sample can be inserted directly into the ionisation source, or can undergo some type of chromatography en route to the ionisation source. This latter method of sample introduction usually involves the mass spectrometer being coupled directly to a high pressure liquid chromatography (HPLC), gas chromatography (GC) or capillary electrophoresis (CE) separation column, and hence the sample is separated into a series of components which then enter the mass spectrometer sequentially for individual analysis.

Methods of sample ionisation

Many ionisation methods are available and each has its own advantages and disadvantages .The ionisation method to be used should depend on the type of sample under investigation and the mass spectrometer available.

Ionisation methods include the following:

Atmospheric Pressure Chemical Ionisation (APCI)

Chemical Ionisation (CI)

Electron Impact (EI)

Electrospray Ionisation (ESI)

Fast Atom Bombardment (FAB)

Field Desorption / Field Ionisation (FD/FI)

Matrix Assisted Laser Desorption Ionisation (MALDI)

Thermospray Ionisation (TSP)

The ionisation methods used for the majority of biochemical analyses are *Electrospray Ionisation (ESI)* and *Matrix Assisted Laser Desorption Ionisation (MALDI)*, and these are described in more detail in Sections 5 and 6 respectively.With most ionisation methods there is the possibility of creating both positively and negatively charged sample ions, depending on the proton affinity of the sample. Before embarking on an analysis, the user must decide whether to detect the positively or negatively charged ions (see section 7).

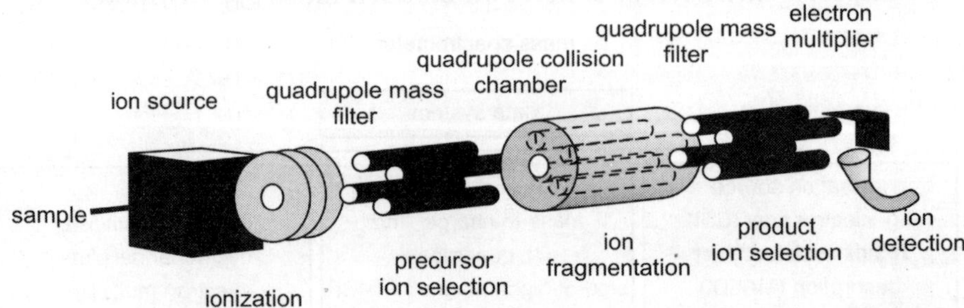

Fig. 1.80 : Showing the Schematic Diagram of the Triple Quadruple Mass Spectrometry Process

Analysis and Separation of Sample Ions

The main function of the *mass analyser* is to *separate* , or *resolve*, the ions formed in the ionisation source of the mass spectrometer according to their *mass-to-charge (m/z) ratios*. There are a number of mass analysers currently available, the better known of which include *quadrupoles* , *time-of-flight (TOF)* analysers, *magnetic sectors*, and both *Fourier transform* and *quadrupole ion traps*. These mass analysers have different features, including the m/z range that can be covered, the mass accuracy, and the achievable resolution. The compatibility of different analysers with different ionisation methods varies. For example, all of the analysers listed above can be used in conjunction with electrospray ionisation, whereas MALDI is not usually coupled to a quadrupole analyser.

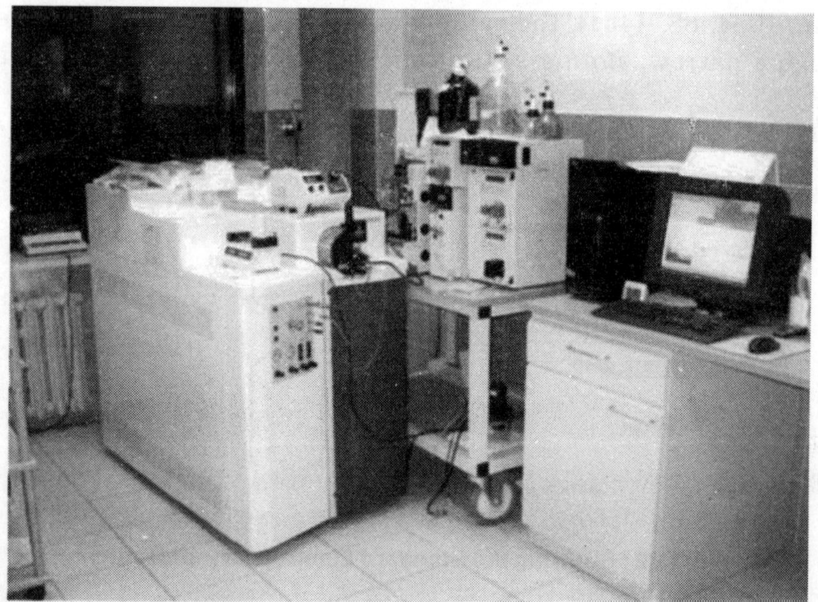

Fig. 1.81 : Showing the Tandem Mass Spectrophotometer in Author's Lab

Tandem (MS-MS) mass spectrometers are instruments that have more than one analyser and so can be used for structural and sequencing studies. Two, three and four analysers have all been incorporated into commercially available tandem instruments, and the analysers do not necessarily have to be of the same type, in which case the instrument is a hybrid one. More popular tandem mass spectrometers include those of the *quadrupole-quadrupole, magnetic sector-quadrupole*, and more recently, the *quadrupole-time-of-flight* geometries.

Detection and recording of Sample Ions

The *detector* monitors the ion current, amplifies it and the signal is then transmitted to the data system where it is recorded in the form of *mass spectra*. The *m/z* values of the ions are plotted against their *intensities* to show the *number of components* in the sample, the *molecular mass* of each component, and the *relative abundance* of the various components in the sample. The type of detector is supplied to suit the type of analyser; the more common ones are the *photomultiplier*, the *electron multiplier* and the *micro-channel plate* detectors.

Electrospray ionization and Electrospray Ionisation

Electrospray Ionisation (ESI) is one of the *Atmospheric Pressure Ionisation (API)* techniques and is well-suited to the analysis of polar molecules ranging from less than 100 Da to more than 1,000,000 Da in molecular mass. During standard electrospray ionisation (J. Fenn, J. Phys. Chem., 1984, 88, 4451), the sample is dissolved in a polar, volatile solvent and pumped through a narrow, *stainless steel capillary* (75 - 150 micrometers i.d.) at a flow

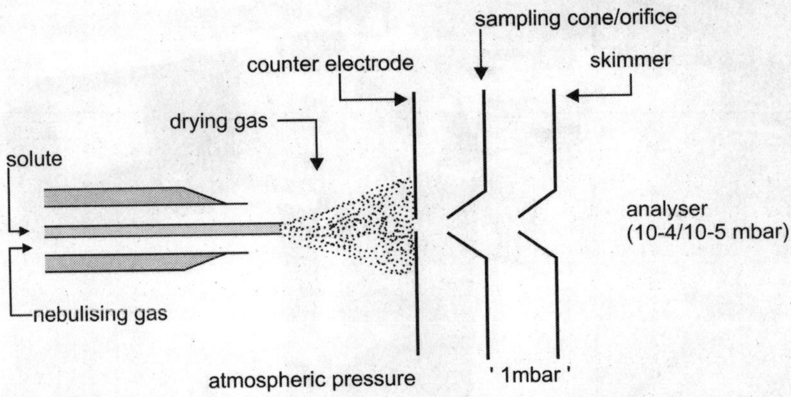

Fig. 1.82 : Showing the Standard Electrospary Ionization

rate of between 1 μL/min and 1 mL/min. A *high voltage* of 3 or 4 kV is applied to the tip of the capillary, which is situated within the ionisation source of the mass spectrometer, and as a consequence of this strong electric field, the sample emerging from the tip is dispersed into an *aerosol of highly charged droplets*, a process that is aided by a co-axially introduced *nebulising gas* flowing around the outside of the capillary. This gas, usually nitrogen, helps to direct the spray emerging from the capillary tip towards the mass spectrometer. The charged droplets diminish in size by solvent evaporation, assisted by a warm flow of nitrogen known as the *drying gas* which passes across the front of the ionisation source. Eventually charged sample ions, free from solvent, are released from the droplets, some of which pass through a *sampling cone* or orifice into an *intermediate vacuum region*, and from there through a small aperture into the analyser of the mass spectrometer, which is held under *high vacuum*. The lens voltages are optimised individually for each sample.

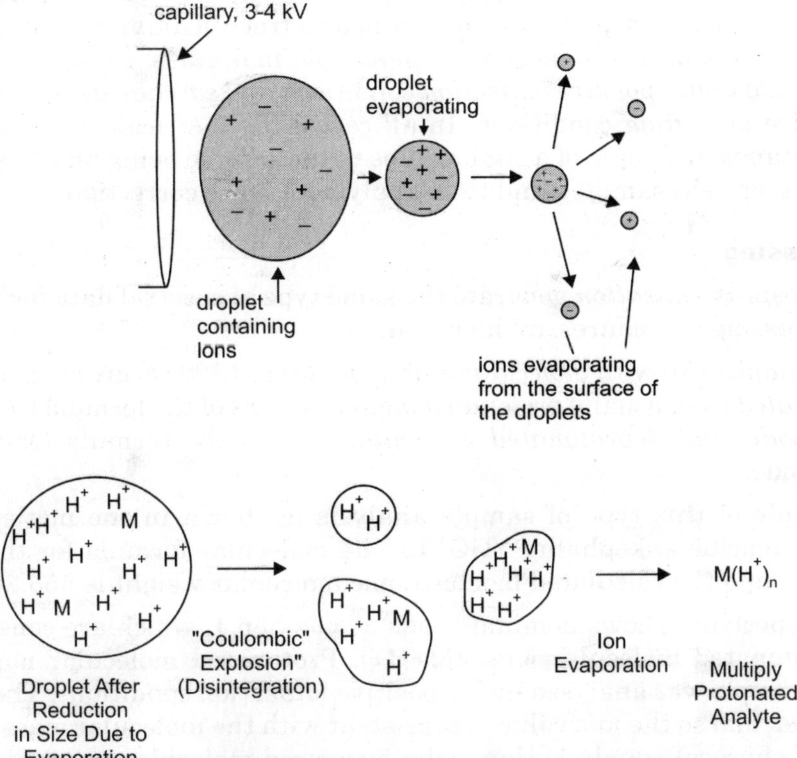

Fig. 1.83 and 183A: The electrospray ionisation process

Nanospray Ionisation

Nanospray ionisation (M. Wilm, M. Mann, Anal. Chem., 1996, 68, 1) is a *low flow rate* version of electrospray ionisation. A *small volume* (1-4 microL) of the sample dissolved in a suitable volatile solvent, at a concentration of ca. *1 - 10 pmol/microL*, is transferred into a miniature *sample vial*. A reasonably *high voltage* (ca. 700 - 2000 V) is applied to the specially manufactured gold-plated vial resulting in *sample ionisation* and spraying. The flow rate of solute and solvent using this procedure is very low, *30 - 1000 nL/min*, and so not only is far less sample consumed than with the standard electrospray ionisation technique, but also a small volume of sample lasts for several minutes, thus enabling *multiple experiments* to be performed. A common application of this technique is for a *protein digest* mixture to be analysed to generate a list of *molecular masses* for the components present, and then each component to be analysed further by *tandem mass spectrometric (MS-MS) amino acid sequencing* techniques.

ESI and *nanospray ionisation* are very sensitive analytical techniques but the sensitivity deteriorates with the presence of non-volatile buffers and other additives, which should be avoided as far as possible.

In *positive ionisation* mode, a trace of formic acid is often added to aid protonation of the sample molecules; in *negative ionisation* mode a trace of ammonia solution or a volatile amine is added to aid deprotonation of the sample molecules. *Proteins and peptides* are usually analysed under *positive ionisation* conditions and *saccharides and oligonucleotides* under *negative ionisation* conditions. In all cases, the m/z scale must be calibrated by analysing a standard sample of a similar type to the sample being analysed (e.g. a protein calibrant for a protein sample), and then applying a mass correction.

Data Processing

ESI and *nanospray ionisation* generate the same type of spectral data for samples, and so the data processing procedures are identical.

In ESI, samples (M) with *molecular masses up to ca. 1200 Da* give rise to *singly charged molecular-related ions*, usually *protonated molecular ions* of the formula (M+H)+ in *positive ionisation mode*, and *deprotonated molecular ions* of the formula (M-H)- in *negative ionisation* mode.

An example of this type of sample analysis is shown in the m/z spectrum of the pentapeptide leucine enkephalin, YGGFL. The molecular formula for this compound is C28H37N5O7 and the calculated monoisotopic molecular weight is 555.2692 Da.

The m/z spectrum shows dominant ions at m/z 556.1, which are consistent with the expected protonated molecular ions, (M+H+). Protonated molecular ions are expected because the sample was analysed under positive ionisation conditions. These m/z ions are *singly charged*, and so the m/z value is consistent with the molecular mass, as the value of z (number of charges) equals 1. Hence the measured molecular weight is deduced to be 555.1 Da, in good agreement with the theoretical value.

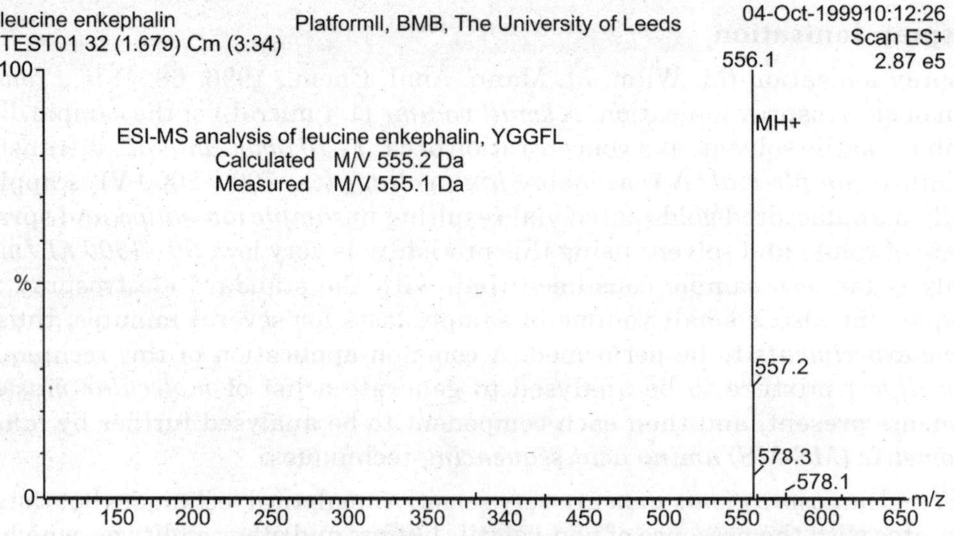

Fig. 1.84 : Positive ESI-MS m/z spectrum of leucine enkaphalin, YGGFL

The m/z spectrum also shows other ions of lower intensity (ca. 25 % of the m/z 556.1 ions) at m/z 557.2. These represent the molecule in which one 12C atom has been replaced by a 13C atom, because carbon has a naturally occurring isotope one atomic mass unit (Da) higher. The intensity of these isotopic ions relates to the relative abundance of the naturally occurring isotope multiplied by the total number of carbon atoms in the molecule. Additionally the fact that the 13C ions are one Da higher on the m/z scale than the 12C ions is an indication that z = 1, and hence the sample ions are singly charged. If the sample ions had been doubly charged, then the m/z values would only differ by 0.5 Da as z, the number of charges, would then be equal to 2.

The m/z spectrum also contains ions at m/z 578.1, some 23 Da higher than the expected molecular mass. These can be identified as the sodium adduct ions, (M+Na)+, and are quite common in electrospray ionisation. Instead of the sample molecules being ionised by the addition of a proton H+, some molecules have been ionised by the addition of a sodium cation Na+. Other common adduct ions include K+ (+39) and NH4+ (+18) in positive ionisation mode and Cl- (+35) in negative ionisation mode.

Electrospray ionisation is known as a 'soft' ionisation method as the sample is ionised by the addition or removal of a proton, with very little extra energy remaining to cause fragmentation of the sample ions.

Samples (M) with molecular weights greater than ca. 1200 Da give rise to multiply charged molecular-related ions such as (M+nH)n+ in positive ionisation mode and (M-nH)n- in negative ionisation mode. Proteins have many suitable sites for protonation as all of the backbone amide nitrogen atoms could be protonated theoretically, as well as certain amino acid side chains such as lysine and arginine which contain primary amine functionalities.

An example of multiple charging, which is practically unique to electrospray ionisation, is presented in the positive ionisation m/z spectrum of the protein hen egg white lysozyme.

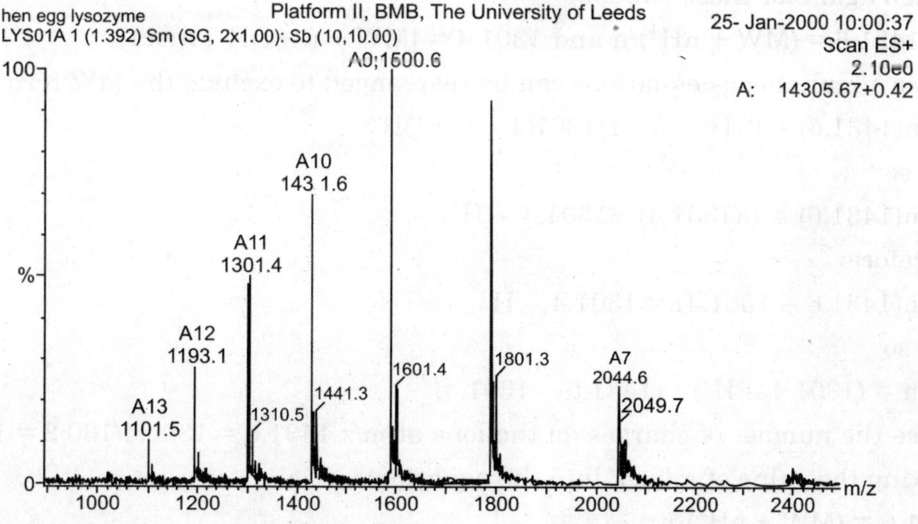

Fig. 1.85 : Positive ESI-MS m/z spectrum of the protien hen egg white lysozyme

The sample was analysed in a solution of 1:1 (v/v) acetonitrile : 0.1% aqueous formic acid and the m/z spectrum shows a Gaussian-type distribution of multiply charged ions ranging from m/z 1101.5 to 2044.6. Each peak represents the intact protein molecule carrying a different number of charges (protons). The peak width is greater than that of the singly charged ions seen in the leucine enkephalin spectrum, as the isotopes associated with these multiply charged ions are not clearly resolved as they were in the case of the singly charged ions. The individual peaks in the multiply charged series become closer together at lower m/z values and, because the molecular weight is the same for all of the peaks, those with more charges appear at lower m/z values than do those with fewer charges (M. Mann, C. K. Meng, J. B. Fenn, Anal. Chem., 1989, 61, 1702).

The m/z values can be expressed as follows:

$m/z = (MW + nH^+)/n$

where m/z = the mass-to-charge ratio marked on the abscissa of the spectrum;

MW = the molecular mass of the sample

n = the integer number of charges on the ions

H = the mass of a proton = 1.008 Da.

If the number of charges on an ion is known, then it is simply a matter of reading the m/z value from the spectrum and solving the above equation to determine the molecular weight of the sample. Usually the number of charges is not known, but can be calculated if the assumption is made that any two adjacent members in the series of multiply charged ions differ by one charge.

For example, if the ions appearing at m/z 1431.6 in the lysozyme spectrum have 'n' charges, then the ions at m/z 1301.4 will have "n+1" charges, and the above equation can be written again for these two ions:

$$1431.6 = (MW + nH^+)/n \text{ and } 1301.4 = [MW + (n+1)H^+]/(n+1)$$

These simultaneous equations can be rearranged to exclude the MW term:

$$n(1431.6) - nH+ = (n+1)1301.4 - (n+1)H^+$$

and so:

$$n(1431.6) = n(1301.4) + 1301.4 - H^+$$

therefore:

$$n(1431.6 - 1301.4) = 1301.4 - H^+$$

and so:

$$n = (1301.4 - H^+) / (1431.6 - 1301.4)$$

hence the number of charges on the ions at m/z 1431.6 = 1300.4/130.2 = 10.

Putting the value of n back into the equation:

$$1431.6 = (MW + nH^+)\ n$$

gives $1431.6 \times 10 = MW + (10 \times 1.008)$

and so $MW = 14{,}316 - 10.08$

therefore MW = 14,305.9 Da

The observed molecular mass is in good agreement with the theoretical molecular mass of hen egg lysozyme (based on average atomic masses) of 14305.14 Da. The individual isotopes cannot be resolved when the ions have a large number of charges, and so for proteins the average mass is measured.

This may seem long-winded but fortunately the molecular mass of the sample can be calculated automatically, or at least semi-automatically, by the processing software associated with the mass spectrometer. This is of great help for multi-component mixture analysis where the m/z spectrum may well contain several overlapping series of multiply charged ions, with each component exhibiting completely different charge states.

Using *electrospray* or *nanospray ionisation*, a *mass accuracy of within 0.01%* of the molecular mass should be achievable, which in this case represents +/- 1.4 Da.

In order to clarify electrospray/nanospray data, *molecular mass profiles* can be generated from the m/z spectra of high molecular mass, multiply charged samples. To achieve this, all the components are transposed onto a true molecular mass (or *zero charge state*) profile from which molecular masses can be read directly without any amendments or calculations.

The m/z spectrum of lysozyme has been converted to a molecular mass profile using Maximum Entropy processing and the data are shown. The mass profile is dominated by

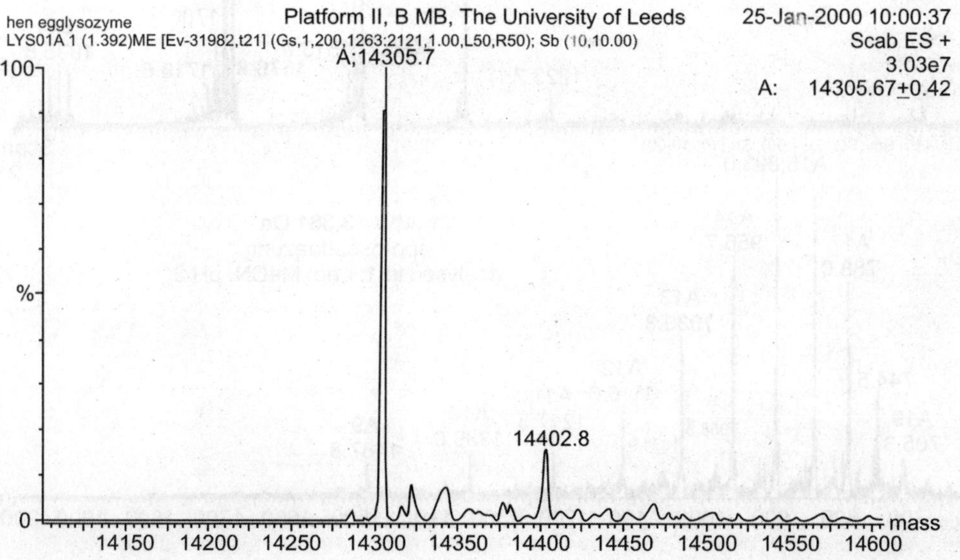

Fig. 1.86 : Molecular mass profile of lysozyme obtained by maximum entropy processing of the m/z spectrum

a component of molecular mass 14,305.7 Da, with a series of minor peaks at higher mass, which is usually indicative of salt adducting *e.g.* Na (M+23), K (M+39), H_2SO_4 or H_3PO_4 (M+98). The molecular masses can be read easily and unambiguously, and a good idea of the purity of the protein is obtained on inspection of the molecular mass profile.

Proteins in their native state, or at least containing a significant amount of folding, tend to produce multiply charged ions covering a smaller range of charge states (say two or three). These charge states tend to have fewer charges than an unfolded protein would have, due to the inaccessibility of many of the protonation sites. In such cases, increasing the *sampling cone voltage* may provide sufficient energy for the protein to begin to unfold and create a wider charge state distribution centering on more highly charged ions in the lower m/z region of the spectrum.

The differences in m/z spectra due to the folded state of the protein are illustrated with the m/z spectra of the protein apo-pseudoazurin acquired under different solvent conditions.

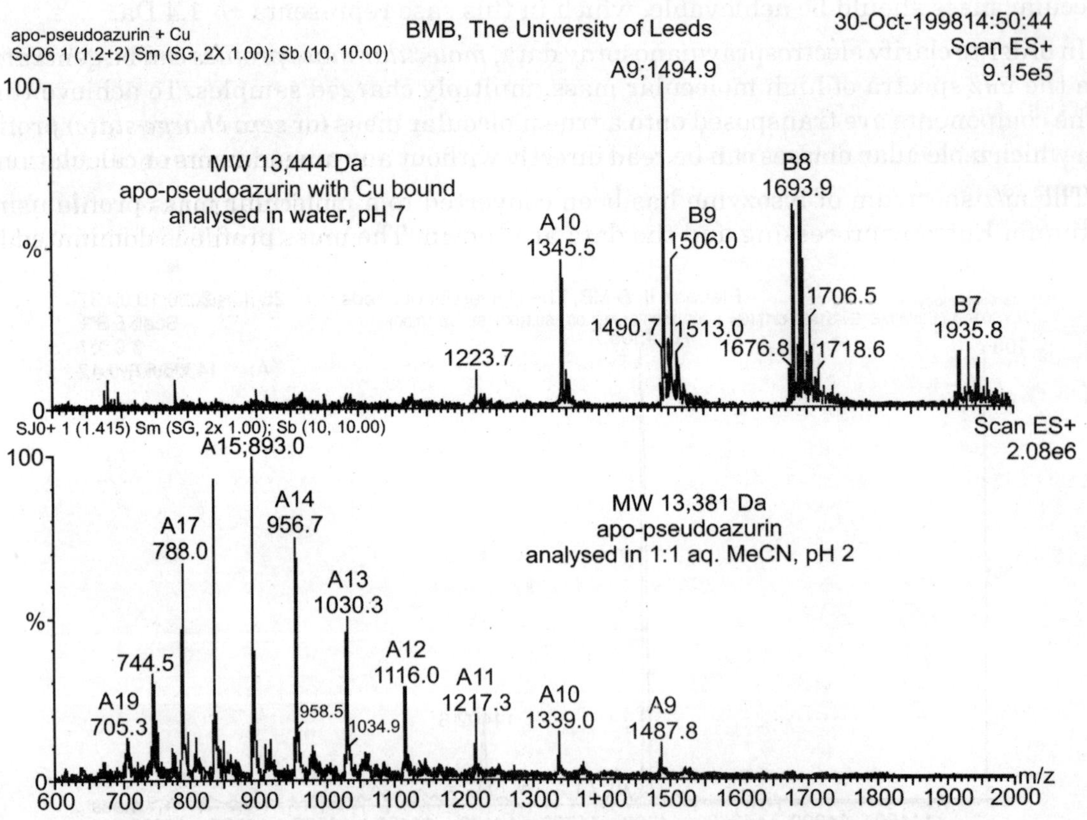

Fig. 1.87 : Positive ESI-MS m/z spectra of the protein apo-pseudoazurin analysed in water at pH7 (upper trace) and in 1:1 acetonitrile:0.1% aq. formic acid at pH2 (lower trace).

Analysis of the protein in 1:1 acetonitrile : 0.1% aqueous formic acid at pH2 gave a Gaussian-type distribution with multiply charged states ranging from n = 9 at m/z 1487.8 to n = 19 at m/z 705.3, centering on n = 15 (lower trace). The molecular mass for this protein was 13,381 Da. Analysis of the protein in water gave fewer charge states, from n = 7 at m/z 1921.7 to n = 11 at m/z 1223.7, centering at n = 9 (upper trace). Not only has the charge state distribution changed, the molecular weight is now 13,444 Da which represents an increase of 63 Da and indicates that copper is remaining bound to the protein. Many types of *protein complexes* can be observed in this way, including *protein-ligand, protein-peptide, protein-metal and protein-RNA macromolecules.*

Matrix Assisted Laser Desorption Ionisation (MALDI) (F. Hillenkamp, M. Karas, R. C. Beavis, B. T. Chait, Anal. Chem., 1991, 63, 1193) deals well with thermolabile, non-volatile organic compounds especially those of high molecular mass and is used successfully in biochemical areas for the analysis of *proteins, peptides, glycoproteins, oligosaccharides,* and *oligonucleotides*. It is relatively straightforward to use and reasonably tolerant to buffers and other additives. The mass accuracy depends on the type and performance of the analyser of the mass spectrometer, but most modern instruments should be capable of measuring masses to within 0.01% of the molecular mass of the sample, at least up to ca. 40,000 Da.

MALDI is based on the *bombardment* of sample molecules with a *laser* light to bring about *sample ionisation*. The sample is pre-mixed with a highly absorbing *matrix* compound for the most consistent and reliable results, and a low concentration of sample to matrix works best. The matrix transforms the laser energy into *excitation energy* for the sample, which leads to sputtering of analyte and matrix ions from the surface of the mixture. In this way energy transfer is efficient and also the analyte molecules are spared excessive direct energy that may otherwise cause decomposition. Most commercially available MALDI mass spectrometers now have a pulsed nitrogen laser of wavelength 337 nm.

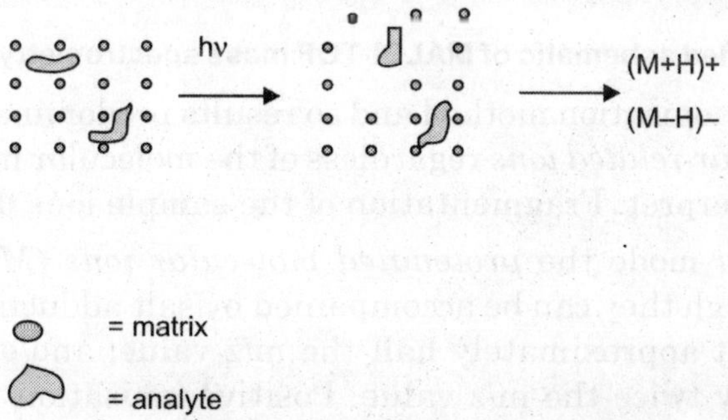

Fig. 1.88 : Matrix assisted laser desorption ionisation (MALDI)

The sample to be analysed is dissolved in an appropriate volatile solvent, usually with a trace of trifluoroacetic acid if positive ionisation is being used, at a concentration of ca. 10 pmol/mL and an aliquot (1-2 mL) of this removed and mixed with an equal volume of a solution containing a vast excess of a matrix. A range of compounds is suitable for use as matrices: *sinapinic acid* is a common one for protein analysis while alpha-cyano-4-hydroxycinnamic acid is often used for peptide analysis. An aliquot (1-2 mL) of the final solution is applied to the sample target which is allowed to dry prior to insertion into the high vacuum of the mass spectrometer. The laser is fired, the energy arriving at the sample/matrix surface optimised, and data accumulated until a m/z spectrum of reasonable intensity has been amassed. The time-of-flight analyser separates ions according to their *mass(m)-to-charge(z) (m/z)* ratios by measuring the time it takes for ions to travel through a field free region known as the flight, or drift, tube. The heavier ions are slower than the lighter ones.

The m/z scale of the mass spectrometer is *calibrated* with a known sample that can either be analysed independently (external calibration) or pre-mixed with the sample and matrix (internal calibration).

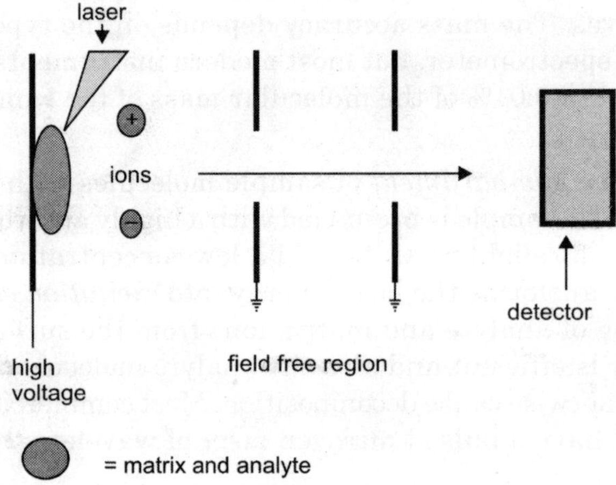

Fig. 1.89 : Simplified schematic of MALDI-TOF mass spectrometry (linear mode)

MALDI is also a 'soft' ionisation method and so results predominantly in the generation of *singly charged molecular-related ions* regardless of the molecular mass, hence the spectra are relatively easy to interpret. Fragmentation of the sample ions does not usually occur.

In *positive ionisation* mode the *protonated molecular ions (M+H+)* are usually the dominant species, although they can be accompanied by salt adducts, a trace of the doubly charged molecular ion at approximately half the m/z value, and/or a trace of a dimeric species at approximately twice the m/z value. Positive ionisation is used in general for *protein* and *peptide* analyses.

In *negative ionisation* mode the *deprotonated molecular ions (M-H-)* are usually the most abundant species, accompanied by some salt adducts and possibly traces of dimeric or doubly charged materials. Negative ionisation can be used for the analysis of *oligonucleotides* and *oligosaccharides*.

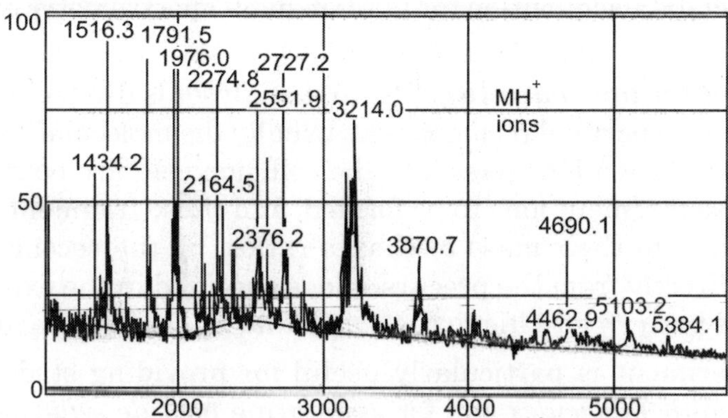

Fig. 1.90 : Positive ionisation MALDI m/z spectrum of a peptide mixture using alpha-cyano-4-hydroxycinnamic acid as matrix. Positive or negative ionisation?

If the sample has functional groups that readily accept a proton (H+) then positive ion detection is used e.g. amines R-NH2 + H+ = R-NH3+ as in proteins or peptides.

If the sample has functional groups that readily lose a proton then negative ion detection is used *e.g. carboxylic acids* $R\text{-}CO_2H = R\text{-}CO_2$- and *alcohols R-OH = R-O-* as in *saccharides* or *oligonucleotides.*

Tandem mass spectrometry (MS-MS): Structural and sequence information from mass spectrometry.

Tandem mass spectrometry (MS-MS) is used to produce *structural information* about a compound by fragmenting specific sample ions inside the mass spectrometer and identifying the resulting fragment ions. This information can then be pieced together to generate structural information regarding the intact molecule. Tandem mass spectrometry also enables specific compounds to be detected in complex mixtures on account of their specific and characteristic fragmentation patterns.

A *tandem mass spectrometer* is a mass spectrometer that has more than one analyser, in practice usually two. The two analysers are separated by a collision cell into which an inert gas (e.g. argon, xenon) is admitted to collide with the selected sample ions and bring about their fragmentation. The analysers can be of the same or of different types, the most common combinations being:

- quadrupole - quadrupole
- magnetic sector - quadrupole
- magnetic sector - magnetic sector
- quadrupole - time-of-flight.

Fragmentation experiments can also be performed on certain single analyser mass spectrometers such as ion trap and time-of-flight instruments, the latter type using a post-source decay experiment to effect the fragmentation of sample ions.

The basic modes of data acquisition for tandem mass spectrometry experiments are as follows:

Product or daughter ion scanning: The first analyser is used to select user-specified sample ions arising from a particular component; usually the molecular-related (i.e. (M+H)+ or (M-H)-) ions. These chosen ions pass into the collision cell, are bombarded by the gas molecules which cause fragment ions to be formed, and these fragment ions are analysed i.e. separated according to their mass to charge ratios, by the second analyser. All the fragment ions arise directly from the precursor ions specified in the experiment, and thus produce a fingerprint pattern specific to the compound under investigation.

This type of experiment is particularly useful for providing structural information concerning *small organic molecules* and for generating *peptide sequence* information.

Precursor or parent ion scanning: He first analyser allows the transmission of all sample ions, whilst the second analyser is set to monitor specific fragment ions, which are generated by bombardment of the sample ions with the collision gas in the collision cell. This type of experiment is particularly useful for monitoring groups of compounds contained within a mixture which fragment to produce common fragment ions, *e.g. glycosylated peptides* in a tryptic digest mixture, *aliphatic hydrocarbons* in an oil sample, or *glucuronide conjugates* in urine.

***Constant neutral loss scanning*:** This involves both analysers scanning, or collecting data, across the whole m/z range, but the two are off-set so that the second analyser allows only those ions which differ by a certain number of mass units (equivalent to a neutral fragment) from the ions transmitted through the first analyser. *e.g.* This type of experiment could be used to monitor all of the carboxylic acids in a mixture. Carboxylic acids tend to fragment by losing a (neutral) molecule of carbon dioxide, CO_2, which is equivalent to a loss of 44 Da or atomic mass units. All ions pass through the first analyser into the collision cell. The ions detected from the collision cell are those from which 44 Da have been lost.

***Selected/multiple reaction monitoring*:** Both of the analysers are static in this case as user-selected specific ions are transmitted through the first analyser and user-selected specific fragments arising from these ions are measured by the second analyser. The compound under scrutiny must be known and have been well-characterised previously before this type of experiment is undertaken. This methodology is used to confirm unambiguously the presence of a compound in a matrix e.g. drug testing with blood or urine samples. It is not only a highly specific method but also has very high sensitivity.

Peptide Sequencing by Tandem Mass Spectrometry

The most common usage of MS-MS in biochemical areas is the *product or daughter ion scanning* experiment which is particularly successful for *peptide* and *nucleotide sequencing.*

Peptide sequencing: $H_2N\text{-}CH(R')\text{-}CO\text{-}NH\text{-}CH(R'')\text{-}CO_2H$

Peptides fragment in a reasonably well-documented manner (P. Roepstorrf, J. Fohlmann, Biomed. Mass Spectrom., 1984, 11, 601; R. S. Johnson, K. Biemann, Biomed. Environ. Mass Spectrom., 1989, 18, 945). The protonated molecules fragment along the *peptide backbone* and also show some *side-chain fragmentation* with certain instruments (Four-Sector Tandem Mass Spectrometry of Peptides, A. E. Ashcroft, P. J. Derrick in "Mass Spectrometry of Peptides" ed. D. M. Desiderio, CRC Press, Florida, 1990).

There are three different types of bonds that can fragment along the amino acid backbone: the *NH-CH, CH-CO*, and *CO-NH* bonds. Each bond breakage gives rise to two species, one neutral and the other one charged, and only the charged species is monitored by the mass spectrometer. The charge can stay on either of the two fragments depending on the chemistry and relative proton affinity of the two species. Hence there are six possible fragment ions for each amino acid residue and these are labelled as in the diagram, with the *a, b,* and *c''* ions having the charge retained on the *N-terminal fragment*, and the *x, y''*, and *z ions* having the charge retained on the *C-terminal fragment*. The most common cleavage sites are at the CO-NH bonds which give rise to the b and/or the *y''* ions. The mass difference between two adjacent b ions, or *y''*; ions, is indicative of a particular amino acid residue (see Table of amino acid residues at the end of this document).

X3 Y3 Z3 X2 Y2 Z2 X1 Y1 Z1

R1 O R2 O R3 O R4

H2N — CH- -C- -NH -CH -C- -NH -CH -C- -NH- -CH — COOH

A1 B1 C1 A2 B2 C2 A2 B3 C3

b2–b1 = amino acid

B2 – B1 = amino acid

R1 R3 O R4

H2N— CH — C ≡ O (+) H3N(+)— CH — C — NH — CH — COOH

b and y" ions are

B1 Y2"

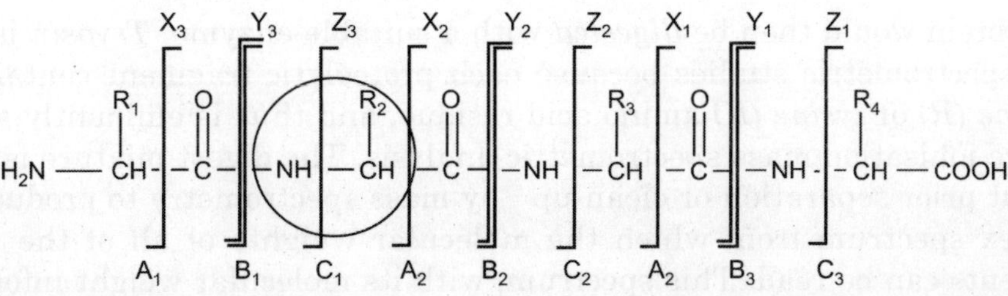

Fig. 1.91 : Peptide sequencing by tandem mass spectrometry - backbone cleavages

The extent of *side-chain fragmentation* detected depends on the type of analysers used in the mass spectrometer. A magnetic sector - magnetic sector instrument will give rise to *high energy* collisions resulting in many different types of side-chain cleavages. Quadrupole - quadrupole and quadrupole - time-of-flight mass spectrometers generate low energy fragmentations with fewer types of side-chain fragmentations.

Immonium ions (labelled '*i*') appear in the very low m/z range of the MS-MS spectrum. Each amino acid residue leads to a diagnostic immonium ion, with the exception of the two pairs leucine (L) and iso-leucine (I), and lysine (K) and glutamine (Q), which produce immonium ions with the same m/z ratio, *i.e.* m/z 86 for I and L, m/z 101 for K and Q. The immonium ions are useful for detecting and confirming many of the amino acid residues in a peptide, although no information regarding the position of these amino acid residues in the peptide sequence can be ascertained from the immonium ions.

An example of an *MS/MS daughter or product ion spectrum* is illustrated below. The molecular mass of the peptide was measured using standard mass spectrometric techniques and found to be 680.4 Da, the dominant ions in the MS spectrum being the protonated molecular ions ($M+H^+$) at m/z 681.4. These ions were selected for transmission through the first analyser, then fragmented in the collision cell and their fragments analysed by the second analyser to produce the following MS/MS spectrum. The *sequence* (*amino acid backbone*) ions have been identified, and in this example the peptide fragmented predominantly at the *CO-NH* bonds and gave both *b* and *y* ions. (Often either the b series or the *y*" series predominates, sometimes to the exclusion of the other). The *b* series ions have been labelled with blue vertical lines and the *y*" series ions have been labelled with red vertical lines. The mass difference between adjacent members of a series can be calculated *e.g.* b3 – b2 = 391.21 – 262.16 = 129.05 Da which is equivalent to a glutamine (E) amino acid residue; and similarly *y*4 - *y*3 = 567.37 – 420.27 = 147.10 Da which is equivalent to a phenylalanine (F) residue. In this way, using either the b series or the *y*" series, the amino acid sequence of the peptide can be determined and was found to be NFESGK (n.b. the *y*" series reads from right to left!). The immonium ions at m/z 102 merely confirm the presence of the glutamine (E) residue in the peptide.

A protein identification study would proceed as follows:

(*a*) The *protein* under investigation would be analysed by mass spectrometry to generate a molecular mass to within an accuracy of 0.01%.

(*b*) The protein would then be *digested* with a suitable enzyme. *Trypsin* is useful for mass spectrometric studies because each proteolytic fragment contains a basic *arginine (R)* or *lysine (K)* amino acid residue, and thus is eminently suitable for positive ionisation mass spectrometric analysis. The digest mixture is analysed - without prior separation or clean-up - by mass spectrometry to produce a rather complex spectrum from which the molecular weights of all of the proteolytic fragments can be read. This spectrum, with its molecular weight information, is called a *peptide map*. (If the protein already exists on a *database*, then the peptide

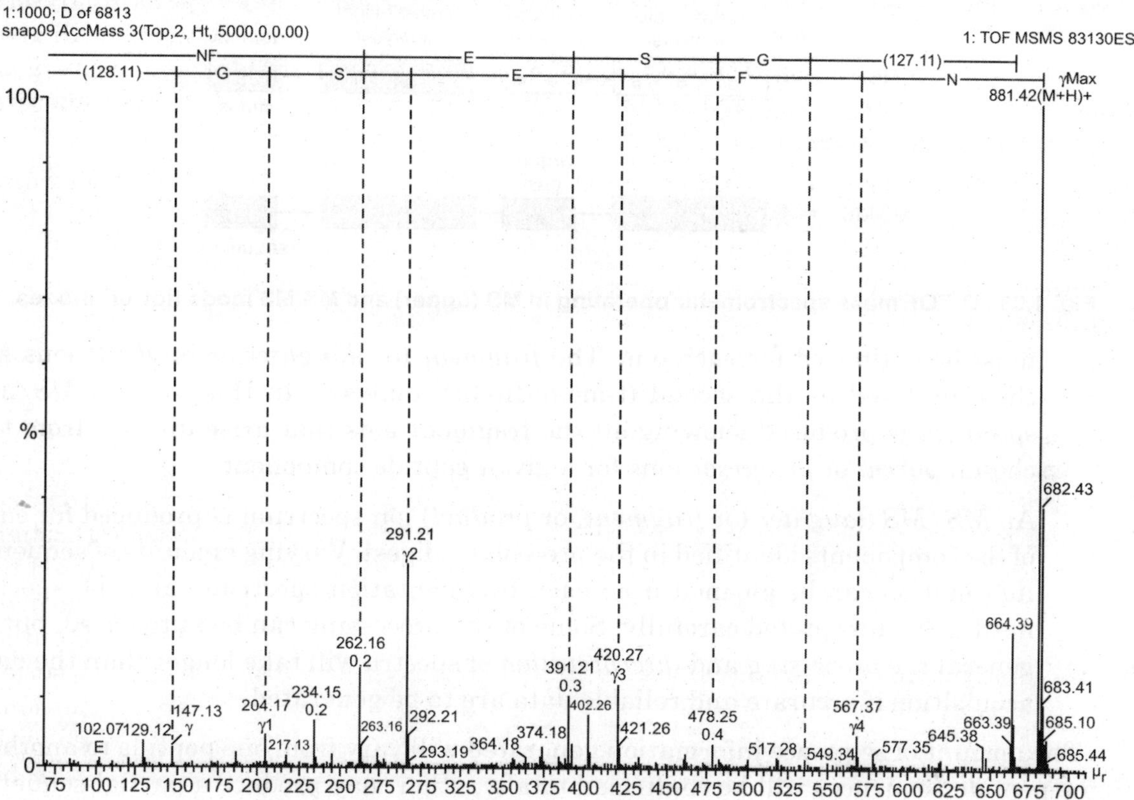

Fig. 1.92 : Peptide sequencing by tandem mass spectrometry—an MS-MS daughter or product ion spectrum

map is often sufficient to confirm the protein.) For these experiments the mass spectrometer would be operated in the "MS" mode, whereby the sample is sprayed and ionised from the nanospray needle and the ions pass through the sampling cone, skimmer lenses, Rf hexapole focusing system, and the first (quadrupole) analyser. The quadrupole in this instance is not used as an analyser, merely as a lens to focus the ion beam into the second (time-of-flight) analyser which separates the ions according to their mass-to-charge ratio.

(*c*) With the digest mixture still spraying into the mass spectrometer, the Q-Tof mass spectrometer is switched into *'MS/MS'* mode. The protonated molecular ions of each of the digest fragments can be independently selected and transmitted through the quadrupole analyser, which is now used as an analyser to transmit solely the ions of interest into the *collision cell* which lies inbetween the first and second analysers. An inert gas such as argon is introduced into the collision cell and the sample ions are bombarded by the collision gas molecules which cause them to fragment. The optimum collision cell conditions vary from peptide to peptide and

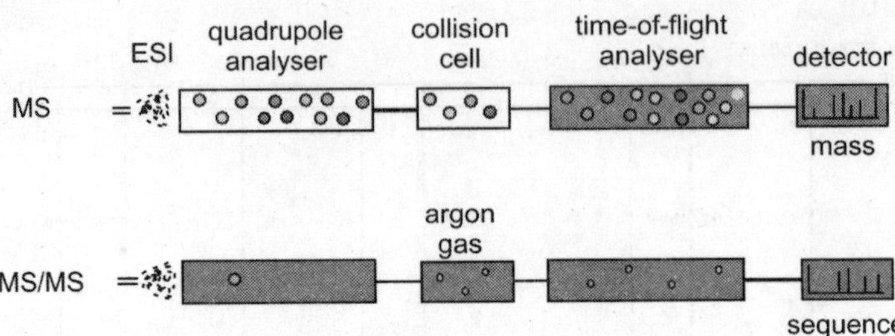

Fig. 1.93 : Q-TOF mass spectrometer operating in MS (upper) and MS/MS mode (lower) modes.

must be optimised for each one. The *fragment* (or *daughter* or *product*) ions are then analysed by the second (time-of-flight) analyser. In this way an *MS/MS spectrum* is produced showing all the fragment ions that arise directly from the chosen *parent* or *precursor* ions for a given peptide component.

An *MS/MS daughter* (or *fragment*, or *product*) ion spectrum is produced for each of the components identified in the proteolytic digest. Varying amounts of sequence information can be gleaned from each fragmentation spectrum, and the spectra need to be interpreted carefully. Some of the processing can be automated, but in general the *processing* and *interpretation* of spectra will take longer than the data acquisition if accurate and reliable data are to be generated.

The amount of sequence information generated will vary from one peptide to another, Some peptide sequences will be confirmed totally, other may produce a partial sequence of, say, 4 or 5 amino acid residues. Often sequence 'tag' of 4 or 5 residues is sufficient to search a protein database and confirm the identity of the protein.

Peptide Sequencing in Summary

Peptides fragment along the amino acid backbone to give sequence information.

Peptides ca. 2500 Da or less produce the most useful data.

The amount of sequence information varies from one peptide to another. Some peptides can generate sufficient information for a full sequence to be determined; others may generate a partial sequence of 4 or 5 amino acids.

A protein digest can be analysed as an entire reaction mix, without any separation of the products, from which individual peptides are selected and analysed by the mass spectrometer to generate sequence information.

About 4 mL of solution is required for the analysis of the digest mixture, with a concentration based on the original protein of ca. 1-10 pmol/mL. MS/MS sequencing is a sensitive technique consuming little sample.

Sometimes the full protein sequence can be verified; some proteins generate sufficient information to cover only part of the sequence. 70 - 80% coverage is reasonable.

Often a sequence 'tag' of 4/5 amino acids from a single proteolytic peptide is sufficient to identify the protein from a database.

The final point in this summary means that mass spectrometers have been found to be extremely useful for *proteomic* studies, as illustrated below.

The proteomics procedure usually involves excising individual spots from a *2-D gel* and independently enzymatically digesting the protein(s) contained within each spot, before analysing the digest mixture by mass spectrometer in the manner outlined above. Electrospray ionisation or MALDI could be used at this step.

The initial *MS spectrum* determining the *molecular masses* of all of the components in the digest mixture can often provide sufficient information to search a *database* using just several of the molecular weights from this *peptide map*.

If the database search is not fruitful, either because the protein has not been catalogued, is previously uncharacterised, or the data are not accurate or comprehensive enough to distinguish between several entries in the database, then further information is required.

This can be achieved by sample clean-up and then MS/MS studies to determine the amino acid sequences of the individual proteolytic peptides contained in the digest mixture, with which further database searching can be carried out.

Oligonucleotide Sequencing by Tandem Mass Spectrometry

Oligonucleotide sequencing: P-S(B)-P-S(B)-P-S(B)

Oligonucleotide sequencing can also be achieved by *tandem mass spectrometry* although it is not so well documented. However *fragmentation patterns* have been established and reported (S. Pomerantz, J. A. Kowalak, J. A. McClosky, J. Amer. Soc. Mass Spectrom., 1993, 4, 204). The experimental principle is similar to that of peptide sequencing, in that individual species are mass measured in *MS mode* of instrument operation, and then their *molecular-related ions* selected by the first (*quadrupole*) analyser to be transmitted into the collision cell where they undergo *fragmentation* after bombardment with a *collision gas*. The fragments are analysed by the second (*time-of-flight*) analyser to produce an *MS/MS product*, or *daughter, ion spectrum* showing all the fragment ions that arise directly from the chosen *parent* or *precursor ions*.

Negative electrospray ionisation is often the preferred ionisation method. The optimisation of the fragmentation conditions varies from component to component and diligence must be taken to ensure the best conditions are employed.

Data processing and interpretation is again of paramount importance for accurate, reliable results and hence sequence information.

Table of amino acid residues

Symbol	Structure	Mass (Da)
Ala A	$-NH.CH.(CH_3).CO-$	71.0
Arg R	$-NH.CH.[(CH_2)_3.NH.C(NH).NH_2].CO-$	156.1
Asn N	$-NH.CH.(CH_2CONH_2).CO-$	114.0
Asp D	$-NH.CH.(CH_2COOH).CO-$	115.0
Cys C	$-NH.CH.(CH_2SH).CO-$	103.0
Gln Q	$-NH.CH.(CH_2CH_2CONH_2).CO-$	128.1
Glu E	$-NH.CH.(CH_2CH_2COOH).CO-$	129.0
Gly G	$-NH.CH_2.CO-$	57.0
His H	$-NH.CH.(CH_2C_3H_3N_2).CO-$	137.1
Ile I	$-NH.CH.[CH.(CH_3)CH_2.CH_3].CO-$	113.1
Leu	$-NH.CH.[CH_2CH(CH_3)_2].CO-$	113.1
Lys K	$-NH.CH.[(CH_2)_4NH_2].CO-$	128.1
Met M	$-NH.CH.[(CH_2)2.SCH_3].CO-$	131.0
Phe F	$-NH.CH.(CH_2Ph).CO-$	147.1
Pro P	$-NH.(CH_2)_3.CH.CO-$	97.1
Ser S	$-NH.CH.(CH_2OH).CO-$	87.0
Thr T	$-NH.CH.[CH(OH)CH_3).CO-$	101.0
Trp W	$-NH.CH.[CH_2.C_8H_6N].CO-$	186.1
Tyr Y	$-NH.CH.[(CH_2).C_6H_4.OH].CO-$	163.1
Val V	$-NH.CH.[CH(CH_3)_2].CO-$	99.1

MALDI PROCESS AND ITS APPLICATIONS

Introduction

Matrix-assisted laser desorption/ionization (MALDI) is one of the two 'soft' ionization techniques besides electrospray ionization (ESI) which allow for the sensitive detection of large, non-volatile and labile molecules by mass spectrometry. Over the past 15 years, MALDI has developed into an indispensable tool in analytical chemistry, and in analytical biochemistry in particular. This subhead will introduce the reader to the technology as it stands now, and will discuss some of the underlying physical and chemical mechanisms as far as they have been investigated and clarified to date. It will concentrate on the central issues of MALDI, necessary for the user to understand for an efficient application of the technique. An in-depth discussion of these topics would be beyond the scope of this chapter, and hence the reader is referred to recent reviews]. The details about the current state of instrumentation including the lasers and their coupling to the mass spectrometers will be presented in following subheads.

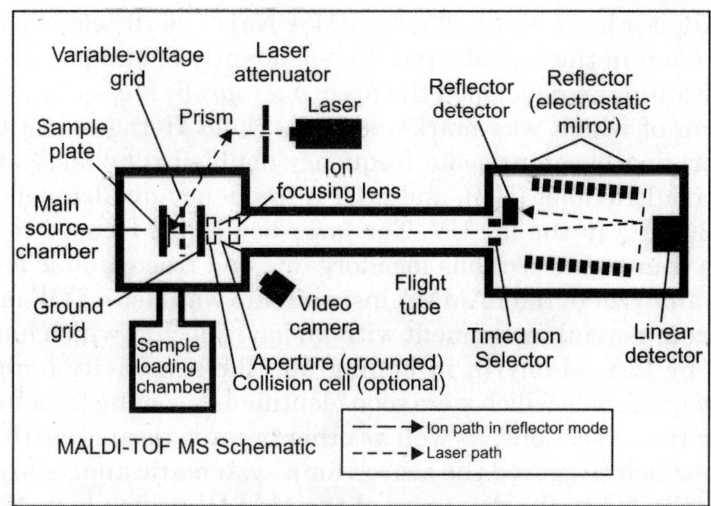

Fig. 1.94 : Showing the Schematic Diagram of MALDI Process

As with most new technologies, MALDI came as a surprise even to the experts in the field on the one hand, but also evolved from a diversity of prior art and knowledge on the other hand. The original notion had been that (bio) molecules with masses in excess of about 500-1000 Da could not be isolated out of their natural (*e.g.,* aqueous) environment, and even less be charged for an analysis in the vacuum of a mass spectrometer without excessive and unspecific fragmentation. During the late 1960s, Beckey introduced *field desorption* (FD), the first technique which opened a small road into the territory of mass spectrometry (MS) of bioorganic molecules. Next came *secondary ion mass spectrometry* (SIMS), and in particular static SIMS, introduced by A. Benninghoven in 1975. This development was taken a step further by M. Barber in 1981 with the introduction of SIMS of organic compounds dissolved in glycerol, which he coined *fast atom bombardment* (FAB). It was in this context, and in conjunction with first attempts to desorbs organic molecules with laser irradiation, that the concept of a 'matrix' as a means of facilitating desorption and enhancing ion yield was born. The principle of desorption by a bombardment of organic samples with the fission products of the 252Cf nuclear decay, later called *plasma desorption* (PD) was published by R. Macfarlane in 1974. Subsequently, the groups of Sundqvist and Roepstoff greatly improved the analytical potential of this technique by the addition of nitrocellulose, which not only cleaned up the sample but was also suspected of functioning as a signal-enhancing matrix. The first attempts to use laser radiation to generate ions for a mass spectrometric analysis were published only a few years after the invention of the laser. Vastola and Pirone had already demonstrated the spectra of organic compounds, recorded with a time-of-flight (TOF) mass spectrometer. Several groups continued to pursue this line of research, mainly R. Cotter at Johns Hopkins University in the USA and P. Kistemaker at the FOM Institute in Amsterdam, the Netherlands. For a number of years the Amsterdam group held the high mass record for a bioorganic analyte with a spectrum of underivatized digitonin at mass 1251Da ([M + Na]+), desorbed with a CO_2-laser at a wavelength of 10.6/μm in the far infrared. Independently of and parallel to these groups, Hillenkamp and Kaufmann developed the *laser microprobe mass analyzer* (LAMMA), the commercial version of which was marketed by Leybold Heraeus in Cologne, Germany. The instrument originally comprised a frequency-doubled ruby laser at a wavelength of 347 nm in the near ultraviolet (UV), and later a frequency-quadrupled ND:YAG-laser at a wavelength of 266 nm in the far UV. The laser beam was focused to a spot of <1/m in diameter to probe thin tissue sections for inorganic and trace atomic ions such as Na, K, and Fe. The mass analyzer of the LAMMA instruments was also a TOF mass spectrometer, and was the first commercial instrument with an ion reflector, which had been invented a few years earlier by B.A. Mamyrin in Leningrad. The sensitivity-limiting 'noise' of the LAMMA spectra were signals which were soon identified as coming from the organic polymer used to embed the tissue sections, as well as other organic tissue constituents. It was this background noise which triggered the search for a systematic analysis of organic samples and which eventually led to the discovery of the MALDI principle in 1984. The principle and its acronym were published in 1985 and the first spectrum of the non-volatile bee venom mellitin, an oligopeptide at mass 2845 Da in 1986. Spectra of proteins with masses exceeding 10 kDa and 100 kDa were published in 1988 and presented at the International Mass Spectrometry Conference in Bordeaux in 1988, respectively. ESI and MALDI were developed independently but concurrently, and when their potential for the desorption of non-volatile, fragile (bio)molecules was discovered people were mostly impressed by their ability to access the high mass range, particularly of proteins. However, FAB- and PD-MS had at that time already generated spectra of trypsin at mass 23 kDa and other high-mass proteins. What reallybmade the difference in particular for the biologists was the stunning sensitivity which, for the first time, made MS compatible with sample preparation techniques used in these fields. For MALDI, the minimum amount of protein needed for a spectrum of high quality was reduced from 1 pmol in 1988 to a few femtomoles only about a year later. Today, in favourable cases, the level is now down in the lowomole range. Many other developments - both instrumental as well as specific sample preparation recipes and assays - took place during the following decade, and the joint impact of all of these together has today made MALDI-MS an indispensable tool not only in the life sciences but also in polymer analysis. The use of a chemical matrix in the form of small, laser-absorbing organic molecules in large excess over the analyte is at the core of the MALDI principle. Several developments for laser desorption schemes took place in parallel to and following publication of the MALDI principle. These all attempt to replace the chemical matrix by a more easy-to-handle physical matrix, or a more simple combination of the two. The best known of

these is the system of Tanaka and coworkers, which was first presented at a Sino-Japanese conference in 1987; details were subsequently published in 1988. The matrix comprises Co-nanoparticles suspended in glycerol as the basic system into which the analyte is dissolved, similar to the sample preparation of FAB. Several other nano- and micro-particles were tested later. For his technique, *surface-assisted laser desorption/ionization* (SALDI), Sunner and co-workers used dry carbon and graphite substrates. This method, termed *desorption/ionization on silicon* (DIOS), uses preparations of neat organicsamples on porous silicon. Several other methods and acronyms use similar systems such as nanowires or sol-gel systems. All of these methods use the substrate on which the analyte is prepared for the absorption of the laser energy, and are characterized by a sensitivity lower than that of MALDI by several orders of magnitude, as well as a strongly increased ion fragmentation which limits the accessible mass range to somewhere between 2000 and 30000Da, depending on the method. There is reason to believe that all of these methods are based on a thermal desorption at the substrate/analyte interface with the high internal excitation of the ions and low ion yield typical for thermal desorption processes. The very high heating and cooling rates, together with high peak temperatures of the substrates as well as the suspension of the absorbers in glycerol, apparently somewhat soften the desorption, the latter most probably through adiabatic cooling in the expanding plume; derivatization of the surfaces can up-concentrate the analyte of interest at the surfaces to increase the sensitivity. Indeed, a yoctomole (10–21 mole) sensitivity has been achieved in this way with a perfluorophenyl-derivatized DIOS system for a small hydrophobic peptide
.

Analyte Incorporation

What, then is so special about the chemical matrix in MALDI? Some of its important features such as the absorption of the laser energy are easily understood, but surprisingly the overall process of the desorption and ionization has not yet

Analyte Incorporation been fully described, almost 20 years after the invention. As a result, the search for better matrices in general or for specific application still remain mostly empirical. One important feature is the way in which the matrix and analyte interact in the MALDI sample. In a typical UV-MALDI sample preparation small volumes of an about 10–6 M solution of the analyte and a near-saturated (ca. 0.1 M) solution of the matrix are mixed; the solvent is then evaporated before the sample can be introduced into the vacuum of the mass spectrometer. Upon solvent evaporation, the matrix crystallizes to form a bed of small crystals that range in size from a few to a few hundred micrometers, depending on the matrix and the details of the preparation. The typical molar analyte to matrix ratio ranges from about 10–2 for small molecules to ca. 10–4 for large proteins. The sample preparation is discussed in more detail in Section 1.8. One of the early surprises in the MALDI development was that all of the well-functioning matrices incorporate the analyte in the crystals quantitatively (up to a maximum concentration) and in a homogeneous (on the light microscopic resolution level of 0.5μm) distribution. This was shown for the UV-MALDI matrices 2,5-dihydroxybenzoic acid (2,5-DHB), sinapinic acid and 4-hydroxy-α-cyanocinnamic acid (HCCA), 3-hydroxy-picolinic acid and the IR-MALDI matrix succinic acid. This homogeneous incorporation, in conjunction with the also homogeneous energy deposition and material ablation result in the co-desorption of intact non-volatile and labile molecules with the matrix and, in addition, to their cooling of internal energy in the expanding plume of material. The mechanisms and driving force for this incorporation are still largely unknown. Horneffer *et al.* have shown in a systematic study of different position isomers of dihydroxybenzoic acids that only 2,5-DHB incorporates homogeneously and quantitatively, whereas other isomers such as 2,6-DHB do not incorporate at all, while some others incorporate only randomly. Confocal laser scan images of the protein avidin, labeled with the fluorochrome Texas red for single crystals of 2,5-DHB and 2,6-DHB are shown in Figure 1.95. No obvious correlation between the incorporation and the crystal structure of these isomers was found. The state of the incorporated analyte molecules in the matrix crystals is another interesting question. Based on results obtained for the incorporation of pH-indicator dye molecules, Krueger *et al.*

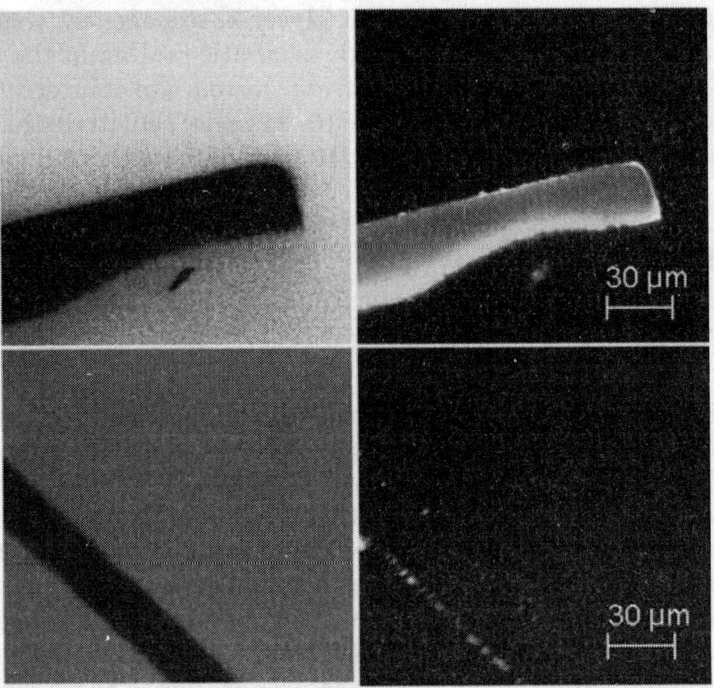

Fig. 1.95 : Confocal laser scan fluorescence images of single crystals of 2,5- dihydroxybenzoic acid (top panels) and 2,6- dihydroxybenzoic acid (bottom panels). Both matrices were doped with the protein avidin, labeled with a Texas red (TR) fluorescent dye. The images were recorded at an x,y-plane 12μm into the crystals. The left panels show dark shadowgraphs of the shape of the crystals against the bright green Bodipy 493/503 nm fluorescence of the immersion liquid. The right panels show the red TR fluorescence of the labeled protein

have concluded that molecules retain their solution charge state in the crystal, which implies that they also retain their solvation shell. Horneffer *et al.* have found a high density of cavities of 10-2000 nm size in crystals of both 2,5-DHB and 2,6-DHB by electron microscopy. At first sight, these cavities could be assumed to contain analyte molecules with residual solvent. However, if this is the case it is difficult to understand why 2,5-DHB - but not 2,6-DHB - incorporates analytes into these cavities; attempts to localize gold-labeled protein in the cavities of 2,5-DHB were also inconclusive. A solventless method for sample preparation was developed originally for the MALDI-MS of synthetic polymers which are often not soluble in standard solvents. In this method, matrix and analyte powders are mixed and ground in a mortar or ball-mill and then applied to a MALDI target support. In a recent report it was shown, that analyte spectra can be obtained from such preparations, even though the analyte is only chemisorbed at the matrix crystal surfaces. However, the desorption is much less "soft" than MALDI-MS from samples with incorporated analytes, leading to a strongly increased metastable fragmentation of the ions and an upper mass limit for proteins of 30-55kDa.

Absorption of the Laser Radiation

$$H = H_0 * e^{az} \qquad \text{eq. 1.1}$$

The role of the optical absorption of the matrix in the transfer of energy from the laser beam to the sample is governed by Beer's law, as described previously in 1985 where H is the laser fluence at depth z into the sample, H_0 is the laser fluence atthe sample surface, and α is the absorption coefficient for a definition of the fluence). The absorption coefficient α equals the product of the molar absorption coefficient αn and the concentration cn of the absorbing molecules in the sample. The wavelength-dependent molar absorption coefficient αn is a property of the matrix compound and, for UV-MALDI, has a maximum value of typically between 5×10^3 and 5×10^4 l mol^{-1} cm^{-1} at the peak absorption wavelength. Molar absorption coefficients of this order of magnitude are only provided by molecules with aromatic rings; the exact wavelength of maximum absorption and its magnitude are determined by the ligands of the core ring and are tabulated in a variety of reference sources. Some care should be exercised in using the tabulated values for αn, because they have all been measured for dilute solutions of the compounds. In the solid state of a typical MALDI sample the absorption bands are typically broadened and slightly red-shifted. The concentration cn of absorbers (chromophores) is unusually high in MALDI samples, about 10 mol? l–1, because all the solvent is evaporated before the sample is introduced into the vacuum. As a result, the absorption coefficient α ranges from about 5×10^4 to $5 \times 10^{5\ cm-1}$. The inverse of α is called the penetration depth δ, and has values of only 20 to 200 nm. It is the depth into the sample, at which the fluence has decreased to about 30% of the value at the surface. It is also an order of magnitude estimate of the depth of material ablated (desorbed) per single laser pulse in MALDI. Because of this very shallow ablation depth, a given location of the sample can usually be irradiated many times before the material is exhausted. For the MALDI process the 'density' of energy, absorbed per unit volume Ea/V of the sample is the process-determining quantity. This can be derived from Eq. above by simple differentiation to:

$$Ea/V = \alpha * H \qquad \text{eq 1.2}$$

Equation 1.2 is at the core of the MALDI process. If a matrix is chosen with asufficiently high absorption coefficient α, a relatively low fluence H_0 can be applied. Values for H_0 of 20-200 Jm^{-2} are representative for most UV-MALDI applications. Pulsed lasers with a pulse width of a few nanoseconds are employed in UV-MALDI. At a fluence of 100 Jm^{-2} and a pulse width of 2 ns, the 'intensity' (irradiance) of the laser beam at the sample surface is only 1011Wm^{-2} or 107Wcm^{-2}, not enough to induce any non-linear absorption such as non-resonant two-photon absorption. For the linear absorption the absorbed energy per unit volume can be controlled meticulously with a suitable variable attenuator in the laser beam, a feature which has turned out to be crucial for the successful MALDI of large molecules, because the desorption of non-volatile, labile molecules can only be achieved in a narrow range of energy 'density'. The other essential feature of this laser absorption is that the energy is transferred more or less uniformly to a macroscopic sample volume (except for the attenuation of the fluence into the sample and the fluence profile, This is very different from the situation in SIMS or PD, where incident particles create minute tracks of atomic dimensions of very high energy density in the sample, with a strong radial decline of energy density. This strongly heterogeneous energy distribution is the main reason for the limitation of these methods for the desorption of larger molecules. The fluence can also be converted into a value for the photon flux—that is, the number of photons impinging on the sample per single laser pulse. A fluence of 100 Jm^{-2} corresponds to a photon flux of 1.7 × 1016 photons per cm^2; each carrying an energy of 3.7 eV at the wavelength of 337nm of the N2 laser. A molar absorption coefficient of 104 $lmol^{-1}$ cm^{-1} represents a physical absorption cross-section of the chromophore of 1.6 × 10^{-1}7 cm^2, resulting in an average of 0.7 photons absorbed per matrix molecule for any given laser exposure. This is, on the one hand, a very high density of excitation energy, close to the solid-state energy stored in all of the intermolecular bonds. It is, therefore not surprising that it leads to an explosive ablation of the excited sample volume. On the other hand, it renders even resonant two-photon absorption by the matrix rather unlikely. The high density of excited molecules does, however, result in a rather high rate of energy pooling in the sample, in which two neighboring excited molecules pool their energy, with one of them acquiring twice the photon energy and the other falling back to the ground state. This energy pooling is an important feature in some models for the ionization of the molecules which requires at least the energy of two photons for an initial photoionization of the matrix molecules. The situation is similar, but not equal, for IR-MALDI. Optical absorption in the infrared region of the spectrum represents a transition between vibrational or rotational molecular states. These transitions are typically weaker than the electronic transitions in the UV by one to two orders of magnitude. The strongest such transitions are those of the O-H and N-H stretch vibrations near a 3 μm wavelength. The absorption coefficient not only of water or vacuum-stable ice, but also of the common IR-MALDI matrix glycerol, in this wavelength region reaches peak values of 104 cm^{-1}, corresponding to a penetration depth of about 1 μm—more than 20-fold that of typical penetration depths in the UV. As a result, the ablated mass per laser exposure in IR-MALDI exceeds that of UV-MALDI by at least a factor of 10, and the sample consumption rate is accordingly higher. Typical laser fluences for IR-MALDI range from 103 to 5 × 103Jm^{-2}.

Non-linear absorption processes are even less likely for such fluences in the infraredas compared to UV-MALDI, and for the photon energy of only 0.3 eV or less even the absorption of several photons by a given chromophore or energy pooling cannot possibly excite single molecules to anywhere near their ionization energy.

The Ablation/Desorption Process

As discussed above, every laser exposure of a sample leads to the removal of a bulk volume—that is, many monolayers of matrix molecules of the sample. The term 'desorption' is, therefore, somewhat ill-chosen for this process, and was so even for the field desorption for which it was originally coined. Ablation is the more correct term, and this is used interchangeably with desorption throughout this chapter. The processes of material ablation and the ionization of a minor fraction of the matrix and analyte molecules are, no doubt, intimately intertwined, and both take place on a micrometer geometrical and a nanosecond time scale. It is experimentally very difficult—if not impossible—to sort out the complex contributions of the physical processes induced by the laser irradiation in all detail. Despite this complexity, it is of considerable merit to treat the two mechanisms separately, and some basic understanding can be derived from such a discussion, this particularly, because the vast majority of material comes off as neutrals. As was pointed out above, even at the threshold fluence for the detection of MALDI ions each laser pulse transfers an amount of energy to the sample, close to the sum of all bond energies in the solid (equivalent to the sum of the heat of fusion and evaporation). Even though this energy will in all cases lead to ablation of the excited volume, different energy dissipation processes need to be taken into account. Energy dissipation by heat conduction during the laser pulse can be neglected in all cases of UV- as well as IR-MALDI. For a penetration depth of laser radiation of 100 nm, the time constant for heat conduction of typical UV-MALDI matrices is about 10 ns—still a factor of three longer than the typical laser pulse width. In the infrared, the heat conduction time constant for 1μm penetration depth is about 1μs, a factor of about 10 longer than the longest pulse width of lasers (Er:YAG) used in that case. The very rapid heating of the sample by the laser radiation will also generate a thermoelastic pressure pulse in the absorbing sample volume which travels out of the excited volume with the speed of sound, carrying away part of the deposited energy. With a speed of sound in typical crystalline matrices of 2000-3000ms^{-1} and depth of 100nm in the UV, the acoustic time constantis less than 100 ps, much shorter than the laser pulse width of a few nanoseconds. Even though energy is constantly carried away by the pressure wave, this amounts only to a very small fraction of the total deposited energy, and the pressure in the excited volume never reaches values high enough to substantially influence the ablation process. For IR-MALDI, the situation can be very different because of the larger penetration depth. For the desorption with an Er:YAG laser the pulse width of 100 ns is long compared to the acoustic time constant, with only a negligible pressure build-up in the excited volume. The pulse width of the optical parametric oscillator (OPO) laser of only 6 ns, however, is rather close to the acoustic time constant, and the system stays close to what is called the 'acoustic confinement'. In this case a very high pressure of several tens of MegaPascal can build up in the excited volume. Rohlfing have investigated the ablation processes by measuring the recoil pressure of the ablated material with a fast acoustic transducer onto which the sample was prepared, while Leisner have studied the expanding plume of ablated material with high-speed time-lapse photography, both at a wavelength of 2.94μm. Both measurements were much easier for IR-MALDI and glycerol as a matrix, because of the higher amount of material ablated. For the short pulse width and near-acoustic confinement, It is been seen that the pressure pulses of very high amplitude as expected, and time durations comparable to the laser pulse. For the 100-ns pulses of the Er:YAG laser, the pressure amplitude was low, but lasted for several microseconds. The plume photographs revealed that material is removed from the sample for times of up to over 100μs in both cases. This is certainly somewhat of a surprise, because the TOF analysis had revealed that the ions are only generated during an initial phaseof not longer than about 300 ns. Similar experiments were conducted by Under UV-MALDI conditionns, using the liquid matrix nitrobenzyl alcohol for better sample homogeneity and a desorption wavelength of 266 nm.

Expectedly, the recoil pressure was very low—lower even than that of the long pulse IR-laser—because of the smaller amount of removed material. The recoil pressure pulse lasted for only less than 25 ns, the time resolution of the detection. The plume photographs revealed a material ejection for up to at least several microseconds, again much longer than the ion generation time of at most a few nanoseconds. Some typical plume photographs are shown in Figures 1.96 and 1.97. The results of these experiment can tentatively be explained by the following models. In IR-MALDI with 100 ns-long ER:YAG-laser pulses, the absorbing volume is superheated to a temperature that is substantially above the boiling temperature,followed by a volume ejection of material through boiling by heterogeneous nucleation. The situation is similar for UV-MALDI. The longer time course of material ejection in the infrared as compared to the UV is caused by a deeper penetration of the radiation into the sample, and a correspondingly higher inertia and residual heat of the excited volume. For the 6-ns pulses in IR-MALDI of the OPO-laser, the ablation process is substantially different. The strong thermoelastic wave is reflected at the sample vacuum interface, thereby reversing its phase.

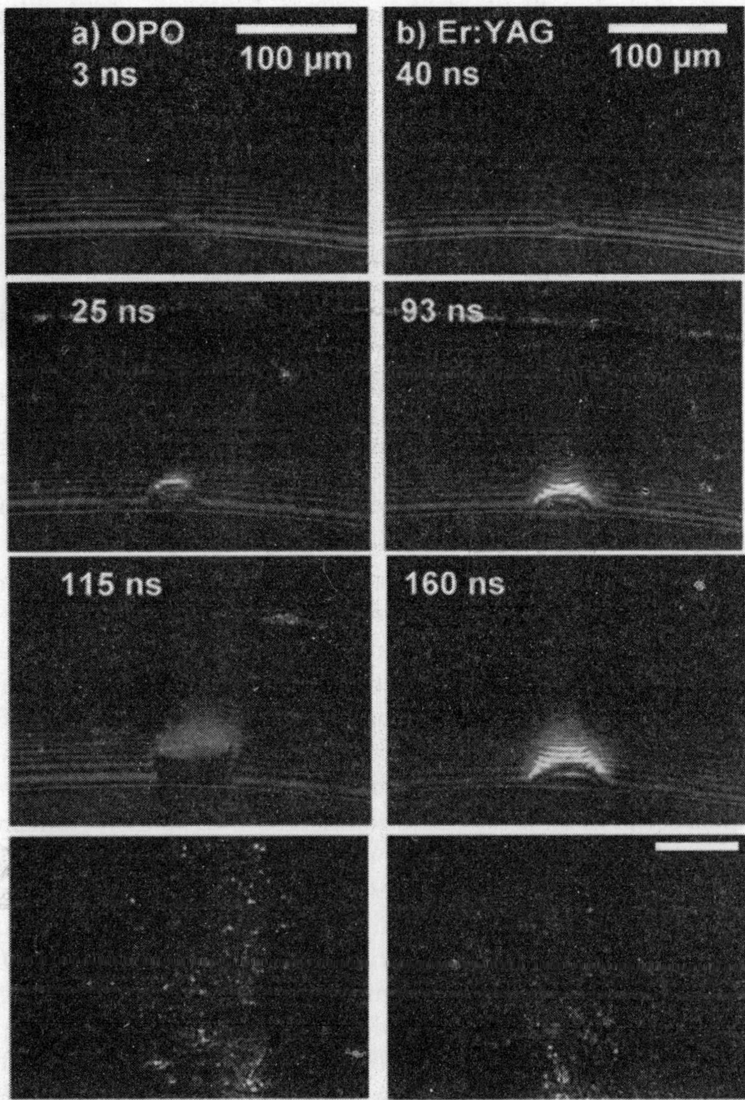

Fig. 1.96 : Showing the High-speed time-lapse photographs of IR-MALDI plumes generated with an optical parametric oscillator (OPO) laser with 6-ns pulse width and an Er:Yag-laser with 100-ns pulse width. Both lasers were operated at 2.94μm wavelength. Matrix: glycerol; time resolution 8 ns; spatial resolution 4μm. The top three panels represent gradients of gaseous material density creating gradients of the index of refraction in the plume, recorded in a dark-field illumination mode. The lowest panel represents particle emission in the plume recorded with light scattered at 90° to the illumination beam. The thin lowest line indicates the top surface of the glycerol drop; the other striations in the dark-field *images are artifacts of optical interference*.

Fig. 1.97 : Showing High-speed photographs of UVMALDI plumes generated with a frequency quadrupled Nd:YAG laser of 266nm wavelength and 8 ns pulse width. Matrix: nitrobenzyl alcohol; time resolution 8 ns; spatial resolution 4μm. Left panel: dark-field image, 45 ns after laser exposure. Right panel: 90° scattered light image, 311 ns after exposure. The thin lowest line indicates the top surface of the glycerol drop; the other striations in the dark-field image are artifacts of optical interference

It then travels back into the sample as a tensile wave, transferring the material beyond the liquid spinodal, as described by Vogel and Venugopalan for soft-tissue ablation. Upon this transition, the material goes through a phase explosion by homogeneous nucleation. Even though all of these experiments were conducted on liquid samples to keep reproducibility high, they reflect, most probably, also the situation for crystalline solid samples. A contribution by the gaseous components such as CO_2 through thermal decomposition of matrix molecules is also discussed as a source of pressure build-up in the excited volume. Theoretical models for the ionization as well as molecular modeling suggest that the ablation process generates clusters and material particles besides gaseous components. Particles are indeed seen in the plume photographs, though only at times late during the ablation, when the generation of ions is long over. Thus, this particle emission does not seem to be relevant for the MALDI ion generation. During the early expansion phase of the plume, dark-field images reveal homogeneous gradients of the index of refraction. However, the spatial resolution of the plume photographs is only a few micrometers; a distribution of clusters of different size, expected during the early phase of the plume expansion, is, therefore, not excluded by the experimental observations. Garrison, Zhigilei and co-workers as well as Knochenmuss have modeled the ablation process using molecular dynamics simulation. Qualitatively, these simulations correctly predict many of the features observed experimentally. Particularly interesting is the consistent prediction that, while clusters are formed early during the ablation process, their internal energy does not seem to suffice for a decay by matrix evaporation, one of the assumptions of the 'lucky survivor' model for ionization. It must also be observed that these simulations contain significant simplifications and, most probably more restrictive, must be scaled to very small volumes and short time regimes because of limited computation capacity. These models have become significantly refined over the past few years and will, no doubt, continue to do so. In this respect they will clearly contribute to our understanding of MALDI processes in the future.

Ionization

The mechanisms which lead to the formation of charged matrix and analyte molecules in the MALDI process are even more poorly understood than the physics of the material ablation/desorption. For a better understanding, it is important to distinguish between the ionization of matrix molecules and that of the analytes. Although no precise numbers have been determined experimentally, it is, most probably, safe to assume that the ion yield for the matrix (*i.e.*, the ratio of ions to neutrals) is somewhere in the range of 10^{-5} to 10^{-3}. The ion yield of the analytes can be much higher, in the order of 0.1-1% for typical cases, and above 10% in exceptional cases. The intensity of the ion signals, as determined from the spectra, are not independent of each other, because charge transfer processes between the two species are, in all likelihood, taking place in the expanding plume and possibly already in the solid state upon laser irradiation. In favorable cases, the spectra even show intense analyte ion signals with negligible matrix ions, despite a typical 104 excess of the matrix. Two models for ion formation have been proposed. The older model assumes neutral analyte molecules in the matrix crystals and a photoionization of the matrix molecules as the initial step, followed by charge transfer to the analyte molecules in the plume. The more recent 'lucky survivor' model assumes that proteins are incorporated into the matrix as charged species, most of which become re-neutralized within desorbed clusters of matrix and analyte. For a laser wavelength of 337 or 355 nm (*i.e.*, photon energies of 3.6 and 3.3eV, respectively), at least two photons are needed for a photoionization of matrix molecules. The typical MALDI laser photon fluxes are too low for any significant resonant two-photon absorption to take place, but very efficient energy pooling between excited neighboring molecules in the crystals has been demonstrated. In the gas phase, even the energy of two photons does not suffice for ionization, but in the solid phase of the crystals the ionization potential may be somewhat lower, and/or thermal energy may make up for the difference. A reaction of the photoelectron with neutral matrix molecules will give rise to negative ions beside the positive ones. The frequent observation of radical matrix ions such as M^+ and/or $[M^+2H]^+$ and a $[M^-2H]^-$ ion besides the expected even-electron ions, among them $[M^+H]^{+-}$ or $[M–H]^-$ as well as a prominent $[2M+H–2H_2O]^+$ for 2,5-DHB and [2MH]+- for CHCA is at least in agreement with the photoionization model, if not a strong indication (Fig. 1.98). As for the model prediction of the relative yield of positive versus negative analyte ions of peptides/proteins, it must be considered that the protonated matrix molecules with proton affinities between 180 and 215kcalmol^{-1} are strong gas-phase acids in comparison to basic amino acids with a much higher proton affinity (up to 245 kcalmol–1 for arginine), resulting in an efficient charge transfer and formation of positively charged analyte ions. In contrast, no such difference in basicity between negatively charged ions of matrix and peptides exists, because both are typically carboxylate anions with very close proton affinities; this should limit the yield of analyte anions.

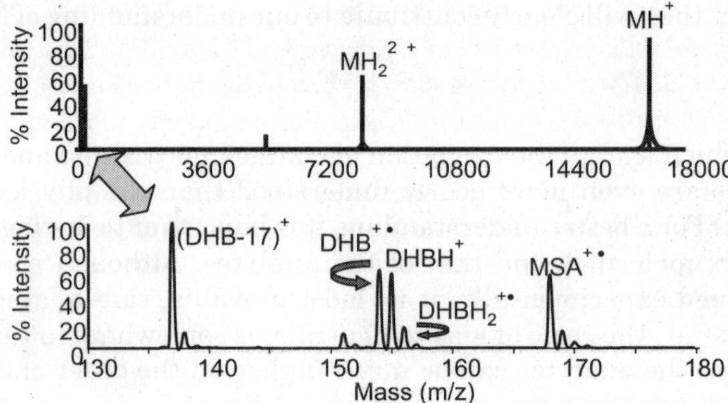

Fig. 1.98: Showing UV-MALDI mass spectrum of myoglobin. Matrix: DHBs (2,5-dihydroxybenzoic acid (DHB) plus 2-hydroxy-5- methoxysalicylic acid (MSA); 9 : 1). Wavelength, 337nm; Mass analyzer, Reflectron TOF

Recently, Knochenmuss has developed a quantitative model based on the matrix photoionization model. One argument against this model is the observation that MALDI spectra, obtained with infrared lasers at a 1.94μm wavelength, closely resemble the UV-MALDI spectra, including radical matrix ions observed (e.g., for the succinic acid matrix). The photon energy of only 0.4 eV at this wavelength certainly excludes photoionization. Similarity of the spectra alone does, however, not suffice as proof of identical ionization processes at the two wavelengths, and indeed the ion yield for analytes in the infrared is about an order of magnitude lower than in the UV. The more recent 'lucky survivor' model of Karas *et al.* proposes that proteins retain their solution charge state upon incorporation into the matrix. This assumption is based on the observation that pH-indicator molecules retain their color and charge state upon crystal incorporation for acidic, neutral, or basic matrices. For most common acidic matrices, almost all peptides will carry a (multiple) positive excess charge; counterions will then typically be either trifluoroacetate or matrix anions. In order to maintain the positive charges of the peptides and to keep the negative counterions separate, the analytes must be incorporated at least in a partially solvated form. In a second step, the model assumes a break-up of the crystal lattice into small clusters upon desorption, some of them with only a single analyte ion. Statistically, some of these clusters are assumed to carry a positive or negative charge by deficit, or an excess of a single counterion. In the expanding plume the clusters are assumed to lose neutral matrix and solvent molecules as well as counterions as free acids or bases after their proton-transfer neutralization with analyte (de)protonation sites. This results in a neutralization of the peptide charges except for the only remaining excess charge:

(1a) $\{(M + nH)n^{+} + (n - 1)A-\}1+ \rightarrow [M + H]^{+} + (n - 1)HA$

(1b) $\{(M - nH)n^{-} + (n - 1)BH+\}1- \rightarrow [M - H]^{-} + (n - 1)B$

These singly charged analyte ions are the lucky survivors of the neutralization process. The model elegantly explains the observation of mostly singly charged ions in MALDI spectra, and would work equally well for UV- as well as IRMALDI. The formation of matrix/ analyte clusters in the desorption process is also predicted by molecular modeling. However, these model calculations also predict that the clusters have not enough internal energy for the proposed evaporation of the neutrals. One of the strengths of the lucky-survivor model is that it can be equally well applied to account for the formation of negative ions from acidic conditions (2a), or the formation of positively charged ions of polyanionic (in solution) species such as nucleic acids (2b) with matrices such as 3-hydroxypicolinic acid or the trihydroxyacetophenones.

(2a) $\{[M + nH]n^{+} + (n + 1)A^{-}\}- \rightarrow [M + A]^{-} + nHA \rightarrow [M - H]^{-} + (n + 1)HA$

(2b) $\{(M - nH)n^{-} + (n + 1)BH^{+}\}+ \rightarrow [M + BH]^{+} + nB \rightarrow [MH]+ + (n + 1)B$

with {} as a symbol for the intermediate cluster, A^{-} and HA for the anion and respective conjugate acid (such as TFA–/HTFA) and B and BH+ for a base and its conjugate acid (such as NH_3/NH_4^{+}). While these ionic cluster ions {. . . . .} never show up in the MALDI spectra with the typical solutes used (*e.g.*, trifluoroacetic acid (TFA) or ammonium salts), they have been detected for extremely strong acids ; their conjugate anions are extremely weak bases and thus stabilize the formed ion pairs with protonated analyte sites. Even though the relative abundance of positive to negative ions of a given analyte under typical MALDI conditions seems never to have been carefully determined, the postulate of an intermediate anion adduct $[M + A]^{-}$ in (2a) rationalizes the general observation that the formation of negative peptide ions out of typically acidic matrix solution is substantially less effective, because the proton-transfer step necessary to form the $[M\text{-}H]^{-}$-ion competes with the simple dissociation of the adduct ion. Similar arguments hold for the polyanionic nucleic acids. Whilst the addition of ammonium ions result in a quantitative detection of the free acids, a substitution of the ammonium by alkyl-quaternary ammonium ions leads to the observation of adduct ions, increasing in intensity with increasing length of the alkyl chains. Besides the processes suggested for the lucky survivor model, matrix photoionization is also probable as a parallel process, as documented by the observed matrix ions. In UV-MALDI, both processes may therefore contribute to the observed analyte ions to an as-yet unknown degree. For analytes of very low proton affinity such as neutral carbohydrates and many synthetic polymers, cationization by Na^{+}, K^{+} or other metal cations is usually observed in MALDI. The cationization in all likelihood takes place in the expanding plume. It requires a co-desorption of the analyte, and the cations and best results are therefore obtained from sample locations where both species exist in close neighborhood, such as in the center of DHB-dried droplet preparations. Specific protocols have been developed for the MALDI of such analytes.

Fragmentation of MALDI Ions

Fragmentation of MALDI ions is a mixed blessing, as in all of MS. It can, on the one hand, lead to a substantial loss of spectra quality such as loss of mass resolution or even complete loss of the signal of the intact parent ion, as has been shown for the loss of sialic acids in the analysis of glycoconjugates in reflectron- TOF analyzers. On the other hand, intrinsic or induced fragmentation is an indispensable tool for the acquisition of structural information in MSn experiments. The nomenclature for the fragmentation - particularly the differentiationin post-source-decay (PSD) and in-source-decay ions—is closely related to timeof- flight analyzers, because they still constitute the majority of spectrometers used for the analysis of MALDI ions. The details of how to analyze fragment ions with different types of instrument are discussed. Even though some limited ion stability—and thus fragmentation—was obvious in the early days of MALDI by peak tailing on the low mass side, and was attributed to small neutral losses of peptide and protein ions, the fact that MALDI can generate substantial prompt and metastable fragmentation of analyte ions was obscured at an early stage. This was due to two facts: the laser microprobe instrument (LAMMA 1000) used for the initial experiments indeed minimized fragmentation because of a very week acceleration field strength and low total (3keV) ion energy; the next-generation MALDI-TOF instruments were linear instruments in which metastable fragment ions cannot be observed directly. It was only when Kaufmann and Spengler started careful investigations of ion stability using a deceleration stage in a linear TOF instrument that the potentially high degree of metastable fragmentation was detected. This was the starting point for the development of the so-called PSD analysis of metastable ions which led to today's MALDI-TOF/TOF instruments. The character of the PSD fragmentation—that is, the classes of fragment ions observed is in full agreement with a collisional activation process. Despite this general agreement, PSD mass spectra are often more complex than CID mass spectra, showing internal fragments and products of consecutive fragmentations, and pointing to more complex excitation mechanisms of the intramolecular degrees of freedom. Besides collisional excitation through collisions of the ions with neutrals in the plume, a direct excitation in the matrix crystal after absorption of the laser energy and excess energy of chemical reactions in the plume such as proton transfer must be considered. All of these processes depend in complex fashion on instrumental parameters such as laser fluence and focus, ion extraction field strength and delay, as well as on the choice of matrix. Information about the different contributions to ion excitation have been listed in a report which compares vacuum MALDI to atmospheric-pressure MALDI; this report provides a comprehensive summary of the current knowledge of MALDI fragmentation. The effect of collisional excitation upon acceleration was demonstrated for matrix ions. These AP-MALDI investigations were later extended to determine initial MALDI plume excitation processes, including the application to more representative test samples than thermometer molecules, such as a model peptide and a nucleoside. Here, matrix softness yielded the best agreement with matrix proton affinity. In general, matrix proton affinities have been used with only limited success to rank matrices with respect to their effectiveness for fragmentation. In a practical approach, matrices are classified and ranked from 'hard' to 'soft' α-cyano-4- hydroxycinnamic acid, the matrix preferentially applied for 'peptide-mass fingerprint' analyses in proteomics because of its rather homogeneous sample morphology, is one of the hardest matrices in that ranking. Because of its degree of fragmentation induction, it is also the matrix of choice for PSD- or TOF/TOFexperiments. 'Super DHB' (DHBs; 2,5-DHB with a 5-10% addition of 2-hydroxy-m5-methoxybenzoic acid) is on the soft end of the list and, therefore, preferentially applied for the analysis of larger proteins. By using such a soft matrix and optimizing all instrumental parameters (low extraction field, long delay times), smallneutral loss can be minimized and a good mass resolution (close to the theoretical limit) is obtainable for a linear TOF configuration, even for medium size proteins up to bovine serum albumin. Common for PSD and the low-energy CID mechanisms is the randomization of the internal energy among all internal degrees of freedom before the (metastable) fragmentation. Interestingly, it was found that the order of matrices from hard to soft agrees with the initial ion velocities determined in a linear TOF. Hard matrices correlate with low initial velocities, and vice versa. This points to a role for expansion cooling in the MALDI desorption process. A very different fragmentation mechanism was first reported by R.S. Brown, whereby fragment ions are formed 'promptly' upon ion generation excitation with a time delay of less than at most 100 ns—substantially less than the typical delay times in delayed-extraction TOF instruments. Therefore, these are referred to as in-source-decay (ISD) ions. ISD spectra contain signals of c- and sometimes z-type fragment ions, in addition to some a-, b- and y-ions. This type of fragmentation is observed for both positive and negative ions, indicating that ISD is independent of proton transfer, and 2,5-DHB is the matrix with the highest ISD yields [63-65]. The analogy to electron capture dissociation prompted a discussion on the possible role of electrons in ISD, although it appears clear today that ISD is mediated by hydrogen radical. ISD yields a substantially more complete fragment-ion series as compared to PSD, although hopes to use it for practical applications (*e.g.*, in proteomics have not materialized, mostly because of the low intensity of the signals. An additional problem is that true MS/MS experiments cannot be carried out as a precursor selection for peptides from a mixture is not possible.

MALDI of Non-Covalent Complexes

After about 20 years' use of MALDI-MS, it is clear that the successful analysis ofnon-covalent interactions and complexes is rather the exception than the rule. Considering most typical MALDI protocols, this cannot be a surprise. Most 'classical' matrices are organic acids and typically used in water/organic solvent mixtures, often acidified by TFA, *i.e.*, in conditions which should result in the dissociation of most (if not all) non-covalent complexes. However, signals of non-covalent complexes have indeed been obtained from such preparations . At least forsome such systems, the dissociation seems to be sufficiently slow that a fast evaporation of the solvent conserves at least a certain fraction of the complexes. Unfortunately, adjustment of the pH and the omission of organic solvent is often not a viable alternative, as acidic matrices will be deprotonated and totally change their crystallization and incorporation properties as salts. Many salts and buffers used to adjust ionic strength/pH are, therefore, not MALDI-compatible in the desired concentration, or at least compromise the performance with respect to sensitivity and mass resolution.The incorporation of analytes into the matrix crystals, which has been shown generally to make the desorption process softer or altogether possible, is another step which might lead to dissociation of the complexes. This question has been addressed in order to understand the so-called 'first-shot phenomenon', which had been observed much earlier but only recently had been resolved. For a number of selected matrices, the signals of protein-protein complexes are observed only in the spectra of first exposures of a given sample spot. Subsequent exposures yield only signals of the monomer units. By a combination of MALDIMS and confocal laser scanning microscopy (CLSM) of complexes with fluorochromes, which exhibit a fluorescence resonance energy transfer (FRET), it was shown that in these systems the complexes dissociate upon incorporation, whereas intact complexes are precipitated at the surface of matrix crystals. The next crucial step is the intact desorption and ionization of the complex and their survival in the gas phase of the expanding plume. Such dissociation upon desorption is even more likely if the complexes are localized at the crystal surface rather thanbeing incorporated. The type of interaction within the complex is also a decisive parameter. Fromenergetic considerations it is obvious that gas-phase stability of non-covalent complexes is highest for ionic interactions, followed by hydrogen bonding. Interestingly, the formation of strong ionic complexes has even been used to facilitate MALDI measurement of highly acidic and thus negatively charged biocompounds, such as oligonucleotides and heparin-derived oligosaccharides, by admixing highly basic peptides, followed by a mass determination of the intact stable complex. Hydrophobic interaction should be particularly labile, because it is based on the hydrophilic environment of the solvent water, lost in the vacuum. The simple detection of non-covalent complexes by ESI shows, that the transfer of the molecule into the vacuum does not necessarily result in a dissociation, if the internal energy does not suffice for the transition to the very different conformational state. It would also appear that complexes with large contact areas between the constituents of the complex and corresponding contribution of salt and hydrogen bridges, as well as hydrophobic interaction typical of many protein-protein complexes help to stabilize the complex. Complexes between small and large molecules, as are typical for ligand-receptor or antigen-antibody systems, are much more difficult to analyze by MALDI-MS. Their affinity depend on the exact conservation of the conformation in small epitopes of the protein, which is more easily lost in the MALDI process than the complete quaternary structure. Interestingly,spectra of the intact biotin-streptavidin complex, one of the strongest complexes known to date, have never been obtained by MALDI. Another issue which complicates the use of MALDI for the analysis of non-covalent complexes is the formation of non-specific multimeric and adduct ions. This effect is even more pronounced for the analysis of non-covalent protein complexes, as high concentrations (10pmolμl–1 or higher) of analyte are typically used to overcome the reduced sensitivity of TOF instruments in the high mass range. Furthermore an elevated laser fluence, as well as deviation from optimal preparationprotocols, are aggravating effects. It is, therefore, most important clearly to differentiate specific from non-specific interactions, and this is typically achieved by using a known non-binding/non-interacting control compound. Because of these limitations, analyses of non-covalent interactions by MALDI are typically qualitative rather than quantitative. Within these boundary conditions, a number of reports have described the successful detection of several types of non-covalent complex. During theearly days of MALDI, high-intensity signals of non-covalent protein complexes usinga nicotinic acid matrix and a laser wavelength of 266 nm were reported, for example of the tetrameric glucose isomerase and a trimeric porin. Comprehensive reviews have been provided by Hillenkamp and Farmer andCaprioli on this subject. In addition, a recent report by Zehl and Allmaier on the influence of instrumental parameters for the detection of quaternary protein structures starts from a careful review of the state of the art, and provides acritical discussion on the above-described problems. These authors used 2,6- dihydroxyacetophenone as (non-acidic) matrix with the addition of ammoniumacetate or diammonium citrate (DAHC) to adjust solution conditions for the stabilization of protein complexes. Another only slightly acidic matrix which tolerates even high additive amounts such as DAHC is 6-azathiothymine (ATT); this was also used to investigate nucleic acids and their non-covalent complexes and adducts. Superior results for double-stranded DNA were, however, obtained when using glycerol as a matrix for IR-MALDI. In summary, the use of MALDI to investigate non-covalent interaction is far less straightforward than typical applications for peptides and proteins under denaturing conditions. Success is not predictable, and careful control experiments must be implemented to differentiate specific from non-specific interactions. It appears, however, that the potential of MALDI in this area is far from being fully explored. Recently, a new approach was presented investigating the formation of non-covalent complexes, based on the detection of the 'intensity fading' of one complex partner, rather than of the intact complex. This approach avoids the problems related to detection of the intact complex in the high mass range, and can be carried out at analytically relevant micromolar and sub-micromolar concentration levels.

The Correct Choice of Matrix: Sample Preparation

Unfortunately or expectedly, there is no single MALDI matrix or sample preparation protocol which is suited to all analytical problems and analytes in MALDIMS. A few of the more general considerations are discussed in the following section, though more specific information is provided in the applications chapters of this book. A representative list of commonly used matrices and their main propertiesis provided in Table 1.15. There are different matrices of first choice for different classes of analytes and analytical problems. For example, CHCA is used in the majority of proteomics applications for the analysis of peptide-mass-fingerprints generated by protein enzymatic digests (as discussed later). On the other hand, 2,5-DHB—and especially DHBs (*i.e.*, DHB with an admixture of 5-10% 5-methoxy-2-hydroxybenzoic acid)—with its pronounced crystallization into large crystals of ca. 100μm size is particularly suited to protein analysis. The reasons for this are, first, because its softness prevents strong small-neutral losses and peak tailing; and second, because the crystals incorporate the proteins, but exclude the majority of common

Table 1.15: Showing A selection of Commonly used MALDI matrices

Matrix	Structure	Wavelength	Major applications
Nicotinic acid	Pyridine ring with COOH (N in ring)	UV 266 nm	Proteins, peptides, adduct formation
2,5-Dihydroxybenzoic acid (plus 10% 2-hydroxy-5-methoxybenzoic acid)	Benzene ring with COOH, OH, OH	UV 337 nm, 353 nm	Proteins, peptides, carbohydrates, synthetic polymers
Sinapinic acid	CH=CH—COOH on benzene ring with H_3CO, OCH_3, OH	UV 337 nm, 353 nm	Proteins, peptides
α-Cyano-4-hydroxycinnamic acid	CH=C(CN)—COOH on benzene ring with OH	UV 337 nm, 353 nm	Peptides, fragmentation
3-Hydroxy-picolinic acid	Pyridine ring (N) with OH, COOH	UV 337 nm, 353 nm	Best for nucleic acids
6-Aza-2-thiothymine	Triazine ring (N, N, N) with OH, CH_3, HS	UV 337 nm, 353 nm	Proteins, peptides, non-covalent complexes; near-neutral pH
k,m,n-Di(tri)hydroxy-acetophenone	Benzene ring with $COCH_3$ and X substituents; X = OH or H	UV 337 nm, 353 nm	Protein, peptides, non-covalent complexes; near-neutral pH
Succinic acid	$HOOC—CH_2\text{-}CH_2\text{-}COOH$	IR 2.94 μm, 2.79 μm	Proteins, peptides
Glycerol	$H_2C—CH—CH_2$ (each with OH)	IR 2.94 μm, 2.79 μm	Proteins, peptides, liquid matrix

IR = infrared; UV = ultraviolet

contaminants. A practical overview of the various matrices and preparation techniques can be found, for example, on the Internet at: http://www.chemistry.wustl.edu/~msf/ damon/ sample_prep_toc.html, as well as on the Internet pages of commercial suppliers of chemicals. The "dried droplet" standard MALDI sample preparation is very simple. Here, the sample and matrix are dissolved in a common solvent or solvent system, andmixed either before deposition onto or directly on the MALDI sample support. The matrix-analyte droplet of typically 1μL volume is then slowly dried in air, or under a forced flow of cold air. This results in a deposit of crystals which, depending on the matrix, vary between submicrometer and several hundred micrometers in size. In many cases, surface tension leads to a non-homogeneous distribution of the individual crystals near the rim of the preparation. The best MALDI performance is usually achieved only at certain locations of the crystals, which often requires manual interference and active control by the experimenter; this is why most MALDI instruments are equipped with a microscopic observation system. The cause of these 'sweet spots' has been the subject of much speculation, the commonly held notion being that of an inhomogeneous distribution of analyte within the crystals. However, this has been disproved by Horneffer *et al.*, who found a homogeneous distribution of .uorescently labelled analyte in the crystals of a representative number of different matrix crystals by CLSM studies. A different (ionization) state of the analyte molecules in different locations, or heterogeneous orientation of the matrix crystal surfaces relative to the spectrometer axis and perpendicular to which the ions are ejected in conjunction with the limited angular acceptance of the mass spectrometer, might also cause the observed sweet spots. As a rule of thumb, the addition of the analyte solution should not noticeably change the crystallization behavior of the neat matrix; this already indicates that the solution excess of the matrix with respect to the analyte is maintained in the crystals, and that the contaminant level is low enough. Any solute component which dramatically changes the appearance of the matrix crystals or prevents crystallization altogether—for example, low-volatility solvents such as glycerol or dimethyl sulphoxide - will prohibit a successful MALDI analysis. Over the years, a large number of modi.cations of, or alternatives to, the drieddroplet technique have been developed. These many variations are often the personal preferences of MALDI users for sample preparation, and the subject may appear to be an art or a even a 'black art'. However, dried-droplet protocols are still the most widely used with high success. It also appears that instrumental developments using lasers with higher frequencies, together with the automation of the entire MALDI measurements, have eased the problems of heterogeneity to some extent. Among the many modifications and variations of the simple dried droplet preparation, two alternatives stand out as particularly useful and widespread, namely 'surface preparation' and 'anchor sample plates'.

Surface Preparation

Surface preparation or predeposited matrix crystal layers were also often called thin layer preparation introduced to enhance sensitivity, homogeneity of the preparation, automation, and liquid chromatography (LC)-spotting. Surface preparation was a true innovation. It was shown that for the CHCA matrix, rapid evaporation of the organic solvent generates a relatively homogeneous, microcrystalline seed layer. Upon addition of the aqueous peptide analyte solution, only the very top layers of the nearly water-insoluble matrix redissolve and incorporate the analyte. The concentration of the whole analyte into only a limited depth layer at the radiation-accessible top of the preparation results in an improved sensitivity, and the structurally relatively homogeneous crystal layer improves the mass resolution, particularly in linear TOF mass spectrometers. Unfortunately, this approach is restricted to matrices which do not fully dissolve in the usually aqueous analyte solvent. However, it is generally believed that, despite its limited solubility, the matrix is partially dissolved by the analyte solution and that true incorporation of the analyte into the matrix takes place. It was, moreover, shown that contaminants such as salts could be rinsed from the surface with a splash of ice water, without any major loss in sensitivity. Hence, surface preparation became the starting point for the development of disposable MALDI targetswith predeposited matrix spots. The generation of more homogeneous micro- crystalline sample layers by rapid evaporation of the solvent (*e.g.*, in vacuo) hasalso been used for a variety of other matrices.

Anchor Sample Plates

Anchor plates for the preparation of multiple samples have small hydrophilic islands, typically of 100-500ìm diameter, placed on a hydrophobic surface. The hydrophobic surface prevents spreading of the sample solution over alarge area, as otherwise observed for dried-droplet preparations. Instead, before and/or during crystallization of the matrix, the solution contracts onto these islands, thereby concentrating the matrix and analyte into a de.ned volume. This up-concentration is particularly useful for low-concentration analyte and matrix solutions, and also facilitates automated analyses of the fixed location samples. A few other modi.cations of the sample preparation have also proven useful in specific cases:

- Mixtures of several different matrices have been reported for an improved performance, but so far only DHBs (a mixture of 90-95% 2,5-DHB and 5-10% 2-hydroxy-5-methoxybenzoic acid) has found relatively widespread application for proteins. It softens the desorption and limits the small neutral loss and thereby improves mass resolution. A mixture of different trihydroxyacetophenones is sometimes used for the analysis of nucleic acids.
- Additives to matrix preparations are mostly used for sample clean-up. These additives do not absorb the laser radiation, but may influence the crystallization behaviour of the matrix to some extent. The most frequently used method is to add DAHC as a cation scavenger to preparations of highly anionic samples such as nucleic acids. The addition of ammoniumphosphate to improve peptide-mass-.ngerprint mass spectra by suppression of matrix cation clusters, and the use of phosphoric acid to improve DHB analysis of phosphopeptides, are two recent successful examples of this approach.

Modified surfaces, for example of sample plates, can be used for the affinity capture of analytes from crude mixtures. These can significantly enhance detectionsensitivity and can be used for a simple sample clean-up. Titanium dioxide (TiO_2) -coated surfaces or sol-gel systems, for example, have been shown to very selectively concentrate phosphopeptides from peptide .ngerprint samples. SELDI ("surface-enhanced laser desorption ionization") uses so-called proteinchips for the detection of peptides and proteins from complex biological fluids such as blood. These protein chips contain various chromatographic media immobilized on a MALDI sample plate for the selective enrichment of constituents of the complex mixture applied. Unfortunately, a large number of unsubstantiated claims for the detection of disease-related biomarkers, mostly as a result of poormass spectrometric performance, has discredited this approach.Liquid matrices could avoid the undesirable heterogeneity of crystalline MALDI samples. Liquid matrices (*e.g.,* nitrobenzylalcohol and nitrophenyloctlyether)were introduced in the early UV-MALDI reports, but never found widespread applicationbecause their performance proved to be signi.cantly inferior to that ofthe solid matrices, particularly because of extensive adduct formation. A more recentdevelopment is the synthesis of ionic liquid matrices, which are synthesized by preparing a 1:1 solution of a classical organic acid matrix and an organic base. A comprehensive review on the first few years of ionic-liquid matrices was recently published. Unfortunately, the products with the best performance for MALDI are either solid or very highly viscous liquids. To date, these matrices seem to be mostly restricted to the MALDI-MS of small, stable analytes. A solvent-free preparation is of particular interest for the analysis of synthetic polymers for which a common solvent with a suitable matrix is not available, and for which sizeable amounts of material are usually available . In this protocol, the analyte and matrix are ground thoroughly in a mortar or ball-mill and loaded onto a MALDI target as powders, or after having been pressed into pellets. Good mass spectra can be obtained for analytes up to a mass of ca. 30 kDa, even though the analytes are not incorporated into the matrix crystals.

Abbreviations

CLSM Confocal Laser Scan Microscopy

DAHC Diammonium Citrate

DHB/2,5-DHB (2,5-) dihydroxybenzioc acid

2,6-DHB 2,6-dihydroxybenzioc acid

DHBs 'super' DHB (mixture of 95% DHB and 5% 2-hydroxy-5-methoxy-benzoic acid

DIOS Desorption/Ionzation On Silicon

ESI Electrospray Ionization

FAB Fast Atom Bombardment

FD Field Desorption

FRET Fluorescence Resonant Energy Transfer
HCCA 4-hydroxy-α-cyanocinnamic acid
ISD In Source Decay
LAMMA Laser Microprobe Mass Analyzer
MALDI Matrix Assisted Laser Desorption/Ionization
UV-MALDI MALDI with ultraviolet laser wavelengths
IR-MALDI MALDI with infrared laser wavelengths
AP-MALDI MALDI at Atmospheric Pressure
MS Mass Spectrometry
PD Plasma Desorption
PSD Post Source Decay
SALDI Surface Assisted Laser Desorption/Ionization
SELDI Surface Enhanced Laser Desorption/Ionization
SIMS Secondary Ion Mass Spectrometry
TOF Time-Of-Flight
TOF-MS Time-Of-Flight Mass Spectrometer

CHAPTER 2

Post-Translational Modifications

Introduction

Post-translational modification (PTM) is the chemical modification of a protein after its translation. It is one of the later steps in protein biosynthesis for many proteins.

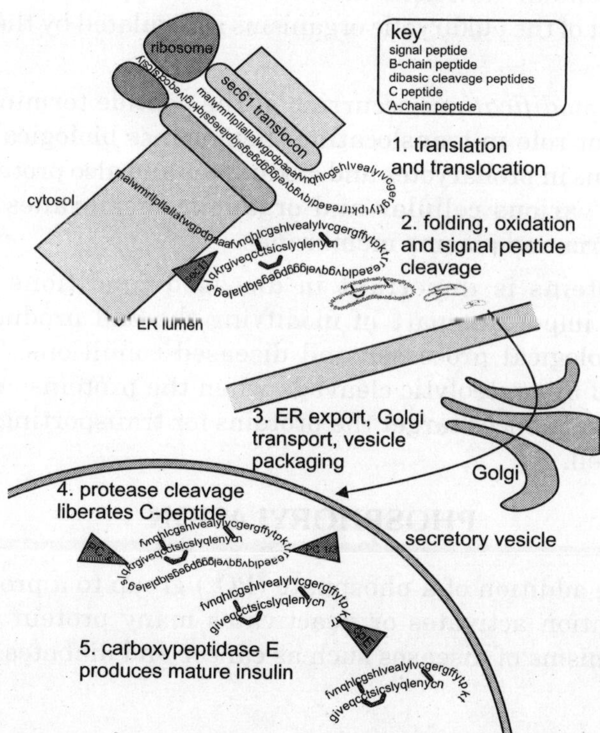

Fig. 2.1 : Showing The bottom of this diagram shows the modification of primary structure of insulin, as described

A protein (also called a polypeptide) is a chain of amino acids. During protein synthesis, 20 different amino acids can be incorporated in proteins. After translation, the posttranslational modification of amino acids extends the range of functions of the protein by attaching to it other biochemical functional groups such as acetate, phosphate, various lipids and carbohydrates, by changing the chemical nature of an amino acid (*e.g.* citrullination) or by making structural changes, like the formation of disulfide bridges.

Also, enzymes may remove amino acids from the amino end of the protein, or cut the peptide chain in the middle. For instance, the peptide hormone insulin is cut twice after disulfide bonds are formed, and a propeptide is removed from the middle of the chain; the resulting protein consists of two polypeptide chains connected by disulfide bonds. Also, most nascent polypeptides start with the amino acid methionine because the 'start' codon on mRNA also codes for this amino acid. This amino acid is usually taken off during post-translational modification.

Most of the proteins that are translated from mRNA undergo chemical modifications before becoming functional in different body cells. The modifications collectively, are known as post-translational modifications. The protein post translational modifications play a crucial role in generating the heterogeneity in proteins and also help in utilizing identical proteins for different cellular functions in different cell types. How a particular protein sequence will act in most of the eukaryotic organisms is regulated by these post translational modifications.

Post Translational modifications occurring at the peptide terminus of the amino acid chain play an important role in translocating them across biological membranes. These include secretory proteins in prokaryotes and eukaryotes and also proteins that are intended to be incorporated in various cellular and organelle membranes such as lysosomes, chloroplast, mitochondria and plasma membranes.

Expression of proteins is important in diseased conditions. *Post translational modifications* play an important part in modifying the end product of expression and contribute towards biological processes and diseased conditions. The amino terminal sequences are removed by proteolytic cleavage when the proteins cross the membranes. These amino terminal sequences target the proteins for transporting them to their actual point of action in the cell.

PHOSPHORYLATION

Phosphorylation is the addition of a phosphate (PO_4) group to a protein or other organic molecule. Phosphorylation activates or deactivates many protein enzymes, causing or preventing the mechanisms of diseases such as cancer and diabetes.

History

In 1906, Phoebus A. Levene at the Rockefeller Institute for Medical Research identified phosphate in the protein vitellin (phosvitin), and by 1933 had detected phosphoserine in casein, with Fritz Lipmann.[2] However, it took another 20 years before Eugene P. Kennedy described the first 'enzymatic phosphorylation of proteins'. Protein phosphorylation in particular plays a significant role in a wide range of cellular processes. Its prominent role in biochemistry is the subject of a very large body of research (as of March 2009, the Medline database returns nearly 160,000 articles on the subject, largely on *protein* phosphorylation).

Function

Reversible phosphorylation of proteins is an important regulatory mechanism that occurs in both prokaryotic and eukaryotic organisms. Enzymes called kinases (phosphorylation) and phosphatases (dephosphorylation) are involved in this process. Many enzymes and receptors are switched 'on' or 'off' by phosphorylation and dephosphorylation. Reversible phosphorylation results in a conformational change in the structure in many enzymes and receptors, causing them to become activated or deactivated. Phosphorylation usually occurs on serine, threonine, and tyrosine residues in eukaryotic proteins. In addition, phosphorylation occurs on the basic amino acid residues histidine or arginine or lysine in prokaryotic proteins. The addition of a phosphate (PO_4) molecule to a polar R group of an amino acid residue can turn a hydrophobic portion of a protein into a polar and extremely hydrophilic portion of molecule. In this way it can introduce a conformational change in the structure of the protein via interaction with other hydrophobic and hydrophilic residues in the protein.One such example of the regulatory role that phosphorylation plays is the p53 tumour suppressor protein. The p53 protein is heavily regulated and contains more than 18 different phosphorylation sites. Activation of p53 can lead to cell cycle arrest, which can be reversed under some circumstances, or apoptotic cell death. This activity occurs only in situations wherein the cell is damaged or physiology is disturbed in normal healthy individuals.

Upon the deactivating signal, the protein becomes dephosphorylated again and stops working. This is the mechanism in many forms of signal transduction, for example the way in which incoming light is processed in the light-sensitive cells of the retina.

Regulatory roles of phosphorylation include

- Biological thermodynamics of energy-requiring reactions
  - Phosphorylation of Na^+/K^+-ATPase during the transport of sodium (Na^+) and potassium(K^+) ions across the cell membrane in osmoregulation to maintain homeostasis of the body's water content.
- Mediates enzyme inhibition
  - Phosphorylation of the enzyme GSK-3 by AKT (Protein kinase B) as part of the insulin signaling pathway.

- Phosphorylation of src tyrosine kinase (pronounced 'sarc') by C-terminal Src kinase (Csk) induces a conformational change in the enzyme, resulting in a fold in the structure, which masks its kinase domain, and is thus shut 'off'.

• Important for protein-protein interaction via 'recognition domains.'
  - Phosphorylation of the cytosolic components of NADPH oxidase, a large membrane-bound, multi-protein enzyme present in phagocytic cells, plays an important role in the regulation of protein-protein interactions in the enzyme.

• Important in protein degradation.
  - In the late 1990s, it was recognized that phosphorylation of some proteins causes them to be degraded by the ATP-dependent ubiquitin/proteasome pathway. These target proteins become substrates for particular E3 ubiquitin ligases only when they are phosphorylated.

Signaling Networks

Elucidating complex signaling pathway phosphorylation events can be difficult. In a cellular signaling pathways, a protein A phosphorylates protein B, and B phosphorylates C. However, in another signaling pathway, protein D phosphorylates A, or phosphorylates protein C. Global approaches such as phosphoproteomics the study of phosphorylated proteins, which is a sub-branch of proteomics combined with mass spectrometry-based proteomics, have been utilised to identify and quantify dynamic changes in phosphorylated proteins over time. These techniques are becoming increasingly important for the systematic analysis of complex phosphorylation networks. They have been successfully used to identify dynamic changes in the phosphorylation status of more than 6000 sites after stimulation with epidermal growth factor.

Protein Phosphorylation Sites

There are thousands of distinct phosphorylation sites in a given cell since: 1) There are thousands of different kinds of proteins in any particular cell (such as a lymphocyte). 2) It is estimated that 1/10th to 1/2 of proteins are phosphorylated (in some cellular state). 3) Phosphorylation often occurs on multiple distinct sites on a given protein.Since phosphorylation of any site on a given protein can change the function or localization of that protein, understanding the 'state' of a cell requires knowing the phosphorylation state of its proteins. For example, if amino acid Serine-473 ('S473') in the protein AKT is phosphorylated, AKT is, in general, functionally active as a kinase. If not, it is an inactive kinase.

Types of Phosphorylation

Within a protein, phosphorylation can occur on several amino acids. Phosphorylation on serine is the most common, followed by threonine. Tyrosine phosphorylation is relatively rare. However, since tyrosine phosphorylated proteins are relatively easy to purify using antibodies, tyrosine phosphorylation sites are relatively well understood. Histidine and aspartate phosphorylation occurs in prokaryotes as part of two-component signaling and in some cases in eukaryotes in some signal transduction pathways.

Detection and Characterization

Antibodies can be used as powerful tools to detect whether a protein is phosphorylated at a particular site. Antibodies bind to and detect phosphorylation-induced conformational changes in the protein. Such antibodies are called phospho-specific antibodies; hundreds of such antibodies are now available. They are becoming critical reagents both for basic research and for clinical diagnosis.

PTM (Post-translational Modification) isoforms are easily detected on 2D gels. Indeed, phosphorylation replaces neutral hydroxyl groups on serines, threonines, or tyrosines with negatively-charged phosphates with pKs near 1.2 and 6.5. Thus, below pH 5.5, phosphates add a single negative charge; near pH 6.5, they add 1.5 negative charges; above pH 7.5, they add 2 negative charges. The relative amount of each isoform can also easily and rapidly be determined from staining intensity on 2D gels. In some very specific cases, the detection of the phosphorylation as a shift in the protein's electrophoretic mobility is possible on simple 1-dimensional SDS-PAGE gels, as it's described for instance for a transcriptional coactivator by Kovacs et al. Strong phosphorylation-related conformational changes (that persist in detergent containing solutions) are thought to underlie this phenomenon. Most of the phosphorylation sites for which such a mobility shift has been described fall in the category of SP and TP sites (*i.e.* a proline residue follows the phosphorylated serine or threonine residue). More recently large scale mass spectrometry analyses have been used to determine sites of protein phosphosphorylation. Over the last 4 years dozens of studies have been published each identifying thousands of sites, many of which were previously undescribed. Mass spectrometry is ideally suited for such analyses as the addition of phosphorylation results in an increase in the mass of the protein and the phosphorylated residue. However, advanced highly accurately mass spectrometers are needed for these studies limiting the technology to labs with high-end mass spectrometers. A detailed characterization of the sites of phosphorylation is very difficult, and the quantitation of protein phosphorylation by mass spectrometry requires isotopic internal standard approaches. A relative quantitation can be obtained with a variety of differential isotope labelling technologies. There are also several

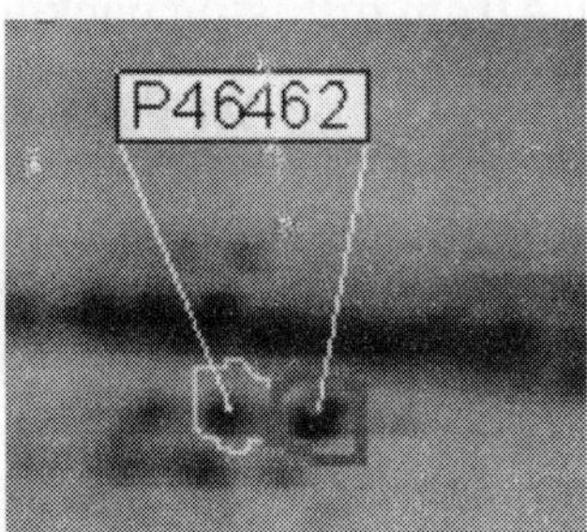

Fig. 2.2 : Showing Example of post-translational modification detected on a 2D gel yui (spot boundaries delimited by analysis software, identification by mass spectrometry, P46462 is the protein ID in Expasy)

quantitative protein phosphorylation methods including fluorescence immunoassays, FRET, TRF, fluorescence polarization, fluorescence-quenching, mobility shift, bead-based detection, and cell-based formats.

Other Kinds

ATP, the 'high-energy' exchange medium in the cell, is synthesized in the mitochondrion by addition of a third phosphate group to ADP in a process referred to as oxidative phosphorylation. ATP is also synthesized by substrate-level phosphorylation during glycolysis. ATP is synthesized at the expense of solar energy by photophosphorylation in the chloroplasts of plant cells. Phosphorylation of sugars is often the first stage of their catabolism. It allows cells to accumulate sugars because the phosphate group prevents the molecules from diffusing back across their transporter.

APPLICATION OF PHOSPHORYLATION

Phosphorylation is the well-established post-translational event that regulates subcellular localization, dimerization, DNA binding, coregulator interaction and transcriptional activity of nuclear receptors [Orti *et al.*, 1992]. Understanding the role of phosphorylation in nuclear receptor function is limited by receptor expression levels, intracellular phosphatase activity, and low stoichiometry and/or rapid turnover of some phosphorylation sites.

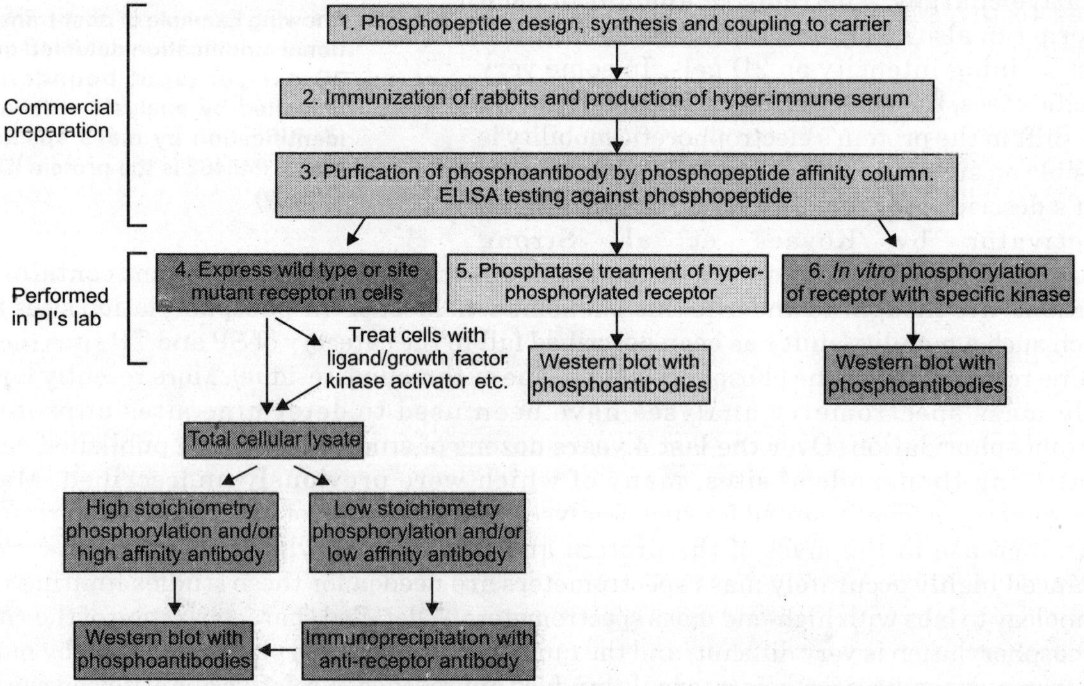

Fig. 2.3 : The following section describes six key steps in development and characterization of phosphoantibodies to study nuclear receptor phosphorylation

Several approaches may be used to study previously identified phosphorylation sites in nuclear receptors [Rowan *et al.*, 2003]. Cells may be labeled *in vivo* with ^{32}P orthophosphate followed by immunopurification and phosphopeptide mapping. Similarly, purified receptor may be phosphorylated *in vitro* with different kinases and individual sites assessed by phosphopeptide mapping [Rowan *et al.*, 2003]. However these approaches are labor intensive, time consuming, and require radioactive material and large amounts of purified receptor. Mass spectrometry is another approach to study protein phosphorylation [Garcia *et al.*, 2005]. This non-quantitative approach requires large amounts of purified receptor and is limited primarily by costly instrumentation and the need for a highly skilled operator.

The phosphoantibody approach to study receptor phosphorylation overcomes several limitations inherent in other approaches and provides the additional benefit of allowing rapid assessment of combinations of receptor phosphorylation sites by Western blotting [Rowan *et al.*, 2003]. The advantages of the phosphoantibody approach include: 1) a highly sensitive assay that can detect phosphorylation in crude extracts containing low receptor levels and/or low stoichiometry of phosphorylation without the need for purified receptor; 2) the ability to profile total receptor phosphorylation and to quantify relative levels of each phosphorylation site; 3) immunoprecipitation of receptors phosphorylated at specific sites to investigate the recruitment of phosphoproteins to promoters (chromatin immunoprecipitation (ChIP)) and to identify phosphorylation sites involved in specific protein-protein interaction (co-immunoprecipitation); 4) identification of phosphorylation sites associated with real time dynamics of receptor subcellular localization and recycling and other cellular processes (immunofluorescence; flow cytometry sorting); 5) the ability to monitor changes in the total receptor phosphorylation profile during disease processes such as the progression from benign to malignant cancer (immunohistochemistry).

The phosphoantibody approach has been widely applied to characterize nuclear receptor activity and subcellular localization [Wang *et al.*, 2002]. Glucocorticoid receptor (GR) GR-P-S203 and GR-P-S211 phosphoantibodies have been used by immunoblotting to study GR activation by different ligands and by indirect immunofluorescence to investigate the subcellular localization of the active GR. Progesterone receptor (PR) phosphospecific antibodies to sites S400 [Pierson-Mullany and Lange, 2004], S162, S190 and S294 [Narayanan *et al.*, 2005] were used by immunoblotting to study the ligand independent activation of PR and to correlate PR transcriptional activity and cell-cycle progression. Androgen receptor (AR) phosphoantibody to site S81 was used by immunoblotting to study the mechanism of ligand-dependent arrest of the AR in subnuclear foci [Black *et al.*, 2004]. Phosphoantibodies to ERα sites S118 and S167 [Chen *et al.*, 2002; Shah and Rowan, 2005]were used by immunoblotting to study crosstalk between ERα and several kinases. In addition, these phosphoantibodies have been used by immunohistochemistry to detect

ERα phosphorylation in human breast tumors [Murphy *et al.*, 2004; Yamashita *et al.*, 2005].

The following section describes six key steps in development and characterization of phosphoantibodies to study nuclear receptor phosphorylation (Figure 2.2). The first three steps include preparation, purification and initial testing of phosphoantibodies and are generally performed by commercial vendors. The remaining three steps to validate and confirm specificity of the phosphoantibody for specific phosphorylation sites are performed by the investigator in the laboratory and are the major focus of this review.

Peptide Design and Immunogen Preparation

The synthetic phosphopeptide used for immunization is recommended to be 10-20 amino acids in length and conjugated with a suitable carrier that will solicit a strong immune response and produce a large quantity of the antibody [Eisele *et al.*, 1999; Frank, 1984; Harlow and Lane, 1988]. The most widely used carriers in antibody production are keyhole limpet hemacyanin (KLH) and bovine serum albumin (BSA) [Harlow and Lane, 1988]. It is important to be aware of the conjugated carrier used during immunization to anticipate any false positives that may occur during antibody testing. For example if the conjugated carrier is BSA, a false positive may arise if BSA was used as a blocking agent for Western blotting. Immunogenicity of the peptide-protein carrier can be verified by an enzyme linked immunosorbent assay (ELISA) to identify the most appropriate protein carrier dose.

Producing Hyper-immune Serum

For broad specificity it is recommended that phosphoantibodies be prepared as polyclonal antibodies [Burns, 2005; Harlow and Lane, 1988; Leenaars and Hendriksen, 2005; Lipman *et al.*, 2005]. Rabbits are the host of choice to avoid self-recognition of the immunogen and since rabbits provide high amounts of sera. The immunogen is mixed with adjuvant prior to immunizing animals. The immunogen mixture is injected subcutaneously and re-administered at day 14 and 44 post immunization. At day 54 sera is collected by bleeding of the marginal ear vein. Bleeding is repeated on day 60 and then every 4 weeks until the antibody titer has declined. A booster dose of immunogen should be administered to re-enhance animal immunity and produce more sera [Burns, 2005]. After each bleeding, antibody titer should be measured by ELISA.

Affinity Purification

Following harvest of the hyper-immune sera, the phosphoantibody can be enriched by an affinity purification against the phosphorylated peptide [Harlow and Lane, 1988]. The affinity purification is validated by ELISA screening against the phosphopeptide in which phosphoantibody purity should exceed 95%.Numerous commercial suppliers will produce custom, affinity purified phosphoantibodies (Bethyl Laboratories, Invitrogen, Global Peptide, ABGENT, Open Biosystems and others).

Phosphoantibody specificity assessed by receptor phosphorylation site mutations

Affinity purified phosphoantibody must be validated as phosphorylation site specific. In mammalian cells that do not express the receptor of interest, wild type receptor expression plasmids or plasmids containing phosphorylation site mutations (Serine (S) to Alanine (A), Threonine (T) to A, Tyrosine (Y) to Phenylalanine (F)) should be transfected in cells to achieve high level protein expression. Total cell extracts from wild-type and phosphorylation site mutant transfected cells should be prepared for Western blotting with the phosphoantibody and peptide-competed phosphoantibody to assess specificity for the phosphorylation site. High receptor levels may be required to measure phosphorylation sites that exhibit low stoichiometry. For other sites that require an activation event, cells may first need to be incubated with ligand, growth factor, kinase activator, etc. prior to detection of the specific phosphorylation with a phosphoantibody.

The ideal phosphoantibody should recognize receptor from cells transfected with wild type but not the site-specific mutant protein. However depending on cell context, protein expression and stoichiometry, some phosphoantibodies may fail to detect a signal in total cellular extract. If this occurs, enrichment of receptor by immunoprecipitation with a receptor-specific antibody is recommended prior to Western blotting with the phosphoantibody. It is critical that immunoprecipitation be carried out over a brief period (no more than a few hours) since dephosphorylation may occur over longer periods. Regardless, phosphatase inhibitors should always be included in lysis buffers whether receptor is immunoprecipitated or not.

A critical step when first using phosphoantibodies for Western blotting is to empirically determine the optimal phosphoantibody concentration that will: 1) exhibit reactivity with wild type, but not phosphorylation site mutant receptor; and 2) not result in high general background on Western blots. In our experience, some phosphoantibodies exhibit specificity for wild type and not phosphorylation site mutant receptor only at high antibody dilutions. The appropriate antibody dilution must be determined empirically using serial dilutions of the affinity purified antibody in Western blot analysis. We have found that some affinity purified phosphoantibodies (stock concentration of 1 mg/ml) require dilution as high as 1:10,000 to eliminate non-specific reactivity with the phosphorylation site mutant receptor.

Absence of Phosphoantibody Reactivity with de-phosphorylated Receptor

A second step for validation of phosphoantibodies is to confirm the antibody does not react with receptor that has been de-phosphorylated. In this context, the hyper-phosphorylated form of the purified receptor should be incubated in the presence or absence of ë phosphatase, followed by Western blotting with the phosphoantibody. Phosphatase treatment should prevent reactivity of the phosphoantibody with the receptor.

in vitro Receptor Phosphorylation to measure Phosphoantibody Reactivity

In some cell/tissue contexts that lack a specific kinase or have inactive kinase, some phosphoantibodies may not react with receptor due to absence or very low stoichiometry of phosphorylation at a particular site. In this scenario, *in vitro* phosphorylation of purified receptor with a kinase known to phosphorylate the specific site can be used prior to incubation with ë phosphatase. Phosphoantibody reactivity with the purified protein should increase following *in vitro* phosphorylation and signal should be lost following ë phosphatase treatment. A kinase that is not specific for the site in question should be used as a control for the *in vitro* phosphorylation.

Reactivity and Specificity: Phosphoantibodies to ERα as an example

In this study, phosphoantibodies developed against eight different phosphorylation sites of ERα were characterized (Figure 2.3). ERα is phosphorylated upon ligand binding and/ or crosstalk with kinases. Although there are eight identified phosphorylation sites in ERα, (S104, S106, S118, S167, S236, S305, T311, and Y537 [Lannigan, 2003; Michalides *et al.*, 2004], only phosphoantibodies against S118 and S167 have been widely applied for receptor functional studies. Phosphoantibodies directed against S104, S106 and Y537 are also commercially available although application of these antibodies to receptor functional studies is limited. This may be due to lower stoichiometry of phosphorylation at these sites, rapid turnover of tyrosine phosphorylation sites and/or poorer affinity of these antibodies compared to the S118 and S167 phosphoantibodies.

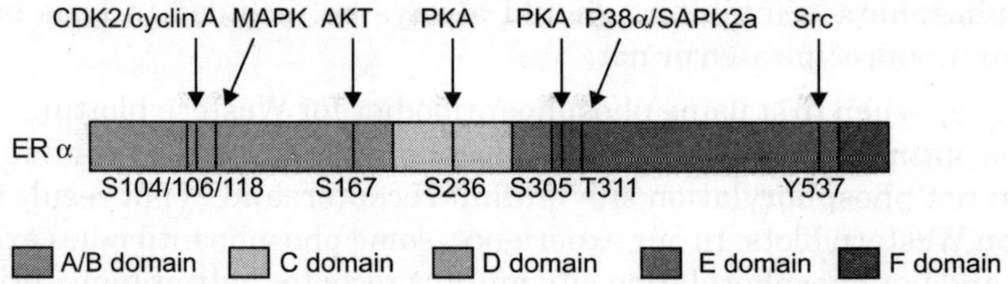

Fig. 2.4 : Phosphoantibodies developed against eight different phosphorylation sites of ERα were characterized

Antibodies

Bethyl Laboratories (Montgomery, TX) provided complimentary phosphoantibodies: ERα ER-P-S104 (Cat. # BL1637), ER-P-S106 (Cat. # BL1638), ER-P-S118 (Cat. # BL1641), ER-P-S167 (Cat. # BL1643), ER-P-S236 (Cat. # 1645), ER-P-S305 (Cat. # 1665), ER-P-T311 (Cat. # BL1667) and ER-P-Y537 (Cat. # BL1647). Antibody D12 for ERα immunopreciptitation (Cat. # sc-8005) was purchased from Santa Cruz Biotechnology (Santa Cruz, CA). ERα antibody clone 6F11 for Western blots of total ERα (Cat. # VP-E613), peroxidase conjugated anti-mouse (Cat. # π-2000) and peroxidase conjugated anti-rabbit antibodies (Cat. # π-1000) were purchased from Vector Laboratories (Burlingame, CA).

Purified ERα, Phosphatase and Kinases

Baculoviral expressed ERα (Cat. # P2187) was purchased from Invitrogen (Carlsbad, CA). λ protein phosphatase (Cat. # P0753S) and active recombinant full length human CDK2-cyclin A complex expressed in E. coli (Cat. # P6025S) were purchased from New England Biolabs (Ipswich, MA). Baculoviral expressed, active recombinant full length human protein kinase A (PKA) catalytic subunit β (Cat. # PPK-448) was purchased from Stressgen (San Diego, CA). Baculoviral expressed, active recombinant full length human Src kinase (Cat. # 14-326) and active recombinant human full length p38α/SAPK2a kinase expressed in E. coli (Cat. # 14-587) were purchased from Upstate (Charlottesville, VA).

Methods

Cell culture and transfection

COS-1 cells were maintained in DMEM phenol red free medium containing 10% Fetal Bovine Serum (FBS), 2% glutamine and 1% penicillin/streptomycin. Cells were plated in 15 cm dishes for 48 hrs in DMEM phenol red-free medium containing 5% FBS that was treated with dextran-coated charcoal to remove endogenous steroids. Wild type or phosphorylation site mutant ERα constructs (6 μg) were transiently transfected in cells for 48 hrs using Fugene 6 (Roche, Indianapolis, IN). Cells were incubated with 17β-estradiol (E2) (10 nM) or Forskolin (10 μM) + IBMX (100 μM) (F/I) for 2 hrs. Cells were harvested and cellular pellets were incubated in high salt lysis buffer (10 mM Tris pH 8.0, 0.4 M NaCl, 2 mM EDTA pH 8.0, 2 mM EGTA, 10 mM β-mercaptoethanol, 0.1% Triton X100, 1 mM sodium orthovanadate, 20 mM β-glycerophosphate, 25 mM sodium fluoride, 0.1 mM PMSF) containing protease inhibitor mixture (σ, St. Louis, MO) for 10 min in ice.

Immunoprecipitation of ERα

Protein A sepharose beads (Amersham Biosciences, Piscataway, NJ) were re-swelled in phosphate buffer saline (PBS) and incubated with ERα antibody (D12, Santa Cruz) by rotating the beads at room temperature for 2 hrs. Beads were washed three times with PBS, followed by incubation with the total COS-1 cellular extract for 3 hrs at 4 C with rotation. Beads were washed three times with PBS, followed by addition of 5X SDS-PAGE loading buffer. Beads were incubated at 100 C for 5 min to elute ERα. Samples were electrophoresed by SDS-PAGE and phosphorylation of ERα was detected by Western blotting using site specific phosphoantibodies. Phosphoantibody signals obtained by Kodak Image analysis of Western blots were normalized to total ERα level by incubating the membrane in stripping buffer (2% SDS, 100 mM β-mercaptoethanol, 62.5 mM Tris HCl pH 6.8) at 55 C for 30 min with rotation and re-probing the membrane by Western blot with antibody against total ERα (clone 6F11, Vector Laboratories).

λ Phosphatase Analysis

200 ng purified ERα was incubated with 200ng λ phosphatase in reaction buffer (50mM Tris-HCl, 100 mM NaCl, 2 mM MnCl2 2mM dithiothreitol (DTT), 0.1 mM EGTA, 0.01 %

Brij 35, pH 7.5) for 1 hr at 30 C. To terminate the reaction, 5X SDS-PAGE loading buffer was added and samples were incubated at 100 C for 5 min., followed by SDS-PAGE and Western blots using site specific phosphoantibodies

in vitro Phosphorylation

Purified ERα (200 ng) was incubated with the site specific kinase or kinase complex, ATP, and kinase buffer for 1 hr at 30 C in the presence or absence of ë phosphatase. Kinases used were: CDK2-cyclin A (100 ng; (kinase buffer 50 mM Tris-HCl, 10 mM MgCl2, 1 mM EGTA, 2 mM DTT, 0.01% Brij 35, pH 7.5); PKA (100 ng) or inactive PKA (PKA incubated at 100 C for 2 min.; kinase buffer (20 mM MOPS pH 7.0, 1 mM sodium orthovanadate, 25 mM β-glycerophosphate, 1 mM EGTA, 1 mM DTT, 7 mM MgCl2); P38α/SAPK2a (100 ng; (kinase buffer 25 mM Tris-HCl pH 7.5, 0.02 mM EGTA); and Src kinase (100 ng; kinase buffer 8 mM MOPS pH 7.0, 0.2 mM EDTA). *in vitro* phosphorylation reactions were terminated by addition of 5X SDS-PAGE loading buffer and incubation of samples at 100 C for 5 min. Following SDS-PAGE, phosphorylation of S104, S236, S305, T311, and Y537 were detected by Western blotting with phosphoantibodies.

Results

The initial step for characterization of phosphoantibodies is to prove the antibody is site specific. For this purpose, wild type ERα and site mutant ERα constructs were separately transfected into ERα-negative COS-1 cells. Cells were then incubated with 17β-estradiol (10-8M) or forskolin (10μM) + IBMX (100μM) for 2 hrs and cell extracts were prepared for Western blotting. Phosphorylation sites with low stoichiometry or antibodies with low affinity may not detect receptor in crude cellular extracts. For this reason ERα was first immunoprecipitated with a separate ERα antibody (D12, Santa Cruz) and then the immunopurified receptor was subjected to Western blotting with the phosphoantibodies. Phosphoantibodies to ERα-P-S104 (Figure 2.5A), ERα-P-S106 (Figure 3B), ERα-P-S118 (Figure 2.5C), ERα-P-S167 (Figure 2.5D), ERα-P-S236 (Figure 2.5E), ERα-P-S305 (Figure 2.5F), ERα-P-T311 (Figure 2.5G) and ERα-P-Y537 (Figure 2.5H) detected wild type ERα, but not phosphorylation site ERα mutants, indicating that antibodies were site specific. For some phosphoantibodies serial dilutions were prepared to determine the optimal antibody concentration for detection of wild type, but not mutant ERα. At high concentration (2 μg/ml) the ERα-P-S167 phosphoantibody recognized both wild-type ERα and mutant S167A (data not shown). This nonspecific interaction with mutant S167A was absent when the antibody concentration was decreased to 0.25 μg/ml (Figure 2.5D).

Specificity of the antibodies was verified by ë phosphatase treatment of the hyper-phosphorylated purified ERα or by *in vitro* phosphorylation of ERα with specific kinases. Phosphoantibodies to sites S106, S118 and S167 recognized purified, baculoviral expressed ERα, indicating that kinase pathways that phosphorylate these sites are conserved in insect Sf9 cells (Figure 2.6 A-C, lane 1).

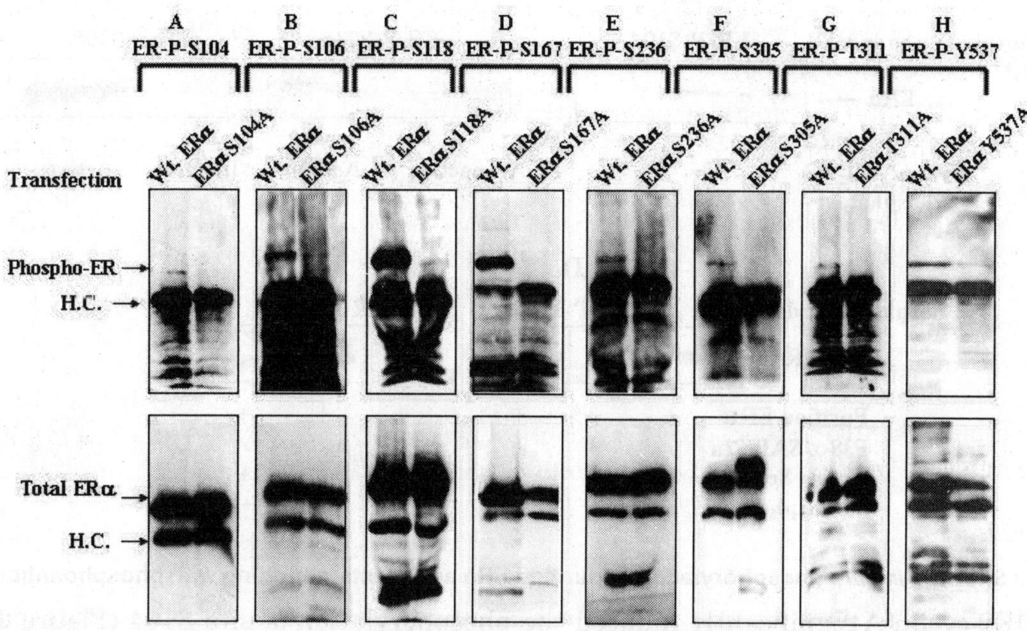

Fig. 2.5 : This non-specific interaction with mutant S167A was absent when the antibody concentration was decreased to 0.25 μg/ml

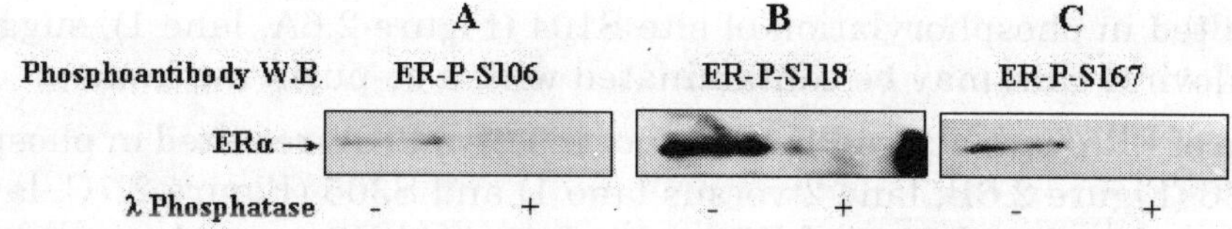

Fig. 2.6 : Showing Phosphatase treatment of purified ERα and Western blotting with phosphoantibodies

A similar conservation between mammalian and Sf9 insect cells for receptor phosphorylation was observed with baculoviral expressed progesterone receptor [Beck *et al.*, 1996]. Purified ERα was incubated with λ phosphatase for 1 hr at 30 C and the phosphorylation of S106, S118, and S167 was assessed by Western blotting with the phosphospecific antibodies. ë phosphatase treatment of ERα resulted in loss of Western blot signal with phosphoantibodies to sites S106 (Figure 2.5A), S118 (Figure 2.5B) and S167 (Figure 2.5C). Unlike phosphoantibodies to S106, S118, and S167, phosphoantibodies to sites S104, S236, S305, T311 and Y537 exhibited no reactivity with purified ERα (data not shown). The antibody specificity was assessed by *in vitro* phosphorylation of ERα with CDK2-cyclin A, PKA, p38α/SAPK2a and Src kinases followed by Western blotting with phosphoantibodies to sites S236, S305, T311 and Y537.

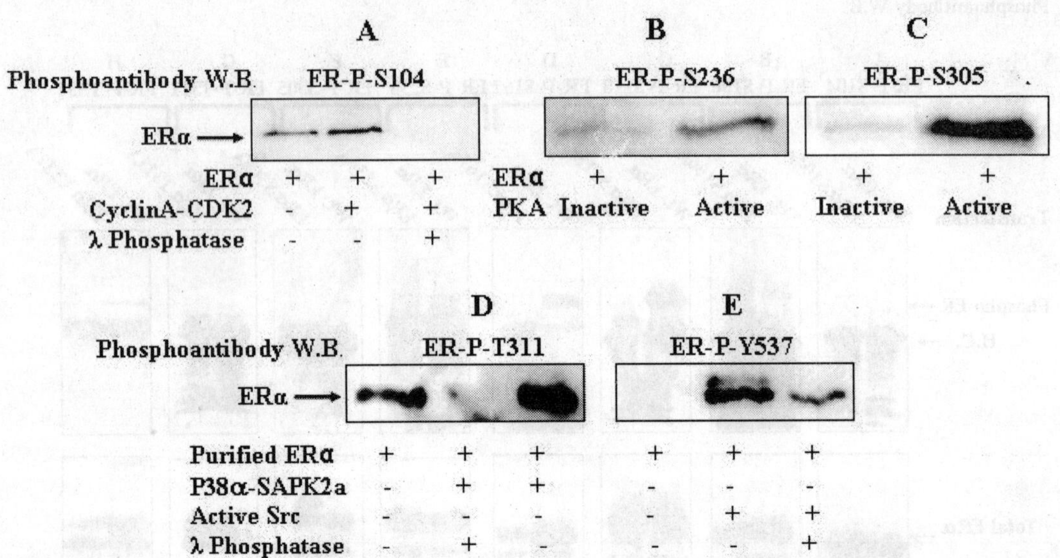

Fig. 2.7 : Showing *in vitro* phosphorylation of purified ERα and Western blotting with phosphoantibodies

CDK2-cyclin A significantly induced the phosphorylation of site S104 (Figure 2.7A, lane 2) and subsequent λ phosphatase treatment (Figure 73A, lane 3) abolished the phosphorylation as assessed by Western blotting with the ERα-P-S104 phosphoantibody. In the absence of kinase, incubation of purified baculoviral ERα with kinase buffer and ATP also resulted in phosphorylation of site S104 (Figure 2.6A, lane 1), suggesting that purified, baculoviral ERα may be contaminated with a co-purifying kinase.

Incubation of ERα with active PKA, but not inactive PKA, resulted in phosphorylation of ERα at S236 (Figure 2.6B, lane 2 versus lane 1) and S305 (Figure 2.7C, lane 2 versus lane 1). *in vitro* phosphorylation of ERα with P38α/SAPK2a complex resulted in T311 phosphorylation (Figure 2.7D, lane 3), and this phosphorylation was lost with subsequent ë phosphatase incubation (Figure 2.6D, lane 2). Incubation of ERα with Src kinase resulted in phosphorylation of ERα at Y537 (Figure 2.7E, lane 2) and this phosphorylation was markedly reduced with subsequent ë phosphatase incubation (Figure 2.7E, lane 3).

Discussion

Although there are several different methods to characterize changes in receptor phosphorylation, the phosphoantibody approach is particularly useful for simultaneously measuring each phosphorylation site. In this report the general steps in characterizing and validating phosphoantibodies are described using the example of phosphoantibodies raised against eight phosphorylation sites in ERα. Validation of each phosphoantibody was assessed in two steps; first the site specificity of the phosphoantibody was validated by expressing ERα wild type or site mutant plasmids into receptor negative cell lines. Second, the phosphoantibody specificity was validated by incubating the hyper-phosphorylated purified ERα with λ phosphatase and by performing *in vitro* phosphorylation with a specific kinase or kinase complex that is known to phosphorylate a specific site.

Although all eight phosphoantibodies raised against each ERα phosphorylation site were site specific, these phosphoantibodies reacted differently with the hyper-phosphorylated, baculoviral expressed ERα. Only phosphoantibodies to sites S106, S118 and S167 recognized the baculoviral expressed ERα. This may have occurred because some sites are not phosphorylated in insect Sf9 cells due to either the absence of kinase activity or the presence of phosphatases that prevent ERα phosphorylation at these sites.

CDK2-cyclin A is a specific kinase complex previously shown to phosphorylate both S104 and S106 of ERα [Rogatsky *et al.*, 1999]. Because of the close proximity of S104 and S106, it is possible that phosphorylation of one site may be required for phosphorylation of the adjacent site (currently under investigation). Serine 236 and Serine 305 are located within consensus sequences for PKA and phosphorylation of these sites by PKA has been demonstrated [Chen *et al.*, 1999; Michalides *et al.*, 2004]. The direct kinase that phosphorylates ERα at T311 has not been identified. Lee and Bai [Lee and Bai, 2002] reported that T311 is phosphorylated by a p38 MAPK kinase complex that contained both p38α and SAPK2a. Since T311 does not lie within a consensus sequence for MAPK phosphorylation (the T residue is not followed by a proline residue), it is highly unlikely that p38 directly phosphorylates T311. A more likely explanation is that the kinase that directly phosphorylates T311 is a kinase that copurified with p38 in the present and previous study. Y537 is present within a Src kinase consensus sequence and is phosphorylated by Src kinase *in vitro* [Arnold and Notides, 1995; Arnold *et al.*, 1995].

In summary, development of phosphoantibodies to assess the functional role of nuclear receptor phosphorylation is a powerful approach that has distinct advantages over other more labor intensive and costly approaches. However, rigorous validation experiments must precede use of phosphoantibodies to ascertain both reactivity with the phosphorylated receptor and absence of cross reactivity with non-phosphorylated receptor. Phosphoantibody specificity is determined using several complimentary approaches, including expression of wild type and mutant receptor in cells, phosphatase treatment of receptor, and *in vitro* phosphorylation of receptor. Using phosphoantibodies that are specific for each identified phosphorylation site will permit investigators to simultaneously measure the entire profile of receptor phosphorylation during studies that probe nuclear receptor mechanisms of action.

Phosphorylation State-Specific Antibodies

Applications in Investigative and Diagnostic Pathology

Protein phosphorylation was discovered more than 50 years ago. The study of intracellular signaling is nearly synonymous with the study of protein phosphorylation. In a recent review, Philip Cohen[2] asserted that "the reversible phosphorylation of proteins regulates nearly every aspect of cell life." Phosphorylation and its reverse reaction, dephosphorylation, are carried out by more than 2000 kinases and a smaller number of phosphatases, respectively. Phosphorylation of proteins can modify function in two main ways. Phosphorylation at specific residues may induce conformational changes that lead to altered enzymatic activity, or of ion channel permeability. Alternatively or in parallel, phosphorylation can generate specific binding sites for other proteins, leading to the assembly of functional complexes of proteins. Phosphorylation of transcription factors is central to gene regulation whereas phosphorylation of cytoskeletal proteins is important for control of cell shape and motility. Finally, recent advances point to phosphorylation as an initial step in targeted protein degradation. The importance of protein phosphorylation in cancer was made apparent by the identification of several oncogenes as mutated and constitutively activated kinases. Malfunction of signal transduction pathways is also implicated in non-neoplastic diseases including immunological, endocrine, cardiovascular, cerebrovascular, and neurodegenerative disorders.

The development of phosphorylation state-specific antibodies (PSSAs) now makes possible the study of protein phosphorylation *in situ*, allowing glimpses of dynamic protein phosphorylation reactions in the spatially complex structures of cells and tissues. I will review the historical development of PSSAs, briefly describe current methodologies for their production, and address potential pitfalls and artifacts, along with a case study from our laboratory. I will then present selected applications of PSSAs, limiting the review to studies on human disease or animal models and including immunohistochemical approaches.

Development of PSSAs

The first PSSAs were monoclonal antibodies raised against neurofilament proteins. Their recognition as PSSAs was a serendipitous discovery followed by rigorous analysis. In this elegant landmark paper, the authors showed not only that PSSAs could discern between phosphorylated and dephosphorylated proteins in biochemical assays, but that they could be applied to fixed brain tissue sections to reveal information about the subcellular heterogeneity of neurofilament protein phosphorylation. The panel of Sternberger antibodies remains a mainstay in diagnostic and investigative neuropathology.

In the 1980s, researchers succeeded in developing monclonal and polyclonal antibodies specific for phosphotyrosine, and with somewhat more limited success to phosphothreonine These antibodies, because they bind to any protein containing the phosphorylated amino acid, were most useful in Western blotting experiments, where the multiple phosphoproteins could be resolved by their molecular weight. Nevertheless, investigators have applied these generic PSSAs in immunohistochemical studies of human cancers and revealed elevated accumulation of phosphotyrosyl-containing proteins in cancers. Anti-phosphotyrosine antibodies were instrumental in defining the signaling protein complex localized to focal adhesions More recently, a phosphotyrosine antibody was successfully used to screen anaplastic lymphoma specimens for evidence of activating ALK tyrosine kinase mutations.

This could be a general approach for cancer geneticists who wish to identify subsets of tumors likely to harbour mutationally activated tyrosine kinases.

More targeted approaches to develop sequence-specific PSSAs yielded success in the early 1990s. Again focusing on the cytoskeleton, Inagaki and colleagues produced monoclonal antibodies specific for phosphorylated forms of glial fibrillary acidic protein (GFAP) by injecting mice with enzymatically phosphorylated peptides, and screening resultant hybridomas for reactivity against the phospho-, but not the dephospho-peptide. The phosphopeptide immunization approach was also taken by the Greengard group, but with the production of polyclonal antisera instead of monoclonal antibodies. Polyclonal PSSA production is less labor intensive, in that the extensive post-immunization screening step is omitted, but does require an affinity purification step. The most effective procedure is to first remove those antibodies in the antisera that bind to the dephosphorylated antigen by using a dephospho-peptide affinity column, followed by positive selection of the flow-through on a phospho-peptide column. It should be noted that it is just as feasible to produce dephospho-specific antibodies (those that bind to a specfic site only when dephosphorylated). To do so, animals are immunized with the appropriate dephospho-peptide, and the resultant antisera are affinity purified to remove antibodies reactive to the phosphopeptide. Although early methods often relied on enzymatic phosphorylation of peptide antigens, a very inefficient process, advances in peptide chemistry allowing chemical phosphorylation have largely obviated the inefficient enzymatic phosphorylation procedures. The first PSSAs developed using synthetic tyrosine-containing phosphopeptides were used to study activation of erbB-2.

Commercially available PSSAs now are available for more than 300 different phosphoproteins and/or phosphorylation sites (Table 2.1; obtained by metasearch of catalogs using http://www.biocompare.com). The majority of commercial PSSAs are produced by immunization of animals (usually rabbits or goats) with a synthetic phosphorylated peptide. In theory, it would be possible to generate a PSSA against every possible phosphoepitope by synthesizing all possible phosphopeptides. Even if the peptide length is limited to 11 amino acids, the number of peptides needed for complete coverage of all sequences in the form $XXXXXA_pXXXXX$, where X is any amino acid and A_p is either phosphothreonine, phosphoserine, or phosphotyrosine is 3×10^{20}. Unfortunately, this would require unachievable manpower, not to mention a rabbit population covering the face of the earth. More realistic approaches might limit the universe of phosphopeptides to those that actually occur in nature, perhaps on the order of tens of thousands, assuming a handful of sites per phosphoprotein. In fact, large-scale identification of phosphorylation sites is now possible using mass spectrometric techniques, and this method has the potential to eventually map the entire phosphoproteome

4E-BP1 (S65)

4E-BP1 (T37/46)

4E-BP1 (T70)

Acetyl-CoA Carboxylase (S79)
Adducin (S724)
AFX (S193)
Akt (S473)
Akt (T308)
ALK (Y1604)
AMPK-alpha (T172)
APP (T668)
ASK1 (S83)
ATF-2 (T 69/71)
ATF-2 (T71)
Aurora 2 (T288)
Bad (S112/136)
Bad (S136)
Bad (S155)
Bcl-2 (S70)
Bcr (Y177)
beta-Arrestin 1 (S412)
beta-Catenin (S33/37/T41)
beta-Catenin (T41/S45)
BLNK (Y96)
BRCAI (S1189)
BRCAI (S1280)
BRCAI (S1387)
BRCAI (S1423)
BRCAI (S1457)
BRCAI(S466)
Btk (S180)
Btk (Y223)
C/EBP beta (S105)
c-Abl (T735)
c-Abl (Y245)
c-Cbl (Y731)

c-Cbl (Y774)
c-Jun (S63)
II c-Jun (S73)
c-Jun (S73)
c-Kit (Y719)
c-Kit (Y703)
c-Kit (Y936)
c-Myc (T58/S62)
Caldesmon (S789)
CaMKII (T286)
Caveolin-1 (Y14)
CD19 (Y531)
cdc2 (T161)
cdc25 C (T48)
cdc25C (S216)
cdk2 (T160)
Chk1 (S296)
Chk1 (S317)
Chk1 (S345)
Chk2 (S19)
Chk2 (S33/35)
Chk2 (T387)
Chk2 (T432)
Chk2 (T68)
Cofilin (S3)
Connexin 43 (S368)
CPI-17 (T38)
cPLA2 (S505)
CREB (S133)
CrkII (Y221)
CrkL (Y207)
DARPP-32 (T34)
DARPP-32 (T75)

delta-Opioid Receptor (S363)

DNA-topoisomerase II alpha

eEF2 (T56)

eEF2k (S366)

EGF Receptor (Y1045)

EGF Receptor (Y1068)

EGF Receptor (Y845)

EGF Receptor (Y992)

eIF2 alpha (S51)

eIF4 G (S1108)

eIF4E (S209)

Elk-1 (S383 eNOS (S1177)

eNOS (T495)

eNOS (S116)

EphA3 (Y596/Y602)

Ephrin B (Y324/329)

ERK1/2 (T202/Y204)

Erk5 (T218/Y220)

Estrogen Receptor alpha (S104/106)

Estrogen Receptor alpha (S118)

Estrogen Receptor alpha (S167)

Ezrin (T567)/Radixin (T564)/Moesin (T558)

Etk (Y40)

FADD (S191)

FADD (S194)

FAK (Y397)

FAK (Y576/577)

FAK (Y925)

FGF Receptor (Y653/654)

FKHR (T24)

FKHR (S256)

FKHRL1 (S 253)

FKHRL1 (T 32)

P FLT3 (Y591)
FLT3 (Y591)
FRS2-alpha (Y436)
Gab1 (Y627)
GABA-B ReceptorR2 (S892)
GFAP GluR1 (S831)
GluR1 (S845)
GluR2 (S880)
Glycogen Synthase (S640)
GRF1 (S916)
GSK-3 alpha/beta (S21/9)
GSK-3 alpha (S21)
GSK-3 beta (S9)
GSK3 (Y279/Y216)
HER2/ErbB2 (Y1112)
HER2/ErbB2 (Y1248)
HER2/ErbB2 (Y877)
Histone H3 (S10)
Histone H2A.X (S139)
Histone H2B (S14)
H3 (S28)
Histone H3 (T3)
HMGN1/HMG 14 (S6)
HSP27 (S15)
HSP27 (S78)
HSP27 (S82)
IGF-IR (Y1131)/Insulin Receptor (Y1146)
IKK alpha/beta (S180)
I kappa B-alpha (S32/36)
IRS-1 (S307)
IRS-1 (S612)
IRS-1 (S636/639)
Jak1 (Y1022/1023)

Jak2 (Y1007/1008)
JNK/SAPK (T183/Y185)
KDR (Y1212)
Keratin 18 (S33)
Keratin 8 (S431)
Keratin 8 (S73)
LAT (Y171)
LAT (Y191)
LAT (Y226)
Lck (Y505)
Leptin Receptor (Y985)
Leptin Receptor (Y1138)
Lyn (Y507)
M-CSF Receptor (Y723)
M-CSF Receptor (Y809)
MAPKAPK-2 (T222)
MAPKAPK-2 (T334)
MARCKS (S152/156)
MDM2 (S166)
MEK1 (T292)
MEK1 (S298)
MEK1/2 (S 217/221)
Met (Y1234/1235)
Met (Y1349)
MKK3/MKK6 (S 189/07)
Mnk1 (T 197/02)
MSK1 (S360)
MSK1 (S376)
MSK1 (T581)
mTOR (S2448)
mTOR (S2481)
Myelin Basic Protein Myosin Light Chain 2 (S19)
MYPT1 (T696)

Neurofilament H,M,L Neurogranin (S36)
NF-kappa B p65 (S536)
Nibrin/nbs1 (S343)
NMDAR1 (S890)
NMDAR1 (S896)
NMDAR1 (S897)
nNOS (S1416)
NR1 (S896)
NR2B (S1303)
NPM (T199)
p38 MAP Kinase (T180/Y182)
p53 (S15)
p53 (S20)
p53 (S37)
p53 (S392)
p53 (S46)
p53 (S6)
p53 (S9)
p70 S6 Kinase (T389)
p70 S6 Kinase (T421/S424)
p70 S6 Kinase (T 412)
p90RSK (S380)
p90RSK (T359/S363)
p90RSK (T573)
p95/NBS1 (S343)
PAK2 (S20)
Paxillin (Y118)
PDGF Receptor beta (Y751)
PDGF Receptor beta (Y716)
PDK1 (S241)
PDK1 (Y373/376)
PERK (T980)
Phospholamban (S16)

SAPK/JNK (T183/Y185)
PAK1 (S144)/PAK2 (S141)
PAK1/2 (S199/204)
PAK1 (T423)/PAK2 (T402)
PRK1 (T778)/PRK2 (T816)
PKA RII (S96)
PKC alpha (S657)
PKC alpha/beta II (T638/641)
PKC delta/theta (S643/676)
PKC delta (T505)
PKC Epsilon (S 729)
PKC theta (T538)
PKC zeta/lambda (T410/403)
PKD/PKC mu (S 744/748)
PKD/PKC mu (S916)
PKD2 (S876)
PKR (T446/451)
PLC beta 3 (S1105)
PLC beta 3 (S537)
PLC gamma1 (Y783)
PP1 alpha (T320)
PP2A (Y307)
Presenilin-2 (S327/330)
Progesterone Receptor (S190)
Progesterone Receptor (S294)
PTEN (S380/T382/383)
Pyk2 (Y402)
Rac1/cdc42 (S71)
Rad17 (S645)
Raf (S259)
Raf (S338)
Rb (S780)
Rb (S795)

Rb (S807/811)
Ret (Y905)
RNA polymerase II
RSK3 (T 353/356)
S6 Ribosomal Protein (S235/236)
S6 Ribosomal Protein (S 240/244)
SEK1/MKK4 (T261)
SGK
Shc (Y239/240)
Shc (Y317)
SHP-2 (Y542)
SHP-2 (Y580)
Smad1/5 (S 463/465)
Smad2 (S465/467)
Src (Y416)
Src (Y527)
Stat1 (Y701)
STAT1 (S727)
STAT2 (Y689)
Stat3 (S727)
Stat3 (Y705)
Stat5 (Y694)
STAT5A/B (S726/S731)
Stat6 (Y641)
Syk (Y323)
Syk (Y525/526)
Synapsin (S9)
Tau (S199/S202/T205)
Tau (T212/S214)
Tau (S231)
Tau (S396/S404)
Tau (dephospho S199/S202)
TrkA (Y490)

Tuberin (T1462)
Tuberin (Y1571)
Tyk2 (Y 1054/1055)
Tyrosine Hydroxylase (S40)
VASP (S157)
VASP (S239)
VEGF Receptor-2 (Y951)
VEGF Receptor-2 (Y996)
Zap-70 (Y319)
Zap-70 (Y493)

Tests of Antibody Specificity

The principles of testing for PSSA specificity are generally similar to conventional antibodies. The most important additional controls involve experimentally altering the phosphorylation state of the target protein and demonstrating the ability of the PSSA to document this alteration in fixed cells or tissues. An example of a rigorously controlled immunohistochemical study using a monoclonal PSSA was recently published. The authors used a phospho-Stat5 antibody to examine phosphorylation in a culture model as well as mouse and human breast tissue specimens. Several independent methods were used to validate antibody specificity, including Western blotting, immunostaining of stimulated *versus* unstimulated cultured cells, immunostaining of tissue with peptide preincubation controls, and genetic (knockout) controls. Each of these approaches is discussed briefly below.

Western Blotting

As for any antibody, the first step is validation by Western blot to show that it detects a single band (or multiple bands if family members share phosphorylation motifs) of appropriate molecular weight in homogenates of tissues and cells. The antibody should also report phosphorylation and dephosphorylation in response to appropriate stimuli in cell culture models.

Immunocytochemical Staining of Fixed Cultured Cells

The next step is to show that the phosphorylation state changes observable on Western blots are also observable on immunostaining of fixed cultured cells undergoing the same stimulation paradigm. The fixation should mirror that which takes place in the surgical pathology lab (*e.g.*, typically 10% buffered formalin). Additional assurance that the PSSA in hand will work on formalin-fixed, paraffin-embedded (FFPE) sections can be had by demonstration that fixed cultured cell preps, after paraffin-embedding and sectioning, still retain the expected changes in immunoreactivity. Methods for preparation of cultured cells for paraffin-embedding have been compared for the purpose of cell and tissue microarray construction.

Phosphopeptide Preincubation and Enzymatic Dephosphorylation Controls

A common test of specificity for antibodies in general is preincubation of the diluted antibody with molar excess of the immunizing antigen. The same can be done for PSSAs, with additional specificity provided by the use of phospho- and dephosphopeptides. Immunizing phosphopeptides are often available from antibody suppliers. An important control is to show that the phosphopeptide, but not the otherwise identical dephosphopeptide, abolishes immunoreactivity A less specific but still useful control is to show that immunoreactivity for a phospho-dependent antibody is abolished by pretreatment of sections with alkaline phosphatase. In contrast, dephospho-specific antibodies, for example tau-1, which only binds to a specific dephosphorylated epitope, should show enhanced immunoreactivity after alkaline phosphatase treatment.

Molecular Genetic Controls

An elegant control at the molecular level is to perform site-directed mutagenesis of the phospho-acceptor amino acid within the protein of interest. Expression of the mutated protein in cells, followed by immunoprecipitation and probing with the PSSA should reveal complete loss of immunoreactivity compared to the wild-type protein. This approach has been taken for a phosphorylation-specific phospholipase C-γ2 antibody[21] and the phospho-specific Stat5 antibody.

Immunohistochemical Artifacts Specific to PSSAs

As with immunohistochemistry in general, the most common problem encountered in the application of PSSAs to fixed tissue sections is a false-negative reaction. Tissues that are known to contain the phosphorylated protein of interest, as determined by Western blot with the PSSA, sometimes fail to exhibit immunoreactivity by immunohistochemistry. This can be due to inaccessibility of antigen to antibody, 'antigen masking,' or sensitivity (signal-to-noise ratio). Antigen retrieval techniques may improve detection of phosphoepitopes, especially within dense cellular matrices, such as the nucleus. Systematic testing of various antigen retrieval techniques for use with PSSAs has not been reported. The problem of sensitivity is especially apparent for some phosphorylated signaling proteins and transcription factors which are present at low copy number and may not be detectable by standard immunohistochemical methods. An obvious warning sign that a PSSA is probably not suitable for immunohistochemical applications is when the manufacturer recommends a two-step procedure (immunoprecipitation followed by Western blotting) for phosphorylation detection on blots. This generally indicates a relatively low affinity and/or selectivity of the PSSA. A key concept to keep in mind when using PSSAs is that protein phosphorylation is a highly dynamic process *in vivo*. At best, immunohistochemical detection of phosphorylation captures a true snapshot of phosphorylation at a moment in time. At worst, the snapshot captures only a fleeting trace of reality. In fact, there is potential for both under-representation and over-representation of the true phosphorylation state. A good case example is PSSAs directed against tau, the microtubule-associated protein that accumulates in Alzheimer's disease (AD) neurofibrillary tangles. A widely accepted notion in the field was that tau deposited in AD tangles had qualitatively and quantitatively aberrant phosphorylation. PSSAs were developed that detected hyperphosphorylated tau in AD but not normal brain. However, the subsequent discovery that biopsy-derived tau from normal non-AD brain (rapidly procured surgical tissue) was phosphorylated at many of the sites considered AD-specific shook up the field. From this study the authors concluded that the phosphorylation sites under study were not AD-specific, but that AD neurons appeared to have deficient phosphatase activity relative to normal brain neurons, such that the phosphoepitopes disappeared from normal neurons by the time of autopsy, whereas AD neurons retained high levels of phospho-tau. To make matters more complicated, a comprehensive study of simulated postmortem conditions revealed that tau initially underwent increased phosphorylation on at least one AD site, followed by a slow decrease. Morevover, total protein phosphorylation underwent changes following tissue removal, with peaks of phosphorylation at 30 and 90 minutes postmortem, followed by a slow decline. The mechanism of these changes occurring in devitalized tissue is not completely understood. The obvious explanation for the slow decline is the loss of cellular ATP, required for kinase activity, in the face of continued phosphatase action (ATP-independent). However, the biphasic increases in total phosphorylation remain to be explained. We have observed a related artifact in gathering data for a study on ERK/MAP kinase activation in human gliomas. In rapidly procured but large (>1 cm) surgical specimens, phospho-ERK/MAPK immunoreactivity was sometimes limited to the outer few millimeters of tissue compared to the uniform preservation of total (phospho-independent) ERK/MAPK immunoreactivity (Figure 2.8). This was observed in both low-and high-grade gliomas. Our interpretation of this observation is that due to time-dependent penetration of the formalin fixative, the outer rim of large specimens shows preservation of the phosphorylation state, whereas tissue deep in the core has lost phosphorylation by the time that the fixative has permeated. For this reason, we limit our analysis of PSSA immunoreactivity to either small biopsy specimens (<5 mm) or to the outer few millimeters of large specimens.

These observations, taken together with the clearly documented lability of phospho-tau epitopes, raise the issue of phosphoepitope lability as a critical one in the field. Once fixed and paraffin-embedded, it seems likely that phosphoepitopes, like other antigens, are extremely stable in room temperature archives. However, this should be examined in an objective fashion, by comparing results from specimens over a several decade span of storage. Most important is the lability of protein phosphorylation in surgical specimens, both during the time of specimen handling and during fixation. There is a need for a controlled study of the dephosphorylation kinetics of representative phosphoepitopes in various human tissue specimens. This could be assessed both by quantitative Western blot as well as semi-quantitative immunohistochemistry. Clearly, it will not be possible to control the exact handling time for all surgical specimens, with variable handling times necessitated

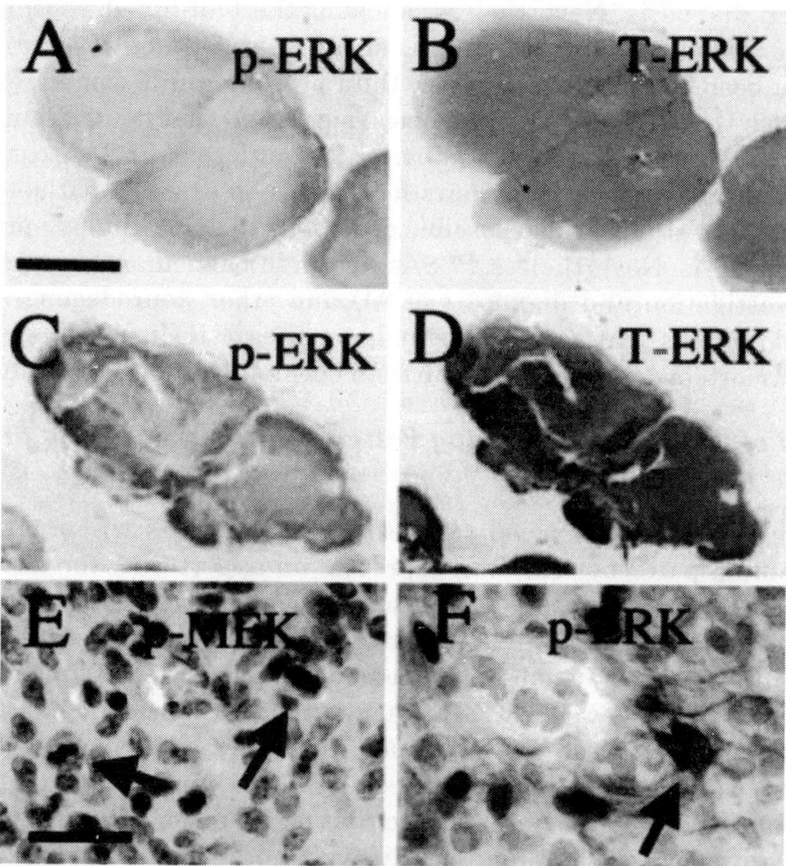

Fig. 2.8 : Illustration of potential pitfalls and unexpected spatiotemporal complexity of protein phosphorylation using PSSAs. A–D: Artifactual loss of phospho-ERK immunoreactivity in large tissue specimens. Glioma specimens larger than 1 cm sometimes showed strong phospho-ERK staining in the peripheral few millimeters but not the core (A, anaplastic astrocytoma; C, glioblastoma multiforme). Immunoreactivity for a phosphorylation-independent ERK antibody was always preserved throughout the tumor specimen (B and D), suggesting that phosphorylated epitopes may be lost due to ongoing dephosphorylation in the core of large specimens due to slow fixation. Bar in A, 1 cm, applies to A–D. E–F: Comparison of phospho-MEK and phospho-ERK immunohistochemistry reveals unexpected complexity of component activation within a signaling cascade. A phospho-MEK antibody (Cell Signaling Technology) shows strong and selective staining of mitotic cells in a human glioblastoma (E, arrows). In contrast, phospho-ERK immunostaining of an adjacent section revealed cytoplasmic and nuclear staining in non-mitotic cells (F). These patterns were confirmed in several non-neoplastic tissues, in both human and rodent (J.W. Mandell, unpublished data). Antibody specificity was confirmed by both Western blot and peptide competition controls (data not shown). The apparent paradox was recently revealed to be due to a mitosis-specific cleavage of MEK which renders it highly phosphorylated in mitosis, but uncoupled to ERK activation. Bar in E, 50 μm, applies to E–F.

by frozen section diagnosis. Nevertheless, knowing the half-life of phosphorylation will give more confidence in interpreting results using PSSAs. Optimal fixation conditions for PSSAs have not been rigorously addressed. Data presented in a commercial publication (*Signals* 1:4, 2002; Cell Signaling Technologies) suggested that neutral-buffered formalin was the best all-around fixative for a panel of four different PSSAs, compared to 70% ethanol and paraformaldehyde: good news for studies on archival pathology specimens. Taken together, these studies raise possible objections to using autopsy-procured tissues for studies with PSSAs. Nevertheless, PSSAs to tau, in particular, have proven powerful tools in the investigation and diagnosis of AD and other neurodegenerative diseases. Phosphorylated proteins that accumulate in aggregates or inclusions may be much more resistant to postmortem dephosphorylation than normally localized phosphoproteins.

Interpretation of Unexpected Staining Patterns: Potential Pitfalls or Opportunity for Discovery

Investigators using PSSAs in novel tissues or tumour types will occasionally reveal unexpected staining patterns. This can represent an opportunity for discovery but can also result from aberrant antibody cross-reaction. One approach to such an unexpected result from our laboratory is illustrated (Figure 2.8) . We had used a commercially available phospho-MEK antibody (Cell Signaling Technology, Beverly, MA) to complement a phospho-ERK antibody study of RasRafMEKERK pathway activation in human gliomas. Since ERK is the only known substrate of MEK, and all culture models suggested simultaneous activation of the two components, it was expected that the immunostaining pattern of the phospho-MEK antibody would be identical to that for phospho-ERK. To our surprise, the phospho-MEK antibody labeled almost exclusively mitotic cells. This was true in both neoplastic gliomas (Figure 2.7E) and all non-neoplastic tissues examined, such as developing brain (not shown). The staining pattern of the phospho-MEK antibody was identical to a well-characterized mitosis-specific monoclonal antibody, MPM-2 (data not shown). The same tissues stained with two different phospho-ERK antibodies (Sigma, St. Louis, MO) showed cytoplasmic and nuclear immunoreactivity that was largely excluded from mitotic cells (Figure 2.8F) Activated and phosphorylated ERK has been reported to localize at the kinetochores of mitotic cells. Thus it seemed possible that there might be a role for phosphorylated and activated MEK in mitosis. Nevertheless, the largely discordant staining patterns of phospho-ERK and phospho-MEK were confusing and raised the question of aberrant antibody cross-reactivity. Resolution of the paradoxical difference in phospho-ERK and phospho-MEK immunoreactivity came from a series of biochemical experiments (J.W. Mandell, M. Zecevic, and M.J. Weber, unpublished data) and was also confirmed by a recent publication. MEK1 (but not MEK2) appears to undergo a mitosis-specific cleavage, dependent on cyclin-B/Cdc-2 activity. This cleavage physically and functionally dissociates MEK from ERK activity, thus accounting for the discordant staining we observed.

Applications of PSSAs to Human Neoplasia

Cancer research is the most active field for applications of PSSAs, due to the central role of protein phosphorylation in cancer cell growth and survival signaling. A practical reason for the great progress in this area is that most tumor specimens are rapidly procured by surgical biopsy or resection, rather than at autopsy. A sampling of recent studies in human neoplasms is presented, grouped according to the general class of phosphoprotein target studied (Table 2.1). Some important phosphoproteins are notably absent, because there

Table 2.1: Some Published Studies of Human Neoplasms Utilizing Phosphorylation State-Specific Antibodies

Phosphoprotein	Neoplasms	References
Transmembrane receptor tyrosine kinases		
ErbB-2	Breast carcinoma	28-32
EGFR	Non-small cell lung carcinoma (NSCLC), pancreatic carcinoma, testicular erm cell tumors	33-35, 62
IGF-1R	Breast carcinoma, medulloblastoma	36-38
CSF-1R	Breast carcinoma	39
Intracellular kinases		
ERK/MAP kinase	Gliomas, carcinomas (prostate, breast, pancreatic, head/neck)	19, 40-42, 62
AKT	Carcinomas (epithelial ovarian, endometrial, breast, papillary thyroid, pancreatic, NSCLC), multiple myeloma	43-48, 62
Transcription factors/ nuclear proteins		
STAT3/6	Hodgkin lymphoma, multiple myeloma, prostate carcinoma	49-52
Beta-catenin	Colorectal carcinoma53	
Smad2/4	Breast carcinoma	54
I-kappaB alpha	Gynecologic squamous intraepithelial neoplasia/carcinoma	55
P53	Transitional cell carcinoma	56
Rb	Uveal melanoma, retinoblastoma	57, 58
Histone H1	Gynecologic squamous intraepithelial neoplasia/carcinoma	59
c-jun	Breast carcinoma, astrocytoma	60,61

are no reports of their immunohistochemical study using PSSAs. An example is c-Kit, which is mutationally activated in mast cell tumors, chronic myelogenous leukemia, germ cell tumours, and gastrointestinal stromal tumors. Presumably, lack of a suitable specific PSSA has prevented immunohistochemical study of c-Kit activation *in situ*.

Transmembrane Receptor Tyrosine Kinases

ErbB Receptors

One of the first successful applications to human tumors was a monoclonal PSSA to tyrosine-phosphorylated erbB-2 (also known as HER-2/neu). Activation was observed in a subset of breast cancers which overexpress the receptor. Similar findings were confirmed in an independent study. More recent studies have shown significant correlations between erbB-2 phosphorylation and long-term clinical outcome Interestingly, erbB-2 was found to be more frequently activated in ductal carcinoma *in situ* than in invasive carcinoma, suggesting that erbB-2 signalling is important in the early stages of breast tumorigenesis.

Epidermal Growth Factor Receptor

Although well-documented as an overexpressed or mutated protein in human cancers, relatively few studies of epidermal growth factor receptor (EGFR) phosphorylation in human tumours have been presented. A study of non-small cell lung cancer revealed that phosphorylation, but not overexpression, of EGFR is strongly correlated with worse clinical outcomes. This suggests that assessment of EGFR phosphorylation could be used for therapeutic decision-making, especially for EGFR-directed chemotherapies. Non-seminomatous germ cell testicular tumours also showed significant EGFR activation. A recently developed antibody enabled confirmation that the constitutively activated EGFR variant III was also hyperphosphorylated in human lung cancers.

Insulin-Like Growth Factor 1 Receptor

An antibody specific for the phosphorylated insulin-like growth factor 1 receptor (IGF-1R) was applied to breast carcinoma specimens, suggesting overactivation in cancer cells. This antibody was used in a separate study on medulloblastomas, also revealing high levels of receptor phosphorylation relative to normal cerebellum A similar result was obtained in an independent study, which also interrogated the downstream signaling molecules ERK1/2 and AKT, all of which were much more highly phosphorylated in medulloblastoma than control cerebellar tissue.

Colony Stimulating Factor-1 Receptor

A polyclonal PSSA directed against the macrophage colony stimulating factor receptor (CSF-1R), the product of the c-fms proto-oncogene, was shown to faithfully report activation by ligand in cell culture. Subsequently, application of this antibody to breast tumours revealed activation in 52% of invasive human breast tumors (72% of CSF-1R-positive cases) in a sample of 114 cases and in 38% of carcinoma *in situ*.

Intracellular Kinases

ERK/MAP Kinase

The first study to assess activation of a cytoplasmic kinase in archival tumor specimens was performed on human gliomas. PSSAs to ERK/MAPK revealed widespread activation in astrocytomas, regardless of grade, but much lower levels of activation in oligodendrogliomas. Anaplastic progression in oligodendrogliomas was associated with a larger number of cells with active ERK/MAPK. Within glioblastomas, interesting patterns of activation were observed, including around foci of microvascular hyperplasia and necrosis, suggesting possible paracrine signaling relationships. An unexpected observation was that mitotic and actively cycling tumor cells showed diminished activation relative to cells in G_0, suggesting functional roles other than cell proliferation. ERK/MAPK activation was found to be associated with prostate cancer progression Compared to a low level of activation in non-neoplastic prostate, the level of activated ERK/MAPK increased with increasing Gleason score and tumor stage in cancer specimens. Tumour samples from two patients showed no activation of ERK/MAPK before androgen ablation therapy; however, following androgen ablation treatment, high levels of activated ERK/MAPK were detected in the recurrent tumours. A similar study in breast cancers revealed 72% of tumours to have high nuclear phospho-ERK/MAPK immunostaining relative to normal breast epithelium. Phospho-ERK/MAPK status was found to be a significantly independent predictor for hormonal therapy response duration and patient survival. Head and neck cancers were found to have elevated ERK/MAPK activation, and expression of the EGFR, its ligand transforming growth factor, and erbB2 correlated with activation of ERK/MAPK. Activation was also spatially associated with a higher Ki-67 proliferative index

Protein Kinase B

Given its widely studied roles in anti-apoptotic signaling, protein kinase B (AKT) has been the subject of several investigations using PSSAs. AKT is normally kept inactive and unphosphorylated by the phosphatase PTEN. In a series of primary epithelial ovarian carcinomas, loss of PTEN expression was highly correlated with elevated AKT phosphorylation. A similar inverse relationship was documented in breast cancers and endometrial carcinomas. AKT was found to be frequently activated in non-small cell lung cancers, irrespective of the histological subtypes. Papillary thyroid cancers also showed evidence of high AKT activation. A study on bone marrow biopsies from patients with multiple myeloma (MM) demonstrated phospho-AKT staining of malignant plasma cells in a cell membrane-specific pattern, compared to no staining in non-neoplastic hematopoietic cells .

Transcription Factors and Other Nuclear Proteins

STATs

The STATs (signal transducer and activator of transcription) are a family of key transcription factors involved in cytokine signaling. Constitutive STAT6 phosphorylation was found to be a common and distinctive feature of Hodgkin and Reed-Sternberg cells in classical Hodgkin lymphoma, whereas STAT3 activation was regularly present in both Hodgkin and non-Hodgkin lymphomas.

Multiple myeloma specimens revealed constitutive activation of STAT3 in almost one-half of cases. However, this did not seem to have a major impact on the expression of anti-apoptotic proteins or proliferation. Prostate carcinomas also show increased phosphorylation of STAT3 relative to non-malignant samples.

β-Catenin

The power of tissue microarray technology was applied to test the expression, localization, and phosphorylation status of β-catenin, a protein involved in both in cell-cell adhesion and the wnt signaling pathway . Examination of 650 colorectal cancer specimens revealed that the majority of cancers retained some β-catenin membranous staining, whereas cytoplasmic or nuclear expression was seen in 42.5% and 20.4% of specimens, respectively. Phospho-β-catenin showed nuclear staining in only 9.5% of specimens, and there was no apparent membranous or cytoplasmic staining. There was no significant association between β-catenin or phospho-β-catenin and grade or stage. Nuclear expression of phospho-β-catenin, was associated with an improved survival.

Smads

Another tissue microarray study compared the patterns of expression and activation of the Smads in breast cancers. The Smads are a family of signal transduction molecules that can transmit signals from cell surface receptors for TGF-β to the nucleus. Among 456 cases of human breast carcinoma assembled in tissue microarrays, the majority expressed Smad2, phospho-Smad2, and Smad4. Among patients with stage II breast cancer, lack of phospho-Smad2 expression in the tumor was strongly associated with shorter overall survival.

NF-κB/I-κB

In a series of gynecologic squamous lesions, high-grade lesions and carcinomas were found to have increased nuclear translocation of the subunits p50 and RelA as well as loss of I-κB α immunoreactivity. Phosphorylation of I-κB-α occurred in the squamous intraepithelial lesions but not in the advanced stages of squamous cell carcinoma. Since phosphorylation of I-κB-α is a prerequisite for its degradation, allowing NF-κB activity, these findings are consistent with activation of the NF-κB pathway in disease progression.

p53

Given that p53 is regulated by phosphorylation, and the overwhelming quantity of basic and applied research on the role of p53 in human neoplasia, it is surprising how few translational studies have used PSSAs to p53. This may be due in part to the complexity of p53 phosphorylation and the paucity of PSSAs suitable for immunohistochemistry. The majority of transitional cell carcinomas that harbored missense mutations were found to exhibit immunopositivity with a Ser392 phospho-specific p53 antibody. Phosphorylation at Ser392 activates specific DNA binding functions by stabilizing p53 tetramer formation.

Rb

Given the central and historically important role of this tumor suppressor in cancer research, there are surprisingly few studies on Rb phosphorylation in tumors using PSSAs. A study on uveal melanomas documented increased phosphorylation at carboxy-terminal residues Ser807 and Ser811. Phosphorylation at these sites was also shown to be important for Rb inactivation in cultured melanoma cells. A study on non-familial retinoblastoma tumours also suggested increased Rb phosphorylation in tumor cells that had not lost expression of the protein, consistent with inactivation.

Histones

Examination of a series of gynecologic squamous intraepithelial lesions using a phospho-histone 1 antibody revealed patterns generally similar to those observed using MIB-1. However, differing proportion of cells were stained by MIB-1 and the phospho-H1 antibody, suggesting that histone1 phosphorylation, likely due to a cyclin-dependent kinase activity, reveals a different subpopulation of cycling cells.

c-jun

c-jun, a component of the activating protein-1(AP-1) complex, is a target of many growth factor and cytokine signaling pathways. In breast cancer specimens, phosphorylation of c-jun was found to be tightly correlated with ERK1/2 phosphorylation, shortened duration of endocrine response in estrogen receptor-positive patients, but not correlated with proliferation or histological grade. A study on infiltrating astrocytomas demonstrated elevated phoshorylated c-jun, as well as another AP-1 component, c-Fos in the majority of glioblastomas (grade IV astrocytomas), but not in lower grade (II-III) astrocytomas.

Roles for PSSAs in Assessing Efficacy of Signaling Pathway-Targeted Chemotherapies

One of the most exciting potential applications of PSSAs is the assessment of therapeutic efficacy for drugs targeted to specific intracellular signaling pathways. Given the explosion of candidate small molecule inhibitors, and many more in the pharmaceutical pipeline, this is bound to be a growth area. Proof-of-principle for this application was obtained in a xenograft model of human pancreatic adenocarcinoma. In this study, the efficacy of an epidermal growth factor receptor (EGFR) inhibitor alone and in combination with wortmannin was tested by quantitative immunofluorescence analysis of the phosphorylation state of EGFR, ERK, and PKB. Microscopic quantitation allowed selection of only viable tumor for assay. Immunofluorescence microscopy enabled direct measurement of the ratio of phosphorylated to total kinase protein in the same section, thus normalizing for differences in kinase protein expression. The approach successfully documented the pathway blockade predicted by the drugs administered. The ability to test tumour biopsies for signaling pathway activation state, both before and after initiation of chemotherapy, should allow both prediction of tumoricidal sensitivity and documentation of efficacy in the clinical oncology arena. A remarkable study used skin biopsies of cancer patients to assess the efficacy of another EGFR inhibitor, ZD1839 (Iressa; AstraZeneca Pharmaceuticals, Wilmington, DE). By using skin as the sentinel tissue in patients with head and neck cancers, the authors were able to show convincingly that the inhibitor blocked not only EGFR phosphorylation, but also reduced downstream ERK/MAPK activation and keratinocyte proliferation index. Concomitantly, patients treated with the drug showed increased dermal expression of p27(KIP1) and maturation markers and increased apoptosis. These effects were observed at all dosage levels, before reaching dose-limiting toxicities. The authors suggested that *in vivo* pharmacodynamic assessments using PSSAs on skin biopsies could be used to select optimal effective doses instead of using the maximum-tolerated dose for efficacy and safety trials.

Applications of PSSAs in Degenerative, Inflammatory, and Toxin-induced Diseases

Phosphorylation state-specific anti-tau protein antibodies have revolutionized the diagnosis and investigation of Alzheimer's disease and a set of distinctive neurodegenerative diseases termed the 'tauopathies,' including Pick's disease, corticobasal degeneration, progressive supranuclear palsy, progressive subcortical gliosis, and frontotemporal dementia with Parkinsonism. Tau phosphorylation has been the subject of excellent reviews and will not be discussed here. The ERK/MAPK signaling pathway has been the focus of several translational studies, given its importance in proliferation, differentiation, and survival signalling. A series of non-neoplastic human neurosurgical specimens revealed consistent activation of ERK/MAP kinase in reactive astrocytes in both subacute and chronic lesions, including infarct, mechanical trauma, chronic epilepsy, and progressive multifocal leukoencephalopathy. In a mouse model of asbestosis, increased phosphorylated ERK immunoreactivity was found in pulmonary epithelial cells at sites of developing fibrotic lesions after 14 and 30 days of asbestos inhalation. Insight into the pathogenesis of sporadic inclusion body myositis, a common form of inflammatory myopathy, was obtained by studying MAP kinase pathway activation in muscle biopsies. Phosphorylated ERK/MAPK, but not JNK or p38 MAPK was detected in the diseased vacuolated fibers that are the hallmark of this disease. The authors hypothesized that the activated ERK/MAPK could be responsible for phosphorylating cytoskeletal proteins that form the filamentous inclusions also characteristic of this disease. A study of human Lewy body diseases, including both classical Parkinson's and diffuse Lewy body disease revealed striking granular cytoplasmic aggregates of phospho-ERK in the substantia nigra, involving almost one-third of surviving neurons, which were largely absent in control cases. Double-labelling studies and examination of preclinical cases suggested that these phosphorylation changes might occur relatively early in the disease process, preceding actual Lewy body formation. Non-neoplastic inflammatory diseases are largely unstudied using PSSAs. Inflammatory bowel disease tissues revealed activation of the STAT1 pathway in inflammatory cells of ulcerative colitis, but not in Crohn's disease or normal colon, suggesting disease-specific signalling mechanisms. An unexpected connection between the trinucleotide repeat diseases and aberrant protein phosphorylation was suggested by a study using a general phosphoserine antibody. Anti-phosphoserine staining of tissue sections from brains affected by trinucleotide repeat disease revealed high reactivity in neuronal inclusions and affected nuclei, but not normal neurons. The regional distribution of the phosphorylated nuclei in neurons correlated with other pathological changes. Using the same antibody to immunopurify the phosphorylated protein(s) in neuronal inclusions, the authors found the major phosphoprotein to be histone H3. This finding has interesting implications for potential mechanisms by which the trinucleotide repeat gene products could interfere with gene transcription. Another disease characterized by abnormal protein aggregation is alcoholic hepatitis, in which cytokeratins 8 and 18 accumulate as cytoplasmic inclusions (Mallory bodies). To investigate roles for cytokeratin phosphorylation in Mallory body formation, PSSAs to cytokeratins were used to probe diseased and normal liver tissue sections. Hepatocyte cytokeratins were found to be hyperphosphorylated at multiple sites in a Mallory body mouse model, even in hepatocytes that had yet to develop Mallory bodies. Again the suggestion was that aberrant hyperphosphorylation might precede inclusion formation.

Concluding Remarks

Studies of protein phosphorylation previously ignored the spatial complexity inherent in tissue and cell signaling. The advent of PSSAs now makes possible the probing of intact tissues and cells, both in experimental models and human specimens, for patterns of specific protein phosphorylation. In studies on tumor biology, PSSAs will allow analysis of protein phosphorylation within neoplastic cells independently of the non-neoplastic stroma. The potential complexity of staining patterns obtained when using PSSAs raises interpretive problems. Comparison of results of studies using PSSAs will require some level of quantitation, such as is routine with proliferation markers such as Ki-67. This will be straightforward where staining is discrete and easily separated from background, such as a nuclear transcription factor, but may be less objective when the staining pattern is more complex. For example, a PSSA may label both angiogenic blood vessels as well as tumour cells, so it would not be appropriate to report results simply as "percentage of cells positive." An additional layer of complexity may appear as we learn more about the functional significance of multiple phosphorylation sites on single proteins. Evidence for differential phosphorylation of adjacent tyrosine residues of the erbB2 receptor in breast cancers raises the issue of heterogeneity at the molecular as well as cellular level. PSSAs may prove to be especially useful for demonstrating chemotherapeutic efficacy, when the targets are known players in phosphorylation cascades. Applications of PSSAs to non-neoplastic diseases are in their infancy, but show great potential. Just as the development of comprehensive gene chips has allowed near genome-saturating studies of gene expression, the eventual development of PSSAs for virtually all phosphoproteins will make feasible a similar large-scale approach to phosphorylation cascades. Novel applications of PSSAs, especially in combination with the power of tissue microarrays, should reveal new paradigms for disease classification and diagnosis based on protein activation state.

GLYCOSYLATION

Glycosylation is the enzymatic process that attaches glycans to proteins, lipids, or other organic molecules. This enzymatic process produces one of the fundamental biopolymers found in cells (along with DNA, RNA, and proteins). Glycosylation is a form of co-translational and post-translational modification. Glycans serve a variety of structural and functional roles in membrane and secreted proteins. The majority of proteins synthesized in the rough ER undergo glycosylation. It is an enzyme-directed site-specific process, as opposed to the non-enzymatic chemical reaction of glycation. Glycosylation is also present in the cytoplasm and nucleus as the O-GlcNAc modification. Five classes of glycans are produced:

- *N*-linked glycans attached to a nitrogen of asparagine or arginine side chains;
- *O*-linked glycans attached to the hydroxy oxygen of serine, threonine, tyrosine, hydroxylysine, or hydroxyproline side chains, or to oxygens on lipids such as ceramide;
- phospho-glycans linked through the phosphate of a phospho-serine;
- *C*-linked glycans, a rare form of glycosylation where a sugar is added to a carbon on a tryptophan side chain;
- glypiation, which is the addition of a GPI anchor that links proteins to lipids through glycan linkages.

Purpose

The carbohydrate chains attached to the target proteins serve various functions. For instance, some proteins do not fold correctly unless they are glycosylated first. Also, polysaccharides linked at the amide nitrogen of asparagine in the protein confer stability on some secreted glycoproteins. Experiments have shown that glycosylation in this case is not a strict requirement for proper folding, but the unglycosylated protein degrades quickly. Glycosylation may play a role in cell-cell adhesion (a mechanism employed by cells of the immune system), as well.

Mechanisms

There are various mechanisms for glycosylation, although most share several common features:

- Glycosylation, unlike glycation, is an enzymatic process;
- The donor molecule is often an activated nucleotide sugar;
- The process is site-specific.

Types of Glycosylation

N-linked glycosylation

N-linked glycosylation is important for the folding of some eukaryotic proteins. The *N*-linked glycosylation process occurs in eukaryotes and widely in archaea, but very rarely in bacteria.In Eukaryotes, most *N*-linked oligosaccharides begin with addition of a 14-sugar precursor to the asparagine in the polypeptide chain of the target protein. The structure of this precursor is common to most eukaryotes, and contains 3 glucose, 9 mannose, and 2 *N*-acetylglucosamine molecules. A complex set of reactions attaches this branched chain to a carrier molecule called dolichol, and then it is transferred to the appropriate point on the polypeptide chain as it is translocated into the ER lumen.

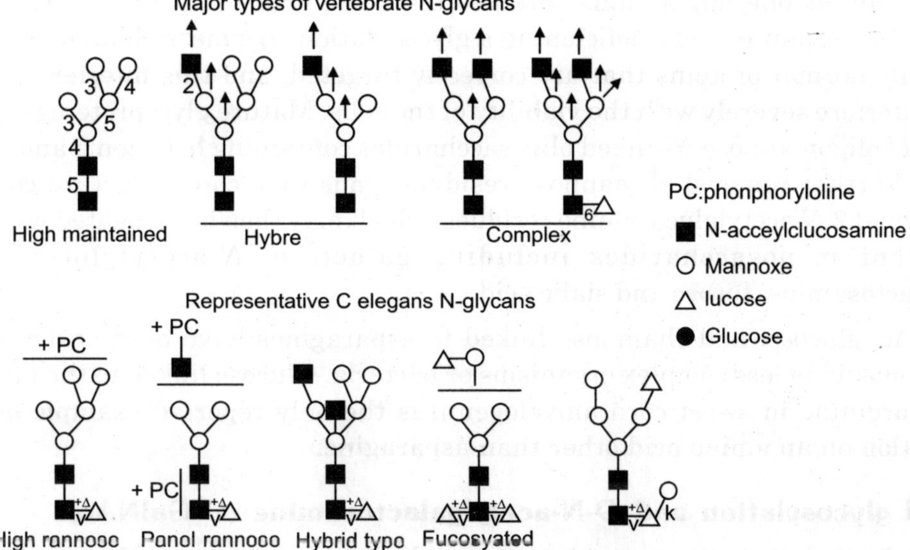

Fig. 2.9 : Comparative overview of the major types of vertebrate N-glycan subtypes and some representative *C. elegans* N-glycans

There are three major classes of *N*-linked saccharides resulting from this core: high-mannose oligosaccharides, complex oligosaccharides and hybrid oligosaccharides.

- High-mannose is, in essence, just two *N*-acetylglucosamines with many mannose residues, often almost as many as are seen in the precursor oligosaccharides before it is attached to the protein.
- Complex oligosaccharides are so named because they can contain almost any number of the other types of saccharides, including more than the original two *N*-acetylglucosamines.

Proteins can be glycosylated by both types of oligosaccharides on different portions of the protein. Whether an oligosaccharide is high-mannose or complex is thought to depend on its accessibility to saccharide-modifying proteins in the Golgi. If the saccharide is relatively inaccessible, it will most likely stay in its original high-mannose form. If it is accessible, then it is likely that many of the mannose residues will be cleaved off and the saccharide will be further modified by the addition of other types of group as discussed above.The oligosaccharide chain is attached by oligosaccharyltransferase to asparagine occurring in the tripeptide sequence Asn-X-Ser or Asn-X-Thr where X could be any amino acid except Pro. This sequence is known as a glycosylation *sequon*. After attachment, once the protein is correctly folded, the three glucose residues are removed from the chain and the protein is available for export from the ER. The glycoprotein thus formed is then transported to the Golgi where removal of further mannose residues may take place. However, glycosylation itself does not seem to be as necessary for correct transport targeting of the protein, as one might think. Studies involving drugs that block certain steps in glycosylation, or mutant cells deficient in a glycosylation enzyme, still produce otherwise-structurally-normal proteins that are correctly targeted, and this interference does not seem to interfere severely with the viability of the cells. Mature glycoproteins may contain a variety of oligomannose *N*-linked oligosaccharides containing between 5 and 9 mannose residues. Further removal of mannose residues leads to a 'core' structure containing 3 mannose, and 2 *N*-acetylglucosamine residues, which may then be elongated with a variety of different monosaccharides including galactose, *N*-acetylglucosamine, *N*-acetylgalactosamine, fucose and sialic acid.

GalNAc, glucose, and rhamnose linked to asparagines have been observed as well, although mostly in less complex organisms or bacteria. Glucose linked to the guanidinium group of arginine in sweet corn amyelogenin is the only reported example of *N*-linked glycosylation on an amino acid other than asparagine.

O-linked glycosylation and *O*-N-acetylgalactosamine (*O*-GalNAc)

O-linked glycosylation occurs at a later stage during protein processing, probably in the Golgi apparatus. This is the addition of N-acetyl-galactosamine to serine or threonine residues by the enzyme *UDP-N-acetyl-D-galactosamine:polypeptide N-acetylgalactosaminyltransferase* (EC 2.4.1.41), followed by other carbohydrates (such as galactose and sialic acid). This process is important for certain types of proteins such as proteoglycans, which involves the addition of glycosaminoglycan chains to an initially unglycosylated 'proteoglycan core protein.' These additions are usually serine *O*-linked glycoproteins, which seem to have one of two main functions. One function involves secretion to form components of the extracellular matrix, adhering one cell to another by interactions between the large sugar complexes of proteoglycans. The other main function is to act as a component of mucosal secretions, and it is the high concentration of carbohydrates that tends to give mucus its 'slimy' feel. Proteins that circulate in the blood are not normally *O*-glycosylated, with the exception of IgA1 and IgD (two types of antibody) and C1-inhibitor.

O-fucose

O-fucose is added between the second and third conserved cysteines of EGF-like repeats in the Notch protein, and other substrates by GDP-fucose protein *O*-fucosyltransferase 1, and to Thrombospondin repeats by GDP-fucose protein *O*-fucosyltransferase 2. In the case of EGF-like repeats, the *O*-fucose may be further elongated to a tetrasaccharide by sequential addition of N-acetylglucosamine (GlcNAc), galactose, and sialic acid, and for Thrombospondin repeats, may be elongated to a disaccharide by the addition of glucose. Both of these fucosyltransferases have been localized to the endoplasmic reticulum, which is unusual for glycosyltransferases, most of which function in the Golgi apparatus.

O-glucose

O-glucose is added between the first and second conserved cysteines of EGF-like repeats in the Notch protein, and possibly other substrates by protein:*O*-glucosyltransferase (Poglut). This enzyme is known as Rumi in *Drosophila*, and is also localized to the ER like the O-fucosyltransferases. The O-glucose modification appears to be necessary for proper folding of the EGF-like repeats of the Notch protein, and increases secretion of this receptor.

O-*N*-acetylglucosamine (*O*-GlcNAc)

O-GlcNAc is added to serines or threonines by *O*-GlcNAc transferase. *O*-GlcNAc appears to occur on most serines and threonines that would otherwise be phosphorylated by serine/threonine kinases. Thus, if phosphorylation occurs, *O*-GlcNAc does not, and *vice versa*. This is an incredibly important finding because phosphorylation/dephosphorylation has become a scientific paradigm for the regulation of signaling within cells. A massive amount of cancer research is focused on phosphorylation. Ignoring the involvement of this form of glycosylation, which clearly appears to act in concert with phosphorylation, means that a lot of current research is missing at least half of the picture. *O*-GlcNAc addition and removal also appears to be a key regulator of the pathways that are disrupted in diabetes mellitus. The gene encoding the *O*-GlcNAcase enzyme has been linked to non-insulin dependent diabetes mellitus. It is the terminal step in a nutrient-sensing hexosamine signalling pathway.

O-*N*-acetylglucosamine in Other Contexts

Recently, *O*-GlcNAc was reported to occur between the fifth and sixth conserved cysteines in some EGF-like repeats from the Notch protein. It would seem unlikely that this modification would be due to the same enzyme involved with addition of *O*-GlcNAc to cytoplasmic and nuclear localized proteins. Considering that *O*-fucose and *O*-glucose addition to EGF-like repeats is due to ER localized enzymes, presumably an ER localized protein *O*-GlcNAc transferase exists.

O-mannose

During *O*-mannosylation, a mannose residue is transferred from mannose-p-dolichol to a serine/threonine residue in secretory pathway proteins. O-mannosylation is common to both prokaryotes and eukaryotes.

Collagen Glycosylation

Many lysines in collagen are hydroxylated to form hydroxylysine, and many of these hydroxylysines are then glycosylated by the addition of galactose. This galactose monosaccharide can then be further elongated by the addition of a glucose. This glycosylation is required for the proper functioning of collagen. Glycosylation of hydroxlysine occurs in the ER.

Hydroxyproline Glycosylation

Proline is also hydroxylated in collagen, however, no glycosylation occurs here as the hydroxyprolines are necessary for hydrogen bonding in the collagen triple helix. There is one protein named Skp1 in *Dictyostelium discoideum* that carries a GlcNAc on hydroxyproline, but this would appear to be an extremely rare form of glycosylation. Otherwise, only plants appear to carry glycans on hydroxyproline, with both galactose and arabinose glycans being reported in the literature.

Glycosylation of Glycogenin

Liver and muscle glycogenin carries a glucose on a tyrosine side chain. This is the only known example of glycosylated tyrosine in nature.

Glycosylation of Ceramide

Either a galactose or a glucose can be added to a hydroxyl on the lipid ceramide. The glucose can be further elongated to a disaccharide by the addition of a galactose.

Proteoglycans

The large and complex glycans that modify proteoglycans are initiated by addition of xylose to serine. This is the only form of glycan so far reported to begin with xylose addition directly to protein apart from the xylose seen on phospho-serine in *Dictyostelium discoideum* described below.

Phospho-Serine Glycosylation

Xylose, fucose, mannose, and GlcNAc phospho-serine glycans have been reported in the literature. Fucose and GlcNAc have been found only in *Dictyostelium discoideum*, mannose in *Leishmania mexicana*, and xylose in *Trypanosoma cruzi*.

C-mannosylation

A mannose sugar is added to the first tryptophan residue in the sequence W-X-X-W (W indicates tryptophan, X is any amino acid). Thrombospondins are one of the most commonly modified proteins, however this form of glycosylation appears elsewhere as well. This is an unusual modification because the sugar is linked to a carbon rather than a reactive atom like a nitrogen or oxygen.

GPI Anchors (Glypiation)

A special form of glycosylation is the *GPI anchor*. This form of glycosylation functions to attach a protein to a hydrophobic lipid anchor, via a glycan chain.

Application of Glycosylation

Numerous factors that influence cell-surface carbohydrate composition remain to be elucidated. The combination of novel biochemical and metabolism-based approaches with emerging genomic methods promises to accelerate efforts to understand glycosylation.

The surface of a mammalian cell is decorated with complex carbohydrates. These sugars, known individually as glycans and collectively as the glycocalyx, are biosynthetically assembled from simple monosaccharides into a diverse array of oligo- and poly-saccharides (*See Fig. 2.10 on next page*). Glycans mediate a cell's communications with the outside world and play a crucial role in the events at fertilization that initiate the life of a multicellular organism. Carbohydrates continue to play a critical role throughout development and contribute to the healthy life of the mature organism. Abnormalities in glycan expression are implicated as causative or incidental factors in both relatively rare congenital diseases and widespread acquired diseases, such as cancer. The recent revelation that fewer genes than originally thought comprise the human genome has further highlighted the importance of post-translational modifications, such as glycosylation, as determinants of higher eukaryotic functions.

Deciphering the molecular details of oligosaccharide synthesis and biological activity is one of the major challenges now confronting the cell biologist. Unlike other structural biomolecules such as proteins and nucleic acids, synthesis of which is template-driven and well defined at a molecular level, oligosaccharides are not primary gene products. An understanding of their biosynthesis remains rudimentary. This review briefly describes current understanding of glycan biosynthesis and the methods that have been used to garner this information. It then addresses the exciting prospects that emerging genomic and metabolic techniques, coupled with established methodologies, offer for rapid discovery of the glycosylation processes of a cell.

Conversion of Monosaccharides into Complex Oligosaccharides

The common sugars, requisite co-substrates, and many of the enzymes necessary for the synthesis of complex carbohydrates are already known. Knowing the complete human

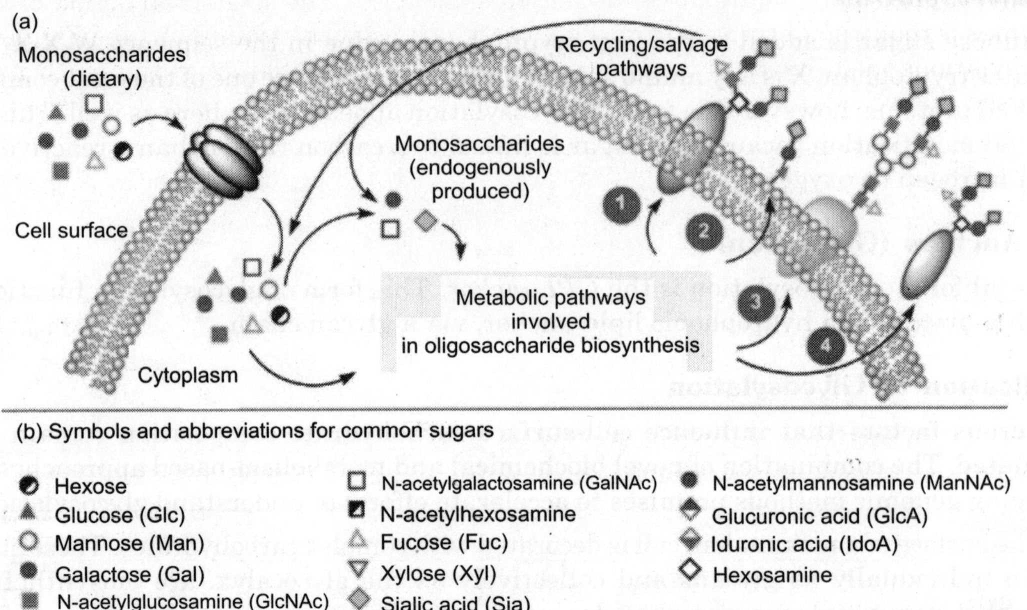

Fig. 2.10 : An overview of the glycosylation process. (*a*) Complex carbohydrates are biosynthetically assembled from sugars obtained from dietary sources, from endogenous conversion from other monosaccharides, or from recycling and salvage pathways. Oligosaccharides of various composition can be attached to various proteins embedded in the plasma membrane (1 and 3) or directly to lipids (2). Collectively, these cell-surface sugars (1, 2, and 3) comprise the glycocalyx that gives each cell a unique molecular identity. Oligosaccharides can also be attached to secreted proteins (4). (*b*) Symbols and abbreviations used in this paper for common sugars

genome ensures that the remaining enzymes involved will be identified soon. What remains mysterious is how these molecular players work in concert to convert a few simple monosaccharides into the exact pattern of complex cell-surface glycans that gives each cell type a unique and reproducible identity (Fig. 1.1). This gap in knowledge not only precludes a detailed understanding of how these molecules are regulated during the healthy lifespan of an organism but, more importantly, also hinders our ability to intervene in pathological situations. Answering questions about glycan biosynthesis will lead to insights into basic biological processes and also opens the door to therapeutic intervention in disease processes.

For the purposes of this review, the metabolic pathways responsible for endowing each cell with its unique complement of oligosaccharides are divided into two stages (Figure 1.2a). The early steps involve the conversion of monosaccharides obtained by the cell from dietary sources, or from recycling and salvage processes (Figure 2.10), into nucleotide-sugar donors. This stage typically entails the phosphorylation of one or more of the hydroxyl groups of the monosaccharides. In addition, it often involves the inversion of stereocenters to convert one sugar to a related epimer. In some cases, the sequential action of several enzymes is required to transform one monosaccharide (such as ManNAc; see Figure 76 for abbreviations used in sugar names) into a considerably different sugar (such as sialic acid; see Figure 2.11b.

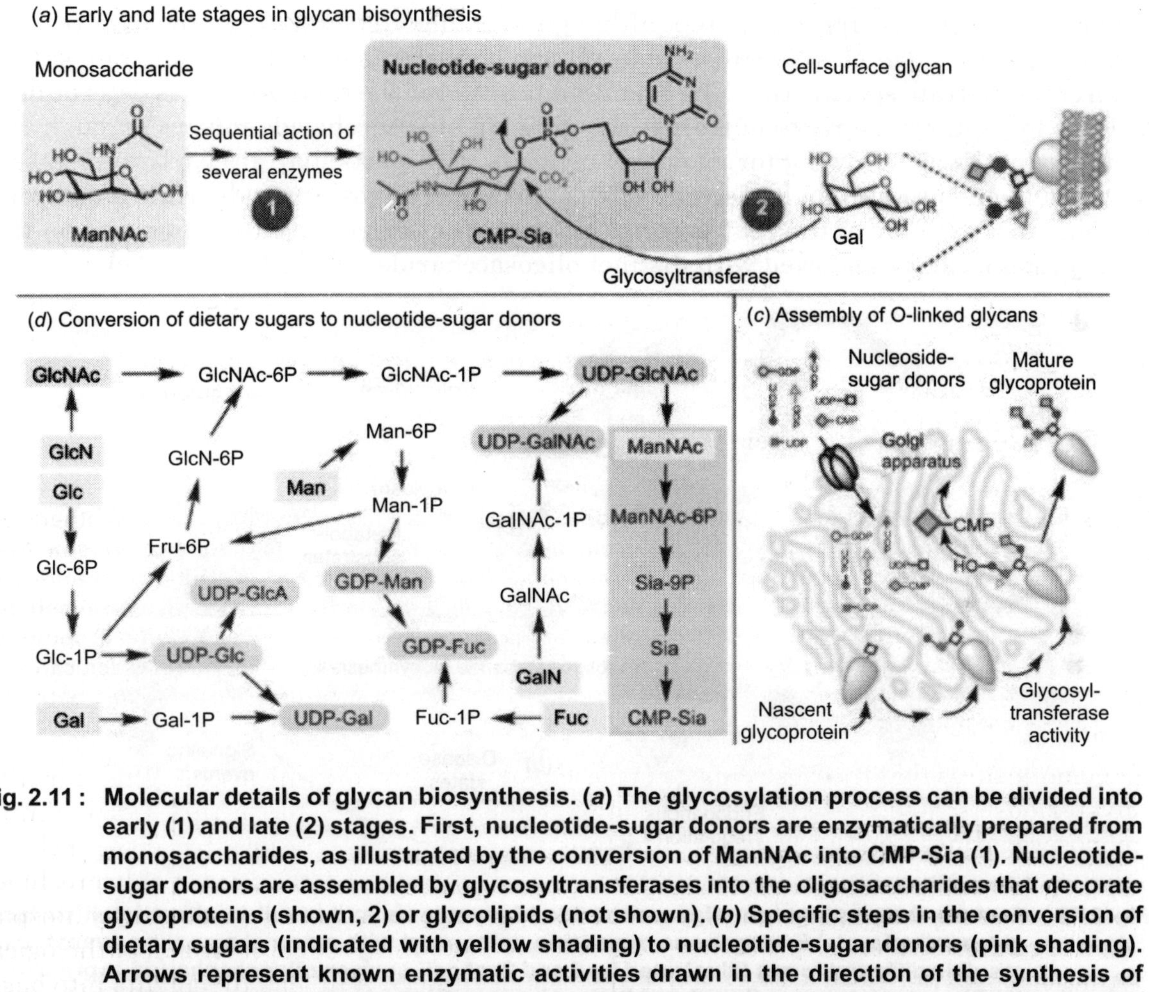

(*a*) Early and late stages in glycan bisoynthesis

Monosaccharide

Nucleotide-sugar donor

Cell-surface glycan

Sequential action of several enzymes

ManNAc

CMP-Sia

Gal

Glycosyltransferase

(*d*) Conversion of dietary sugars to nucleotide-sugar donors

GlcNAc → GlcNAc-6P → GlcNAc-1P → UDP-GlcNAc

GlcN, Glc, Glc-6P, Glc-1P, GlcN-6P, Fru-6P, Man, Man-6P, Man-1P, GDP-Man, GDP-Fuc, UDP-GlcA, UDP-Glc, UDP-Gal, Gal, Gal-1P, Fuc-1P, Fuc, UDP-GalNAc, GalNAc-1P, GalNAc, GalN, ManNAc, ManNAc-6P, Sia-9P, Sia, CMP-Sia

(*c*) Assembly of O-linked glycans

Nucleoside-sugar donors

Mature glycoprotein

Golgi apparatus

CMP

Nascent glycoprotein

Glycosyl-transferase activity

Fig. 2.11 : Molecular details of glycan biosynthesis. (*a*) The glycosylation process can be divided into early (1) and late (2) stages. First, nucleotide-sugar donors are enzymatically prepared from monosaccharides, as illustrated by the conversion of ManNAc into CMP-Sia (1). Nucleotide-sugar donors are assembled by glycosyltransferases into the oligosaccharides that decorate glycoproteins (shown, 2) or glycolipids (not shown). (*b*) Specific steps in the conversion of dietary sugars (indicated with yellow shading) to nucleotide-sugar donors (pink shading). Arrows represent known enzymatic activities drawn in the direction of the synthesis of nucleotide-sugar donors. It should be noted that the reverse reactions are typically also possible, catalyzed either by the same or other enzymes (*c*) Nucleotide-sugar donors enter the endoplasmic reticulum (ER) or Golgi lumen through the action of specific antiport transporters. Oligosaccharides are synthesized by sequential action of the appropriate glycosyltransferases as they traverse the secretory apparatus. The process shown is typical of *O*-linked (serine- or threonine-attached) glycoprotein biosynthesis. For *N*-linked glycoproteins (not shown), a core oligosaccharide is assembled in the cytosol, then transported into the ER where it is processed by glycosidases, and then further elaborated by glycosyltransferases; details of this complex process are described elsewhere

Once a phosphorylated monosaccharide of the desired stereochemical configuration is achieved, conversion to the UDP, GDP, or CMP analog (depending on the sugar) creates a nucleotide-sugar donor. The nucleotide functions as a high-energy leaving group to facilitate the assembly of the monosaccharides into complex carbohydrates by the stepwise action of a group of enzymes, known as glycosyltransferases, most of which reside in the Golgi apparatus (Figure 2.11c). Each step, although seemingly straightforward, involves the correct choice of one of several possible glycosyltransferases with similar, but subtly different, substrate specificities. The exact composition of the final product is determined, at least in part, by the route of transit the growing oligosaccharide follows through the secretory pathway, allowing (or avoiding) contacts with particular glycosyltransferases. As a result, one protein can be decorated by a particular oligosaccharide while a different protein, another copy of the first protein, or even an alternate glycosylation site on the same protein, can be endowed with distinct oligosaccharides (Figs. 1.1 and 1.2c).

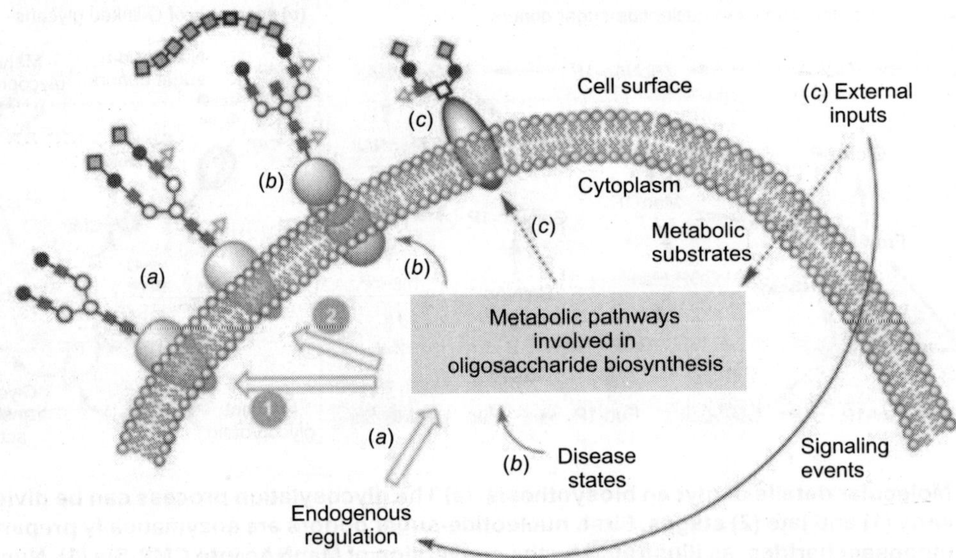

Fig. 2.12 : Factors that impinge on oligosaccharide biosynthesis and result in altered cell surface glycan display. (*a*) Endogenous regulation, in concert with external signaling events, can result in different forms (illustrated by 1 and 2) of cell-surface oligosaccharide expression. (*b*) Disease states are often characterized by specific, and in some cases multiple, changes in glycosylation that can be attributed to abnormalities in the metabolic pathways involved in oligosaccharide biosynthesis. (*c*) External inputs, such as exogenously delivered metabolites, in addition to the previously mentioned signaling events, can modulate cell-surface glycan composition

A fruitful method for determining the internal workings of a cell is the isolation and analysis of subpopulations of cells with distinct properties Molecular and genetic characterization of such cells has illuminated the function of enzymes responsible for a wide range of cellular characteristics, including oligosaccharide biosynthesis. Continued progress in unraveling glycosylation depends on judicious selection of cell populations with variations in surface glycan expression. Variation in the output of the glycosylation pathways can result from endogenous regulatory mechanisms, abnormalities associated with specific diseases, or external inputs (Figure 2.12). We next discuss the benefits and limitations of using each of these sources of variation in oligosaccharide composition for further study of glycan biosynthesis.

Endogenous Regulatory Mechanisms

The glycoconjugate diversity found on different cell types in a healthy organism is a consequence of intracellular metabolic mechanisms responding, in many cases, to external stimuli (Fig. 1.3). In theory, the entire human genome sequence, coupled with methods to measure the expression level of each gene, provides tools for thorough study of glycan biosynthesis. For example, microarray analysis of cell populations selected at various stages in development, or derived from different tissues, promises to explain the distinct oligosaccharide expression pattern of each cell type. Despite the fact that different cell populations also experience gross morphological changes involving many genes that are not related to glycosylation, the development of sophisticated computational algorithms should allow glycosylation-specific effects on gene expression to be deconvoluted from irrelevant secondary effects. This type of genome-wide approach will provide an elegant picture of how the internal glycosylation processes of a cell are reflected on the cell surface as a diverse array of oligosaccharides. Nevertheless, such an approach, by itself, may leave a number of key issues in glycan biosynthesis unresolved.

Microarray studies have the remarkable ability to describe the interplay of numerous enzymes comprising multiple metabolic pathways and reveal system-wide perturbations in gene expression. But, unfortunately, the overwhelming volume of data generated from these studies presents difficulties in distinguishing a primary molecular defect from ensuing secondary (and higher order) effects. As a consequence, subtle changes affecting enzymes that play key regulatory roles may be obscured amid quantitatively larger, but functionally less significant, alterations. The molecular defects responsible for a pathology may be similarly concealed. If so, it will be difficult to identify candidate enzymes as targets for pharmaceutical intervention, or for replacement by gene therapy. Accordingly, a more traditional study of disease states leading to the exact identification of a molecular defect responsible for a pathological phenotype remains a sensible experimental route to complement more recent methods to assess genome-wide changes in gene expression.

Glycosylation Changes Associated with Disease States

Abnormalities associated with disease states are major contributors to diversity in glycan expression (Figure 2.12c). These defects, in many cases, ultimately arise from the dysfunction of an individual enzyme, often as the consequence of a single amino-acid mutation. Determination of the molecular defect responsible for a disease phenotype can therefore reveal the normal function of a particular gene product. A fundamental limitation, however, of relying on human-disease or whole-animal models is that the critical role of glycans in fertilization and development means that many glycosylation defects are embryonic-lethal. Although fortunate from the perspective of human health, this situation prevents potentially interesting metabolic perturbations from being observed clinically (or in animal models) and results in an incomplete understanding of the glycosylation processes of a cell.

To circumvent limitations inherent in the study of animal disease models, researchers have found that it is possible to mutagenize large cell populations and select rare-event mutant cell lines that often mimic disease states at a molecular level. The experimental advantage of such cell-based 'forward genetics' screens is that requirements for cell-surface glycosylation are significantly less stringent in cell monocultures than for whole organisms. Consequently, cells with potentially embryonic-lethal mutations can survive to be isolated and studied, resulting in an enhanced picture of the glycosylation machinery.

The most straightforward method for selecting a rare cell harboring a glycosylation defect is through the use of toxic lectins. Lectins are proteins that recognize and bind to specific sugar residues when presented in certain conformational contexts within an oligosaccharide. Certain lectins are bifunctional: in addition to a sugar-binding domain they also contain a cytotoxic (usually ribosome-inactivating) domain. Incubation of a large, mutagenized cell population with a toxic lectin rapidly results in the isolation of rare mutant cell subpopulations that lack the targeted binding motif and therefore escape death (Figure 2.13). As in animal disease models, molecular characterization leads to the identification of the particular molecular defect responsible for the cell-surface aberration.

The use of toxic lectins, while experimentally easy, can lead to unintended selection outcomes. For example, most of these toxins require retrograde transport into the Golgi or endoplasmic reticulum before they can be translocated into the cytoplasm. Not surprisingly, selection outcomes therefore include transport defects that have little relevance to glycosylation processes. A superior cell selection method, with mutational outcomes more closely targeted to the intended glycosylation pathways, is the use of fluorescently labeled, non-toxic lectins (or carbohydrate-specific antibodies) coupled with a cell-sorting method based on flow cytometry or magnetic particles (Figure 2.13b). These sophisticated, high-throughput methods allow the selection and subsequent propagation of living cells, thereby avoiding the multiple mechanisms that cells can exploit to reduce the deleterious effects of exposure to toxins. Also, such methods permit both positive and negative selection for the desired glycosylation phenotype (Figure 2.13b).

A final concern with current selection techniques is that mutational outcomes are biased toward the later steps in glycoconjugate biosynthesis, typically either the Golgi transporter or glycosyltransferase stages (Figure 2.13c). As illustrated in Figure 1.2b, the earlier stages of glycosylation involve multiple interconversions between structurally related monosaccharides. Many early-stage defects can be 'masked' by re-adjustment of metabolic flux through these intersecting pathways. Clearly, experimental access to such masked mutations is crucial to gaining a complete understanding of the glycosylation processes of a cell. An emerging metabolism-based method that we have developed has the potential to illuminate this class of masked molecular abnormalities.

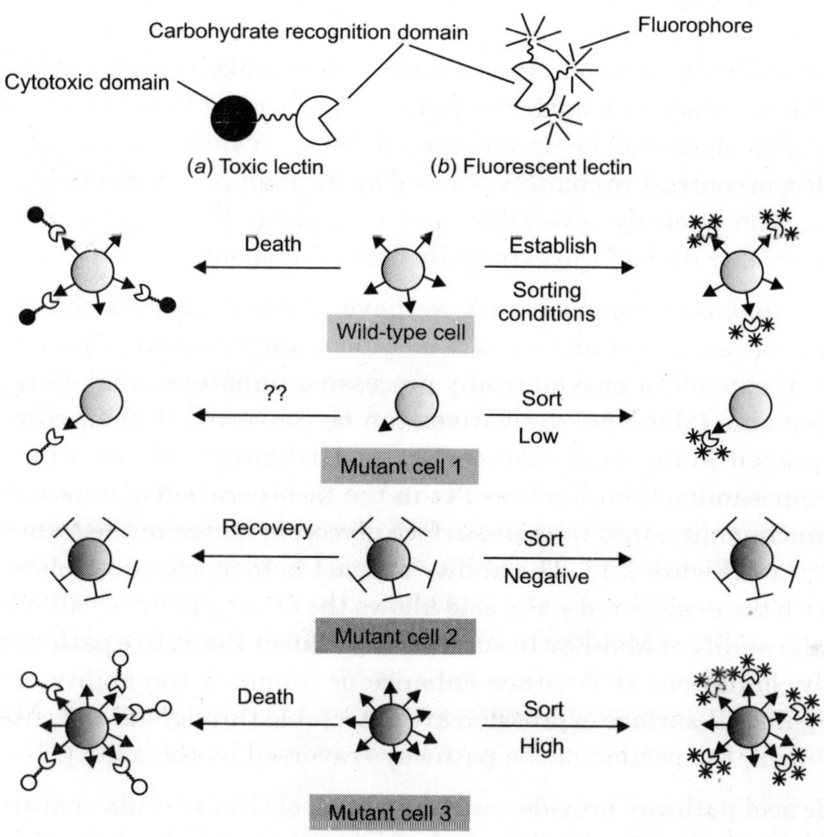

Fig. 2.13 : Lectin-based cell-selection strategies. Two lectin-based strategies can separate cells with glycosylation abnormalities from predominantly wild-type populations. (*a*) The first strategy uses a bifunctional toxic lectin that binds to a carbohydrate ligand expressed on wild-type cells thereby causing cell death. Reduced (Mutant cell 1) or altered (Mutant cell 2) expression of the target epitope can abrogate lectin binding allowing cell recovery. A drawback of this strategy is that over-expression phenotypes (Mutant cell 3) are targeted for death, preventing their isolation; in addition, intermediate levels of lectin binding (Mutant cell 1) may or may not cause cell death. (*b*) A superior selection strategy uses fluorescently labeled lectins that allow separation of cell types by flow cytometry (FACS). In this case, sorting conditions are established with wild-type cells and these subsequently allow separation of cells with low, no, or even excess, lectin binding by using low, negative, or high FACS parameters. As a result, each of the mutant cell populations can be isolated with a level of precision not readily attained with the toxic lectin approach

Externally Supplied Substrates can Illuminate 'masked' Metabolic Defects

External inputs can modulate the glycosylation pathways of a cell (Figure 1.3c). As mentioned above, extracellular signals can trigger changes in oligosaccharide biosynthesis by as-yet poorly understood regulatory processes. External manipulation of glycosylation can also be achieved by the direct delivery of small molecule metabolites into biosynthetic pathways. For example, compounds as simple as ammonia can have a profound effect on the display of cell-surface carbohydrate epitopes. A substrate-based approach can establish linkages, many of which may be unanticipated, between various components of metabolic pathways. Also, in contrast to changes effected by the manipulations of enzymes, substrate-based intervention is easily reversible, and it is amenable to quantitative analysis by altering the concentration of the externally delivered agent.

The substrate-based approach that we have pursued involves the interception of a pathway with an unnatural analog of a metabolic intermediate. Specifically, the sialic acid pathway is capable of enzymatically processing unnatural analogs (Figure 2.14). *N*-acetylmannosamine (ManNAc) derivatives can be converted to their corresponding cell-surface-displayed sialic acid counterparts. Utilization of an analog such as *N*-levulinoylmannosamine (ManLev) results in the incorporation of a unique chemical tag, the ketone functionality, into the cell-surface glycoconjugates in the form of the modified sialic acid SiaLev (Figure 2.14. The ability to react ketone-specific probes, such as biotin hydrazide, with the engineered sialic acid allows the development of cell selection schemes that exploit the ability of ManLev to successfully transit the entire pathway (Figure 2.14). Consequently, mutations that either enhance or diminish the ability of the unnatural substrate to gain cell-surface expression are detectable throughout the entire length of, or even upstream of, the portion of the pathway traversed by the analog.

The sialic acid pathway provides an illustration of the molecular nature of early stage 'masked' mutations that can be illuminated by an unnatural substrate-based approach (Figure 2.15). One of the mutational outcomes yielded by ManLev-based selection in human Jurkat (T-lymphoma derived) cells is a mutant form of the UDP-GlcNAc epimerase. The mutant enzyme is refractory to allosteric feedback inhibition because of loss of binding of the downstream metabolite, CMP-Sia (Figure 2.15, 1). The causative molecular defect, a single amino-acid substitution identical to that found in the inborn human disease sialuria, results in overproduction of ManNAc, thereby competitively excluding ManLev from the pathway and abolishing SiaLev expression on the cell surface. Because flux of the natural substrate, ManNAc, continues through the pathway, there is no change in cell-surface glycan expression in the absence of ManLev. Consequently, this molecular defect could not have been isolated using established lectin or antibody approaches, and it demonstrates one advantage of the unnatural substrate-based method.

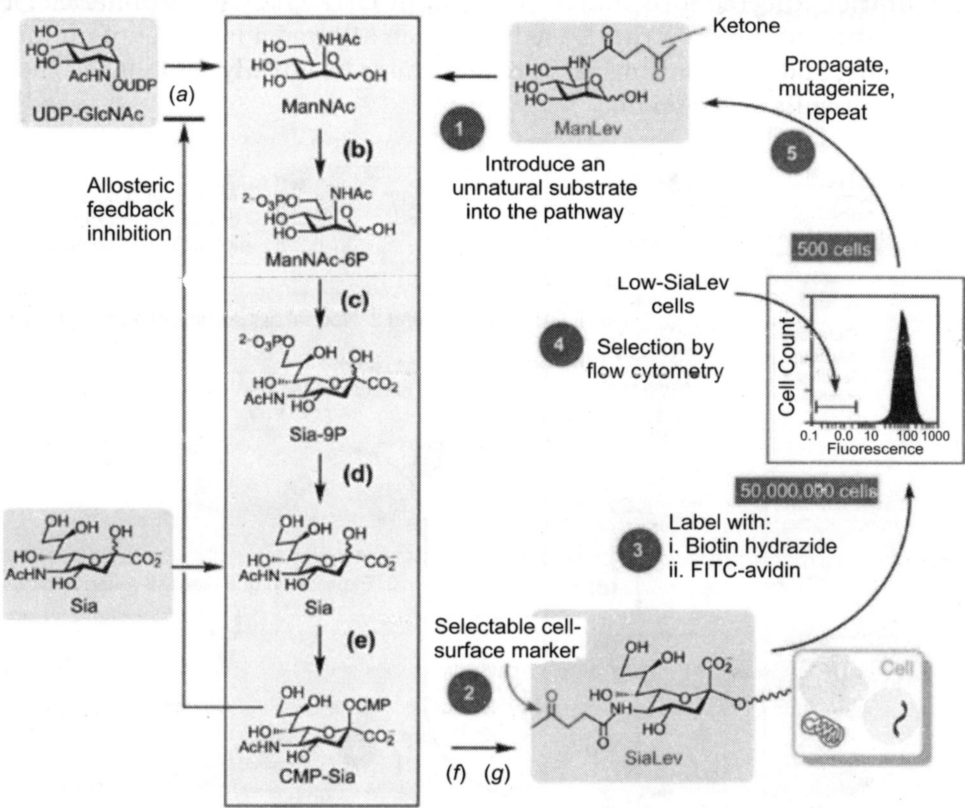

Fig. 2.14 : Strategy for metabolic cell selection for defects in the sialic acid pathway. The sialic acid pathway beginning with UDP-GlcNAc proceeds by the sequential action of (*a,b*) UDP-GlcNAc 2-epimerase/ManNAc 6-kinase; (*c*) sialic acid 9-phosphate synthase; (*d*) sialic acid 9-phosphatase; (*e*) CMP-sialic acid synthetase; (*f*) CMP-sialic acid Golgi transporter; and (*g*) sialyltransferase (several in human); to install a sialic acid on glycoconjugates destined for the cell surface. The substrate-based cell selection approach begins with (1) the interception of the pathway with ManLev, an unnatural analog of ManNAc. The pathway converts this unnatural substrate into glycan-bound SiaLev containing a selectable marker, the ketone (2). The ketone can be selectively labeled with biotin hydrazide and the cells stained with FITC-labeled avidin (3). Sorting of low-SiaLev cells (shown, or high-SiaLev cells, not shown) by flow cytometry (4) allows for the high-throughput selection of cells harboring rare metabolic mutations. After sorting, cells are allowed to recover and then the sorted cell population is analyzed for ketone expression (5). These five steps are repeated iteratively until the desired phenotypic endpoint of high- or low-SiaLev expression is obtained

Another advantage of substrate-based metabolic selection is the ability to rapidly compile comprehensive libraries of mutations. To continue the sialuria example, only three mutations have been characterized from human patients, because the disease is rare]. In the absence of structural characterization, this limited data set led to the tentative suggestion that the mutation affected a regulatory domain in UDP-GlcNAc 2-epimerase. The high-throughput nature of the substrate-based approach allowed a large set of mutations to be obtained rapidly, and the resulting array of mutations has firmly established the existence of the putative regulatory domain.

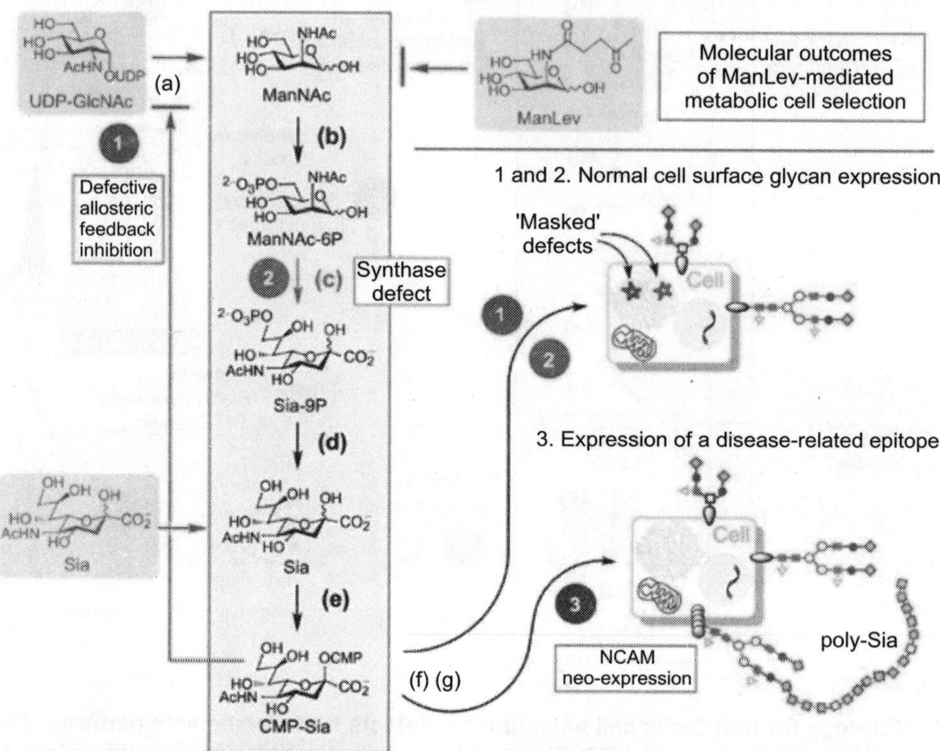

Fig. 2.15 : Molecular outcomes of ManLev-based selection. Three mutational outcomes of metabolic selection include (1, red) a defect in UDP-GlcNAc 2-epimerase (*a*) that renders this enzyme refractory to feedback inhibition by CMP-Sia. The consequent increase in endogenous ManNAc production competitively excludes the unnatural substrate ManLev from the pathway, accounting for the 'low-SiaLev' phenotype. The continued flux of natural substrate through the pathway also explains the normal cell-surface glycan expression of these mutant cells. Another possible mutational outcome of a low-SiaLev selection is a defect in the sialic acid synthase (2, green). Like the mutant epimerase cells, these cells also have normal cell-surface glycan expression, with the internal defect being 'masked' by acquisition of exogenous Sia downstream of the defect. Finally, a 'high-SiaLev' phenotype results from neo-expression of poly-Sia (3, blue), as a result of upregulation of NCAM. Unlike the first two cell lines, these cells have aberrant cell-surface carbohydrate presentation, having gained expression of a carbohydrate epitope characteristic of highly metastatic cancer (Enzymes a through g are identified in the legend to Figure 2.14)

Another early-stage masked molecular abnormality that is only accessible by using the metabolic selection method is a defect in sialic acid synthase (Figure 2.15, 2). In normal cell culture conditions, this mutation would be complemented by intake of sialic acid from the serum in culture media. In an animal model, the inability to produce sialic acid is likely to be embryonic-lethal because of the crucial role of this sugar in development. A substrate-based approach is therefore the only strategy capable of detecting this abnormality in a 'forward genetics' screen. Another important feature of the substrate-based approach is its suitability for selection of gain-of-function or overexpression mutants. To give a specific example, ManLev-based selection produced mutant Jurkat cells that had begun to express polysialic acid (poly-Sia), as a consequence of upregulation of NCAM expression (Figure 2.15c). This abnormality parallels changes in cell-surface carbohydrates observed in highly metastatic cancers.

In the future, application of metabolic substrate-based forward genetics methods will extend beyond the sialic acid biosynthetic pathway. Our recent demonstration that cells can incorporate 'ketoGal', a ketone-containing analog of GalNAc, into cell-surface glycans has opened the door for selection strategies that explore molecular defects affecting internal positions of a complex polysaccharide chain. Together, selection strategies based on unnatural substrates that target the terminal sialic acid residues (accessed by ManLev) and the position proximal to the peptide backbone in *O*-linked glycoproteins (accessed by ketoGal) promise to facilitate the identification of new genes and regulatory control points that impinge on the target pathways.

Future Challenges

Currently, characterization of molecular abnormalities uncovered by genetic screens proceeds largely by using classical molecular biological and biochemical techniques. This process has been compared to a search for a needle in a haystack, requiring a large input of manpower and resources per gene that is hard to reconcile with the wealth of genetic information now available. Now that the entire human genome is (nearly) in hand, the exact sequence of a gene suspected of harbouring a glycosylation-related defect can be determined with relative ease by direct sequencing methods. Nevertheless, with dozens, and potentially hundreds, of enzymes involved in oligosaccharide biosynthesis, a direct sequencing approach remains daunting. Even more problematic are situations in which the cause of a glycosylation abnormality is distant from the enzymes directly involved in carbohydrate metabolism.

The up-regulation of NCAM in ManLev-selected Jurkat cells exemplifies molecular defects that do not occur directly in the oligosaccharide biosynthetic pathways yet nevertheless affect the composition of cell-surface sugars. Neo-expression of NCAM, leading to cell-surface polysialic acid display, may result from regulatory perturbations in one or more currently unidentified transcription factors. In this case, no single gene can be readily implicated as a causative factor. Instead, molecular resolution awaits the exploitation of genome-wide methods that have yet to reach maturation. For example, microarray analysis based on comprehensive libraries of single-nucleotide polymorphisms (SNPs) that are now being compiled, and developing proteomic approaches, will shed light on how the molecular players physically interact with each other and their environment.

A final necessity is to translate the effects of the primary molecular defect to the overall metabolism of the cell and functioning of the entire organism. As discussed previously, a genome-wide approach, when used alone, faces the challenge of identifying a primary metabolic defect amidst an overwhelming number of compensatory secondary and tertiary effects. Conversely, traditional approaches used to identify a primary, causative defect typically ignore overall effects on cellular metabolism. As an illustration, we again consider the 'sialuria' cells (Figure 2.15a). The effects of a single amino-acid mutation in the UDP-GlcNAc 2-epimerase are likely to reverberate throughout the cell, affecting metabolic events far removed from the glycosylation pathways. For example, the increased sialic acid synthesis in these cells requires a large diversion of phosphoenolpyruvate (PEP) from its normal role in energy production. Similarly, production of CMP-Sia diverts CTP from its normal cellular functions that include RNA and DNA synthesis. Nevertheless these mutant cells continue to thrive, probably as a consequence of rearrangement of flux throughout multiple metabolic pathways, a type of change that can only be assessed through a genome-wide approach.

In conclusion, the ultimate goal of studying glycosylation is to learn the role of glycans in a whole animal. Methods that extend lessons learned from cell models to multicellular organisms are therefore crucial. In the future, with the entire genomes of higher organisms becoming known, the molecular defects observed in single cells can be introduced into the analogous enzymes in stem cells. Already these 'reverse genetic' methods are feasible in the nematode *Caenorhabditis elegans*. With efforts to sequence the mouse genome well underway and the rat genome now in progress, such methods will soon be extended to mammalian systems. When necessary, sophisticated temporal and tissue-specific gene expression systems can be used to avoid the problem of embryonic lethality. We conclude that the integration of constantly improving molecular biology techniques with emerging substrate-based and genome-wide approaches promises rapid progress in determining the molecular forces that govern oligosaccharide biosynthesis.

OTHER PTMS

Other modifications, like phosphorylation, are part of common mechanisms for controlling the behaviour of a protein, for instance activating or inactivating an enzyme.

Post-translational modification of proteins is detected by mass spectrometry or Eastern blotting.

Protein Post-translational modifications and applications may happen in several ways. Some of them are listed below:

1. *Glycosylation*: Many proteins, particularly in eukaryotic cells, are modified by the addition of carbohydrates, a process called glycosylation. Glycosylation in proteins results in addition of a glycosyl group to either asparagine, hydroxylysine,

serine, or threonine. Software for studying glycosylation by glycan structure prediction.

2. *Acetylation*: the addition of an acetyl group, usually at the N-terminus of the protein.
3. *Alkylation*: The addition of an alkyl group (*e.g.* methyl, ethyl).
4. *Methylation*: The addition of a methyl group, usually at lysine or arginine residues. (This is a type of alkylation.)
5. *Biotinylation*: Acylation of conserved lysine residues with a biotin appendage.
6. *Glutamylation*: Covalent linkage of glutamic acid residues to tubulin and some other proteins.
7. *Glycylation*: Covalent linkage of one to more than 40 glycine residues to the tubulin C-terminal tail of the amino acid sequence.
8. *Isoprenylation*: The addition of an isoprenoid group (*e.g.* farnesol and geranylgeraniol).
9. *Lipoylation*: The attachment of a lipoate functionality.
10. Phosphopantetheinylation, The addition of a 4'-phosphopantetheinyl moiety from coenzyme A, as in fatty acid, polyketide, non-ribosomal peptide and leucine biosynthesis.
11. Phosphorylation, the addition of a phosphate group, usually to serine, tyrosine, threonine or histidine.
12. *Sulphation*: The addition of a sulphate group to a tyrosine.
13. Selenation
14. C-terminal amidation

CHAPTER

Clinical Proteomics 3

Biomarkers of drug efficacy and toxicity are becoming a key need in the drug development process. Mass spectral-based proteomic technologies are ideally suited for the discovery of protein biomarkers in the absence of any prior knowledge of quantitative changes in protein levels. The success of any biomarker discovery effort will depend upon the quality of samples analyzed, the ability to generate quantitative information on relative protein levels and the ability to readily interpret the data generated. This review will focus on the strengths and weaknesses of technologies currently utilized to address these issues. Better biomarkers are urgently needed to improve diagnosis, guide molecularly targeted therapy and monitor activity and therapeutic response across a wide spectrum of disease. Proteomics methods based on mass spectrometry hold special promise for the discovery of novel biomarkers that might form the foundation for new clinical blood tests, but to date their contribution to the diagnostic armamentarium has been disappointing. This is due in part to the lack of a coherent pipeline connecting marker discovery with well-established methods for validation. Advances in methods and technology now enable construction of a comprehensive biomarker pipeline from six essential process components: candidate discovery, qualification, verification, research assay optimization, biomarker validation and commercialization. Better understanding of the overall process of biomarker discovery and validation and of the challenges and strategies inherent in each phase should improve experimental study design, in turn increasing the efficiency of biomarker development and facilitating the delivery and deployment of novel clinical tests.

Introduction

Advances in protein analytical technologies are finding broad application in drug discovery programmes. One area of intense interest is in the area of biomarker discovery. Biomarkers are indicators of a biological process and may be genes, proteins, small molecules or metabolites. Intense effort has been applied to the discovery of genetic associations in complex diseases. Single nucleotide polymorphisms (SNPs) have been used as biomarkers of disease association and susceptibility.1 SNPs provide valuable information that may be used in the selection of treatments and prediction of outcomes, although they are not useful for measurement of these outcomes. While SNPs indicate the potential for disease susceptibility, it is the activity of the resultant protein that actually determines this. Biomarkers of drug efficacy and toxicity have the potential to speed the process of drug development, as they may provide indications of drug action at earlier stages than clinical endpoints. When successfully applied, biomarker analysis can have an impact on the length and cost of clinical trials. With the wealth of information generated from genomic sequencing projects, attention has begun to shift to the study of the resultant protein component. Protein biomarkers also provide predictive information, but will also be useful in monitoring the effects of drug treatments. Measurement of protein changes can be accomplished in body fluids as well as tissues and cells, which is a particular advantage in a clinical setting. The large volume of data acquired in protein-based studies demands application of higher throughput, more sensitive techniques for the discovery of suitable biomarkers. Until recently, biomarker discovery resulted from intensive study of individual proteins, development of enzyme-linked immunosorbent assay-type assays and measurements on control and perturbed systems. It is becoming increasingly clear that the predictive utility of individual biomarker proteins may be limited. As an alternative, panels of proteins may be required to accurately gauge the level of perturbation of a biological system. While a variety of multiplex assay technologies are being developed to facilitate the rapid analysis of multiple protein biomarkers simultaneously from a single sample,2–6 most are limited by the need to know which protein is required to be monitored and to develop specific reagents (most frequently specific antibody pairs) for these proteins. A few approaches, which do use non-antibody binding agents, rely on non-specific interactions (ion exchange), which complicates the identification of potential biomarkers. The problem is finding all of the relevant biomarkers without knowing in advance what they are. Integration of protein separation technologies, some of which have been in use for decades, with high throughput mass spectral techniques are providing solutions to this need. Numerous strategies have been applied in the area of biomarker discovery. Mass spectral technologies have been widely used in concert with separations technologies such as two-dimensional polyacrylamide gels and chromatographic techniques. Mass spectrometry has also been used to identify and quantify proteins in complex mixtures without prior separations. Recent developments in quantification using mass spectral techniques provide examples of how this technology may be utilized to identify biomarkers in complex samples in a high throughput fashion. Application of this technology to biological fluids may afford the ability to measure and identify protein changes without a priori knowledge of protein changes occurring in response to a particular perturbation. While quite powerful, protein changes identified by these strategies will still only provide candidate biomarkers. Validation of these candidates will require sophisticated bioinformatics technologies to analyze the data and assign statistical significance and confidence to protein measurements. Validation will ultimately provide tools by which experts in the biology of a particular system may visualize the data and draw meaningful conclusions as to the context of a biomarker or panel of biomarkers. This review will focus on strategies for the identification of protein biomarker candidates, with emphasis on the issues surrounding the adaptation of separations and identification technologies to high throughput analysis of complex biological fluids. Biological fluids are preferred in biomarker measurements because samplesn may be obtained by relatively noninvasive methods such as drawing blood. They also have the advantage over cell or tissue samples that the protein components are all in a soluble form in a single compartment. The fluids most frequently studied are serum, plasma and cerebrospinal fluid (CSF). The process of biomarker discovery in these fluids may be subdivided into three areas: (1) sample collection and preparation; (2) separation and quantification; and (3) data analysis. It is essential in the effective identification of valid biomarkers that the error inherent in each of these components be accurately determined and that only quantitative changes that have statistical significance be used to suggest biomarker candidates. Otherwise, a huge amount of effort can be spent exploring changes that are simply noise in the complex system under analysis.

SAMPLE COLLECTION AND PREPARATION: One of the largest sources of variability in the biomarker discovery process is subject-to-subject variability. Many factors influence the protein concentration of a biological fluid, including normal metabolism, circadian rhythms of protein production, degradation and environmental conditions. In addition, following sample collection, modifications of proteins may occur via proteolysis, protein aggregation and chemical modifications, such as oxidation. In order to minimize these variations, sample collection and storage conditions must be standardized within any study. Factors to be considered include the time of day the samples are collected, the length of time samples are kept at room temperature and whether to process the samples immediately or freeze them. If samples are to be stored frozen, the number of thaws should be minimal. As a result, it may be necessary to sub aliquot samples such that large volumes do not need to be thawed in order to remove small aliquots for analysis at different times. Without attention to sample quality, differences in protein levels resulting from external factors may be misinterpreted as biological effects. Prior to analysis by mass spectral techniques, most biological fluids will need to be processed to reduce protein complexity. Fluids like serum and plasma are comprised of thousands of different proteins but a relative few proteins dominate. Albumin and the immunoglobulins (Igs) represent about 75 per cent of the protein concentration of these fluids. These proteins are similarly abundant in CSF. Removal of these proteins prior to analysis allows visualisation of proteins of lower abundance. A number of strategies have been developed around removal of these two proteins. Many of these involve affinity chromatography steps. For example, protein A and protein G are bacterial proteins that have affinities primarily for the constant region of the IgG heavy chain. Resins on which these proteins are immobilised can remove most of the IgG in a sample with fairly high specificity. Albumin removal is not as easily accomplished. One of the most common methods for albumin removal from fluids is the use of columns containing an immobilised dye such as Cibacron blue. This dye interacts strongly

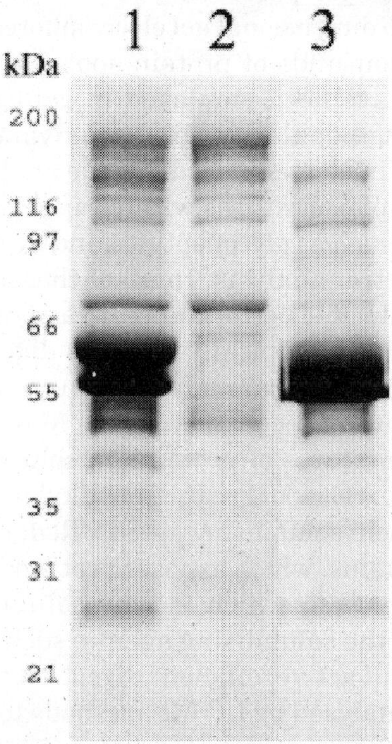

Fig. 3.1 : Removal of albumin from serum with Cibacron blue chromatography. Rat serum was passed over a commercial Cibacron blue resin (Affygel blue, Bio-Rad). The flow through fraction was collected and analysed on a 4–20% sodium dodecylsulphate polyacrylamide gel electrophoresis (SDS-PAGE) gel under reducing conditions. Later, resin with bound protein was treated with SDS sample buffer to remove the retained proteins. *Lane 1*: rat serum. *Lane 2*: proteins not bound to the Cibacron blue resin. *Lane 3*: bound proteins released from the Cibachron blue resin

with albumin and may be used to deplete this protein from samples. Figure 3.1 shows a sodium dodecylsulphate polyacrylamide gel electrophoresis (SDS-PAGE) gel of a serum sample before and after passage over a Cibacron blue column. It is evident that the heavy albumin band at 66 kDa is greatly reduced by the dye resin and that the relative proportions of many lower abundance proteins have been increased. The drawback to this technique is that the dye resin is not absolutely specific for albumin and is known to interact with other proteins possessing a dinucleotide fold. Electrophoresis of the bound fraction reveals that many other proteins have been bound to varying extents (Figure 3.1, lane 3). This could introduce variability and, therefore, the bound fraction should be retained and analysed in any biomarker discovery project. Other albumin removal techniques are being developed and these include anti-albumin antibodies and albumin-specific peptides. Generally, these techniques are more costly than the dye columns, which is why they have not yet been widely adopted. Additional protein fractionation techniques may be performed at this stage of sample processing. The most commonly employed are gel electrophoresis techniques. Two dimensional gel electrophoresis has been utilised for decades and is capable of resolving thousands of protein spots. More recently, chromatographic prefractionation techniques have been employed in gel-free analytical procedures. The gel-free procedures are gaining popularity because advances in liquid chromatography/ mass spectrometry (LC/MS) technologies have made the analysis of highly complex mixtures possible. Simplification of complex mixtures without using gels has been accomplished by isolation of classes of peptides, such as glycopeptides,and by liquid phase isoelectric focusing of mixtures prior to mass spectral analysis. In all of these strategies, great care must be taken in order to ensure reproducible performance, to avoid the introduction of variability. The final step in sample processing typically involves digestion of proteins into peptides using proteolytic enzymes. The most commonly used enzyme is trypsin, since the resultant peptides are compatible with mass spectral analysis. Many different methods have been developed to digest complex mixtures of proteins in solution. Factors that influence the success of the technique include: (1) global reduction/alkylation of proteins; and (2) inclusion of chaotropic salts or other protein solubilising agents. Reduction and alkylation of cysteines facilitates the unfolding of proteins, which exposes protease-sensitive sites. This unfolding also promotes protein aggregation, which is why solubilizing agents are needed. By adjusting the concentration of the solubilising agents, such that aggregation is minimised but proteolytic enzymes are still active, efficient digestion may be achieved. The resulting peptide mixture may now be analysed by LC/MS methods to identify and quantify proteins in the mixture.

Separation Identification Quantification

> Fragmentation and peptides on the mass spectrometer may be used to identify the sequence of the peptide

The analysis of mixtures of peptides by mass spectrometry is possible by interfacing high-performance liquid chromatography (HPLC) separations with electrospray ionization techniques. Reversed-phase solvents and ion pairing agents are volatile and thus compatible with this soft ionization process. In this application, the mass spectrometer functions like an HPLC detector, although much more information may be acquired than with a typical detector. In addition to total ion current, the mass spectrometer continuously acquires mass information on the molecular species that are eluting from the column at any point in time. Many instruments, such as the ion trap mass spectrometer, may be programmed to subject peptides to fragmentation in the tandem mass spectrometric (MS/MS) mode, which generates peptide sequence information that can be used to identify peptides. In this mode, peptides are fragmented by collisions with monoatomic gas molecules. Typically, the weakest bond in peptides is the peptide bond between amino acids, and the fragments that are generated will differ in mass by discrete quantities that are defined by the sequence of amino acids in the peptide. An example of such a chromatogram is shown in Figure 3.2. Figure 3.2A displays the total ion current of a tryptic digest of a serum sample (after removal of albumin and IgG) separated on a C-18 reversed phase column. Figure 83B displays the mass spectrum of a particular time region of the chromatogram, indicating that, at any point in time, multiple peptides may be eluting from the column. In a data dependent mode, the mass spectrometer may alternate between the MS and the MS/MS mode. The computer controller can identify the most abundant peak in the spectrum, select this ion for fragmentation in the MS/MS mode and then return to the MS mode and select the next most abundant ion for fragmentation. Figure 3.2C displays the MS/MS fragmentation pattern collected for ion 980.7 in Figure 3.2B. These fragmentation spectra may be used to search databases of protein sequences utilizing programs such as SEQUEST or Masscot. These algorithms compare theoretical fragmentation patterns of peptides in the database to the actual fragmentation pattern obtained and return the highest

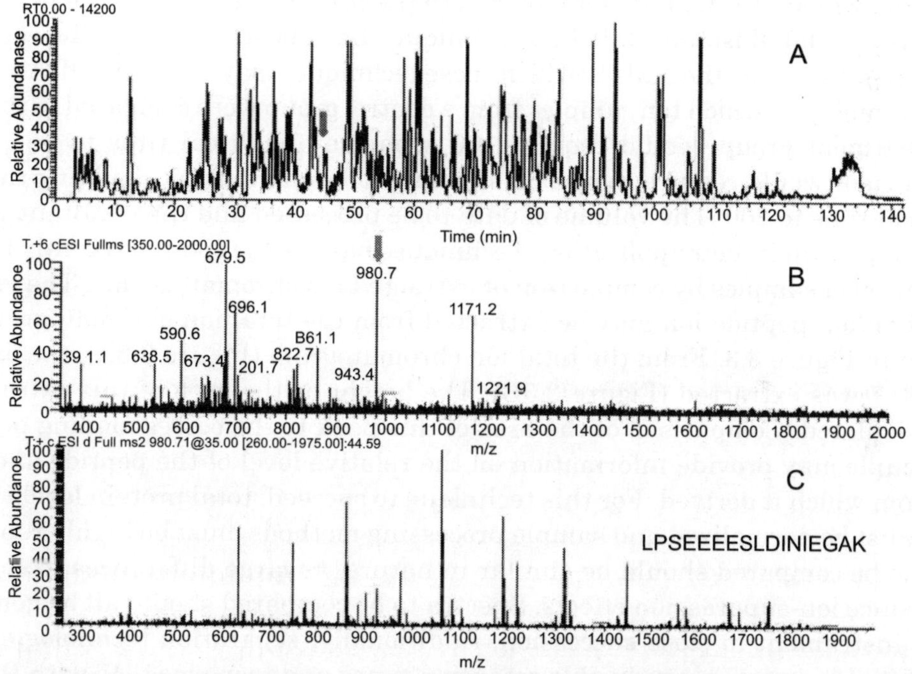

Fig. 3.2 : Liquid chromatography tandem mass spectrometric (LC/MS/MS) analysis of a serum sample. Serum that was spiked with chicken lysozyme was reduced, alkylated and digested with trypsin. The resultant peptides were analyzed on an ion trap mass spectrometer equipped with a 1 mm C-18 column. Peptides were fragmented by collisional induced dissociation (CID) and MS/MS spectra were used to search protein databases with the Sequent program. (*A*) Base peak display of the total ion chromatogram of the LC separation of the peptides. (*B*) Mass spectrum acquired at one time point (indicated by the black arrow in A). (*C*) MS/MS spectrum of ion 980.7 from panel B (denoted by black arrow in B) with sequence LPSEEEESLDINIEGAK

correlation matches. Many spectra may be searched in automated fashion, although some visual inspection is still required for peptide matches with relatively low correlation scores.

Many efforts have been initiated to improve the quality of these correlations 25–28 but much room for improvement exists. While separation and identification techniques are available, quantification of mass spectra is at an earlier stage of development. The most widely utilized technologies for quantification of peptides and proteins by mass spectrometry are the isotope tagging techniques. The most popular of these is the isotope-coded affinity tag (ICAT) technology. This technique allows relative quantification of peptides in two different samples by labeling one sample of protein with a deuterated alkylating agent while the other sample is labeled with the same alkylating agent without deuterium. The two samples are then mixed together, digested with proteolytic enzyme and processed by LC/MS. Peptides from the different samples are separated by 8 mass units and the heights of the peptide pairs are compared to provide information on the relative levels of peptide in each sample, which can then be related back to the protein from which the peptides were derived. Many related isotopic labeling techniques have been reported. The requirement for paired analysis limits the scale to which these techniques may be practiced. A comparison of patient samples, in which ten samples from a control group were compared to the samples from a treatment group, would require 100 separate analytical runs to be conducted. Statistical rigor would require reciprocal labeling to be carried out, doubling the number of analytical runs to 200. The volume of data to be processed and the resultant expense of these techniques limit their application. Techniques have been reported recently for relative quantification of samples by comparison of extracted ion chromatograms. The ion current for an individual peptide ion may be extracted from the total ion chromatogram. This is illustrated in Figure 3.3. From the total ion chromatogram (Figure 3.3A), the ion current for ion 980.7 was extracted (Figure 3.3B). The height or the area of this extracted peak may be calculated. Comparison of the area of this peak to the corresponding peak from a second sample may provide information on the relative level of the peptide and thus the protein from which it derived. For this technique to succeed, total protein levels in the two samples must be normalized and sample processing methods must be highly reproducible. Samples to be compared should be similar in nature, as large differences in composition may introduce ion-suppression effects. Spectra to be compared should all be generated on the same instrument in close succession. Additionally, separation technologies must be well validated to ensure reproducible retention times and responses. As with the isotopic labeling techniques, a wealth of data may be generated. This results in the need for bioinformatics and statistical methods for processing and interpreting the data.

Data Analysis

The initial analysis of mass spectral data typically involves database searching using the algorithms mentioned in the previous section. The resultant tables of identified proteins also contain scoring parameters that assign confidence to individual peptide results. When these scores are high, peptide identifications can be accepted without the need for visual inspection of the spectra. Similarly, very low scores indicate random correlation and may be discarded. The area of difficulty that currently exists is in the intermediate confidence scores. In some cases, peptide assignments with scores in this intermediate range may be correct. These scores may derive from low intensity spectra, peptides with high charge states (. +3) and large peptides, among other factors. The difficulty arises because there will be incorrectly identified peptides in the intermediate scoring range and one must visually inspect MS/MS spectra in this range to determine the difference between correct and incorrect identifications. This is an area of active research and many groups are developing improved scoring parameters and post-search data analysis programs. For quantitative applications, peak heights or peak areas need to be extracted, samples compared and the validity statistically evaluated. This area is far less standardized than database searching and thus not many commercially available software packages exist. Software is available for individual instruments, like the Q-Tof mass spectrometer, to evaluate ICAT experiments.33 Even these packages, however, may need to be adapted to an individual approach. A major challenge is in the application of these techniques in an automated fashion. To generate the statistical power needed for a biomarker discovery programme, many samples must be run and analyzed. Software for automation of MS/MS searching, evaluation of data quality and quantification of MS data must be developed for this to occur. Thus, the mass spectrometrist must work closely with specialists in bioinformatics and software development in order to devise solutions to these barriers. Once primary analysis is accomplished, software packages for additional data manipulation and visualization do exist. Spreadsheet programs like Microsoft Excel or JMP may be used to tabulate data and perform statistical analyses. A second category of tools includes those for table storage and joining. Through these, expanded tables of primary data can be stored directly into a database such as Microsoft Access. The data may then be merged with information about proteins, such as data from the Gene Ontology database, pathway information, experimental details and additional analyses. This will facilitate biological interpretation and begin the data mining process. The data could be parsed at this stage, although it may be unwieldy to manually sift through large tables of data. A third category of tools is therefore required: those for data reduction and visualisation. Graphical tools provide accessible techniques for visualisation of data through pattern recognition. Software packages like Spotfire are well suited for this. Graphical representation of single or multiple tables of data enables interactive queries of the tables' contents using sliders and buttons that update the graphics in real time. Additional tools in Spot fire allow viewers for biological pathways and Gene Ontology to interact with the data in real time. The power of the database architecture is that it enables one database to create multiple views of the same data for different people, or views incorporating different datasets for different applications. At the highest level, tools for cluster analysis are needed. It is increasingly apparent that individual protein changes will only rarely provide biomarkers.

Multiple, interdependent changes in panels of proteins may be more useful in prediction and measurement of outcome applications. Many statistical tools have been developed for analysis of changes in gene expression patterns from microarrays. Approaches building on these tools have begun to be applied to proteomic data sets; however, great care must be taken in the design of the studies and interpretation of the resulting data.

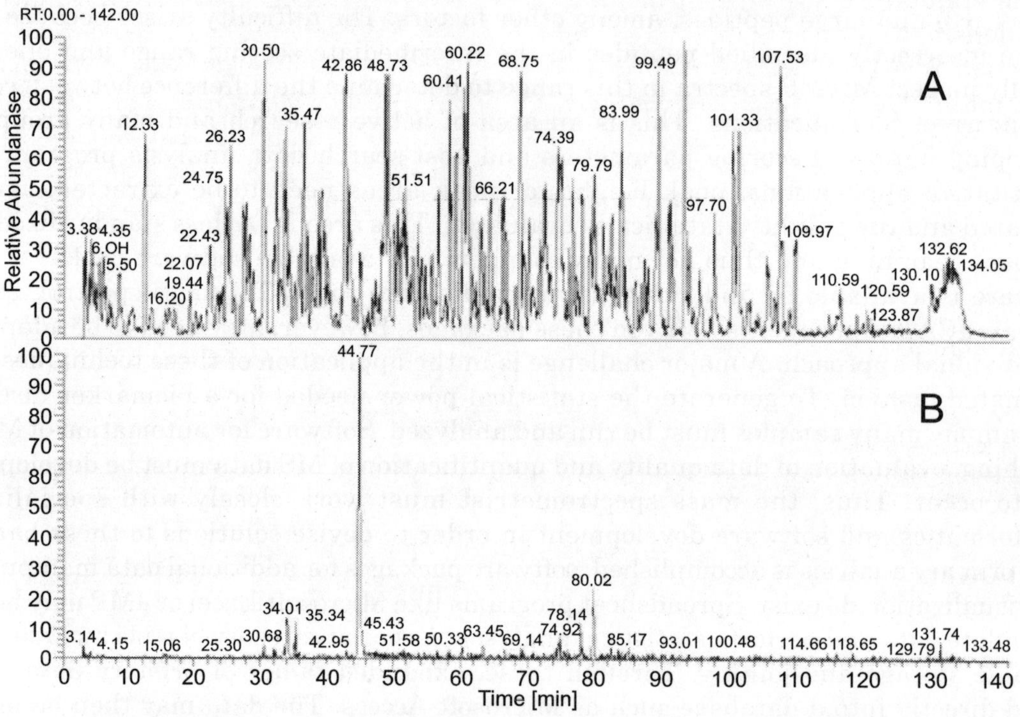

Fig. 3.3: Extracted ion chromatogram of a single peptide from a total serum sample. Liquid chromatography mass spectrometry (LC/MS) spectrum of the serum digest described in Figure 3.2: (*A*) base peak display of the total ion chromatogram of the LC separation of the peptides; (*B*) ion current for m/z 980.7 extracted from the total chromatogram

Conclusion

Applications of mass spectral-based technologies are providing solutions for the discovery of novel biomarkers. Once discovered, these biomarker candidates must be validated and ultimately assayed in a format that lends itself to high throughput analysis. The emerging field of multiplex assay technology offers a complementary approach to the successful implementation of biomarker measurements. Mass spectral approaches will provide information defining the proteins of interest. While these technologies provide the ability to automate separation, identification and quantification technology, and more focussed and higher throughput methods based on multiplexed antibody assays may be designed, based on the information generated from mass spectral approaches. These assays will be capable of handling large numbers of samples in a clinical setting, and the combination of these technologies promises to change the landscape of clinical drug discovery in the near future.

Validation

Biomarker quantifications can be absolute or relative depending upon the characteristics of the standard curve, which include the reference standard, substituted matric and parallelism. Appropriate method validation experiments should be carried out on sample collection, relative accuracy and precision, range finding, parallelism, selectivity, specificity and stability in order to meet the need for exploratory or advanced applications that is specified for a study. The interaction of a biotheraputic with the target ligand or inter-related biomarkers should be taken into consideration for method platform choice and validation. Direct adoption of commercial diagnostic kits can produce confounding data. Therefore kit comparison, modification and appropriate validation experiments are often carried out to meet the specific purpose for drug development. Multiplex assays and physicochemical methods can complement the single ligand – binding assay for protein drugs biomarkers.

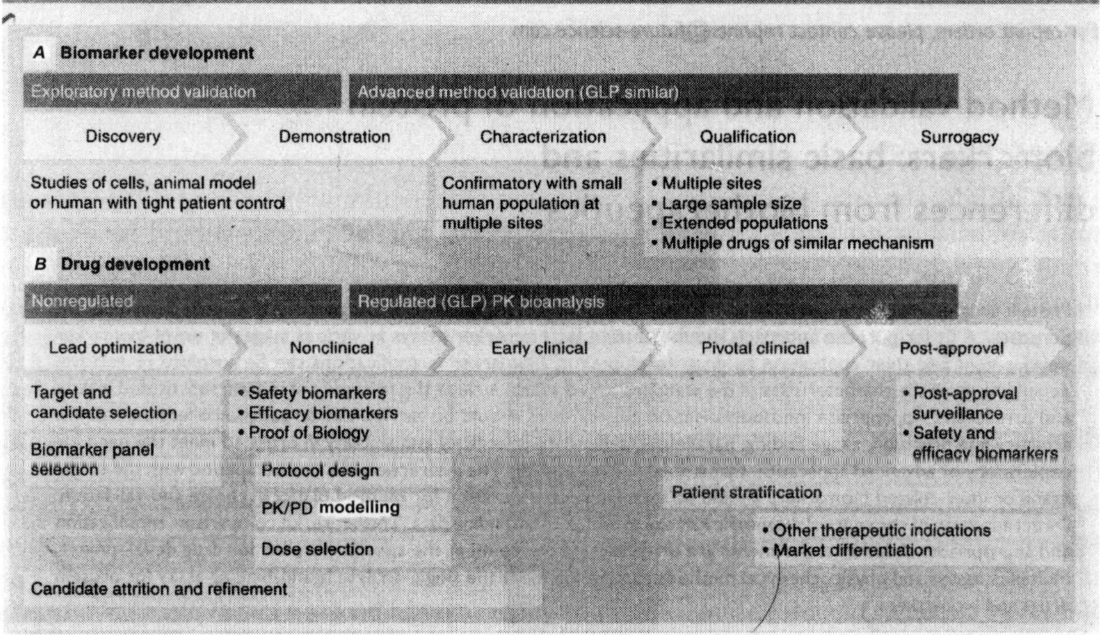

Fig. 3.4 : (*A*) Biomarker (*B*) drug discovery

The purpose of biomarkers are more diverse than those of drug development however method – validation approaches can be roughly categorized into those of exploratory and advanced application Fig. 3.4B depicts the basic concept of fit – for purpose biomarker method validation and how the exploratory and advanced validations are used during biomarker development, validation and documentation for advanced application is more intense and GLP similar, except for a few distinguishing features. The basic similarities and major differences are listed in the table below and discussed in the later subheads.

Table 3.1 : Comparison of Pharmacokinetic and Biomarker Bionalysis

Selectivity	Specificity	Assay acceptance criteria	Stability	Reproducibility
PK study				
Spike recovery test on six matrix lots at LLOQ and one other level	Test against target ligand, in addition to similar structures; measurement of free drug preferred over total	4-6-X rule	Use QC samples	Incurred sample
Biomarker study				
Spike sufficient amount over basal level, test more lots from healthy and disease populations	Test against drug molecule(s) precursor and downstream molecules; measurement of total target biomarker may be the pragmatic option over the free form	Depends on drug effect, disease and biological modulation and method performance	Use sample controls and trend analysis for long term storage	Sample controls

B: Bioavailability; BE: Bioequaivalence; LLOQ: Lower limit of quantification; PD: Pharmocodynamic; PK: Pharmacokinetic; QC: Quality control; VS: Validation samples

(Stability of the analytes in stock solution and biological matrix during the processes of sample collection, storage, shipping, and throughout the last assay should be evaluated for drug compounds and biomarkers. The sample collection stability for monoclonal anti-body drugs in serum has bccn well established; however, the stability of pep tides often depends upon blood collection, anticoagulants and time of exposure to high temperatures, Therefore, plasma or serum sample collection for novel peptide biotherapeutics and biomarkers should be investigated for possible stability issues. Pre-analytic variables have hindered data utility in proteomic biomarker discovery and validation. Errors from variable specimen collection can be higher than those arising from sample analysis itself. The conversion of precursors to the biomarker of interest will lead to overestimation, while degradation will result in underestimation of the analyte. Inhibitors of relevant activation or proteolysis should be included in the collection syringe or added to the sample promptly. Some biomarkers can only be quantified in plasma so as to avoid proteolysis or platelet activation of the coagulation pathway during serum collection. Bulk serum collected into a bag can result in lower recovery than in serum from venipuncture used in a clinical study for some biomarkers. The shearing effect through a small bore needle or the use of high-speed centrifugation on blood cells may cause endothelial cell activation, resulting in analytical artifacts. For biological fluids of *l* relatively low protein content (*e.g.*, urine and cerebral spinal fluid), collection tubes, transfer pipettes and storage containers must be evaluated to minimize adsorption of a peptide/ protein to the contact surfaces.

It is important to standardize techniques for all sample collection and handling and to keep these consistent throughout the duration of the use of the assay [25.26J. For example, the G-force and revolution per minute conversion should be defined for each laboratory's centrifuge in order to avoid mistakes. The standard processes of collections from multiple sites, barcodes and transports to the analytical laboratory should be followed.

Inappropriate collection time and other adverse conditions often lead to confounding or uninterruptable data. If there is a diurnal effect, it is prudent to pool samples or to collect them at the same time of the day. The initial survey of healthy and patient samples provide a rough idea of biological variability. The clinical question is the comparison of the treatment versus placebo. Appropriate clinical (placebo' and/or predose samples) and assay control (sample control or QC) data can be assessed for analytical and biological variability, to produce unbiased clinical answers. However, for cancer studies, placebo or baseline samples may not be available to provide data to parse out the true drug effect versus the biological and assay variability.

Reference Standard: The basic requirement of reference standards hold true for both PK and biomarker assays. The standard is required to be:

- Purified and well characterized
- Representative of the analyte in the unknown samples
- Available on large quantity to support the development programme
- Accessible to the participating laboratories.

Application of Commercial Kits

Commercial kits for diagnostic use have been commonly adopted for drug development since they are readily available. The varieties of kits range from the well-established FDA-approved (or FDA-cleared) kits to less-proven 'for research use only' or 'for investigational use only' kits. As the purposes of drug development are different from that of diagnosis, it is not recommended to directly adopt a kit method for drug development without method validation. The validation experiments should evaluate the reference material and standard matrix, determine performance characteristics, patient range and drug modulation and set up SCs.

The standard calibrators can be a major contrib-utor to confounding data in research kit applica-tion. If there are multiple commercial kit sources, it is prudent to assay the same set of authentic samples using various kits for comparison. It is not surprising to find that the results are totally different from one kit to another because the calibrators (yardsticks) are of different forms. In addition, the calibrators from one supplier can be different with time, due to changes in purification processes and recalibration. If a bulk standard material in sufficient quantity can be acquired from one supplier, standard calibrators should be prepared in-house, in the appropriate matrix, to assure calibrator con-sistency throughout an advanced application, such as in the example of serum CTx. The bulk standard material also allows the preparation of sufficient levels of calibrators with anchor points for appropriate curve fitting with weighting, as well as spiked QCs for accuracy and precision experiments to define the assay range.

The assay range should be evaluated against the population range and the desirable drug effect. When the biomarker levels are extremely low, as is the case with the free soluble recep-tor activator of NFKB ligand, many literature results using a research kit reported concentra-tions below the LLOQ Therefore, most of the population baseline values would actually be assay noise.

For research-grade commercial kits, QCs or authentic sample controls may not be available. It is the analyst's responsibility to set up these con-trols to characterize assay accuracy and precision and to monitor assay performance. For example, method validation using commercial kits for exploratory and advanced biomarker applica-tions have been reported for tartrate-resistant acid phosphatase (TRACP 5b) and serum CTx for bone resorption, respectively the same basic principle of must be applied for the adoption of commercial kits for PK bioana-lysis. Again, the responsibility resides with the bioanalytical laboratory to establish the assay characteristics and determine run-acceptance criteria. Moreover, kit comparison and rigorous specificity tests should be conducted.

Biostatistics and Its Applications

Biostatistics (a contraction of biology and statistics; sometimes referred to as ***biometry*** or ***biometrics***) is the application of statistics to a wide range of topics in biology. The science of biostatistics encompasses the design of biological experiments, especially in medicine and agriculture; the collection, summarization, and analysis of data from those experiments; and the interpretation of, and inference from, the results.

Biostatistics and the History of Biological Thought

Biostatistical reasoning and modeling were of critical importance to the foundation theories of modern biology. In the early 1900s, after the rediscovery of Mendel's work, the conceptual gaps in understanding between genetics and evolutionary Darwinism led to vigorous debate between biometricians such as Walter Weldon and Karl Pearson and Mendelians such as Charles Davenport, William Bateson and Wilhelm Johannsen. By the 1930s statisticians and models built on statistical reasoning had helped to resolve these differences and to produce the neo-Darwinian modern evolutionary synthesis.

The leading figures in the establishment of this synthesis all relied on statistics and developed its use in biology.

- Sir Ronald A. Fisher developed several basic statistical methods in support of his work *The Genetical Theory of Natural Selection*
- Sewall G. Wright used statistics in the development of modern population genetics
- J. B. S Haldane's book, *The Causes of Evolution*, reestablished natural selection as the premier mechanism of evolution by explaining it in terms of the mathematical consequences of Mendelian genetics.

These individuals and the work of other biostatisticians, mathematical biologists, and statistically inclined geneticists helped bring together evolutionary biology and genetics into a consistent, coherent whole that could begin to be quantitatively modelled.

In parallel to this overall development, the pioneering work of D'Arcy Thompson in *On Growth and Form* also helped to add quantitative discipline to biological study.

Despite the fundamental importance and frequent necessity of statistical reasoning, there may nonetheless have been a tendency among biologists to distrust or deprecate results which are not qualitatively apparent. One anecdote describes Thomas Hunt Morgan banning the Friden calculator from his department at Caltech, saying "Well, I am like a guy who is prospecting for gold along the banks of the Sacramento River in 1849. With a little intelligence, I can reach down and pick up big nuggets of gold. And as long as I can do that, I'm not going to let any people in my department waste scarce resources in placer mining.. Educators are now adjusting their curricula to focus on more quantitative concepts and tools.

Education and Training Programmes

Almost all educational programmes in biostatistics are at postgraduate level. They are most often found in schools of public health, affiliated with schools of medicine, forestry, or agriculture or as a focus of application in departments of statistics. In the United States, while several universities have dedicated biostatistics departments, many other top-tier universities integrate biostatistics faculty into statistics or other departments, such as epidemiology. Thus departments carrying the name 'biostatistics' may exist under quite different structures. For instance, relatively new biostatistics departments have been founded with a focus on bioinformatics and computational biology, whereas older departments, typically affiliated with schools of public health, will have more traditional lines of research involving epidemiological studies and clinical trials as well as bioinformatics. In larger universities where both a statistics and a biostatistics department exist, the degree of integration between the two departments may range from the bare minimum to very close collaboration. In general, the difference between a statistics program and a biostatistics one is twofold: (*i*) statistics departments will often host theoretical/methodological research which are less common in biostatistics programs; and (*ii*) statistics departments have lines of research that may include biomedical applications but also other areas such as industry (quality control), business and economics and biological areas other than medicine. The discipline of biostatistics focuses on the examination of healthcare data. Much of the data are collected through the process of randomized, clinical trials. All new medicationsare required to demonstrate safety and effectiveness through randomized, clinical trials before they will be approved for use by the Food and Drug Administration (FDA). For this reason, pharmaceutical companies employ many biostatisticians (and SAS programmers).It is the responsibility of the biostatistician to design the clinical trial. The biostatistician must decide before any subjects are recruited just how many subjects are needed for the study. The statistical method must be clearly specified that is to be used to demonstrate both safety and effectiveness in the patients. It is not always possible to design randomized studies. For example, it is not possibly to test the effects of smoking by randomly assigning subjects to a .smoking. group and to a no smoking group.. Observational studies must be used with the acknowledgement that they can be incomplete and incorrect if confounding factors are not taken into consideration. One of the most lucrative new areas of biostatistics research is to investigate health outcomes in clinical practice. This can only be done observationally aspatients enter into treatment to determine .best practices.. In order to accommodate this observational data, the field of medical informatics has been developed. Its purpose is to work with health information as it exists. The field is strongly advocating the development of electronic patient records. Since physicians are still using chart notes, it is also necessary to be able to analyze unstructured text data. The field of data mining focuses on working with large datasets with hundreds andsometimes thousandsof variables. The field has also developed tools to analyze text data.It is strongly recommended that students interested in biostatistics also learn something about data mining.

Applications of Biostatistics

- Public health, including epidemiology, health services research, nutrition, and environmental health
- Design and analysis of clinical trials in medicine
- Population genetics, and statistical genetics in order to link variation in genotype with a variation in phenotype. This has been used in agriculture to improve crops and farm animals (animal breeding). In biomedical research, this work can assist in finding candidates for gene alleles that can cause or influence predisposition to disease in human genetics
- Anaysis of genomics data, for example from microarray or proteomics experiments. Often concerning diseases or disease stages.
- Ecology, ecological forecasting
- Biological sequence analysis
- Systems biology for gene network inference or pathways analysis

Use of Statistical Software

Spreadsheets have some statistical tools but are extremely limited and should not be used as statistical packages. Small statistical packages can be purchased for use on 1 desktop at cost < $500. Their use is limited and can only perform relatively simple, routine statistical methods. The two main statistical packages used in research are SPSS and SAS. SPSS was developed for use with the social sciences. It still sells primarily to an academic market. SAS now incorporates all the social science methodology of SPSS + database management. It was developed for use in the natural sciences. It is now the primary package used in the business market. The ability to use SAS has now become a very marketable skill. Businesses advertise for SAS experience. For example, FDA statistical guidelines were in part derived with SAS language. Pharmaceutical companies all use SAS as the statistical software package. Other statistical packages (such as S-plus) might be used as add-ons to SAS, but SAS remains the primary package. One of the reasons that SAS remains so popular is that each year in early April, the SAS User.s Group International holds an annual conference attracting approximately 4000 attendees. SAS developers interact with SAS users (mostly from the business environment) to improve the product. Most of the innovations in using statistical methods are now coming from the business world rather than the academic world.

Data Mining Software

There are a number of data mining software packages, including Intelligent Miner by IBM. However, for good data mining software combined with good statistical software, there are two: Clementine by SPSS and Enterprise Miner by SAS. Enterprise Miner as the best integration of statistics with data mining. It contains methods that SPSS does not include: link analysis, text mining, memory-based reasoning. It is the data mining used in the business world.

Data Mining Techniques

- Artificial neural networks
- Rule induction
- Logistic regression
- Association rules
- Data visualization

Artificial Neural Networks are used to classify the observations into categories. The final result is a .black box. in that there is no statistical function that defines the classification rule.

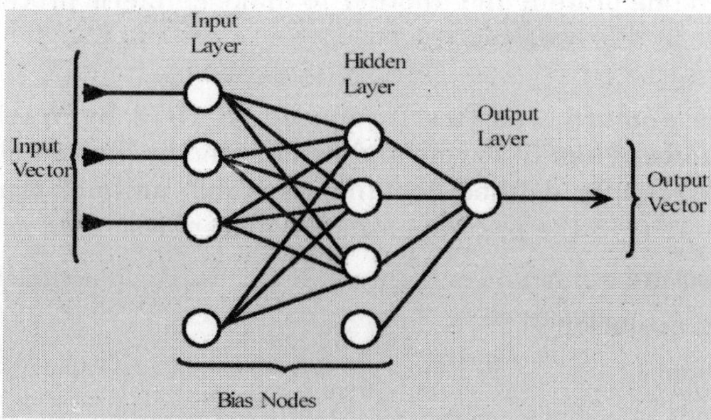

Fig. 3.5 : Showing an Ideal Biostatistical Network

CHAPTER 4

Structural Proteomics

PROTEIN DOMAIN

A *protein domain* is a part of protein sequence and structure that can evolve, function, and exist independently of the rest of the protein chain. Each domain forms a compact three-dimensional structure and often can be independently stable and folded. Many proteins consist of several structural domains. One domain may appear in a variety of different proteins. Molecular evolution uses domains as building blocks and these may be recombined in different arrangements to create proteins with different functions. Domains vary in length from between about 25 amino acids up to 500 amino acids in length. The shortest domains such as zinc fingers are stabilized by metal ions or disulfide bridges. Domains often form functional units, such as the calcium-binding EF hand domain of calmodulin. Because they are independently stable, domains can be 'swapped' by genetic engineering between one protein and another to make chimeric proteins.

Background

The concept of the *domain* was first proposed in 1973 by Wetlaufer after X-ray crystallographic studies of hen lysozyme and papain and by limited proteolysis studies of immunoglobulins. Wetlaufer defined domains as stable units of protein structure that could fold autonomously. In the past domains have been described as units of:

- compact structure
- function and evolution
- folding.

Each definition is valid and will often overlap, i.e. a compact structural domain that is found amongst diverse proteins is likely to fold independently within its structural environment. Nature often brings several domains together to form multidomain and multifunctional proteins with a vast number of possibilities. In a multidomain protein, each domain may fulfil its own function independently, or in a concerted manner with its neighbours. Domains can either serve as modules for building up large assemblies such as virus particles or muscle fibres, or can provide specific catalytic or binding sites as found in enzymes or regulatory proteins.An appropriate example is pyruvate kinase, a glycolytic enzyme that plays an important role in regulating the flux from fructose-1,6-biphosphate to pyruvate. It contains an all-β regulatory domain, an α/β-substrate binding domain and an α/β-nucleotide binding domain, connected by several polypeptide linkers. Each domain in this protein occurs in diverse sets of protein families.The central α/β-barrel substrate binding domain is one of the most common enzyme folds. It is seen in many different enzyme families catalysing completely unrelated reactions. The α/β-barrel is commonly called the TIM barrel named after triose phosphate isomerase, which was the first such structure to be solved. It is currently classified into 26 homologous families in the CATH domain database. The TIM barrel is formed from a sequence of β-α-β motifs closed by the first and last strand hydrogen bonding together, forming an eight stranded barrel. There is debate about the evolutionary origin of this domain. One study has suggested that a single ancestral enzyme could have diverged into several families, while another suggests that a stable TIM-barrel structure has evolved through convergent evolution. The TIM-barrel in pyruvate kinase is 'discontinuous', meaning that more than one segment of the polypeptide is required to form the domain. This is likely to be the result of the insertion of one domain into another during the protein's evolution. It has been shown from known structures that about a quarter of structural domains are discontinuous. The inserted β-barrel regulatory domain is 'continuous', made up of a single stretch of polypeptide. Covalent association of two domains represents a functional and structural advantage since there is an increase in stability when compared with the same structures non-covalently associated. Other, advantages are the protection of intermediates within inter-domain enzymatic clefts that may otherwise be unstable in aqueous environments, and a fixed stoichiometric ratio of the enzymatic activity necessary for a sequential set of reactions.

Domains are Units of Protein Structure

The primary structure (string of amino acids) of a protein ultimately encodes its uniquely folded 3D conformation. The most important factor governing the folding of a protein into 3D structure is the distribution of polar and non-polar side chains. Folding is driven by the burial of hydrophobic side chains into the interior of the molecule so to avoid contact with the aqueous environment. Generally proteins have a core of hydrophobic residues surrounded by a shell of hydrophilic residues. Since the peptide bonds themselves are polar they are neutralised by hydrogen bonding with each other when in the hydrophobic environment. This gives rise to regions of the polypeptide that form regular 3D structural patterns called secondary structure. There are two main types of secondary structure:

α-helices and β-sheets.Some simple combinations of secondary structure elements have been found to frequently occur in protein structure and are referred to as supersecondary structure or motifs. For example, the β-strandsSome simple combinations of secondary structure elements have been found to frequently occur in protein structure and are referred to as supersecondary structure or motifs. For example, the β-hairpin motif consists of two adjacent antiparallel β-strands joined by a small loop. It is present in most antiparallel β structures both as an isolated ribbon and as part of more complex β-sheets. Another common super-secondary structure is the β-α-β motif, which is frequently used to connect two parallel β-strands. The central α-helix connects the C-termini of the first strand to the N-termini of the second strand, packing its side chains against the β-sheet and therefore shielding the hydrophobic residues of the β-strands from the surface.

Structural alignment is an important tool for determining domains.

Tertiary Structure of Domains

Several motifs pack together to form compact, local, semi-independent units called domains. The overall 3D structure of the polypeptide chain is referred to as the protein's tertiary structure. Domains are the fundamental units of tertiary structure, each domain containing an individual hydrophobic core built from secondary structural units connected by loop regions. The packing of the polypeptide is usually much tighter in the interior than the exterior of the domain producing a solid-like core and a fluid-like surface. In fact, core residues are often conserved in a protein family, whereas the residues in loops are less conserved, unless they are involved in the protein's function. Protein tertiary structure can be divided into four main classes based on the secondary structural content of the domain.

- All-α domains have a domain core built exclusively from α-helices. This class is dominated by small folds, many of which form a simple bundle with helices running up and down.
- All-β domains have a core comprising of antiparallel β-sheets, usually two sheets packed against each other. Various patterns can be identified in the arrangement of the strands, often giving rise to the identification of recurring motifs, for example the Greek key motif.
- α+β domains are a mixture of all-α and all-β motifs. Classification of proteins into this class is difficult because of overlaps to the other three classes and therefore is not used in the CATH domain database.
- α/β domains are made from a combination of β-α-β motifs that predominantly form a parallel β-sheet surrounded by amphipathic α-helices. The secondary structures are arranged in layers or barrels.

Domains have Limits on Size

Domains have limits on size. The size of individual structural domains varies from 36 residues in E-selectin to 692 residues in lipoxygenase-1, but the majority, 90%, have less than 200 residues with an average of approximately 100 residues. Very short domains, less than 40 residues, are often stabilised by metal ions or disulfide bonds. Larger domains, greater than 300 residues, are likely to consist of multiple hydrophobic cores.

Domains and Quaternary Structure

Many proteins have a quaternary structure, which consists of several polypeptide chains that associate into an oligomeric molecule. Each polypeptide chain in such a protein is called a subunit. Haemoglobin, for example, consists of two α and two β subunits. Each of the four chains has an all-α globin fold with a heme pocket.

Domain swapping is a mechanism for forming oligomeric assemblies. In domain swapping, a secondary or tertiary element of a monomeric protein is replaced by the same element of another protein. Domain swapping can range from secondary structure elements to whole structural domains. It also represents a model of evolution for functional adaptation by oligomerisation, *e.g.* oligomeric enzymes that have their active site at subunit interfaces.

Domains as Evolutionary Modules

Nature is a tinkerer and not an inventor, new sequences are adapted from pre-existing sequences rather than invented. Domains are the common material used by nature to generate new sequences, they can be thought of as genetically mobile units, referred to as 'modules'. Often, the C and N termini of domains are close together in space, allowing them to easily be "slotted into" parent structures during the process of evolution. Many domain families are found in all three forms of life, Archaea, Bacteria and Eukarya. Domains that are repeatedly found in diverse proteins are often referred to as modules, examples can be found among extracellular proteins associated with clotting, fibrinolysis, complement, the extracellular matrix, cell surface adhesion molecules and cytokine receptors. Molecular evolution gives rise to families of related proteins with similar sequence and structure. However, sequence similarities can be extremely low between proteins that share the same structure. Protein structures may be similar because proteins have diverged from a common ancestor. Alternatively, some folds may be more favored than others as they represent stable arrangements of secondary structures and some proteins may converge towards these folds over the course of evolution. There are currently about 45,000 experimentally determined protein 3D structures deposited within the Protein Data Bank (PDB). However this set contains a lot of identical or very similar structures. All proteins should be classified to structural families to understand their evolutionary relationships. Structural comparisons are best achieved at the domain level. For this reason many algorithms have been developed to automatically assign domains in proteins with known 3D structure, see 'Domain definition from structural co-ordinates'.The CATH domain database classifies domains into approximately 800 fold families, ten of these folds are highly populated and are referred to as 'super-folds'. Super-folds are defined as folds for which there are at least three structures without significant sequence similarity. The most populated is the α/β-barrel super-fold as described previously.

Multidomain Proteins

The majority of genomic proteins, two-thirds in unicellular organisms and more than 80% in metazoa, are multidomain proteins created as a result of gene duplication events. Many domains in multidomain structures could have once existed as independent proteins. More and more domains in eukaryotic multidomain proteins can be found as independent proteins in prokaryotes. For example, vertebrates have a multi-enzyme polypeptide containing the GAR synthetase, AIR synthetase and GAR transformylase modules (GARs-AIRs-GARt; GAR: glycinamide ribonucleotide synthetase/transferase; AIR: aminoimidazole ribonucleotide synthetase). In insects, the polypeptide appears as GARs-(AIRs)2-GARt, in yeast GARs-AIRs is encoded separately from GARt, and in bacteria each domain is encoded separately.

Origin

Multidomain proteins are likely to have emerged from a selective pressure during evolution to create new functions. Various proteins have diverged from common ancestors by different combinations and associations of domains. Modular units frequently move about, within and between biological systems through mechanisms of genetic shuffling:

- transposition of mobile elements including horizontal transfers (between species);
- gross rearrangements such as inversions, translocations, deletions and duplications;
- homologous recombination;
- slippage of DNA polymerase during replication.

Types of Organisation

The simplest multidomain organisation seen in proteins is that of a single domain repeated in tandem. The domains may interact with each other or remain isolated, like beads on string. The giant 30,000 residue muscle protein titin comprises about 120 fibronectin-III-type and Ig-type domains. In the serine proteases, a gene duplication event has led to the formation of a two β-barrel domain enzyme. The repeats have diverged so widely that there is no obvious sequence similarity between them. The active site is located at a cleft between the two β-barrel domains, in which functionally important residues are contributed from each domain. Genetically engineered mutants of the chymotrypsin serine protease were shown to have some proteinase activity even though their active site residues were abolished and it has therefore been postulated that the duplication event enhanced the enzyme's activity. Modules frequently display different connectivity relationships, as illustrated by the kinesins and ABC transporters. The kinesin motor domain can be at either end of a polypeptide chain that includes a coiled-coil region and a cargo domain. ABC transporters are built with up to four domains consisting of two unrelated modules, ATP-binding cassette and an integral membrane module, arranged in various combinations.

Not only do domains recombine, but there are many examples of a domain having been inserted into another. Sequence or structural similarities to other domains demonstrate that homologues of inserted and parent domains can exist independently. An example is that of the 'fingers' inserted into the 'palm' domain within the polymerases of the Pol I family. Since a domain can be inserted into another, there should always be at least one continuous domain in a multidomain protein. This is the main difference between definitions of structural domains and evolutionary/functional domains. An evolutionary domain will be limited to one or two connections between domains, whereas structural domains can have unlimited connections, within a given criterion of the existence of a common core. Several structural domains could be assigned to an evolutionary domain.

Domains are Autonomous Folding Units

Protein folding—the unsolved problem: Since the seminal work of Anfinsen over forty years ago,[19] the goal to completely understand the mechanism by which a polypeptide rapidly folds into its stable native conformation remains elusive. Many experimental folding studies have contributed much to our understanding, but the principles that govern protein folding are still based on those discovered in the very first studies of folding. Anfinsen showed that the native state of a protein is thermodynamically stable, the conformation being at a global minimum of its free energy. Folding is a directed search of conformational space allowing the protein to fold on a biologically feasible time scale. The Levinthal paradox states that if an averaged sized protein would sample all possible conformations before finding the one with the lowest energy, the whole process would take billions of years. Proteins typically fold within 0.1 and 1000 seconds, therefore the protein folding process must be directed some way through a specific folding pathway. The forces that direct this search are likely to be a combination of local and global influences whose effects are felt at various stages of the reaction. Advances in experimental and theoretical studies have shown that folding can be viewed in terms of energy landscapes, where folding kinetics is considered as a progressive organisation of an ensemble of partially folded structures through which a protein passes on its way to the folded structure. This has been described in terms of a folding funnel, in which an unfolded protein has a large number of conformational states available and there are fewer states available to the folded protein. A funnel implies that for protein folding there is a decrease in energy and loss of entropy with increasing tertiary structure formation. The local roughness of the funnel reflects kinetic traps, corresponding to the accumulation of misfolded intermediates. A folding chain progresses toward lower intra-chain free-energies by increasing its compactness. The chains conformational options become increasingly narrowed ultimately toward one native structure.

Advantage of Domains in Protein Folding

The organisation of large proteins by structural domains represents an advantage for protein folding, with each domain being able to individually fold, accelerating the folding process and reducing a potentially large combination of residue interactions. Furthermore, given the observed random distribution of hydrophobic residues in proteins, domain formation appears to be the optimal solution for a large protein to bury its hydrophobic residues while keeping the hydrophilic residues at the surface. However, the role of inter-domain interactions in protein folding and in energetics of stabilisation of the native structure, probably differs for each protein. In T4 lysozyme, the influence of one domain on the other is so strong that the entire molecule is resistant to proteolytic cleavage. In this case, folding is a sequential process where the C-terminal domain is required to fold independently in an early step, and the other domain requires the presence of the folded C-terminal domain for folding and stabilisation. It has been found that the folding of an isolated domain can take place at the same rate or sometimes faster than that of the integrated domain. Suggesting that unfavourable interactions with the rest of the protein can occur during folding. Several arguments suggest that the slowest step in the folding of large proteins is the pairing of the folded domains. This is either because the domains are not folded entirely correctly or because the small adjustments required for their interaction are energetically unfavourable, such as the removal of water from the domain interface.

Domains and Protein Flexibility

The presence of multiple domains in proteins gives rise to a great deal of flexibility and mobility, leading to *protein domain dynamics*. Domain motions can be inferred by comparing different structures of a protein, or they can be directly observed using spectra measured by neutron spin echo spectroscopy. They can also be suggested by sampling in extensive molecular dynamics trajectories. Domain motions are important for:

- catalysis;
- regulatory activity;
- transport of metabolites;
- formation of protein assemblies; and
- cellular locomotion.

One of the largest observed domain motions is the 'swivelling' mechanism in pyruvate phosphate dikinase. The phosphoinositide domain swivels between two states in order to bring a phosphate group from the active site of the nucleotide binding domain to that of the phosphoenolpyruvate/pyruvate domain. The phosphate group is moved over a distance of 45A involving a domain motion of about 100 degrees around a single residue.In enzymes, the closure of one domain onto another captures a substrate by an induced fit, allowing the reaction to take place in a controlled way. A detailed analysis by Gerstein led to the classification of two basic types of domain motion; hinge and shear. Only a relatively small portion of the chain, namely the inter-domain linker and side chains undergo significant conformational changes upon domain rearrangement.

Hinges by Secondary Structures

A study by Hayward found that the termini of α-helices and β-sheets form hinges in a large number of cases. Many hinges were found to involve two secondary structure elements acting like hinges of a door, allowing an opening and closing motion to occur. This can arise when two neighbouring strands within a β-sheet situated in one domain, diverge apart as they join the other domain. The two resulting termini then form the bending regions between the two domains. α-helices that preserve their hydrogen bonding network when bent are found to behave as mechanical hinges, storing 'elastic energy' that drives the closure of domains for rapid capture of a substrate.

Helical to Extended Conformation

The interconversion of helical and extended conformations at the site of a domain boundary is not uncommon. In calmodulin, torsion angles change for five residues in the middle of a domain linking α-helix. The helix is split into two, almost perpendicular, smaller helices separated by four residues of an extended strand.

Shear Motions

Shear motions involve a small sliding movement of domain interfaces, controlled by the amino acid side chains within the interface. Proteins displaying shear motions often have a layered architecture: stacking of secondary structures. The interdomain linker has merely the role of keeping the domains in close proximity.

Domain Motion and Functional Dynamics in Enzymes

The analysis of the internal dynamics of structurally different, but functionally similar enzymes has highlighted a common relationship between the positioning of the active site and the two principal protein sub-domains. In fact, for several members of the hydrolase superfamily, the catalytic site is located close to the interface separating the two principal quasi-rigid domains. Such positioning appears instrumental for maintaining the precise geometry of the active site, while allowing for an appreciable functionally-oriented modulation of the flanking regions resulting from the relative motion of the two sub-domains.

Domain Definition from Structural Co-ordinates

The importance of domains as structural building blocks and elements of evolution has brought about many automated methods for their identification and classification in proteins of known structure. Automatic procedures for reliable domain assignment is essential for the generation of the domain databases, especially as the number of protein structures is increasing. Although the boundaries of a domain can be determined by visual inspection, construction of an automated method is not straightforward. Problems occur when faced with domains that are discontinuous or highly associated. The fact that there is no standard definition of what a domain really is has meant that domain assignments have varied enormously, with each researcher using a unique set of criteria. A structural domain is a compact, globular sub-structure with more interactions within it than with the rest of the protein. Therefore, a structural domain can be determined by two visual characteristics; its compactness and its extent of isolation. Measures of local compactness in proteins have been used in many of the early methods of domain assignment and in several of the more recent methods.

Methods

One of the first algorithms used a Cα-Cα distance map together with a hierarchical clustering routine that considered proteins as several small segments, 10 residues in length. The initial segments were clustered one after another based on inter-segment distances; segments with the shortest distances were clustered and considered as single segments thereafter. The stepwise clustering finally included the full protein. Go also exploited the fact that inter-domain distances are normally larger than intra-domain distances; all possible Cα-Cα distances were represented as diagonal plots in which there were distinct patterns for helices, extended strands and combinations of secondary structures. The method by Sowdhamini and Blundell clusters secondary structures in a protein based on their Cα-Cα distances and identifies domains from the pattern in their dendrograms. As the procedure does not consider the protein as a continuous chain of amino acids there are no problems in treating discontinuous domains. Specific nodes in these dendrograms are identified as tertiary structural clusters of the protein, these include both super-secondary structures and domains. The DOMAK algorithm is used to create the 3Dee domain database. It calculates a 'split value' from the number of each type of contact when the protein is divided arbitrarily into two parts. This split value is large when the two parts of the structure are distinct.

The method of Wodak and Janin was based on the calculated interface areas between two chain segments repeatedly cleaved at various residue positions. Interface areas were calculated by comparing surface areas of the cleaved segments with that of the native structure. Potential domain boundaries can be identified at a site where the interface area was at a minimum. Other methods have used measures of solvent accessibility to calculate compactness. The PUU algorithm incorporates a harmonic model used to approximate inter-domain dynamics. The underlying physical concept is that many rigid interactions will occur within each domain and loose interactions will occur between domains. This algorithm is used to define domains in the FSSP domain database. Swindells (1995) developed a method, DETECTIVE, for identification of domains in protein structures based on the idea that domains have a hydrophobic interior. Deficiencies were found to occur when hydrophobic cores from different domains continue through the interface region. RigidFinder is a novel method for identification of protein rigid blocks (domains and loops) from two different conformations. Rigid blocks are defined as blocks where all inter residue distances are conserved across conformations. A general method to identify *dynamical domains*, that is protein regions that behave approximately as rigid units in the course of structural fluctuations, has been introduced by Potestio *et al.* and, among other applications was also used to compare the consistency of the dynamics-based domain subdivisions with standard structure-based ones. The method, termed PiSQRD, is publicly available in the form of a webserver. The latter allows users to optimally subdivide single-chain or multimeric proteins into quasi-rigid domains based on the collective modes of fluctuation of the system. By default the latter are calculated through an elastic network model; alternatively pre-calculated essential dynamical spaces can be uploaded by the user.

PROTEIN CROSS LINKING

The most common schemes for forming a well-defined heteroconjugate require the indirect coupling of an amine group on one biomolecule to a thiol group on a second biomolecule, usually by a two- or three-step reaction sequence. The high reactivity of thiols and—with the exception of a few proteins such as β-galactosidase—their relative rarity in most biomolecules make thiol groups ideal targets for controlled chemical crosslinking. If neither molecule contains a thiol group, then one or more can be introduced using one of several thiolation methods. The thiol-containing biomolecule is then reacted with an amine-containing biomolecule using a heterobifunctional crosslinking reagent such as one of those described in Amine–Thiol Crosslinking, below.

Introducing Thiol Groups into Biomolecules

Several methods are available for introducing thiols into biomolecules, including the reduction of intrinsic disulfides, as well as the conversion of amine or carboxylic acid groups to thiol groups:

- Disulfide crosslinks of cystines in proteins can be reduced to cysteine residues by dithiothreitol (DTT, D1532) or tris-(2-carboxyethyl) phosphine (TCEP, T2556). However, reduction may result in loss of protein activity or specificity. Excess DTT must be carefully removed under conditions that prevent reformation of the disulfide, whereas excess TCEP usually does not need to be removed before carrying out the crosslinking reaction. TCEP is also more stable at higher pH values and at higher temperatures than is the air-sensitive DTT reagent.
- Amines can be indirectly thiolated by reaction with succinimidyl acetylthioacetate (SATA, S1553), followed by removal of the acetyl group with 50 mM hydroxylamine or hydrazine at near-neutral pH (**Figure 4.1**). This reagent is most useful when disulfides are essential for activity, as is the case for some peptide toxins.
- Amines can be indirectly thiolated by reaction with succinimidyl 3-(2-pyridyldithio)propionate (SPDP, S1531), followed by reduction of the 3-(2-

pyridyldithio)propionyl conjugate with DTT or TCEP (**Figure 88**). Reduction releases the 2-pyridinethione chromophore, which can be used to determine the degree of thiolation.

- Thiols can be incorporated at carboxylic acid groups by an EDAC-mediated reaction with cystamine, followed by reduction of the disulfide with DTT or TCEP; see Amine–Carboxylic Acid Crosslinking below.
- Tryptophan residues in thiol-free proteins can be oxidized to mercaptotryptophan residues, which can then be modified by iodoacetamides or maleimides.

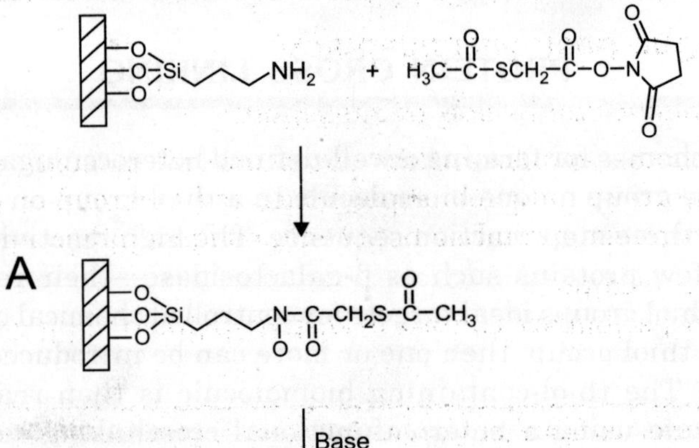

Fig. 4.1 : Schematic illustration of the heterobifunctional crosslinker succinimidyl acetylthioacetate (SATA, S1553): (*A*) attachment to an aminosilane-modified surface, (*B*) deprotection with base and (*C*) reaction with a thiol-reactive biomolecule

Our preferred reagent combination for protein thiolation is SPDP/DTT or SPDP/TCEP. We use SPDP to prepare a reactive R-phycoerythrin derivative (P806, Phycobiliproteins—Section 6.4), providing researchers with the optimal number of pyridyldisulfide groups for crosslinking the phycobiliprotein to thiolated antibodies, enzymes and other biomolecules through disulfide linkages. More commonly, the pyridyldisulfide groups are first reduced to

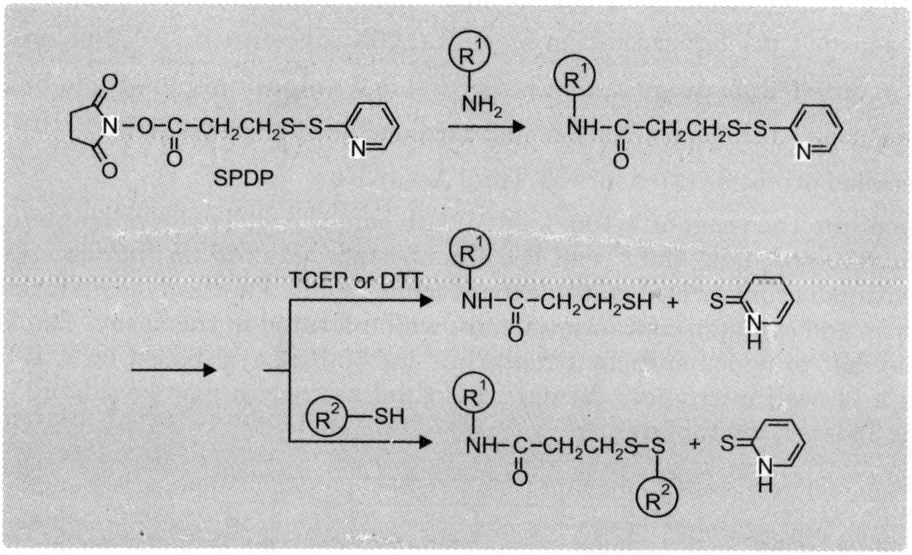

Fig. 4.2 : **SPDP derivatization reactions. SPDP (S1531) reacts with an amine-containing biomolecule at pH 7 to 9, yielding a pyridyldithiopropionyl mixed disulfide. The mixed disulfide can then be reacted with a reducing agent such as DTT (D1532) or TCEP (T2556) to yield a 3-mercaptopropionyl conjugate or with a thiol-containing biomolecule to form a disulfide-linked tandem conjugate. Either reaction can be quantitated by measuring the amount of 2-pyridinethione chromophore released during the reaction**

Measuring Thiolation of Biomolecules

To ensure success in forming heterocrosslinks, it is important to know that a molecule has the proper degree of thiolation. We generally find that two to three thiol residues per protein are optimal. Following removal of excess reagents, the degree of thiolation in proteins or other molecules thiolated with SPDP can be directly determined by measuring release of the 2-pyridinethione chromophore ($EC_{343\ nm}$ ~8000 $cm^{-1}M^{-1}$).

Alternatively, the degree of thiolation and presence of residual thiols in a solution can be assessed using 5,5'-dithiobis-(2-nitrobenzoic acid) (DTNB, Ellman's reagent; D8451), which stoichiometrically yields the 5-mercapto-2-nitrobenzoic acid chromophore ($EC_{410\ nm}$ ~13,600 $cm^{-1}M^{-1}$) upon reaction with a thiol group. DTNB can also be used to quantitate residual phosphines in aqueous solutions, including TCEP; in this case, two molecules of 5-mercapto-2-nitrobenzoic acid are formed per reaction with one molecule of a phosphine.

Measure-iT Thiol Assay Kit

The Measure-iT Thiol Assay Kit (M30550) provides easy and accurate quantitation of thiol. The kit supplies concentrated assay reagent, dilution buffer, and concentrated thiol standard. The assay has a linear range of 0.05–5 ìM thiol (**Figure 4.3**), making it up to 400 times more sensitive than colorimetric methods based on DTNB (Ellman's reagent).

Each Measure-iT Thiol Assay Kit contains:

- Measure-iT thiol quantitation reagent (100X concentrate in 1,2-propanediol
- Measure-iT thiol quantitation buffer (50 mM potassium phosphate buffer)
- Measure-iT thiol quantitation standard (reduced glutathione)
- Detailed protocols (Measure-iT Thiol Assay Kit)

Simply dilute the reagent 1:100, load 100 µL into the wells of a microplate, add 1–10 µL sample volumes, mix, then read the fluorescence. Maximum fluorescence signal is attained within 5 minutes and is stable for at least 1 hour. The assay is performed at room temperature, and common contaminants are well tolerated in the assay. The Measure-iT Thiol Assay Kit provides sufficient materials for 500 assays, based on a 100 µL assay volume in a 96-well microplate format; this thiol assay can also be adapted for use in cuvettes or 384-well microplates.

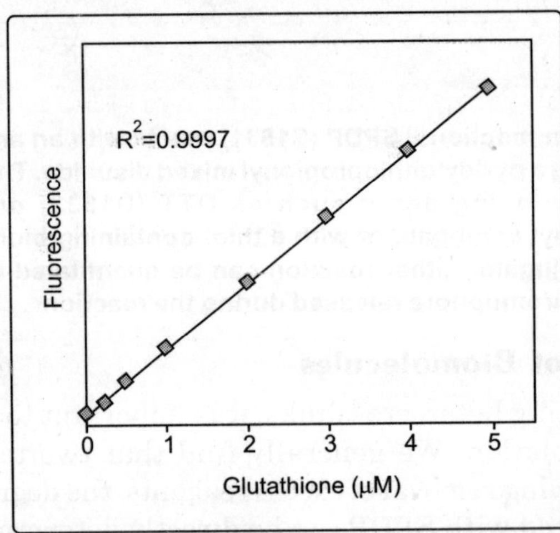

Fig. 4.3 : Linearity and sensitivity of the Measure-iT thiol assay. Triplicate 10 µL samples of glutathione were assayed using the Measure-iT Thiol Assay Kit (M30550). Fluorescence was measured using excitation/emission of 490/520 nm and plotted versus glutathione concentration. The variation (CV) of replicate samples was <2%.

Thiol and Sulfide Quantitation Kit

Ultrasensitive colorimetric quantitation of both protein and nonprotein thiols can also be achieved using the Thiol and Sulfide Quantitation Kit (T6060). In this assay, which is based on a method reported by Singh, thiols reduce a disulfide-inhibited derivative of papain, stoichiometrically releasing the active enzyme. Activity of the enzyme is then measured using the chromogenic papain substrate L-BAPNA via spectrophotometric detection of p-nitroaniline release at 412 nm (**Figure 4.4**). Although thiols can also be quantitated using DTNB (Ellman's reagent), the enzymatic amplification step in this quantitation kit enables researchers to detect as little as 0.2 nanomoles of a thiol—a sensitivity that is about 100-fold better than that achieved with DTNB. Thiols in proteins and potentially in other high molecular weight molecules can be detected indirectly by incorporating the disulfide cystamine into the solution. Cystamine undergoes an exchange reaction with protein thiols, yielding 2-mercaptoethylamine (cysteamine), which then releases active papain. Thiols that are alkylated by maleimides, iodoacetamides and other reagents are excluded from detection and can therefore be assayed subtractively.

The Thiol and Sulfide Quantitation Kit contains:

- Papain–SSCH$_3$, the disulfide-inhibited papain derivative
- L-BAPNA, a chromogenic papain substrate
- DTNB (Ellman's reagent), for calibrating the assay
- Cystamine
- L-Cysteine, a thiol standard
- Buffer
- Detailed protocols for measuring thiols, inorganic sulfides and maleimides (Thiol and Sulfide Quantitation Kit)

A: PAPAIN–S-S-CH$_3$ + R-SH ⇌ PAPAIN–SH + R-S-S-CH$_3$
inactive → active

B: L-BAPNA (colourless) —PAPAIN–SH→ product + H_2N–C$_6$H$_4$–NO_2 (coloured)

C: PROTEIN–SH + S-CH$_2$CH$_2$NH$_2$ / S-CH$_2$CH$_2$NH$_2$ (cystamine) ⇌ PROTEIN–S-S-CH$_2$CH$_2$NH$_2$ + HS-CH$_2$CH$_2$NH$_2$ (cystamine)

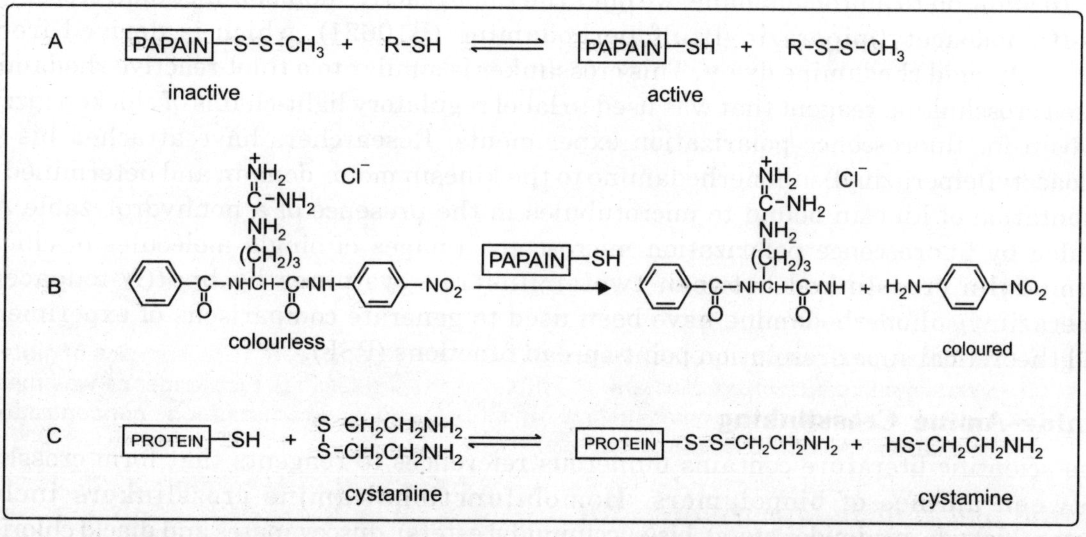

Fig. 4.4 : Chemical basis for thiol detection using the Thiol and Sulfide Quantitation Kit (T6060): (*A*) the inactive disulfide derivative of papain, papain–SSCH$_3$, is activated in the presence of thiols; (*B*) active papain cleaves the substrate L-BAPNA, releasing the *p*-nitroaniline chromophore; (*C*) protein thiols, often poorly accessible, exchange with cystamine to generate 2-mercaptoethylamine (cysteamine), which is easily detected

Sufficient reagents are provided for approximately 50 assays using 1 mL assay volumes and standard cuvettes or 250 assays using a microplate format.

Thiol–Thiol Crosslinking

Oxidation

Thiol residues in close proximity can be oxidized to disulfides by either an intra- or intermolecular reaction. In many circumstances, however, this oxidation reaction is reversible and difficult to control.

Fluorescent Thiol–Thiol Crosslinkers

Dibromobimane (bBBr, D1379) is an interesting crosslinking reagent for proteins because it is unlikely to fluoresce until both of its alkylating groups have reacted. It has been used to crosslink thiols in myosin, actin, hemoglobin, *Escherichia coli* lactose permease and mitochondrial ATPase. It has also been shown to intramolecularly crosslink thiols in a complex of nebulin and calmodulin. In addition, dibromobimane has been used to probe for the proximity of dual-cysteine mutagenesis sites in ArsA ATPase and P-glycoprotein. Dibromobimane, a stimulator of the ATPase activity of a cysteine-free P glycoprotein, was used with cysteine-scanning mutagenesis to identify amino acid residues important for function.

In addition to dibromobimane, we offer the thiol-reactive homobifunctional crosslinker bis-((*N*-iodoacetyl)piperazinyl)sulfonerhodamine (B10621), which is derived from a relatively rigid rhodamine dye. This crosslinker is similar to a thiol-reactive rhodamine-based crosslinking reagent that was used to label regulatory light-chains of chicken gizzard myosin for fluorescence polarization experiments. Researchers have attached bis-((*N*-iodoacetyl)piperazinyl)sulfonerhodamine to the kinesin motor domain and determined the orientation of kinesin bound to microtubules in the presence of a nonhydrolyzable ATP analog by fluorescence polarization microscopy. Images of single molecules of chicken calmodulin crosslinked between two engineered cysteines by bis-((*N*-iodoacetyl) piperazinyl)sulfonerhodamine have been used to generate comparisons of experimental and theoretical super-resolution point-spread functions (PSF).

Amine–Amine Crosslinking

The scientific literature contains numerous references to reagents that form crosslinks between amines of biopolymers. Homobifunctional amine crosslinkers include glutaraldehyde, bis(imido esters), bis(succinimidyl esters), diisocyanates and diacid chlorides. These reagents, however, tend to yield high molecular weight aggregates, making them unsuitable for reproducibly preparing well-defined conjugates between two different amine-containing biomolecules. For example, glutaraldehyde is still used by some companies and research laboratories to couple horseradish peroxidase, which has only six lysine residues, to proteins with a larger number of lysine residues. Unfortunately, this practice can result in variable molecular weights and batch-to-batch inconsistency.

Well-defined conjugates between two amine-containing molecules are more reliably prepared by thiolating one or more amines on one of the biomolecules and converting one or more amines on the second biomolecule to a thiol-reactive functional group such as a maleimide or iodoacetamide, as described below in Amine–Thiol Crosslinking. For example, we prepare our horseradish peroxidase conjugates (Secondary Immunoreagents—Section 7.2, Avidin, Streptavidin, NeutrAvidin and CaptAvidin Biotin-Binding Proteins and Affinity Matrices—Section 7.6) using SPDP- and SMCC-mediated reactions (**Figure 4.2**, **Figure 4.5**).

Direct amine–amine crosslinking routinely occurs during fixation of proteins, cells and tissues with formaldehyde or glutaraldehyde. These common aldehyde-based fixatives are also used to crosslink amine and hydrazine derivatives to proteins and other amine-containing polymers. For example, lucifer yellow CH (L453, Polar Tracers—Section 14.3) is nonspecifically conjugated to surrounding biomolecules by aldehyde-based fixatives in order to preserve the dye's staining pattern during subsequent tissue manipulations. Also, biotin hydrazides (Biotinylation and Haptenylation Reagents—Section 4.2) have been directly coupled to nucleic acids with glutaraldehyde, a reaction that is potentially useful for conjugating fluorescent hydrazides and hydroxylamines to DNA.

Amine–Thiol Crosslinking

Indirect crosslinking of the amines in one biomolecule to the thiols in a second biomolecule is the predominant method for forming a heteroconjugate. If one of the biomolecules does not already contain one or more thiol groups, it is necessary to introduce them using one of the thiolation procedures described above in Thiolation of Biomolecules. Thiol-reactive groups such as maleimides are typically introduced into the second biomolecule by modifying a one or more of its amines with a heterobifunctional crosslinker containing both a succinimidyl ester and a maleimide. The maleimide-modified biomolecule is then reacted with the thiol-containing biomolecule to form a stable thioether crosslink (**Fig. 4.5**). Chromatographic methods are usually employed to separate the higher molecular weight heteroconjugate from the unconjugated biomolecules.

Introducing Maleimides at Amines

Succinimidyl *trans*-4-(maleimidylmethyl)cyclohexane-1-carboxylate (SMCC, S1534) is our reagent of choice for introducing thiol-reactive groups at amine sites because of the superior chemical stability of its maleimide and its ease of use (*See Fig. 4.5 on next page*).

Introducing Disulfides at Amines

Our preferred method for preparing heteroconjugates employs the thiolation reagent SPDP (S1531). The pyridyldisulfide intermediate that is initially formed by reaction of SPDP

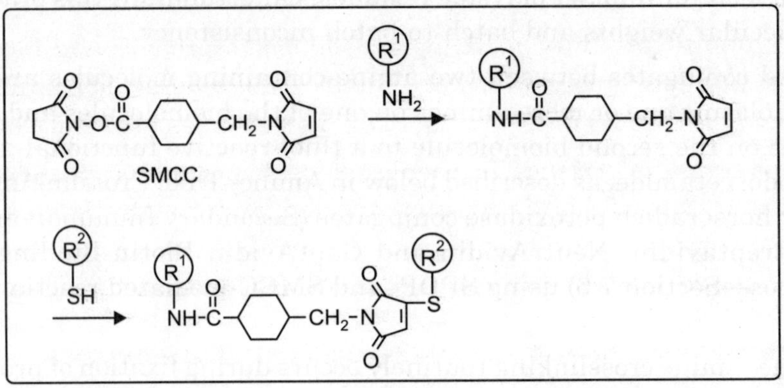

Fig. 4.5 : **Two-step reaction sequence for crosslinking biomolecules using the heterobifunctional crosslinker SMCC (S1534)**

with amines can form an unsymmetrical disulfide through reaction with a second thiol-containing molecule (**Figure 4.5**). The thiol-containing target can be a molecule such as β-galactosidase that contains intrinsic thiols or a molecule in which thiols have been introduced using one of the thiolation procedures described above in Thiolation of Biomolecules. In either case, it is essential that all reducing agents, such as DTT and TCEP, are absent. The heteroconjugate's disulfide bond is about as stable and resistant to reduction as disulfides found in proteins; it can be reduced with DTT or TCEP to generate two thiol-containing biomolecules.

Protein–Protein Crosslinking Kit

Our Protein–Protein Crosslinking Kit (P6305) provides all of the reagents and purification media required to perform three protein–protein conjugations in which neither protein contains thiol residues. The chemistry used to thiolate the amines of one of the proteins with SPDP and to convert the amines of the second protein to thiol-reactive maleimides with SMCC is shown in **Figure 4.5** and **Figure 4.6**, respectively. Included in the kit are:

- SPDP, for thiolating amines
- SMCC, for converting amines to thiol-reactive maleimides
- TCEP, for reducing the pyridyldisulfide intermediate
- *N*-ethylmaleimide (NEM), for capping residual thiols
- Six reaction tubes, each containing a magnetic stir bar
- Spin columns plus collection tubes
- Dimethylsulfoxide (DMSO)

- Detailed crosslinking protocols (Protein–Protein Crosslinking Kit)

The Protein–Protein Crosslinking Kit was designed to prepare and purify protein–protein conjugates; however, it can be readily modified for generating peptide–protein or enzyme–nucleic acid conjugates or for conjugating biomolecules to affinity matrices.

We have considerable experience in preparing protein–protein conjugates and will apply this expertise to a researcher's particular application through our custom synthesis service. We provide custom conjugation services on an exclusive or non-disclosure basis when requested. For more information or a quote, please contact Invitrogen Custom Services.

Assaying Maleimide—and Iodoacetamide-Modified Biomolecules

The potential instability of maleimide derivatives and the photosensitivity of iodoacetamide derivatives may make it advisable to assay the modified biomolecule for thiol reactivity before conjugation with a thiol-containing biomolecule. SAMSA fluorescein (A685), which is currently our only fluorescent reagent that can generate a free thiol group, was designed for assaying whether or not a biomolecule is adequately labeled with a heterobifunctional maleimide or iodoacetamide crosslinker. Brief treatment of SAMSA fluorescein with NaOH at pH 10 liberates a free thiol (SAMSA Fluorescein). By adding base-treated SAMSA fluorescein to a small aliquot of the crosslinker-modified biomolecule, the researcher can check to see whether the biomolecule has been sufficiently labeled before proceeding to the next step. The degree of modification can be approximated from either the absorbance or the fluorescence of the conjugate following quick purification on a gel-filtration column.

Alternatively, thiol reactivity of the modified biomolecule can be assayed using the reagents provided in our Thiol and Sulfide Quantitation Kit (T6060), a product that is described above. Once unconjugated reagents have been removed, a small aliquot of the maleimide- or iodoacetamide-modified biomolecule can be reacted with excess cysteine. Thiol-reactive groups can then be quantitated by determining the amount of cysteine consumed in this reaction with the Thiol and Sulfide Quantitation Kit.

Amine–Carboxylic Acid Crosslinking

1-Ethyl-3-(3-dimethylaminopropyl)carbodiimide (EDAC, E2247) can react with biomolecules to form "zero-length" crosslinks, usually within a molecule or between subunits of a protein complex. In this chemistry, the crosslinking reagent is not incorporated into the final product. The water-soluble carbodiimide EDAC crosslinks a specific amine and carboxylic acid between subunits of allophycocyanin, thereby stabilizing its assembly; We use EDAC to stabilize allophycocyanin in its allophycocyanin conjugates (Phycobiliproteins—Section 6.4). EDAC has also been used to form intramolecular crosslinks in myosin subfragment-1, intermolecular crosslinks in actomyosin, intersubunit crosslinks of chloroplast subunits and DNA–protein crosslinks. Addition of *N*-hydroxysuccinimide or *N*-hydroxysulfosuccinimide (NHSS, H2249) is reported to enhance the yield of carbodiimide-mediated conjugations, indicating the *in situ* formation of a succinimidyl ester–activated protein (**Figure 4.6**). EDAC has been reported to be impermeant to cell membranes, which should permit selective surface labeling of cellular carboxylic acids with fluorescent amines.

Reaction of carboxylic acids with cystamine ($H_2NCH_2CH_2S–SCH_2CH_2NH_2$) and EDAC followed by reduction with DTT results in thiolation at carboxylic acids. This indirect route to amine–carboxylic acid coupling is particularly suited to acidic proteins with few amines, carbohydrate polymers, heparin, poly(glutamic acid) and synthetic polymers lacking amines. The thiolated biomolecules can also be reacted with any of the probes described in Thiol-Reactive Probes—Chapter 2.

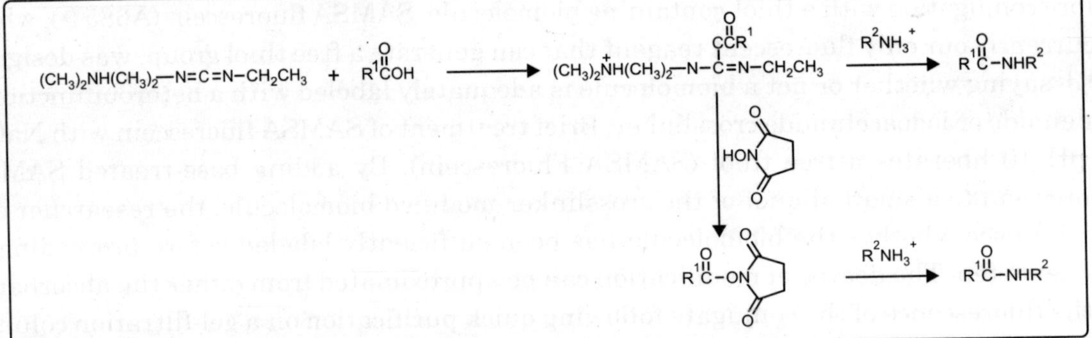

$(CH_3)_2NH(CH_3)_3–N=C=N–CH_2CH_3 + R^1COOH \rightarrow (CH_3)_2\overset{+}{N}H(CH_3)_3–N(CCR^1{=}O)–C=N–CH_2CH_3 \xrightarrow{R^2NH_3^+} R^1C(O)–NHR^2$

HON (N-hydroxysuccinimide) ↓

$R^1C(O)–ON$ (succinimide) $\xrightarrow{R^2NH_3^+} R^1C(O)–NHR^2$

Fig. 4.6 : Stabilization of an unstable *O*-acylisourea intermediate by *N*-hydroxysuccinimide in a carbodiimide-mediated (EDAC, E2247) modification of a carboxylic acid with a primary amine.

Crosslinking Amines to Acrylamide Polymers

The succinimidyl ester of 6-((acryloyl)amino)hexanoic acid (acryloyl-X, SE; A20770) reacts with amines of proteins, amine-modified nucleic acids and other biomolecules to yield acrylamides that can be copolymerized into polyacrylamide matrices or onto surfaces, such as in microarrays and in biosensors. For example, streptavidin acrylamide (S21379, Avidin, Streptavidin, NeutrAvidin and CaptAvidin Biotin-Binding Proteins and Affinity Matrices—Section 7.6) copolymerizes with acrylamide on polymeric surfaces to create a uniform monolayer of the immobilized protein. The immobilized streptavidin can then bind biotinylated ligands, including biotinylated hybridization probes, enzymes, antibodies and drugs.

Cat #	Links	MW	Storage	Soluble	Abs	EC	Em	Solvent	Notes
A685		521.50	F,D,L	pH >6, DMF	491	78,000	515	pH 9	
A20770		282.30	F,D,L	DMSO	<300		none		
B10621		840.47	F,D,L	DMSO	549	88,000	575	MeDH	1
D1379		350.01	L	DMF, MeCN	391	6100	see Notes	MeDH	2
D1532		154.24	D	H_2O	<300		none		
D8451		396.35	D	pH >6	324	18,000	none	pH 8	3
E2247		191.70	F,D	H_2O	<300		none		
H2249		217.13	D	H_2O	<300		none		
S1531		312.36	F,D	DMF, MeCN	282	4700	none	MeDH	4
S1534		334.33	F,D	DMF, MeCN	<300		none		
S1553		231.22	F,D	DMF, MeCN	<300		none		
T2556		286.65	D	pH >5	<300		none		

1. Iodoacetamides in solution undergo rapid photodecomposition to unreactive products. Minimize exposure to light prior to reaction.
2. Bimanes are almost non-fluorescent until reacted with thiols. For monobromobimane conjugated to glutathione, Abs = 394 nm, Em = 490 nm (QY ~0.1–0.3) in pH 8 buffer.
3. D8451 reaction product with thiols has Abs = 410 nm (EC = 14,000 $cm^{-1}M^{-1}$).
4. After conjugation of S1531 the degree of substitution can be determined by measuring the amount of 2-pyridinethione formed by treatment with DTT (D1532) or TCEP (T2556) from its absorbance at 343 nm (EC = 8000 $cm^{-1}M^{-1}$).

PROTEIN CROSS-LINKING PROTOCOLS

To enable elution of protein with little antibody contamination (for cleaner protein preparation and cleaner western blots), it is recommended to cross link the antibody to the beads. An example procedure for this is shown below. The target protein should then be eluted with a mild eluent, such as glycine buffer.

Reagents

Cross linking reagent:

Dimethyl pimelimidate (DMP)

Stock concentration 13 mg/ml DMP.

Working solution should be between pH 8 and pH 9.

Elution reagent

1 M glycine (Add conc. HCl to correct pH to pH 3)

Dilution buffer

PBS + 1 mg/ml BSA

Wash buffer

0.2 M triethanolamine in PBS (3.04 ml triethanolamine per 100 ml buffer)

Quenching buffer

50 mM ethanolamine in PBS (311.7 μl per 100 ml)

Preparation

1. Wash beads twice in PBS. The end concentration should be 50 % bead slurry.
2. Mix well and rotate overnight at 4°C.

Cross-linking:

1. Wash the beads (protein A or protein G) by centrifuging (14,000 rpm, 1 min) into a pellet. Aspirate out the PBS supernatant.
2. Add dilution buffer at 1:1 ratio, mix gently and rotate for 10 minutes at 4°C. Centrifuge and aspirate/discard the supernatant as before.
3. Prepare the antibody solution in dilution buffer at the required concentration (see antibody datasheet for suggested concentration). Add diluted antibody at 1:1 ratio to the beads. Mix gently and rotate 1 hr at 4°C.
4. Centrifuge and aspirate/discard the supernatant.
5. Add dilution buffer to beads at 1:1 ratio. Rotate for 5 min at 4°C. Centrifuge and aspirate/discard the supernatant.
6. Add PBS to beads at 1:1 ratio. Centrifuge and aspirate/discard the supernatant.
7. Cross-linking:

   DMP is unstable in aqueous solution. Prepare solution immediately prior to use.
8. Dissolve 1ml of prepared 13 mg/ml stock of DMP with 1 ml wash buffer. Vortex immediately to mix.

   Add DMP solution to beads at 1:1 ratio. Rotate for 30 min at room temperature.
9. Wash the beads with wash buffer (rotate 5 min RT, then spin and aspirate).

-N/B You will need to verify pH of DMP is between 8-9 before and after addition to beads (cross-linking efficiency is greatly reduced outside this pH range).

Add DMP for second time at 1:1 ratio, rotate 30 min RT, wash as before.

Add DMP for third time at 1:1 ratio, rotate 30 min RT, wash as before.

10. Quench and wash.

    Add quench buffer at 1:1 ratio, rotate 5 min RT, spin and aspirate; repeat.

    Wash with PBS.

11. Remove excess (unlinked) antibody:

    Wash with 1 M glycine pH 3. Rotate 10 min RT. Repeat.

12. Storage washes.

    Wash with buffer to be used for immunoprecipitation (usually PBS+TWEEN). Rotate 5 min RT.

    Wash three times and store in final wash (after rotation). Beads can be stored at 4°C for a few days. Sodium azide can be added to prevent bacterial growth.

Immunoprecipitation: The antibody bound beads can now be used in a normal IP procedure. Elution of bound antigens: To prevent elution of antibody with the target protein, use a gentle glycine elution gradient (up to 1 M

Cross-linking of IgG to Protein A or G Beads

Materials Needed

Protein A (NEB #S1425S) or Protein G (NEB #S1430S) Magnetic Beads

Elution Buffer: 0.1 M glycine-HCl (pH 2.5)

Binding Buffer: 0.1 M sodium borate (pH 8.2)

Dimethyl pimelidate dihydrochloride (Sigma, D-8388) dissolved at 25 mM in Cross-linking Buffer.

Cross-linking Buffer: 0.2 M triethanolamine (pH 8.2)

Blocking Buffer: 0.1 M ethanolamine (pH 8.2)

Immunoglobulin in Binding Buffer

This protocol consists of an IgG purification step followed by covalent cross-linking of the IgG to the Protein A/G solid support. For IgG that has been previously purified, proceed directly to the cross-linking protocol.

Protocol

1. **IgG Purification:** The following protocol is for the binding of 20 µg of purified IgG or isolation of 20 µg IgG from serum. Vortex and thoroughly resuspend Protein A Magnetic Beads.

2. Aliquot 100 μl of bead suspension to a sterile microcentrifuge tube.
3. Add 500 μl 0.1 M NaPhosphate Buffer (pH 8.0) and vortex to resuspend. Apply magnet for 30 seconds, to pull beads to the side of the tube and remove supernatant. Repeat wash.
4. Add to the beads 80 μl of 0.1 M NaPhosphate Buffer (pH 8.0) and 15-25 ìl of serum or 20 μg purified IgG in a maximum volume of 30 μl.
5. Mix thoroughly and incubate at 4°C with agitation for 30 minutes.
6. Apply magnet and remove supernatant.
7. Wash beads three times as in step 3. At this point the purified IgG can be eluted from the beads or used directly for immunoprecipitation of target proteins. The purified IgG can also be cross-linked to the Protein A beads (see cross-linking protocol) to create a reusable immunoprecipitation bead which prevents the co-elution of antibody with target protein.
8. **IgG Cross-linking to Protein A/G Magnetic Beads:** Add 1 ml of Cross-linking Buffer (0.2 M triethanolamine, [pH 8.2]) to the Protein A/G immobilized antibody and vortex to resuspend. Apply magnet for 30 seconds, to pull beads to the side of the tube and remove supernatant. Repeat wash.
9. Resuspend in 1 ml Cross-linking Buffer containing 25 mM DMP (6.5 mg DMP/ml of buffer). Mix thoroughly and incubate at room temperature for 45 minutes with agitation.
10. Apply magnet for 30 seconds, to pull beads to the side of the tube and remove supernatant.
11. Add 1 ml Blocking Buffer (0.1 M ethanolamine, [pH 8.2]) and vortex to resuspend. Apply magnet for 30 seconds, to pull beads to the side of the tube and remove supernatant.
12. Add 1 ml of Blocking Buffer and vortex to resuspend. Incubate for 1 hour at room temperature with agitation.
13. Apply magnet for 30 seconds, to pull beads to the side of the tube and remove supernatant. Add 1 ml of PBS, vortex to resuspend, apply magnet for 30 seconds, to pull beads to the side of the tube and remove supernatant. Repeat wash twice.
14. Add 1 ml Elution Buffer (0.1 M glycine-HCl [pH 2.5]) and vortex to resuspend, apply magnet for 30 seconds, to pull beads to the side of the tube and remove supernatant. This elutes bound antibody that is not cross-linked with DMP.
15. Resuspend and store beads in 100 μl PBS, 0.1% Tween 20, 0.02% sodium azide.

Protein Croslinking Methods

Photo-induced protein cross-linking is a powerful new method for the analysis of protein-protein interactions in vitro. A photo-activated metal-ligand complex mediates the one-electron oxidation of tyrosine or tryptophan residues on a protein. The resultant radical intermediates can cross-link to nearby nucleophilic or aromatic residues rapidly and efficiently. Thus, the metal complex is a mediator or catalyst of cross-linking and the cross-link is the result of direct bond formation between the interacting proteins. In many cases, yields of 20-90% can be obtained with reaction times of one second or less. A detailed protocol and some practical considerations are provided below, along with a list of relevant references.

A. Protein and Buffer Considerations: Purify proteins for Photo Crosslinking through any convenient protein isolation method, such as GST pull-down (such as Protocol ID#417), SDS-PAGE (such as Protocol ID#1919) or sucrose density gradient isolation (such as Protocol ID#951). See Hint #1 for additional details. If possible, proteins should be purified into a solution of Phosphate Buffered Saline (PBS). If the purification process results in the protein being solubulized in a solution other than PBS, dialyze the protein against PBS (see Protocol ID#9054 and use PBS as the dialysis buffer). Buffers other than PBS have been employed successfully; however, easily oxidized buffer components, such as Dithiothreitol or β-Mercaptoethanol should not be included in the buffer. PICUP has proven to be useful in the analysis of protein-protein interactions in more complex settings, such as cell lysates. In such settings, commonly used epitope and affinity tags are usually employed to aid in the analysis of the cross-linked products of interest (see Hint #2). If an antibody that recognizes an unknown epitope is employed to follow PICUP reactions, and the protein of interest appears by Western analysis to be consumed without the production of visible cross-linked products, this probably means that the epitope recognized by the antibody was modified in the course of the reaction.

B. Light Source and Reaction Considerations: The light source used in the contributor's laboratory is a 150-W xenon arc lamp (Oriel, Stamford, CT). The contributor strongly recommends the use of such an intense light source if available. However, a standard flashlight can support the PICUP reaction. Based on comments from those who have used this methodology, the results are highly dependent on the intensity of the light. Light used in the reaction is first filtered through 10 cm of ddH_2 and then a 380 nm to 2,500 nm cut on filter (Oriel). The light exposure time is controlled through the use of the timed shutters of a single lens reflex camera that has had both the lens and back cover removed. If one must use a flashlight, a high-intensity MagLite-type flashlight is recommended. Also, longer irradiation times are necessary (5-30 seconds), and the light source must be closer to the reaction tube (5 cm vs. 50 cm for the 150-W xenon arc lamp). The contributor has not optimized use of flashlight-mediated reactions.

For some substrates, PICUP is too efficient. In cases where the protein of interest is driven by multiple cross-linking events into a high molecular weight species, histidine can be added to the reaction. The contributor has found that histidine reduces the reaction efficiency in a predictable way (*i.e.*, increasing histidine concentration results in decreasing reaction efficiency). Inhibition with histidine appears to be a more convenient way to inhibit an overly efficient cross-linking reaction than experimenting with different metal and APS concentrations.

For some substrates, PICUP is inefficient. In cases where low yields of cross-linked products are obtained, increase the light reaction time.

C. Photo-Induced Crosslinking of Proteins: 1. Add 10 to 30 µl of Protein Solution #1 to a 1.5 ml microcentrifuge tube.

2. Add 10 to 30 il of Protein Solution #2 to the microcentrifuge tube and mix gently (see Hint #3).

3. Immediately prior to exposure to light, add $(Ru(bpy))_3Cl_2$ to a final concentration of 125 µM and mix gently.

4. Then add APS to a final concentration of 2.5 mM and mix gently.

5. Photolyze the reaction mixture for 0.5 to 5 sec (see Hint #4).

6. Quench the reaction by adding one-quarter the reaction volume of 4X Gel Loading Buffer (final concentration 1X).

7. Samples are incubated for 5 min at 95°C and separated by SDS-Polyarcylamide Gel Electrophoreses (see Protocol ID#455).

8. Analyze cross-linked products through Coomassie staining (see Protocol ID#716), silver staining (see Protocol ID#496, Protocol ID#1211, Protocol ID#346, or Protocol ID#435) or Western blot analysis (see Protocol ID#70, Protocol ID#1146 or Protocol ID#251). Alternatively, the protein of interest can be radiolabeled and the cross-linked products can be visualized by autoradiography (see Protocol ID#9036).

Solutions

$(Ru(bpy))_3Cl_2$—Prepare in ddH_2O

$(Ru(bpy))_3Cl_2$—Tris(2,2'-Bipyridyl)Ruthenium(II)Chloride, Hexahydrate (Aldrich)

Gel Loading Buffer (4X)—0.4% (w/v) Xylene Cyanol

40% (v/v) Glycerol

0.2 M Tris

8% (w/v) SDS

0.4% (w/v) Bromophenol Blue

2.88 M β-Mercaptoethanol

Protein Solution #2—1 to 3 μM Purified Protein #2

See Section A for additional details

Prepare in appropriate buffer

Protein Solution #1—See Section A for additional details

1 to 3 μM Purified Protein #1

Prepare in appropriate buffer

PBS–137 mM Sodium Chloride (NaCl)

2.7 mM Potassium Chloride (KCl)

Also see Protocol ID#2152 for additional details

1.4 mM Potassium Phosphate, Monobasic (KH_2PO_4)

4.3 mM Sodium Phosphate, Dibasic (Na_2HPO8sub*4)

BioReagents and Chemicals

SDS

Tris(2,2'-Bipyridyl)Ruthenium(II)Chloride, Hexahydrate

Potassium Phosphate, Monobasic

β-Mercaptoethanol

Tris

Sodium Phosphate, Dibasic

Potassium Chloride

Sodium Chloride

Glycerol

Bromophenol Blue

Xylene Cyanol

Protocol Hints

1. There are numerous protocols for the purification of total protein or a specific protein. Specific protocols identified in the procedure section are examples; browse the Working with Proteinsection of this web site for additional options.
2. S10, myc epitope tags, His_6, and biotin affinity tags have been shown to survive the PICUP reaction in functional form (at least with irradiation times on the order

of 1 second or less using the 150W lamp). These tags are useful for either the identification or isolation of cross-linked products. In contrast, the hemagglutin (HA) and FLAG tags are oxidized to products not recognized by the cognate antibody and are therefore not useful tags with which to visualize the outcome of oxidative cross-linking reactions. Some other oxidatively labile tags, such as GFP and fluorescein, have also been shown to be unsuitable for this purpose.

3. The concentration of proteins used can vary. To avoid the generation of spurious cross-linked products, limit the concentration of a single protein to no more than 20 μM final concentration.
4. The microcentrifuge tube is placed parallel to the light source (*i.e.*, the light beam shines into the opening in the top of the tube) at a distance of 50 cm.

CHAPTER 5

Emerging Technologies the Microfluidics

Microfluidics deals with the behaviour, precise control and manipulation of fluids that are geometrically constrained to a small, typically sub-millimeter, scale. Typically, *micro* means one of the following features:

- small volumes (nl, pi, fl)
- small size
- low energy consumption
- effects of the micro domain

It is a multidisciplinary field intersecting engineering, physics, chemistry, microtechnology and biotechnology, with practical applications to the design of systems in which such small volumes of fluids will be used. Microfluidics emerged in the beginning of the 1980s and is used in the development of inkjet printheads, DNA chips, lab-on-a-chip technology, micro-propulsion, and micro-thermal technologies.

Microscale Behaviour of Fluids

The behaviour of fluids at the microscale can differ from 'macrofluidic' behavior in that factors such as surface tension, energy dissipation, and fluidic resistance start to dominate the system. Microfluidics studies how these behaviors change, and how they can be worked around, or exploited for new uses.

At small scales (channel diameters of around 100 nanometers to several hundred micrometers) some interesting and sometimes unintuitive properties appear. In particular, the Reynolds number (which compares the effect of momentum of a fluid to the effect of viscosity) can become very low. A key consequence of this is that fluids, when side-by-side, do not necessarily mix in the traditional sense; molecular transport between them must often be through diffusion. High specificity of chemical and physical properties (concentration, pH, temperature, shear force, etc.) can also be ensured resulting in more uniform reaction conditions and higher grade products in single and multi-step reactions.

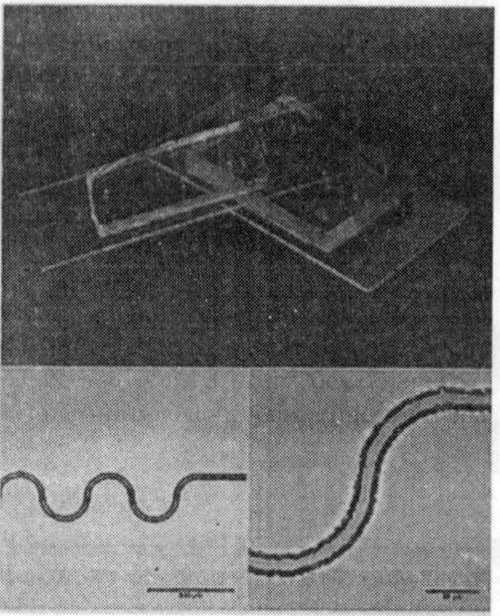

Fig. 5.1 : Silicone rubber and glass microfluidic devices. Top: a photograph of the devices. Bottom: D1C micrographs of a serpentine channel –15 μm wide.

Effects of Micro Domain

- laminar flow
- surface tension
- electrowetting
- fast thermal relaxation
- electrical surface charges
- diffusion

Key Application Areas

Microfluidic structures include micro-pneumatic systems, *i.e.* microsystems for the handling of off-chip fluids (liquid pumps, gas valves, etc), and microfluidic structures for the on-chip handling of nano- and picolitre volumes. To date, the most successful commercial application of microfluidics is the inkjet printhead. Significant research has been applied to the application of microfluidics for the production of industrially relevant quantities of material. Advances in microfluidics technology are revolutionizing molecular biology procedures for enzymatic analysis (*e.g.*, glucose and lactate assays), DNA analysis (*e.g.*, polymerase chain reaction and high-throughput sequencing), and proteomics. The basic idea of microfluidic biochips is to integrate assay operations such as detection, as well as sample pre-treatment and sample preparation on one chip. An emerging application area for biochips is clinical pathology, especially the immediate point-of-care diagnosis of diseases. In addition, microfluidics-based devices, capable of continuous sampling and real-time testing of air/water samples for biochemical toxins and other dangerous pathogens, can serve as an always-on 'bio-smoke alarm' for early warning.

Continuous-flow Microfluidics

These technologies are based on the manipulation of continuous liquid flow through microfabricated channels. Actuation of liquid flow is implemented either by external pressure sources, external mechanical pumps, integrated mechanical micropumps, or by combinations of capillary forces and electrokinetic mechanisms. Continuous-flow microfluidic operation is the mainstream approach because it is easy to implement and less sensitive to protein fouling problems. Continuous-flow devices are adequate for many well-defined and simple biochemical applications, and for certain tasks such as chemical separation, but they are less suitable for tasks requiring a high degree of flexibility or ineffect fluid manipulations.

These closed-channel systems are inherently difficult to integrate and scale because the parameters that govern flow field vary along the flow path making the fluid flow at any one location dependent on the properties of the entire system. Permanently-etched microstructures also lead to limited reconfjgurability and poor fault tolerance capability. Process monitoring capabilities in continuous-flow systems can be achieved with highly sensitive microfluidic flow sensors based on MEMS technology which offer resolutions down to the nanoliter range.

Digital (droplet-based) Microfluidics

Alternatives to the above closed-channel continuous-flow systems include novel open structures, where discrete, independently controllable droplets are manipulated on a substrate using electrowetting. Following the analogy of digital microelectronics, this approach is referred to as digital microfluidics. Le Pesant *et al.* pioneered the use of electrocapillary forces to move droplets on a digital track. The 'fluid transistor' pioneered by Cytonix also played a role. The technology was subsequently commercialized by Duke University. By using discrete unit-volume droplets,[14] a microfluidic function can be reduced to a set of repeated basic operations, i.e., moving one unit of fluid over one unit of distance. This 'digitization' method facilitates the use of a hierarchical and cell-based approach for microfluidic biochip design. Therefore, digital microfluidics offers a flexible and scalable system architecture as well as high fault-tolerance capability. Moreover, because each droplet can be controlled independently, these systems also have dynamic reconfigurability, whereby groups of unit cells in a microfluidic array can be reconfigured to change their functionality during the concurrent execution of a set of bioassays. Although droplets are manipulated in confined microfluidic channels, since the control on droplets is not independent, it should not be confused as 'digital microfluidics'. One common actuation method for digital microfluidics is electrowetting-on-dielectric (EWOD). Many lab-on-a-chip applications have been demonstrated within the digital microfluidics paradigm using electrowetting. However, recently other techniques for droplet manipulation have also been demonstrated using Surface Acoustic Waves, optoelectrowetting, mechanical actuation, etc.

DNA Chips (Microarrays)

Early biochips were based on the idea of a DNA microarray, *e.g.,* the GeneChip DNAarray from Afrymetrix, which is a piece of glass, plastic or silicon substrate on which pieces of DNA (probes) are affixed in a microscopic array. Similar to a DNA microarray, a protein array is a miniature array where a multitude of different capture agents, most frequently monoclonal antibodies, are deposited on a chip surface; they are used to determine the presence and/or amount of proteins in biological samples, *e.g.,* blood. A drawback of DNA and protein arrays is that they are neither reconfigurable nor scalable after manufacture. Digital microfluidics has been described as a means for carrying out Digital PCR.

Molecular Biology

In addition to microarrays biochips have been designed for two-dimensional electrophoresis, transcriptome analysis, and PCR amplification. Other applications include various electrophoresis and liquid chromatography applications for proteins and DNA, cell separation, in particular blood cell separation, protein analysis, cell manipulation and analysis including cell viability analysis and microorganism capturing.

Evolutionary Biology

By combining microfluidics with landscape ecology and nanofluidics, a nano/micro fabricated fluidic landscape can be constructed by building local patches of bacterial habitat and connecting them by dispersal corridors. The resulting landscapes can be used as physical implementations of an adaptive landscape by generating a spatial mosaic of patches of opportunity distributed in space and time. The patchy nature of these fluidic landscapes allows for the study of adapting bacterial cells in a metapopulation system. The evolutionary ecology of these bacterial systems biology. in these synthetic ecosystems allows for using biophysics to address questions in evolutionary biology.

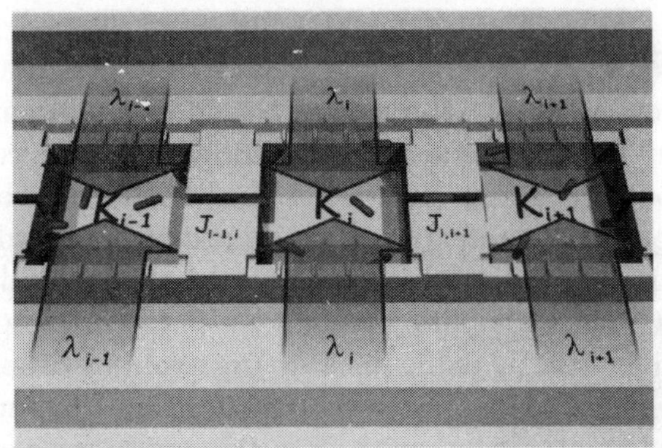

Fig. 5.2 : Three Micro Habitat Patches MHPs connected by dispersal corridors (indicated here as J_{ij}) into a ID lattice. The ecosystem service (of habitat renewal) to each MHP represented here as λ_i (red arrows). Each MHP can also hold different carrying capacity K_i for its supporting local population of bacterial cells (depicted in green)

Cellular Biophysics

By rectifying the motion of individual swimming bacteria, microfluidic structures can be use to extract mechanical motion from a population of motile bacterial ceils.[21J This way, bacteria-powered rotors can be built

Optics

The merger of microfluidics and optics is typical known as Optofluidics. An example of an optofluidic device is a Tuneable Microlens Array

Acoustic Droplet Ejection (ABE)

Acoustic droplet ejection uses a pulse of ultrasound to move low volumes of fluids (typically nanoliters or picoliters) without any physical contact. This technology focuses acoustic energy into a fluid sample in order to eject droplets as small as a millionth of a millionth of a liter (picoliter = 10~12 liter). ADE technology is a very gentle process, and it can be used to transfer proteins, high molecular weight DNA and live cells without damage or loss of viability. This feature makes the technology suitable for a wide variety of applications including proteomics and cell-based assays.

Fuel Cells

Microfluidic fuel cells can use laminar flow to separate the fuel and its oxidant to control the interaction of the two fluids without a physical barrier as would be required in conventional fuel cells

Lab-on-a-chip (LOC) is a device that integrates one or several laboratory functions on a single chip of only millimeters to a few square centimeters in size. LOCs deal with the handling of extremely small fluid volumes down to less than pico liters. Lab-on-a-chip devices are a subset of MEMS devices and often indicated by 'Micro Total Analysis Systems'(uTAS) as well. Microfluidics is a broader term that describes also mechanical flow control devices like pumps and valves or sensors like flowmeters and viscometers. However, strictly regarded 'Lab-on-a-Chip' indicates generally the scaling of single or multiple lab processes down to chip-format, whereas 'uTAS' is dedicated to the integration of the total sequence of lab processes to perform chemical analysis. The term 'Lab-on-a-Chip' was introduced later on when it turned out that uTAS technologies were more widely applicable than only for analysis purposes.

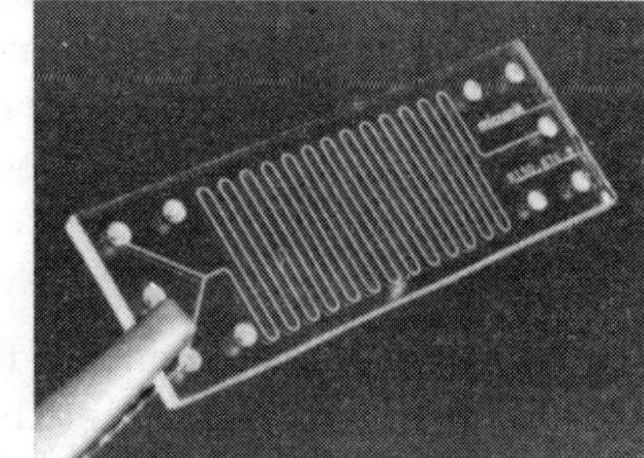

Fig. 5.3 : Lab-on-a-chip made of glass

Digital microfluidics is an alternative technology for lab-on-a-chip systems based upon micromanipulation of discrete droplets. Microfluidic processing is performed on unit-sized packets of fluid which are transported, stored, mixed, reacted, or analyzed in a discrete manner using a standard set of basic instructions.

Basics

In analogy to digital microelectronics, these basic instructions can be combined and reused within hierarchical design structures so that complex procedures (*e.g.* chemical synthesis or biological assays) can be built up step-by-step. And in contrast to continuous-flow microfiuidics, digital microfluidics works much the same way as traditional bench-top protocols, only with much smaller volumes and much higher automation. Thus a wide range of established chemistries and protocols can be seamlessly transferred to a nanoliter droplet format. Electro wetting, dielectrophoresis, and immiscible-flu id flows are the three most commonly used principles, which have been used to generate and manipulate microdroplets in a digital microfluidic device.

Working Principle

Droplets are formed using the surface tension properties of liquid. For example, water placed on a hydrophobic surface will lower its contact with the surface by creating drops whose contact angle with the substrate will increase as the hydrophobicity increases. However, in some cases it is possible to control the hydrophobicity of the substrate by using electrical fields. This is referred to as Electrowetting on dielectric or EWOD. In thin layers of Teflon AF, FluoroPel V-polymer or CYTOP, for example, while no field is applied the surface will be extremely hydrophobic and a droplet of water will try to 'stay away[1] from the surface, resulting in a droplet with steep walls. When a field is applied, a polarized hydrophilic surface is created, and the water droplet tries to 'get closer' to the surface, resulting in much more spread out droplet. By controlling the localization of this polarisation it is possible to control the displacement of the droplet.

Implementation

In one of various embodiments of EWOD-based microfluidic biochips, investigated first by Cytonix in 1987 and subsequently commercialized by Advanced Liquid Logic, there are two parallel glass plates, and the bottom plate contains a patterned array of individually controllable electrodes, and the top plate is coated with a continuous grounding electrode. A dielectric insulator coated with a hydrophobic is added to the plates to decrease the wettability of the surface and to add capacitance between the droplet and the control electrode. The droplet containing biochemical samples and the filler medium, such as the silicone oil, a fluorinated oil or air are sandwiched between the plates; the droplets travel inside the filler medium. In order to move a droplet, a control voltage is applied to an electrode adjacent to the droplet, and at the same time, the electrode just under the droplet is deactivated. By varying the electric potential along a linear array of electrodes, electro-wetting can be used to move droplets along this line of electrodes.

In *flow chemistry,* a chemical reaction is run in a continuously flowing stream rather than in batch production. In other words, pumps move fluid into a tube, and where tubes join one another, the fluids contact one another. If these fluids are reactive, a reaction takes place. Flow chemistry is a well-established technique for use at a large scale when manufacturing large quantities of a given material. However, it is relatively new to use it in the laboratory environment.

Batch *vs.* Flow

Comparing parameters in Batch *vs* Flow:

- Reaction stoichiometry. In batch production this is defined by the concentration of chemical reagents and their volumetric ratio. In Flow this is defined by the concentration of reagents and the ratio of their flow rate.

- Reaction time. In batch production this is determined by how long a vessel is held at a given temperature. In flow this is determined by the volume of the reactor, and the bulk flow rate.

Benefits of Flow

- Reaction temperature can be far above the solvent's boiling point due to easy ability to contain pressure.
- Mixing can be achieved within seconds at the smaller scales used in flow chemistry.
- The thermal mass of the fluid is typically far lower than the thermal mass of the system (and orders of magnitude less than with batch chemistry). This makes controlling the temperature of the media both faster and easier ensuring that exothermic and endothermic process can be conducted without issue.
- Multi step reactions can be arranged in a continuous sequence. This can be especially beneficial if intermediate compounds are unstable, since they will exist only momentarily and in very small quantities.
- Position along the flowing stream and reaction time point are directly related to one another. This means that it is possible to arrange the system such that further reagents can be introduced into the flowing reaction stream at precisely the time point in the reaction that is desired.
- It is possible to arrange a flowing system such that purification is coupled with the reaction. There are three primary techniques that are used:

  — Solid phase scavenging

  — Chromatographic separation

  — Liquid/Liquid Extraction
- By coupling the output of the reactor to a detector system, it is possible with appropriate controls to create an unattended system which can sequentially investigate a range of possible reaction parameters (varying stoichiometry, residence time and temperature) and therefore optimise reactions with little or no intervention.
- Reactions which involve reagents containing dissolved gases are easily handled, whereas in batch a pressurised 'bomb' reactor would be necessary.
- Multi.phase liquid reactions (*e.g.* phase transfer catalysis) can be performed in a straightforward way, with high reproducibi'lity over a range of scales and conditions.
- Scaleup of a proven reaction can be achieved rapidly with little or no process development work, by either changing the reactor volume or by running several reactors in parallel, provided that flows are recalculated to achieve the same residence times.

Continuous Flow Reactor

Fig. 5.4 : Reaction stages of a Coflore ACR multicell flow reactor

Continuous reactors are typically tube like and manufactured from non-reactive materials such as stainless steel, glass and polymers. Mixing methods include diffusion alone (if the diameter of the reactor is small e.g. <1 mm) and static mixers.

Continuous flow reactors allow good control over reaction conditions including heat transfer, time and mixing.

The residence time of the reagents in the reactor (i.e. the amount of time that the reaction is heated or cooled) is calculated from the volume of the reactor and the flow rate through it.

Residence time = Reactor Volume / Flow Rate

Therefore, to achieve a longer residence time, reagents can be pumped more slowly and/or a larger volume reactor used. Production rates can vary from nano litres to litres per minute.

Some examples of flow reactors are spinning disc reactors (Colin Ramshaw); spinning tube reactors; oscillatory flow reactors; microreactors: hex reactors; and 'aspirator reactors'.

In an aspirator reactors is a pump propels one reagent, which causes a reactant to be sucked in. This type of reactor was patented circa 1941 by Nobel companies for used in preparing nitroglycerin.

Flow Reactor Scale

The smaller scale of micro flow reactors can make them ideal for process development experiments. Although it is possible to operate How processes at a Tonne plus scale, synthetic efficiency benefits from improved thermal and mass transfer as well as mass transport.

Use of Gases in Flow

Laboratory scale flow reactors are ideal systems for using gases, particularly those that are toxic or associated with other hazards. The gas reactions that have been most successfully adapted to flow are Hydrogenation and Carbonylation, although work has also been performed using other gases, from ethylene to ozone.

Fig. 5.5 : A micro reactor

Reasons for the suitability of flow systems for hazardous gas handling are:

- Systems allow the use of a fixed bed catalyst. Combined with low solution concentrations, this allows all compound to be adsorbed to catalyst in the presence of gas
- Comparatively small amounts of gas are continually exhausted by the system, eliminating the need for many of the special precautions normally required for handling toxic and/or flammable gases
- The addition of pressure means that a far greater proportion of the gas will be in solution during the reaction than is the case conventionally
- The greatly enhanced mixing of the solid, liquid and gaseous phases allows the researcher to exploit the kinetic benefits of elevated temperatures without being concerned about the gas being displaced from solution

Other uses of Flow

It is possible to run experiments in flow using more sophisticated techniques, such as solid phase chemistries.

Scale up of Microwave Reactions

Microwave reactors are frequently used for small scale batch chemistry. However due to the extremes of temperature and pressure reached in a microwave it is often difficult to transfer these reactions to conventional non-microwave apparatus for subsequent development, leading to difficulties with scaling studies. A flow reactor with suitable high temperature ability and pressure control can directly and accurately mimic the conditions created in a microwave reactor, and since in flow chemistry the quantity of material produced is limited only by the reaction time, scaling can be achieved.

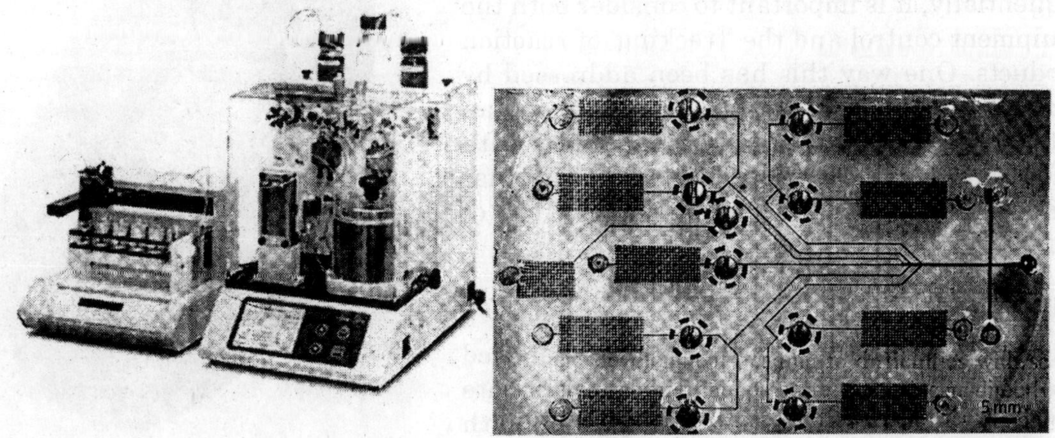

Fig. 5.6 : Showing the Microfluidic System

Running Flow Experiments

The practicalities of running flow experiments in normal chemistry laboratories has not traditionally been simple, requiring either a self-built system of tubes, pumps, heaters, pressurisers and even software, or investing in a space-consuming and expensive commercial solution.

The challenges of controlling flow experiments should also not be underestimated. For example,

- pumps do not always perform at the expected ilow rate due to various causes (incomplete wetting / air bubbles caused by dissolved gas) and without a real time pump monitoring system the user might be completely unaware of this, resulting in inaccurate experiments and limited reproducibility or scaleup success.
- because of the dispersion that occurs as a plug of liquid moves through a long tube reactor, some of the leading and trailing ends of the plug must be rejected, so that only the 'steady state' reaction product is kept. In the absence of a system to compute the extent of the dispersion, or to detect it in real time, it is necessary to discard significant amounts of product to ensure only good output is kept.

Fig. 5.7 : Pump Status Monitoring

Today, several of the commercial systems available address the challenges noted and are now available at a comparatively low price.

Where multiple reactions are being conducted sequentially, it is important to consider both the equipment control and the 'tracking' of reaction products. One way this has been addressed by commercial flow chemistry vendors is to add an eptional autosampler to their instruments with software similar to an LCMS or microwave that graphically depicts the physical location of products from each reaction,

Fig. 5.8 : World's smallest micropump

Micropump

Although any kind of small pump is often referred to as micropump, a more accurate and up-to-date definition restricts this term to pumps with functional dimensions in the micrometre range. Such pumps are of special interest in microfliiidic research, and have become available for industrial product integration in recent years. Their miniaturized overall size, potential cost and improved dosing accuracy compared to existing miniature pumps fuel the growing interest for this innovative kind of pump.

Types and Technology

In this sense, first true micropumps were reported on in 1975. However, the micropumps developed by Jan Smits and Harald Van Lintel in the early 1980's are considered to be the first genuine MEMS micropumps, and sparked the interest in shrinking the size of a fully functional pump to new dimensions.

Within the microfluidic world physical laws change their appearance: As an example, volumetric forces, such as weight or inertia, often become negligible, whereas surface forces can dominate fluidical behaviour, especially when gas inclusion in liquids is present. With only a few exceptions, micropumps rely on micro-actuation principles, which can reasonably be scaled up only to a certain size.Micropumps can be grouped into mechanical and non-mechanical devices: Mechanical systems contain moving parts, which are usually actuation and valve membranes or flaps. The driving force can be generated by utilizing piezoelectric, electrostatic, thermo-pneumatic, pneumatic or magnetic effects. Non-mechanical pumps function with electro-hydrodynamic, electro-osmotic or ultrasonic flow generation, just to name a few of the actuation mechanisms that are currently studied.

Industrial Integration

Any kind of active microfluidic handling or analysis system (µTas, Lab-on-a-Chip System) requires some kind of micropump system. In addition, macro-fluidic systems which rely on miniature pumps might be reduced in size or enhanced in their functionality by integrating a micropump. Emerging technologies, such as portable fuel cell applications will benefit when smaller yet more energy efficient pumps become available on the market. In 2003, the first commercial availability of a micropump was announced. Other companies have followed with their own pumps. All commercially available micropumps depend on piezoelectric actuation and incorporate passive check valves. Micropumps made of polymers appear to yield potentially low unit prices, while silicon micropumps prove to be the smallest pump devices in the world.

It has to be seen which of these pumps will be the first one to be successfully integrated into a commercially available product.

The Coanda effect (pronounced /r"kwflr nda/) is the tendency of a fluid jet to be attracted to a nearby surface.[1] The principle was named after Romanian aerodynamics pioneer Henri Coanda, who was the first to recognize the practical application of the phenomenon in aircraft development.

Discovery

An early description of this phenomenon was provided by Thomas Young in a lecture given to The Royal Society in 1800:

The lateral pressure which urges the flame of a candle towards the stream of air from a blowpipe is probably exactly similar to that pressure which eases the inflexion of a current of air near an obstacle. Mark the dimple which a slender stream of air makes on the surface of water. Bring a convex body into contact with the side of the stream and the place of the dimple will immediately show the current is deflected towards the body; and if the body be at liberty to move in every direction it will be urged towards the current.

A hundred years later, Henri Coanda identified an application of the effect during experiments with his Coanda-1910 aircraft which mounted an unusual engine designed by Coanda. The motor-driven turbine pushed hot air rearward, and Coanda noticed that the airflow was attracted to nearby surfaces. He discussed this matter with leading aerodynamic 1st Theodore von Kantian who named it the Coanda effect. In 1934 Coanda obtained a patent in France for a "Method and apparatus for deviation of a fluid into another fluid". The effect was described as the "Deviation of a plan jet of a fluid that penetrates another fluid in the vicinity of a convex wall."

Causes

The Coanda effect is a result of entrainment of ambient fluid around the fluid jet. When a nearby wall does not allow the surrounding fluid to be pulled inwards towards the jet (i.e. to be entrained), the jet moves towards (he wall instead. The fluid of the jet and the surrounding fluid should be essentially the same substance (a gas jet into a body of gas or a liquid jet into a body of liquid). In one application, a jet of air is blown over the upper surface of an airfoil, which can have a strong influence on the overall lift, especially at high angles of attack when the flow would otherwise separate (stall). See Blown flap.

Applications

The Coanda effect has important applications in various high-lift devices on aircraft, where air moving over the wing can be 'bent down' towards the ground using flaps and a jet sheet blowing over the curved surface of the top of the wing. The bending of the flow results in its acceleration and as a result of Bernoulli's principle pressure is decreased; aerodynamic lift is increased. The flow from a high speed jet engine mounted in a pod over the wing produces enhanced lift by dramatically increasing the velocity gradient in the shear flow in the boundary layer. In this velocity gradient particles are blown away from the surface, thus lowering the pressure there. Closely following the work of Coanda on applications of his research, and in particular the work on his 'Aerodina Lenticular;!' John Frost of Avro Canada also spent considerable time researching the effect, leading to a series of 'inside out' hovercraft-like aircraft where the air exited in a ring around the outside of the aircraft and was directed by being "attached" to a flap-like ring.

This is as opposed to a traditional hovercraft design, in which the air is blown into a central area, the plenum, and directed down with the use of a fabric "skirt". Only one of Frost's designs was ever built, the Avrocar.

The VZ-9 AV Avrocar (often listed as VZ-9) was a Canadian vertical takeoff and landing (VTOL) aircraft developed by Avro Aircraft Ltd. as part of a secret U.S. military project carried out in the early years of the Cold War. The Avrocar intended to exploit the Coanda effect to provide lift and thrust from a single 'turborotor' blowing exhaust out the rim of the disk-shaped aircraft to provide anticipated VTOL-Iike performance. In the air, it would have resembled a Hying saucer. Two prototypes were built as 'proof-of-concept' test vehicles for a more advanced USAF fighter and also for a U.S. Army tactical combat aircraft requirement.

The effect was also implemented during the U.S. Air Force's AMST project. Several aircraft, notably the Boeing YC-14 (the first modern type to exploit the effect), have been built to take advantage of this effect, by mounting turbofans on the top of wing to provide high-speed air even at low flying speeds, but to date only one aircraft has gone into production using (his system to a major degree, the Antonov An-72 'Coaler'.

The McDonneH Douglas YC-15 and its successor the Boeing C-I7 Globemaster III, also employ the effect. The NOTAR helicopter replaces the conventional propeller tail rotor with a Coanda effect tail.

An important practical use of the Coanda effect is for inclined hydropower screens[7], which separate debris, fish, etc., otherwise in the input flow to the turbines. Due to the slope, the debris falls from the screens without mechanical clearing, and due to the wires of the screen optimizing the Coanda effect, the water flows though the screen to the penstocks leading the water to the turbines.

The Coanda effect is also used to make automotive windshield washers which function without moving parts and to create pneumatic logic circuits.

The operation principle of oscillatory flowmetcrs also relies on the Coanda phenomenon. The incoming liquid enters a chamber that contains 2 'islands'. Due to the Coanda effect the main stream splits up and goes under one of the islands. This flow then feeds itself back into the main stream making it split up again, but in the direction of the second isle. This process repeats itself as long as the liquid circulates the chamber, resulting in a self induced oscillation that is directly proportional to the velocity of the liquid and consequently the volume of substance flowing through the meter. A sensor picks up the frequency of this oscillations and transforms it into an analog signal yielding volume passing through.

In air conditioning the Coanda effect is exploited to increase the throw of a ceiling mounted diffuser. Because the Coanda effect causes air discharged from the diffuser to "stick" to the ceiling, it travels farther before dropping for the same discharge velocity than it would if the diffuser was mounted in free air, without the neighbouring ceiling. Lower discharge velocity means lower noise levels and, in the case of variable air volume (VAV) air conditioning systems, permits greater turn-down ratios. Linear diffusers and slot diffusers that present a greater length of contact with the ceiling exhibit greater Coanda effect.

In cardiovascular medicine, the Coanda effect accounts lor the separate streams of blood in the fetal right atrium'. It also explains why eccentric mitral regurgitation jets are attracted and dispersed along adjacent left atria I wall surfaces (so called "wall-hugging jets" as seen on echocardiographic color-doppler interrogation). This is clinically relevant because the visual area (and thus severity) of these eccentric wall-hugging jets is often underestimated compared to the more readily apparent central jets. In these cases, volumetric methods such as the proximal isovelocity surface area (PISA) method are preferred to quantify the severity of mitral regurgiunion.

The Coanda effect is used in medicine as a ventilator.

In meteorology, the Coanda effect theory has also been applied to some air streams flowing out of mountain ranges such as the Carpathian Mountains and Transylvanian Alps, where effects on agriculture and vegetation have been noted. It also appears to be an effect in the Rhone Valley in France and near Big Delta in Alaska.

Demonstration

The Coanda effect can be demonstrated by directing a small jet of air upwards at an angle over a ping pong ball. The jet is drawn to the upper surface and curves around, diverting the flow downwards over the back. This change in the momentum of the air flow is reacted out in the reduced pressure on the upper surface of the ball, this suction being sufficient to overcome the weight of the ball (when there is enough air flow). This demonstration can be performed using a vacuum cleaner if the outlet can be attached to the pipe and aimed upwards at an angle.

A common misconception is that Coanda effect is demonstrated when a stream of tap water flows over the back of a spoon held lightly in the stream and the spoon is pulled into the stream. While the flow looks very similar to the air flow over the ping pong ball above (if one could see the air flow), the cause is not really the Coanda effect. Here, because it is -A flow of water into air, there is no entrainment of the surrounding fluid (the air) into the jet (the stream of water). This particular demonstration is dominated by surface tension.

Another demonstration is to direct the air flow from. e.g.. a vacuum cleaner operating in reverse, tangentially past a round cylinder. A waste basket works well. The air How seems to 'wrap around' the cylinder and can be detected at more than 180° from the incoming ilow. Under the right conditions, flow rate, weight of the cylinder, smoothness of the surface it sits on, the cylinder will actually move. Note that the cylinder will not move directly into the flow as a misapplication of the Bernoulli effect.would predict, but at a diagonal.

The effect can also be seen by placing a can in front of a lit candle. If one blows directly at the can, the air will bend around it and extinguish the candle.

If two lit candles are placed side-by-side, the heated air from each candle rises and entrains surrounding air. Since both 'jets' are trying to entrain common air from the space between the two streams, they are drawn towards one another. This is more apparent if the candles are making a little smoke. This is a demonstration of the Coanda effect without the presence of any surface. In some sense, the plane of symmetry between the two flows can be thought of as the surface.

Problems Caused

The Coanda effect has disadvantages as well as advantages.

In marine propulsion, the efficiency of a propeller or ihrusler can be severely curtailed by the Coanda effect. The force on the vessel generated by a propeller is a function of the speed, volume and direction of the water jet leaving the propeller. Under certain conditions (e.g. when a ship moves through water) the Coanda effect changes the direction of a propeller jet, causing it to follow the shape of the ship's hull. The side force from a tunnel thruster at the bow of a ship decreases rapidly with forward speed. The side thrust may completely disappear at speeds above about 3 knots.

Acoustic droplet ejection (ADE) uses a pulse of ultrasound to move low volumes of fluids (typically nanoliters or picoliters) without any physical contact. This technology focuses acoustic energy into a fluid sample in order to eject droplets as small as a picoliter. ADE technology is a very gentle process, and it can be used to transfer proteins, high molecular weight DNA and live cells without damage or loss of viability. This feature makes the technology suitable for a wide variety of applications including proteomics and cell-based assays.

History

Acoustic droplet ejection was first reported in 1927 by Robert W. Wood and Alfred Loomis. who noted that when a high-power acoustic generator was immersed in an oil bath, a mound formed on the surface of the oil and, like a 'miniature volcano,' ejected a continuous stream of droplets. Ripples that appear in a glass of water placed on a loud speaker show that acoustic energy can be converted to kinetic energy in a fluid. If the sound is turned up enough, droplets will jump from the liquid. This technique was refined in the 1970s

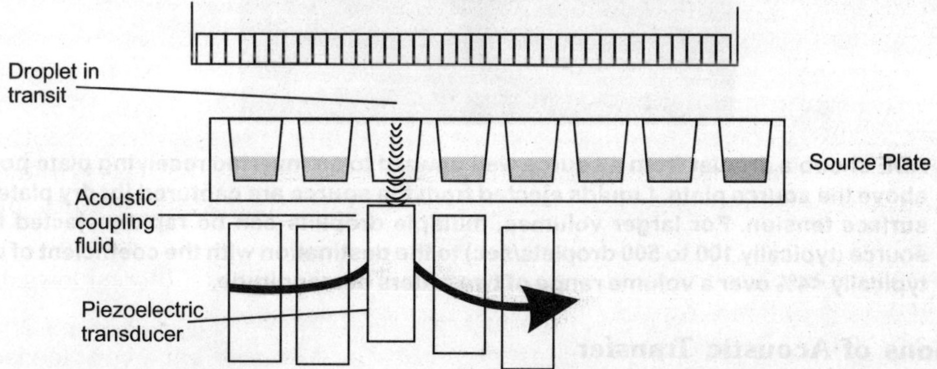

Fig. 5.9 : ADE transfer fluids from source wells to an inverted destination plate. The fluid in any well in the source plate can be transferred to any well or position of the destination. Transfer volumes are adjustable for each well. The transducer travels in the Z axis to keep the focus of the acoustic pulse at the fluid meniscus. Colors are used to suggest dIfferent solutes dissolved in the fluid in each well. Fluid stays in inverted plates.

and 1980s by Xerox and IBM and other organizations to provide a single droplet on-demand for printing ink onto a page. Two California-based companies, EDC Biosystems Inc. and Labcyte Inc., exploit acoustic energy for two separate functions; (1) as a liquid transfer device and (2) as a device for liquid auditing.

Ejection Mechanism

To eject a droplet, a transducer generates and transfers acoustic energy to a source well. When the acoustic energy is focussed near the surface of the liquid, a mound of liquid is formed and a droplet is ejected. [Figure 1J The diameter of the droplel scales inversely with the frequency of the acoustic energy—higher frequencies produce smaller droplets. Unlike other liquid transfer devices, no pipette tips, pin tools, or nozzles touch the source liquid or destination surfaces. Liquid transfer methods that rely on droplet formation through an orifice, *e.g.*, disposable tips or capillary nozzles, invariably lose precision as the transfer volume decreases. Touchless acoustic transfer provides a coefficient of variation-(CYs) that is significantly lower than other techniques and is independent of volume at the levels tested.

Fig. 5.10 : ADE shoob a droplet from a source well upward to an inverted receiving plate positioned above the source plate. Liquids ejected from the source are captured (b) dry plates due to surface tension. For larger volumes, multiple droplets can be rapidly ejected from the source (typically 100 to 500 droplets/sec) to the destination with the coefficient of variation typically <4% over a volume range of two orders of magnitude.

Applications of Acoustic Transfer

The following applications are among those that can benefit from the features of acoustic droplet ejection:

- High throughput screening
- Microelectromechanical systems

Index

S

T

U